BACKYARD Secrets of the GARDEN EXPERTS

BACKYARD Secrets of the GARDEN EXPERTS

Written by Leslie Garisto

Principal Photography by Albert Squillace
Illustrations by Tovah Reznicek

RODALE

 **RODALE**

WE **INSPIRE** AND **ENABLE** PEOPLE TO IMPROVE
THEIR LIVES AND THE WORLD AROUND THEM

A LAYLA PRODUCTIONS BOOK

RODALE GARDEN BOOKS
Executive Editor: Ellen Phillips
Contributing Editors: Erana Bumbardatore, Claire Kowalchik, and Karen Costello Soltys
Associate Art Director: Patricia Field
Photo Editor: Jim Gallucci
Studio Manager: Leslie Keefe
Manufacturing Manager: Mark Krahforst

Backyard Secrets of the Garden Experts was prepared and produced by Layla Productions, Inc.
Project Director: Lori Stein
Editorial Assistant: Elizabeth Luber

We're always happy to hear from you. For questions and comments concerning the editorial content of this book, please write to:

Rodale Inc.
Book Reader's Service
33 East Minor Street
Emmaus, PA 18098

Look for other Rodale books wherever books are sold. Or call us at (800) 848-4735.

For more information about Rodale Inc. and the books and magazines we publish, visit our World Wide Web site at:
http://www.rodalepress.com

Library of Congress Cataloging-in-Publication Data

Garisto, Leslie
  Backyard secrets of the garden experts : discover the pros' tricks for great gardens / written by Leslie Garisto ; principal photography by Albert Squillace ; illustrations by Tovah Reznicek.
    p. cm.
  Includes index
  ISBN 0–87596–802–3 (hardcover)
  1. Gardening. I. Title
  SB450.97.G384 1999
  635'dc21   99–6763

2 4 6 8 10 9 7 5 3   hardcover

ACKNOWLEDGMENTS

This book is the result of the collaborative effort of over 250 professional gardeners from all over the United States and Canada, every one of whom added valuable information and knowledge to the project. It is a testament to the generosity and good nature of gardeners everywhere, to that willingness to share that is so common among people who love to grow things. Even though we knew how generous gardeners are, we were astounded at the amount of time and effort our experts put into answering our questionnaires and talking to us—these busy professionals contributed hours and hours, just because they wanted to pass along a bit of knowledge or a helpful hint to another gardener. We thank each and every one of them from the bottom of our hearts. (Please see page 368 for a complete listing.)

We'd also like to thank the staff at Rodale Inc. for all that they added to this book. Ellen Phillips, Erana Bumbardatore, Trish Field, Karen Costello Soltys, and Jim Gallucci are the most knowledgeable and hardworking book professionals we've ever encountered.

Photographer Albert Squillace, once again, traveled far and wide to get the right photographs. We thank him for his good humor and his talent. Tovah Reznicek provided beautiful illustrations.

We'd also like to thank the following people who in one way or another contributed to the making of this book: Ian Adams, Leo and Cindy Asen, Penelope Byham, Monica Cano, John Glover, Matt Horn, Mr. and Mrs. Bruce Huber, Christl Kogelnik, Mr. and Mrs. Robert Lawrence, Kate Learson, Betty Luber, Maggie Oster, Jerry Pavia, John Pfaff, Lily E. Pfaff, Diane Pratt, Noah Schwartz, Harriet Shapiro, Leigh Sorenson, Mrs. Sverre Sorensen, Loretta Spilker, Al Raimondi, Bobbie Schwartz, Leslie Scott, Bonnie Lane Webber, Chani Yammer, Paul Zakris, Michelle Stein, and Deena Stein.

CONTENTS

FROM GARDENER TO GARDENER

Most of us learn how to garden hands-on, through trial and error, gaining as much from our failures as our successes. But we also learn from the failures and successes of other gardeners, trading hard-won knowledge over the back fence. Imagine, then, how much you could learn if you leaned over that fence and found not one gardening friend but hundreds of them—and not just avid gardeners, but professionals: nursery owners, garden designers, landscape architects, horticulturists from botanic gardens, cooperative extension agents, and university professors. With this book, you can do just that.

We interviewed more than 200 professional gardeners, asking them the sorts of questions you'd ask if you had the chance: how to build the healthiest soil, how to deal with pests and diseases, whether to trellis your cucumbers or stake your saplings. For each question, we approached at least six professionals, and each expert answered roughly a dozen questions. In this way, we were able to assemble a range of information to cover every region and gardening personality.

Even if you're growing edibles, make your garden beautiful, advises John Lee of Allandale Farm in Massachusetts. The better it looks, the better you'll feel while you're working in it, so you'll stay there longer.

Unlike most how-to books on gardening, we don't present a single approach to each problem, but several different approaches. We leave it to you, the reader, to choose the one that best suits you—and your garden. And we believe you'll benefit from knowing the alternatives, even if you don't apply them all in your own backyard.

Backyard Secrets of the Garden Experts is divided into seven chapters, each one covering a crucial aspect of home gardening. Because so many of our contributors stressed the importance of proper planning, we've devoted the first chapter to describing how the experts have started their own gardens. The next three chapters cover different types of plants and how to grow them successfully: edibles (vegetables and herbs); herbaceous flowers (annuals, perennials, and bulbs); and woody plants (trees, shrubs, and vines). The last three chapters are devoted to the essential gardening techniques of soil-building, pest and disease control, and propagation.

Like you, the professional gardeners who participated in this book love to garden, and we think you'll find evidence of that passion on every page and in every tip. We hope you'll use and enjoy the thousands of ideas we've gathered for you. As you go, of course, you'll

Don't rely only on blossoms in your ornamental beds. Foliage—like the leaves of hosta, sweet woodruff, and 'Herman's Pride' yellow archangel below—can be just as attractive. And it lasts so much longer!

QUICK TIPS

🐟 If you have a weed problem, make sure your compost is sterilized—by checking its temperature and making sure it reached above 160°F—before you add it to your garden.
Frederick Held,
Nature's Garden, Oregon.

🐟 Use unwanted branches that have been cut back for natural-looking staking; buddleia works well. Prop well-branched stakes into the perennial border before plants start drooping. The look is natural and the purpose is served.
Ellen Talmage,
The Horticultural Goddess, Inc., New York

🐟 Plant woodland phlox at the base of clumps of tulips and daffodils. They comple-ment each other when in bloom and mark the spot for fall when you want to plant more bulbs and can't remember where the last season's bulbs were.
Gail Korn,
Garden Perennials, Nebraska

change them slightly to suit your own style, and then pass them on to another gardening friend. Whether you do it over the back fence or on the Internet, it's exactly this kind of give-and-take that makes gardening such a rewarding activity, and it's the reason we put this book together, one friend to another.

The Best Advice

In addition to answering specific questions, we asked each of our experts to offer a single secret that makes gardening easier, more productive, or just plain more enjoyable for them. Here's what they had to say:

GENERAL MAINTENANCE It's the day-to-day chores—soil care, weeding, watering, fertilizing—that are the heart and soul of gardening, so it's not surprising that the experts had strong opinions on these subjects. Richard Boonstra, the retired president of Ohio's Bluestone Perennials, stresses the importance of friable (easily worked) soil, recommending regular cultivation to help roots breathe, conserve moisture, and destroy weed seeds just as they're germinating. He also advises gardeners to water deeply, down to a depth of 6 inches or so (you can make sure you've done this by digging into the soil after watering). Depending on soil and weather conditions, you may not need to water for weeks afterward. For even deeper watering (down to a depth of 10 inches), Ward Upham, a horticulturist at Ohio State University, recommends drip irrigation (basically, a series of slender tubes that allow water to seep slowly into the soil, without any loss to evaporation). And to maintain nutrients in the soil, California landscape designer Angela Fabbri offers this advice: "Plant variety. If you've planted something soil-depleting one year, say, tomatoes, switch to something else the next."

MAKING THINGS EASY Like all of us, the experts are eager to find ways to make their jobs easier. Michael Cady of Jackson & Perkins recommends starting from the ground up. "Amend your soil with organic matter," he says. "This will make it easier to dig and to plant: weeds pull easier, plants establish easier, watering is easier because there's less runoff." Many of the experts agreed with this sentiment.

"The single most significant mistake that home gardeners make is neglecting to amend their soil," said Claire Ackroyd, a Maine horticulturist.

For many of the experts, including garden designers Sue Moss of Seattle and Cynthia Rice of North Carolina, the key to ease in the garden is mulch. Sue applies it in the fall, which makes spring weeding a breeze. If autumn leaves are abundant in your yard, Cynthia advises buying an electric leaf mower to shred the leaves and turn them into instant (and inexpensive) mulch.

Both Doris Taylor of Illinois's Morton Arboretum and Tessa Gowans of Washington's Abundant Life Seed Foundation try to group plants according to their soil and water requirements. "I plant tomatoes and

Mulch, mulch, mulch; turn the mulch under the soil; mulch, mulch, mulch, says Peter Borchard of Ohio's Companion Plants. The experts recommend adding organic mulch in and around your beds. Black plastic mulch is useful for vegetables, warming soil and keeping weeds down.

QUICK TIPS

🐦 Use natural fertilizers and controls; in all my years of gardening and advising, I've found that people have longer-lasting success with them.
Ursula Herz, Coastal Gardens, South Carolina

🐦 When edging flower beds or borders with a spade, make a shallow trench at the edge of the lawn. This will stop your mulch from washing onto the lawn in heavy rain.
Peter Linser, Morton Arboretum, Illinois

🐦 Mix quick-maturing radish seeds with beets or carrots. When I harvest the radishes, I save myself the extra work of thinning the beets or carrots.
Donald Ledden, Ledden Brothers, New Jersey

Containers add a new level of flexibility to the garden, bringing spots of color that can change as often as you like.

beans next to each other, because neither likes overhead watering," says Tessa. If you're growing flowers, Celeste Wilson of California's Las Pilitas Nursery suggests that you choose perennials over annuals, which require lots more maintenance. If you grow annuals, she says, keep the beds manageably small.

Gail Korn of Nebraska's Garden Perennials recommends making an even smaller investment: a child's wagon. She uses one in her own garden for toting backyard sundries, from bags of mulch to flats of young plants.

Keeping your plants happy For well-adjusted plants, consider the advice of Washington State grower Hunter Carleton: "Make the soil happy, and the plants will be happy." Before planting, amend your soil with organic matter and make sure it's weed-free. Equally important, according to Douglas Owens-Pike of Minneapolis's EnergyScapes, Inc., is selecting the right plant for the sun and soil conditions your garden offers. If, in addition, you choose only those plants that are native to your area, you can pretty much forget about maintenance once the plants are established, he says.

In a similar vein, Phyllis Farkas of New York's Wildginger Woodlands advises "growing things where they want to grow, not where you want to grow them." When she finds a seedling growing in the lawn, she clears away some of the grass and lets the seedling stay in its chosen place, at least for a season or two.

Making the garden more productive The secret to a thriving garden, says Richard Boonstra of Bluestone Perennials, is a little patience: After amending the soil for a new garden, let it settle for a year; grow a few annuals or vegetables, then add the permanent perennials. And don't forget to compost, urges Frederick Held of Oregon's Nature's Garden. "Recycle all your garden debris, including leaves," he says.

In her own Maine garden, Sarah Gallant of Pinetree Garden Seeds relies on rabbit-power to boost productivity. "Earthworms love rabbit manure, and the kids love the rabbits," she says. And in the Cheyenne Botanic Garden, director Shane Smith relies on his own ruthlessness: "Know when to fold and when to hold," he advises. If a plant isn't thriving, move it, or give it to a guest. ("Tell them you'll throw it out if they don't take it, and they usually will," advises Shane.)

ENItalics-small-caps ENJOYING THE GARDEN It's a given that gardeners love to garden, but sometimes the day-to-day chores, the battles with bugs and weeds and deer, the plants that sprawl when they should stand erect or go to seed before you've had a chance to harvest them, threaten to overwhelm even the most joyous gardener. The experts have faced all this and more and learned along the way how to keep the fun from fading.

If you're gregarious, like Sarah Gallant, try making gardening a cooperative effort, with family and friends. If they're not interested, join a garden co-op. Try to follow garden designer Tory Galloway's advice to plant within your abilities: "If your time (or patience) is limited, start small. Julie Marks of Kentucky's Sleepy Hollow Herb Farm agrees: "So often, I see people starting with grand plans and then getting discouraged," she says. Her simple secret: "Don't do too much."

But just how do you manage that? Robert Caughlan of California's Caughlan & Sons Landscapes does it by choosing low-maintenance shrubs and trees and clustering harder-to-maintain plantings near the house. And Oregon rose grower Louise Clements achieves it by throwing perfectionism roundly on the compost heap. Earlier gardeners —including the Empress Josephine, who boasted one of the world's great rose gardens—had to tolerate a much higher level of pests and diseases, says Louise. "If you look at some of the paintings from that era, they show holes in the leaves and actual bugs—they were all part of the whole environmental event, the complexity of life." Louise's advice: "We need to be more tolerant of imperfections, in our gardens and in ourselves."

In fact, when it comes to enjoying the garden, attitude is key. For horticulturist Claire Ackroyd, that means enjoying the journey, not the destination. "Over the years, you'll acquire an encyclopedic amount of knowledge, and you'll end up with something lovely," she says. And when the weeds and bugs and inevitable failures threaten to turn your lovely journey into a bad trip, consider Robert Caughlan's philosophy: "Think of the garden not as another arena for pressured, overextended hustle and bustle, but as a place to enjoy the gentle rhythms of nature." Dig your hands into the soil and tickle an earthworm. Smell the roses (and the compost). And don't forget to share your garden—and its secrets—with a few good friends.

Start small; you'll enjoy your garden more if you're not overwhelmed by work. A few plants, carefully arranged, can be just as satisfying as a complicated planting.

1
STARTING YOUR GARDEN THE EXPERTS' WAY

"To make a garden 'easy,' plan carefully."
ROBERT CAUGHLAN, CAUGHLAN & SON LANDSCAPES

What's your idea of the perfect garden? Does it include beds overflowing with annuals for cutting? Neat, productive rows of vegetables and herbs? A broad, green lawn surrounded by lush borders of shrubs and perennials? A profusion of native wildflowers? Whatever its purpose, every garden starts with a vision–but some end up short of the mark. So how do you make sure that your finished garden is as spectacular as the vision that inspired it?

In this chapter, the experts prove that it's all in the planning. You'll learn their start-up secrets: the best time to begin your garden, the things you need to do before you start, and how to evaluate your site and soil (and make changes for the better). The experts will give you the lowdown on drainage, climate, and soil tests, and they'll describe the easiest and most efficient methods of weed and sod removal, soil preparation, unearthing tree stumps and rocks, and terracing a slope. You'll even learn where the experts themselves go for advice and what factors gardeners consistently forget.

Here's what you'll find in Chapter 1

YOUR WANT LIST

To help you plan your perfect garden, Indianapolis landscape designer Loretta Spilker developed this series of questions:

❧ What do you like most about your landscape? Least?

❧ Do you want to block or direct traffic?

❧ Which views (from windows, yard, or street) do you especially like? Dislike?

❧ Do you want to block or channel breezes or winds? From which direction or directions?

❧ Do you need screening for privacy? To block poor views? To muffle noise?

❧ Are there community restrictions, neighborhood covenants, or zoning or building codes in effect?

❧ Where are your overhead and underground utility lines or water pipes?

❧ Do you want to accent or camouflage any aspect of your home?

❧ Do you want to create shady, sunny, or quiet areas?

❧ How much work are you willing to do or pay for? How much money have you budgeted for immediate and future landscaping?

THE FIRST STEPS

You're about to start a new garden, and you can't wait to put hoe to ground. But first you must wait, watch, plan, and prepare. By carefully thinking through your garden first, you'll make planting easier and more successful when the time for it finally does come.

Imagine Your Garden

The garden of your dreams, and how to make it real • Decisions and choices • Backyard treasure-hunting • Long-term logic

Every good garden begins in the mind of the gardener. Ask yourself why you're starting this garden: to beautify your yard, to create an outdoor living space, or to harvest vegetables or cut flowers? Think about what you want from your garden and how much time, effort, and money you're willing to put into it.

DETERMINE YOUR NEEDS AND WANTS Most professional garden designers and landscape architects begin by asking clients very specific questions. "I try to find out if my clients want cut flowers, if they plan to use the garden at night, or if they'd like to screen a wall," says Andrea Sessions of Tennessee's Sunlight Gardens. "I ask them which season the garden will be used most, and if they want seating." One of her clients, for example, wanted to create a private spot for a hot tub. You might want an herb garden near the kitchen, or a bed that combines flowers and vegetables, or maybe a vine-covered fence.

CONSIDER THE LANDSCAPE The garden you create will depend not just on what you want but also on what you already have. No matter how small your yard, it probably offers several planting sites. Take a hard look at the features of your yard, and list the advantages and drawbacks.

• Gene Banks of Connecticut's Catnip Acres says, "I sit and cogitate. I throw garden hoses outlining different shapes in different spots to get ideas about where and how to start beds."

• Landscape architect John Buchholz of Sausalito, California, investigates "the lay of the land, its slopes and topography," and he examines the architecture of the house. He identifies special views and vantage points that should either be emphasized (a pond, for example,

This lush perennial border in Akron, Ohio, leaves plenty of room in the front yard for other activities. Its bloom begins in early spring with bleeding hearts, forget-me-nots, and columbines, and lasts through fall with the flowering of ornamental grasses.

or a series of rolling hills) or played down (a smokestack down the road). He also notes styles or themes in the buildings that could be imitated or contrasted in the landscape.

• Gail Haggard of Plants of the Southwest in New Mexico urges gardeners to "use every exposure and niche for its special climate."

THINK LONG-TERM Your garden should make your life more enjoyable. Plan its placement where it won't cause you grief. If you're thinking of placing a new garden near the house or driveway, set some trash cans where you plan to dig, and leave them there for a week or two,

starting your garden

LONG-TERM PLANS

As you plan your backyard landscape, think about all the ways you'll use it.

❧ Do you spend a lot of time outside? Would you like to? In the back or the front yard? Any other area?

❧ Are you gardening for aesthetics, for food, or both?

❧ Do you want a pool, spa, deck, patio, open lawn, dining area, or seating area now or in the future?

❧ Would you like special features such as water gardens, rock gardens, or lighting?

❧ If you have children, do they need play, gardening, or sports areas? Should these be separate areas or part of the landscape?

❧ Will you entertain outdoors? How many people? Day or night?

❧ Does any family member have allergies? Do you need special access for strollers or wheelchairs?

❧ Do you want your garden to increase the value of your home?

❧ How long do you expect to garden on this site?

suggests Cassie Brown, a garden designer from Teaneck, New Jersey. If you find you're knocking the cans down when you drive into the garage, or if you stumble over them every time you throw out the trash, look for an alternate site. At the same time, plan your garden near a water source and not too far from the driveway so that bringing in new plants and maintaining the garden won't be a hassle.

Creating a long-term plan for your entire yard on paper can eliminate problems that might occur if you simply work one area at a time. The sunniest spot in your yard may be a good choice for this year's perennial bed, but it might also be the *only* site for the herb garden you want next year. Shade trees will affect the plants around them. If you know what else you want to grow, you can position everything intelligently. (For more on creating plans, see "Putting It on Paper" on page 76 and "Put It in Writing" on page 165).

Finally, think about whether you will need to contract major work, like installing irrigation or moving lots of soil. You'll save money if you do it all at once.

Know Your Site

Evaluating the environment • Microclimate magic • Creative patience

Whether you're taking over an old established garden or beginning from scratch on a new plot, you'll need to analyze the site before deciding what and where to plant. "Resist the urge to jump into planting your entire landscape," says Kris Bachtell of the Morton Arboretum in Illinois, "or you'll likely be disappointed with the performance of many of the plants."

CHECK OUT THE CLIMATE "Typically, gardeners underestimate the amount of shade their yard receives," says Kris. That's why Bobbie Schwartz of Bobbie's Green Thumb in Ohio asks all of her clients to fill out a "sun chart" (opposite page). After sun, say the experts, consider soil. Ted Lockwood of Connecticut's Highstead Arboretum believes that the secret to a successful garden isn't sun or shade, but good soil. Temperature, wind, humidity, and rainfall also can dictate plant choices. You can get information about your local climate—frost dates, rainfall, and Hardiness Zone—from local nurseries, botanical gardens, or cooperative extension agencies.

SUN AND WIND CHART Date: _____			
	AREA A	**AREA B**	**AREA C**	**AREA D**
7 AM				
9 AM				
11 AM				
12 NOON				
1 PM				
2 PM				
3 PM				
4 PM				
5 PM				
6 PM				
Drainage (see page 28)				
Soil (see page 30)				
Micro-climate conditions (see page 20)				

Plant annuals—like the heliotrope, purple-leaved fountain grass, and 'Victoria' sage above—and watch to see which ones thrive to help you predict how shrubs and perennials will react in your site.

You can get the following information from a local botanical garden, nursery, or cooperative extension agency:

Hardiness Zone: _____   Average local rainfall _____

ENERGYSCAPING

A good landscape design can keep your home cool in summer and warm in winter, thus cutting your energy costs, says Douglas Owens-Pike of EnergyScapes, Inc., in Minneapolis. A well-planned garden also demands less water, fertilizer, and pest control. Here are ways to create an energyscape.

❧ Plant evergreen screens to block winter winds and setting summer sun.

❧ Choose the best locations—usually in the southeast corner—for decks and patios that are used for entertaining.

❧ Shade air conditioners with small trees.

❧ Plant large shade trees on the east and west sides to allow maximum winter solar heat through low sun angles and summer shade early and late in the day.

❧ Substitute one-species lawn with native perennial plants that require much less care.

SEARCH OUT MICROCLIMATES Don't fret if you find out that your zone isn't suitable for some of the plants you want to grow. Nearly every backyard is a combination of small sites with very different climates affected by exposure, nearby structures, and even altitude. Brick, rock, and concrete walls, for instance, hold and radiate warmth; sites near ponds will also stay warm longer. Fences and trees break the flow of wind, and frost gathers first in the low parts of a yard. By finding the right microclimate, you might be successful in growing plants that are recommended for up to three zones warmer than yours.

To locate a warm spot in your yard, look for where the snow melts first, advises Shane Smith, director of Wyoming's Cheyenne Botanic Garden. Cold spots are where the snow lingers. If you live where there's little or no snow, you'll find the coldest sites at the bottom of a hill or in an area that's shaded throughout the winter. Southern exposures will be warmer than northern ones.

Interestingly, a site that's covered by snow during winter often provides the best place for a tender plant. Snow cover protects plants from wind and winter sun, and the soil under a blanket of snow usually stays warmer than exposed ground. The cold also prevents plants from producing early growth that can be killed by frost. "Put a fruit tree in a cold spot," says Shane Smith, "and it will be like going 100 miles south

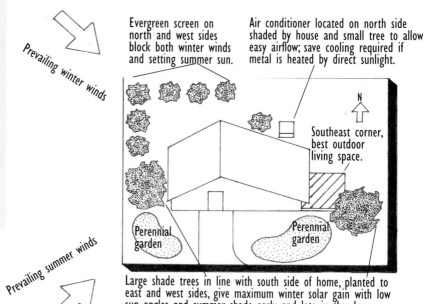

Prevailing winter winds

Evergreen screen on north and west sides block both winter winds and setting summer sun.

Air conditioner located on north side shaded by house and small tree to allow easy airflow; save cooling required if metal is heated by direct sunlight.

N

Southeast corner, best outdoor living space.

Perennial garden

Perennial garden

Prevailing summer winds

Large shade trees in line with south side of home, planted to east and west sides, give maximum winter solar gain with low sun angles and summer shade early and late in the day.

to another zone. The cold will hold off flower-set and increase fruit yield just as a longer growing season would in a warmer climate."

TAKE A WALK No site analysis is complete without a close look at the plants that are already there. "Slowly walk around the property," says Chicago landscape architect Janet Shen, "and consider the effect of grades, slopes, traffic patterns, views, and existing structures." Her secret? Photographing the yard as she goes, so she can analyze it closely later.

Don't forget the best source of information: existing plants. Even if you don't want to keep the plants that are already in your garden, you can learn a lot about your yard by discovering what grows there naturally. If you find mounds of bog plants, like cattails and rushes, you'll know that other moisture-loving plants will thrive in your yard. If tender perennials, like sweet pea vine, last over the winter, you can assume that other tender plants will be hardy as well.

TAKE YOUR TIME How long should your site analysis take? According to Kris Bachtell, it should take at least one growing season so that you can take into account such factors as changing light, seasonal fluctuations in rainfall, and the effects of frost. And if you've recently moved into a home, you'll need time to discover what plants are already there. "If a previous owner was an avid gardener," says Shane Smith, "you'll want to wait and see what comes up." What looks like a patch of hay in March may turn out to be a lush bank of ferns come April, and you may discover that a tree you thought was dead is a late-blooming beauty. In fact, it takes years of gardening to really understand a site intimately. Knowing your yard is an ongoing process of coaxing the secrets out of the landscape.

This doesn't mean that you have to stand around just watching how your garden grows the first year. You can get instant gratification by planting some annuals. Not only will this satisfy your need to get your hands into the ground and give you a quick shot of color, annuals can tell you a lot about the land. If sun-lovers languish in a particular spot, you'll want to consider shade-tolerant shrubs and perennials for that area. If plants droop from wet roots, you may need to drain the site, or consider a bog garden. If everything flourishes, toast your good fortune and get out the garden catalogs.

A closely spaced row of conifers forms a year-round windbreak that keeps in warmth in winter and shades the house in summer. It's also a great backdrop for a bed of flowers or flowering shrubs.

Light

Making sense of sun and shade requirements • Is all sun the same?
• Dappled shade • Shaving away the shade

Unless you plan to grow mushrooms, you'll need to give serious consideration to the available light in your yard when deciding what to plant. Light is the primary source of energy for every growing thing, from the lowest blade of grass to the highest tree. Some plants, like vegetables, are gluttons for light. Others—ferns and hostas, for example—prefer to stay out of the sun. You'll find a plant's light requirements described in garden catalogs as full sun or light, partial, or deep shade. However, there are subtle shades of meaning in their definitions.

FULL SUN What exactly is meant by full sun? The experts offer slightly different definitions:

• "Full sun means no shade at all," says Cynthia Rice, a landscape architect from Raleigh, North Carolina. "Of course, in our world," she

Vibrant reds and yellows, like the flowers of 'Lucifer' crocosmia and yarrow, thrive in full-sun situations.

adds, "there's no such thing." Every yard receives a degree of shade, whether from old, established trees or the shadows of surrounding houses. For her, a site with some shade early and late in the day can safely be considered to be in full sun.

• According to Peter and Jean Ruh, garden experts from the Homestead division of Ohio's Sunnybrook Farms, your yard is in full sun if it receives direct midsummer light from 8:30 A.M. to 7:00 P.M.

• Dorthe Hviid of The Berkshire Botanical Garden in Massachusetts clarifies the Ruhs' definition further: Those 10 to 12 hours of sun need only appear on June 21, the longest day of the year.

• Chicago landscape architect Janet Shen sets a lower limit for full sun at 8 hours, as do Richard Boonstra retired president of Ohio's Bluestone Perennials and Neil Diboll of Wisconsin's Prairie Nursery.

• Seattle garden designer Sue Moss, Aileen Lubin, director of Maine's Merryspring Park, and Mike Shoup of the Antique Rose Emporium in Brenham, Texas, are all comfortable defining "full sun" as 6 hours of direct light a day.

• For Kim Hawks of North Carolina's Niche Gardens, full sun is defined as 6 hours of sun a day, but preferably all in the afternoon.

Most shade-loving plants bear flowers in muted colors, but the lime green foliage of hostas and magenta plumes of astilbes can light up a dark corner.

It would be nice if the nursery industry could get together and decide on a definition. Until that happens, you'll have to question your sources closely when taking advice on sun requirements, or depend on an average of 6 to 8 hours a day that works for many full-sun plants.

"LIGHT" VERSUS "PARTIAL" SHADE If part of your yard is shaded by tall, relatively open trees, the experts consider it to be in light shade (or "speckled" or "dappled" shade), or "filtered sun." Many sun-loving plants grow well in light shade. Mike Shoup has successfully grown an 'Old Blush' rose under a large oak that provides "bright" shade— though it doesn't flower as heavily as its sisters in full sun, it does bloom nicely.

A striking spring combination: bluebells blooming in the shade of a white-flowering crabapple tree.

Most gardens contain areas of sun and shade, like this perennial bed at the New York Botanical Garden. Hydrangeas bloom profusely in the filtered shade of a large oak tree, while sun-loving clary sage and smokebush are planted outside the reach of its branches.

Partial shade means that an area receives periods of both full sun and light shade, including over an hour—2 to 3 hours for most plants—of full sun. Many plants thrive in partial shade, say Peter and Jean Ruh, such as hostas, which like going into shade at about four in the afternoon. A caution: Morning shade followed by a blast of midday sun can stress plants (including some who ordinarily revel in sun), causing them to wilt even when the soil is well irrigated. If plants aren't warmed by morning, the harsh blast of midday sun will be a shocking contrast.

DEEP SHADE If you have deep (or full) shade in your yard, you probably know it. A dense canopy of trees—a stand of conifers, say, or an old American elm—allow little light to penetrate. Some buildings may be so close to each other that the sun can reach the ground only at midday. Douglas Owens-Pike of Minneapolis's EnergyScapes, Inc., defines deep shade as "an hour or less of direct sun daily." It presents a gardening challenge, but by no means an insurmountable one.

MAKING THE MOST OF SHADE You can deal with deep shade in one of two ways, say the experts. You can grow plants that don't require much light (see "Plants for Tough Spots" on pages 36–37 for sugges-tions), or you can limb up your trees (trim off all the lower branches to allow light to penetrate), says Richard Boonstra. Richard remembers visiting a gardener whose grounds were almost entirely shaded by large trees. "He had trimmed all the lower branches," Richard says, "and was growing almost everything in his beds. The trees looked fine, it was shady in his yard all day, but even sun-lovers were growing and giving some bloom." The secret, he says, is to distinguish between moist, dank shade—in which only a limited number of plants will succeed—and dry, bright shade with ample indirect light. If you have the former, a little judicious pruning can help you create the latter.

Galen Gates of the Chicago Botanic Garden advises caution in limbing-up plants. He, too, has had great results in opening up canopies to allow light, but he believes that lopping off all the lower limbs will destroy the shape of a tree and create a lollipop effect. "If I can't open a tree canopy with selective thinning all the way up, I prefer removing a few trees rather than mutilating them all," he says.

A TIME FOR SUN, A TIME FOR SHADE

The amount of sun your yard gets isn't as important as when it gets it and where you live.

In the South, where summer is long and hot, almost all plants, even roses and waterlilies, appreciate relief from the sun's brutal afternoon rays.

Even in the North, you don't need 8 to 12 hours of sun to grow full-sun plants, say Peter Linsner and Kris Bachtell of the Morton Arboretum in Illinois. Most plants shut down in the afternoon because of the heat. Full-sun plants will perform as well in early morning to noon sun as they will when exposed to sun all day.

Another benefit of siting plants to receive early morning sunlight is that it allows leaves to dry off quickly, reducing the chance of fungal diseases. But early morning sun can also in-crease frost damage by heating frozen foliage too quickly.

HANDLING HUMIDITY

In some regions, it's not the cold or heat—it's the humidity that causes most garden problems. "Humidity isn't always bad," says Mercer Arboretum's Linda Gay, who gardens in humid South Texas. In long, dry summers, plants may wilt during the day but recover during the muggy night. However, when humidity is high and temperatures soar into the 90s with not a single breeze, plants can't breathe. Leaves blacken, and moisture breeds fungal disease and rot.

When this happens, Linda trims infected foliage and increases air circulation by removing some tree limbs and thinning or spacing out the plants. She uses small gravel mulch around the plants instead of pine bark. The gravel helps the plants dry out in their centers; pine bark seems to keep everything moist.

Rainfall

Moisture measures • Choosing water-wise plants • Making every drop count

In a gardener's ideal world, an inch of rain would fall every week during the growing season, making hoses obsolete and the garden lush and vibrant. But most of us don't live in an ideal world, and water is a precious resource. However, you can save water by measuring weekly rainfall, watering only as much as your garden needs, and choosing plants appropriate for the climate in your backyard.

GAUGING THE RAIN Whether you live in soggy Seattle or arid Arizona, the amount of rain you get from week to week varies. How do you know if your garden is getting enough rain or if you should water it? Look at your plants, says Bobbie Schwartz of Bobbie's Green Thumb in Ohio. Do they appear healthy and evenly green, or are they wilting? Check them in the early evening or on an overcast day as some plants—especially young tender ones—tend to wilt temporarily under the heat of the sun. Bobbie also recommends looking for water runoff—the water that doesn't get absorbed into the soil but runs off into surrounding areas. Except in downpours, when rain falls too heavily to be fully absorbed, runoff indicates that the soil is well saturated and watering is unnecessary. But don't go by runoff alone. Mike Ruggerio of the New York Botanical Garden points out that runoff also occurs when sod is so dry it can't absorb water.

An easier way to determine if your garden is getting enough water, says Celeste Wilson of California's Las Pilitas Nursery, is with a rain gauge (a small plastic tube calibrated in inches of rainfall) or a moisture gauge (a slightly more sophisticated instrument that lets you know exactly how much water is available to your plants). Or, you can simply leave an empty can in an exposed spot and measure the water level at the end of each week. Most vegetables need about 2 inches of water per week. Established perennials that need about 1 inch per week are considered average, but all plants need more when newly planted.

CHOOSING WATER-SMART PLANTS Hunter Carleton of Washington's Bear Creek Nursery echoes many of the experts when he says that the secret to conserving water and reducing watering chores is to "plant relative to rainfall." That means selecting plants that would thrive in your yard given normal rainfall for your area, without additional watering. This approach, says North Carolina landscape architect Cynthia Rice, is all part of the trend toward landscaping to conserve water (or, as Mary Harrison of Mary's Plant Farm puts it, "using the right plant in the right place"). No matter how dry your site, you can find many plants that will thrive with little or no watering. Of course, adds Cynthia Rice, any plant needs water when it's first put into the ground, and newly planted shrubs and trees need consistent, deep watering for at least the first season.

If your summers tend to be droughty, says Neil Diboll of Wisconsin's Prairie Nursery, consider planting a wildflower meadow (see "Prairie Home Companions" on page 198) instead of a garden. Once established, meadows require no more water than mother nature supplies.

Whether you live in an area that receives 6 inches of rain a year or 60, you'll probably want to consider plants that can survive without additional water during normal years. Some of the most drought-tolerant plants are succulents—such as echeveria and dudleya above—which have thick, fleshy leaves that store water for dry times. Some succulents, like sedum, hens-and-chickens, and yucca, are quite cold-hardy.

THE THIRSTY ONES

If you can't live without exotics that nature clearly meant for another climate, try these tips:

❧ Bobbie Holder of Wyoming's Pawnee Greenhouse and Nursery suggests grouping plants with similar water requirements together "to minimize watering and water wasting."

❧ Mulch deeply—use 2 inches for most perennials, up to 4 inches for trees (see page 209 for mulches).

❧ Give the water that your home and driveway shed to your trees and gardens, says Gail Haggard of New Mexico's Plants of the Southwest. Place a water barrel beneath a downspout to collect rainwater.

❧ Plant exotics with low-light requirements in the shade, suggest Peter and Jean Ruh of Ohio's Sunnybrook Farms, since "shade gardens require less water than those in full sun."

❧ Soak plants in water before planting, says Nelson Sterner of Long Island's Old Westbury Gardens.

Drainage

Why to aim for well-drained soil • Lessons in loosening clay • Plant solutions for soggy spots

Rather than fixing poorly drained soil, consider planting a bog garden, with plants that are happy with wet feet. Cardinal flower and shooting star will thrive in even the wettest spot.

Proper water management in the garden depends not only on how much rain falls each week but also on how well the soil holds water. Experts refer to this as drainage. Well-drained soil has plenty of air space, which allows water to pass through quickly. Poorly drained soils have little air space, so water moves slowly and can cause roots to rot and plants to die. "Poor drainage is the number one cause of plant death," says Ellen Talmage of Long Island's Horticultural Goddess, Inc., especially in winter, when root systems are dormant. Wet soil, she adds, is also the perfect breeding ground for a host of root rot diseases.

IMPROVING DRAINAGE If your soil drains poorly, it probably contains a lot of clay, as is true in many areas of the United States. Made up of extremely fine particles, clay soil acts like a very efficient sponge when wet. When dry, it assumes the consistency of concrete—not the most inviting medium for your average garden plant. You need to add well-composted organic matter to improve the drainage of heavy clay soils, say the experts. Though often recommended for its water-holding

A site that doesn't drain well can be fixed with a drainage pipe leading to a drainage ditch. Dig a trench a few inches deep and line it with gravel. Place the pipe on top, cover it with agricultural fabric, and top with soil.

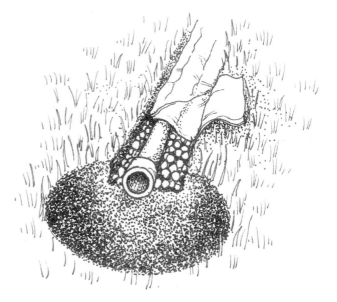

capacities, organic matter also allows the free passage of water and air. "The problem with clay," says Hunter Carleton of Washington's Bear Creek Nursery, "is that it has bonding properties—it tends to stick together. But the acids that are a byproduct of your compost pile break up the clay." Nelson Sterner, director of horticulture at Long Island's Old Westbury Gardens, adds gypsum to break up clay soil.

Kim Hawks of North Carolina's Niche Gardens tills or hand digs the existing soil, then gently builds a layer of topsoil enriched with organic matter or compost on top of the clay to a depth of 1 to 2 feet. Some gardeners till this layer into the soil; others just plant in the top layer. Either way, break up the clay under the organic matter to avoid creating a hard layer underneath.

Mary Irish of Phoenix's Desert Botanical Garden advises gardeners living in the West to beware of another cause of poor drainage: deposits of a calcium carbonate rock called caliche. Caliche may be thick or thin, shallow or deep, but it is always impenetrable to water and roots, and it won't drain at all. If you suspect caliche (see "Drainage Checks," at right), poke down 12 to18 inches and see if you find a layer of hardpan. Dig the caliche out with a spade, then add organic matter.

WIPING AWAY WET SPOTS If your yard drains well, yet water tends to collect in certain areas, the problem may not be the soil but rather that particular site. Wet spots can result from:
• natural depressions in the landscape
• deep shade cast by buildings (shade under trees tends to be dry, since most standing water is taken up by the trees' roots)
• rain running freely off nearby structures
• soil that has been damaged by heavy tilling.

If runoff from something like a garage roof is a problem, simply install gutters and a downspout to direct water away from the garden. In areas where gutters aren't appropriate, you can install tile drainage, says Dr. Richard Lighty, director of Delaware's Mount Cuba Center (see illustration below). An easier way of dealing with wet areas, says Ellen Talmage, is to choose plants that thrive in boggy conditions, keeping in mind that unless the soil is particularly marshy, these plants will need additional water during very dry spells.

DRAINAGE CHECKS

Here are several ways to evaluate how well your soil drains:

🐦 Pick up a handful of soil and squeeze it. If it's gummy and forms a clump that doesn't crumble easily, it will not drain well.

🐦 Take a walk in the yard. If you find yourself sinking into the soil, it's probably holding too much water.

🐦 Dig a hole 18 to 24 inches deep and wide. Fill it to the top with water. If the water is gone in 20 minutes, drainage is good. Two hours drainage is average. If you see water in the hole after 6 to 8 hours—you know what that means.

Keep in mind that after several days of rain, only the best-drained soils will pass the test. In the Midwest and elsewhere, spring soil is often saturated; the same soil in summer can be dry and well-drained.

HOW TO TEST SOIL

When you're ready to test your soil, contact your local cooperative extension agency, which will ask you to send them soil samples collected from the area you plan to garden. Soil can vary from one site in your yard to another, so if you are planning a perennial bed on the south side of your house and a vegetable plot on the west, it pays to have separate tests done.

Be sure to tell the lab what you plan to grow in those areas, and ask them to recommend any necessary additions to the soil. Hint: Most gardeners test their soil in the spring. You'll usually get results back faster if you send samples to be tested in the fall or winter.

Soil

Soil test strategies • Timely testing • Using test results

Soil is more than just dirt underfoot, it's a nearly magical mixture of ground rock, decayed and decaying plant matter, microorganisms, moisture, and air. It holds, nourishes, and sustains plant life. You can determine the quality of your soil with a test, which will tell you its nutrient content and pH level (the measure of its acidity or alkalinity).

WHEN TO TEST When and how often should you test your soil? The experts offer a variety of opinions.
• Peter Borchard of Companion Plants in Ohio tests all his beds every three years to make sure that the soil contains an optimum level of nutrients.
• Horticulturists at Longwood Gardens in Kennett Square, Pennsylvania, recommend testing every other year.
• Dorthe Hviid of The Berkshire Botanical Garden in Massachusetts tests every four to six years.
• Tom Butterworth of Connecticut's Butterbrook Farms considers

Sandy soil (left) is composed of loosely spaced particles that allow water and nutrients to drain too quickly. Clay soil (right) is tightly packed, and allows little drainage. Loam (center) has the largest particles, spaced just right.

soil testing "terribly important when you're putting in a new garden," but he doesn't recommend additional soil tests. "Once you have that baseline test," he says, "you can learn all you need to know from your plants."

• For Sarah Gallant of Maine's Pinetree Garden Seeds, testing is only important if crops become unproductive. Otherwise, she says, she ensures high fertility by adding well-composted organic matter (a combination of manure and garden waste) to all new plantings.

• Seattle garden designer Sue Moss agrees: "To avoid expense and work, I don't bother with soil tests unless things fail to thrive." Because Seattle soils are reliably acidic, Sue simply amends her soil with organic material, which has a neutralizing effect, and a balanced organic fertilizer before planting.

• You may want a soil test, says Dr. Richard Lighty, director of Delaware's Mount Cuba Center, if you're putting in plants with strict requirements—such as rhododendrons, which need a low pH. Otherwise, he says, most new gardens need only an application of organic fertilizer containing nitrogen, potassium, and phosphorus.

MAKING AMENDMENTS Since most plants do best in soil that's neutral to slightly acid, you'll probably want to start amending your soil if your test indicates a high acidity or alkalinity (see "Playing Around with pH" on page 269). As for nutrients, a good test should tell you whether your soil is lacking in the "big three"—nitrogen, phosphorus, and potassium—as well as micronutrients such as magnesium, calcium, and iron. Apply fertilizer as needed. (See also "Creating Fertile Ground" on page 273.)

Existing Plants

New tricks for old plants • *Young and old together*
• *The clean-slate advantage* • *Horticultural health watch*

Unless you've moved into a home on a brand new construction site, your landscape probably has plenty of well-established plants: those you've put in and others that have been around for years. What you keep and what you discard depends on several factors, not the least of which is your attachment to the plants.

WHEN IN DOUBT . . .

If you're having trouble deciding whether to keep a particular plant, Andrea Sessions of Tennessee's Sunlight Gardens suggests that you ask yourself some questions:

❧ Do I love this plant?

❧ Is it too big? (Could it be successfully pruned?)

❧ Has it always had problems?

❧ Does it clash in color or style with the new garden? (And if it does, is there a place for it to live on its own?)

❧ Does it seem to want to take over the rest of the garden?

Don't save an old plant simply because it isn't dead. If you feel guilty about removing it, give it away or remind yourself how much it will enrich your compost.

LESSONS FROM THE WILD

Bob Stewart, owner of Arrowhead Alpines in Michigan, and his colleagues have an interesting alternative to using hardiness zones to determine which plants they'll grow. "We look at a plant's range in the wild and the altitudes at which it occurs, and we draw our own conclusions. We tend to be a bit optimistic; if there's any chance, we try it and see," he says.

"Placement in the garden makes a big difference as well. You need to understand your garden's microclimates to be successful with the tricky ones. It's a good idea to have a few plants to experiment with. Don't give up on the first try. If you're having trouble with a plant, talk to other good growers in your area and ask what they grow and how they do it," suggests Bob.

LET YOUR HEART BE YOUR GUIDE You love the idea of an all-white garden, but you're still carrying a torch for that orange asclepias you nurtured from a seedling. Should you close your eyes and toss it on the compost heap? The experts recommend that you try to work your favorite plants into a new garden design. Marc Stoecklein of Stoecklein's Nursery in Pennsylvania, who's created a number of specialized gardens, usually finds a way to incorporate old plants into the new landscape. "Even in an all-grass or all-blue garden, I mix other plants, such as evergreen backdrops," he says. If a plant really doesn't fit into the new scheme, he makes an effort to find a nook for it somewhere else.

In general, the experts recommend trying to save prize plants, like specimens. California landscape designer John Buchholz tries to work around existing specimen trees, which he defines as "anything tall, with a nice crown and a 3- to 4-inch caliper (the thickness of the trunk), that looks pretty." If you try to move a specimen, he says, it can take several years to come back, and you could end up damaging the plant. Galen Gates of the Chicago Botanic Garden recommends that you call a professional to move large trees.

THE VALUE OF AGE Established plants add a sense of maturity to a new landscape, says Kim Hawks. San Francisco landscape architect Marta Fry tries not to remove plants that add "scale, layering, canopy, shade, or structure to the garden—these elements are hard to achieve." Instead of cutting down a large tree to make way for some desirable saplings, she will often cut it back gradually as the new trees mature. Sometimes, she says, an older tree can be rejuvenated by pruning it to fit into a new planting. She doesn't, however, recommend saving every tree on the property. "Some fast-growing trees may be large, but they're not necessarily long-lived and can be brittle," she says. "I don't mind removing a 'junk' tree." She also recommends that you don't top off a tree to expose a view. Unless the pruning can be done expertly, she says, it won't do justice to the tree or the view.

EVALUATE PLANT HEALTH Love may not be reason enough to save a plant, if the object of your affection is ailing or overgrown. Linda Gay of Mercer Arboretum in Texas considers pest- and disease-resistance the most important criteria to use when evaluating existing plants.

Pat Cook, a horticulturist at Queens Botanic Garden, decided to keep the maple tree she found in her backyard because she liked the look of permanence its broad, round canopy gave the garden, even though it created a lot of shade.

Marc Stoecklein agrees: "If the plant is a host for insects, it can harm an entire garden," he says. On the other hand, a plant may simply need some TLC. "If the problem is one of location or poor planting," says Connecticut cooperative agent Dr. Sharon Douglas, "replanting may cure it." Don't forget, though, that some perennials have a limited useful life. Gene Banks of Connecticut's Catnip Acres replaces any older plants that have become woody (fibrous, with fewer blooms and tougher stems). "After four to five years," she says, "it's best to start fresh with certain plants, including bee balm, lavender, winter savory, and caryopteris." Don't be too quick to give up on a plant, though. For many, some dieback is natural and doesn't indicate problems. Arborvitae branches, for example, often turn brown in winter and are later shed: the tree isn't dying, it's making room for new growth.

Older plants, like this hinoki false cypress, often provide texture as well as size, which is hard to come by in young plants.

THE USDA HARDINESS ZONE MAP

To help gardeners choose plants that can survive winter in their backyards, the United States Department of Agriculture has created a map of plant Hardiness Zones. Each zone represents average annual minimum temperature in a region.

Though the Zone Map is the best guide we have to plant hardiness, experts note that it's not perfect. Arizona, Cape Cod, and Seattle have the same zone classification, but length of winter, length of day, rainfall, and snowfall vary greatly. Use zone classifications when they are helpful; they can give you valuable information on plants that are unsuitable for your climate or that will need extra care. But don't depend solely on that zone number. Ask neighbors, nurserypeople, and other garden experts what works best in your area.

THE RIGHT FIT

Every gardener has to accept some givens, such as climate, local rainfall, and plant requirements, but you can fiddle with certain aspects of your garden, like soil texture, plant hardiness, and length of season. The experts disagree about just how far you should go to change your site so the plants you like will grow on it. Some believe in trying everything, but others think it's wiser to find plants that are happy growing in the conditions you have to offer.

Plant Hardiness

Stretching plants beyond their zones • *Cold-spot ingenuity*
• *Reasonable risks* • *Creative coverage*

A plant's hardiness is its ability to withstand cold. Most plants, even those from the tropics, do well in northern summers; it's the winters that test their mettle. The safe way to choose plants for your garden is to make sure they're recommended for your hardiness zone.

STRETCHING PLANT HARDINESS Gardeners, however, don't necessarily play it safe. There always seems to be some fabulous plant from the zone down the road that just might work in your backyard given a little protection, a little extra effort, a little luck. Few topics generate as much heated debate among the experts as "stretching" a plant into another zone.

• "I plant only what's absolutely going to grow," says Neil Diboll of Wisconsin's Prairie Nursery—an understandable point of view given the harshness of prairie winters.

• Mary Harrison of Mary's Plant Farm in Ohio not only recommends against stretching plants but also questions the need for it. "There are plenty of plants for any given area." she says.

• Massachusetts horticulturist Dorthe Hviid sees both sides of the issue. She encourages "working with nature instead of against it," but empathizes with gardeners who can't live without a particular plant.

• Dr. Richard Lighty, director of Delaware's Mount Cuba Center, compares zone stretching to investing in the stock market. "You should only do it," he advises, "when you have the luxury to play around." Even if you're willing and able to experiment, he believes, the mainstays of the garden should be reliable.

• Guy Sternberg of Starhill Forest Arboretum in Illinois agrees. "The healthiest, most appropriate landscape in most situations is the native landscape."

• But Cindy Reed of Great Plains Native Plant Society in South Dakota, like many home gardeners, is simply a sucker for stretching plants. "I'm unable to resist pushing any attractive plant just to see if it will really die in my yard," she says.

CONSIDER CLIMATE AND MICROCLIMATE Whether you stretch or not depends, in part, on where you live, says Douglas Owens-Pike of EnergyScapes, Inc., in Minnesota, where winter temperatures regularly reach -35° F. If one of his clients is wild about a plant that isn't likely to succeed in the area, he tries to suggest a reasonable alternative. Even in Zone 10, however, there are microclimates (see page 20) whose minimum temperatures may actually be closer to those of Zone 9, 8, or even 7. If you're aware of a "warm spot" in your yard, you may have a microclimate that will suit a plant that's

Hybridizers have created cold-hardy plants such as 'PJM' rhododendron (left), hardy to -45°F; 'Carefree Beauty' shrub rose (center), hardy to Zone 4; and 'Oregon Spring' tomatoes (right), which produce fruit in just 68 days, perfect for a short-season climate.

TOUGH PLANTS FOR TOUGH SPOTS

The experts agree: The best way to keep a plant healthy is to put it in a spot that meets its needs. There are plants that will be happy in even the toughest spots, and we asked our experts to choose the best plants for the most difficult conditions.

TREES, SHRUBS, AND VINES FOR MEDIUM TO HEAVY SHADE

Bearberry (*Arctostaphylos uva-ursi*)

Boston ivy (*Parthenocissus tricuspidata*)

Bunchberry (*Cornus canadensis*)

Drooping leucothoe (*Leucothoe fontanesiana*)

English ivy (*Hedera helix*)

Hemlock (*Tsuga* spp.)

Japanese aucuba (*Aucuba japonica*)

Japanese hydrangea vine (*Schizophragma hydrangeoides*)

Japanese holly (*Ilex crenata*)

Jetbead (*Rhodotypos scandens*)

Kalmia latifolia (*Kalmia* spp.)

Leatherwood (*Cyrilla racemiflora*)

Oakleaf hydrangea (*Hydrangea quercifolia*)

Ratstripper (*Paxistima canbyi*)

Rosebay rhododendron (*Rhododendron maximum*)

Salal (*Gaultheria shallon*)

Sweet box (*Sarcococca* spp.)

Sweetspire (*Itea virginica*)

Virginia creeper (*Parthenocissus quinquefolia*)

Wintercreeper (*Euonymus fortunei*)

ANNUALS, PERENNIALS, AND BULBS FOR MEDIUM TO HEAVY SHADE

Barrenwort (*Epimedium* spp.)

Begonia (*Begonia grandis*, *B. × semperflorens*, *B. × tuberhybrida*)

Bergenia (*Bergenia cordifolia*)

Bleeding heart (*Dicentra* spp.)

Bloodroot (*Sanguinaria canadensis*)

Bugbane (*Cimicifuga spp.*)

Bugleweed (*Ajuga reptans*)

Busy Lizzie (*Impatiens walleriana*)

Cinnamon fern (*Osmunda cinnamonmea*)

Coleus (*Solenostemon scutellarioides*)

Columbine (*Aquilegia* spp. and hybrids)

Corydalis (*Corydalis* spp.)

Foamflower (*Tiarella* spp.)

Foxglove (*Digitalis* spp.)

Gentian (*Gentiana* spp.)

Ginger (*Asarum* spp.)

Goatsbeard (*Aruncus* spp.)

Goldenstar (*Chrysogonum virginianum*)

Hostas (*Hosta* spp. and hybrids)

Interrupted fern (*Osmunda claytoniana*)

Jack-in-the-pulpit (*Arisaema triphyllum*)

Ligularia (*Ligularia* spp.)

Lilyturf (*Liriope* spp.)

Lily-of-the-valley (*Convallaria majalis*)

Liverwort (*Hepatica* spp.)

Lungwort (*Pulmonaria* spp.)

Mayapple (*Podophyllum peltatum*)

Meadowsweet (*Filipendula* spp.)

Meehan's mint (*Meehania cordata*)

Monkshood (*Aconitum* spp.)

New Zealand flax (*Phormium tenax*)

Pachysandra (*Pachysandra* spp.)

Partridgeberry (*Mitchella repens*)

Periwinkle (*Vinca minor*)

Primrose (*Primula* spp.)

Shield fern (*Polystichum* spp.)

Solomon's seal (*Polygonatum spp.*)

Spiderwort (*Tradescantia* spp. and hybrids)

Spotted dead nettle (*Lamium maculatum*)

Strawberry (*Fragaria* spp.)

Sweet woodruff (*Galium odorata*)

Sweet cicely (*Myrrhis odorata*)

Turk's cap lily (*Lilium superbum*)

Turtlehead (*Chelone* spp.)

Virginia bluebells (*Mertensia pulmonarioides*)

Wishbone flower (*Torenia fournieri*)

Wood ferns (*Dryopteris* spp.)

Wood aster (*Aster lateriflorus*)

Yellow waxbells (*Kirengeshoma palmata*)

TREES, SHRUBS, AND VINES FOR WET SOIL

American persimmon (*Diospyros virginiana*)

Bald cypress (*Taxodium distichum*)

Black tupelo (*Nyssa sylvatica*)

Dawn redwood (*Metasequoia glyptostroboides*)

Poplars
(*Populus deltoides, P. nigra*)

River birch
(*Betula nigra*)

Swamp rose
(*Rosa palustris*)

Sweet pepperbush
(*Clethra alnifolia*)

Willow (*Salix* spp.)

Willow oak
(*Quercus phellos*)

Yellowroot
(*Xanthorhiza simplicissima*)

ANNUALS, PERENNIALS, AND BULBS FOR WET SOIL

Astilbe (*Astilbe* spp.)

Black cohosh
(*Cimicifuga racemosa*)

Blue flag (*Iris versicolor*)

Buttercup
(*Ranunculus* spp.)

Calla lily
(*Zantedeschia* spp.)

Cardinal flower
(*Lobelia cardinalis*)

Chameleon plant
(*Houttuynia cordata* 'Chameleon')

Globeflower
(*Trollius* spp.)

Goatsbeard
(*Aruncus* spp.)

Great blue lobelia
(*Lobelia siphilitica*)

Marsh mallow
(*Althaea officinalis*)

Marsh marigold
(*Caltha palustris*)

Meadowsweet
(*Filipendula* spp.)

Milkweed
(*Asclepias* spp.)

Mint (*Mentha* spp.)

Nasturtium
(*Tropaeolum majus*)

Plantain lily
(*Hosta* spp.)

Primrose (*Primula* spp.)

Sweet flag (*Acorus* spp.)

Water forget-me-not
(*Myosotis scorpioides*)

Yellow flag
(*Iris pseudacorus*)

TREES, SHRUBS, AND VINES FOR DRY SOIL

Acacia (*Acacia* spp.)

Barberry
(*Berberis* spp.)

Bearberry
(*Arctostaphylos* spp.)

Black locust
(*Robinia pseudoacacia*)

Cotoneaster
(*Cotoneaster* spp.)

Crape myrtle
(*Lagerstroemia indica*)

English ivy
(*Hedera helix*)

Ginkgo
(*Ginkgo biloba*)

Golden-rain tree
(*Koelreuteria paniculata*)

Heavenly bamboo
(*Nandina domestica*)

Honeylocust
(*Gleditsia* spp.)

Juniper (*Juniperus* spp.)

Lavender
(*Lavandula* spp.)

Oleander
(*Nerium oleander*)

Rock rose (*Cistus* spp.)

Scotch broom
(*Cytisus scoparius*)

Smokebush
(*Cotinus coggygria*)

Tree of heaven
(*Ailanthus altissima*)

Trumpet honeysuckle
(*Lonicera sempervirens*)

Wisteria (*Wisteria* spp.)

ANNUALS, PERENNIALS, AND BULBS FOR DRY SOIL

Adam's-needle
(*Yucca filamentosa*)

African daisy
(*Osteospermum* spp.)

Artemisia (*Artemisia* spp.)

Blanket flower
(*Gaillardia* ×*grandiflora*)

Crown vetch
(*Coronilla varia*)

Daylily (*Hemerocallis* spp.)

Germander
(*Teucrium chamaedrys*)

Globe thistle
(*Echinops ritro*)

Hardy ice plant
(*Delosperma* spp., *Lampranthus* spp.)

Jerusalem sage
(*Phlomis* spp.)

New Zealand flax
(*Phormium tenax*)

Penstemon
(*Penstemon* spp.)

Portulaca
(*Portulaca grandiflora*)

Pot marigold
(*Calendula officinalis*)

Purple coneflower
(*Echinacea purpurea*)

Rudbeckias
(*Rudbeckia* spp.)

Salvias (*Salvia* spp.)

Sand verbena
(*Abronia* spp.)

Sea lavender
(*Limonium latifolium*)

Star-of-Bethlehem
(*Ornithogalum* spp.)

Swan River daisy
(*Brachycome iberidifolia*)

Torch poker
(*Kniphofia* spp.)

Thyme (*Thymus* spp.)

PLANTS FOR SEASHORE CONDITIONS

Adam's-needle
(*Yucca filamentosa*)

Beach plum
(*Prunus maritima*)

Blue fescue
(*Festuca* spp.)

Butterfly weed
(*Asclepias tuberosa*)

Dwarf Mugo pine
(*Pinus mugo* var. *mugo*)

Japanese black pine
(*Pinus thunbergiana*)

Japanese clethra
(*Clethra barbinervis*)

Nippon daisy
(*Chrysanthemum nipponicum*)

Northern bayberry
(*Myrica pensylvanica*)

Ravenna grass
(*Erianthus ravennae*)

Red cedar
(*Juniperus virginiana*)

Sea lavender
(*Limonium latifolium*)

Sea buckthorn
(*Hippophae rhamnoides*)

Seaside goldenrod
(*Solidago sempervirens*)

Serviceberry
(*Amelanchier* spp.)

Sweet bay
(*Laurus nobilis*)

Tibouchina urvilleana, the glorybush, is hardy only in Hawaiilike climates, where it becomes a tall tree. In cooler climates, enjoy this plant indoors in winter and plant it outside when all danger of frost is past.

marginal for your area. However, it pays to be a bit mistrustful of your warm spots, warns Galen Gates of the Chicago Botanic Garden. Often, a warm spot tricks the plant into early growth and then the plant is damaged by cold. Gates places marginally hardy plants in protected areas on the north or east side of the house.

PLACE PLANTS CAREFULLY If you can't resist experimenting, try one or two of the experts' tactics:

• Dr. Lighty advises placing the plant where it will get warmth both from the sun and from a surrounding structure. Bobbie Holder of Wyoming's Pawnee Greenhouse and Nursery agrees, saying that the south side of a building or wall is ideal.

• Sean Hogan, an Oregon designer and horticulturist, finds that in Portland, Oregon, tender fruit trees (such as pomegranate and guava), provide a second crop when they are sitting against a south wall that absorbs heat. Be careful with evergreens, though—they can become dried out in winter by harsh winds and unfiltered sun. It's best to plant vulnerable varieties where they'll receive as little winter sun as possible, says Dr. Lighty.

• When considering a site, remember that wet roots in winter can kill off even plants hardy for your climate. Steven Brack of New Mexico's Mesa Gardens suggests placing marginally hardy plants at the top of a slope, where water can reliably run off and cold air drafts blow away.

SITE FOR DORMANCY Another secret to pushing plants beyond their normal zone, according to Hunter Carleton of Washington's Bear Creek Nursery, is to plant for a long period of dormancy—a state that protects plants. In other words, if your yard doesn't have available warm spots, you might do better planting in a cold spot. Look for a site that remains snow-covered throughout the winter, says Richard Boonstra, retired president of Ohio's Bluestone Perennials, since snow is a natural insulator. If possible, he adds, place a few evergreen boughs over the plant in December to hold the snow. Be careful about applying winter mulches too heavily, though. A thick mulch, says Shane Smith, director of Wyoming's Cheyenne Botanic Garden, can create enough warmth around the roots to send a plant sprouting prematurely. If a cold snap occurs, the plant will be killed. Also, don't mulch too early, warns Boonstra. You can trap moisture around the

Tropical plants in Pennsylvania? Sure, if they are grown as annuals, like the canna above, or brought indoors in winter, like the agaves.

roots, which many plants can't bear during winter. Kim Hawks of North Carolina's Niche Gardens also suggests using a light gravel mulch instead of organic mulch during winter months.

PROTECT THROUGH PROPER PLANTING How and when you plant is also important. Dr. Lighty suggests planting deep, which provides better winter protection for the root systems of some plants. (Deep planting is never a good idea in heavy, clay soil, though. Planting *too* deep can kill plants.) Here are some other expert tips:

• Shane Smith and Bobbie Holder advise planting early to encourage hardiness, preferably in spring before your plants leaf.

• David Bar-Zvi of Fairchild Tropical Garden in Miami finds that some tropical plants survive freezes if given extra potassium. Wood ashes are a good source.

DORMANCY

When a plant becomes dormant, it cuts back or shuts off on breathing, feeding, and photosynthesizing. Plants have an easier time coping with cold during dormancy because they are not actively producing new growth.

To encourage his plants to go dormant early, Bill McKentley of New York's St. Lawrence Nurseries tapers back on watering and fertilizing at summer's end. He also strips some of the leaves off the plant (but not at the stem) as soon as they begin to color in the fall, which stops or reduces photosynthesis, in turn triggering dormancy. This method requires some vigilance, but if it's done at the right time, the plant will go dormant a week or two earlier than it normally would.

A note of caution: Many experts say that stripping leaves stresses the plant and could damage it.

At Chanticleer Gardens in Pennsylvania, tropical plants are grown outdoors through the warm months. Some, like agaves and banana plants, are brought indoors for winter. Most are treated as annuals; cuttings are taken at the end of the summer and the plants are composted.

• Ursula Herz of South Carolina's Coastal Gardens and Nursery offers this hardiness-boosting tip: add ⅛ cup of kelp meal for each gallon of soil in a pot when planting, or spray plants three times in late summer and fall with dehydrated seaweed. Seaweed or kelp are organic fertilizers high in potassium, which is needed for good root production. By ensuring that your plants have good, strong root systems, you're helping them survive in even the harshest conditions.

• Improving soil drainage also boosts winter hardiness, says Mike Ruggerio of the New York Botanical Garden, since well-drained soil freezes less readily than heavy, waterlogged soil does.

MAKE A MICROCLIMATE If you don't mind the way it looks, artificial protection can also help a marginal plant make it through the winter, effectively creating a temporary microclimate. Bill McKentley of St. Lawrence Nurseries in northern New York advises building a simple teepee over small plants and then wrapping the teepee in burlap. In northern climates, gardeners regularly wrap entire fig trees in burlap to help the trees overwinter. Peter and Jean Ruh of the Homestead division of Ohio's Sunnybrook Farms, suggest covering plants with wooden boxes large enough to provide adequate air circulation to prevent breakage and protect the plants from sweeping winds.

TAKING A PLANT SOUTHWARD When gardeners talk about stretching a plant, they're usually referring to moving it northward. There are, however, plants that either thrive in cooler temperatures or require a certain amount of winter dormancy. And many plants can't survive strong sun or high temperatures. In fact, the USDA has created a heat hardiness chart to complement its cold hardiness version (see page 384).

While it's generally easier to move a plant south, says Bill McKentley, you're still changing the plant's environment. Even though the plant may survive, it may not produce good fruit or beautiful blossoms. Summer apple trees, for instance, generally fruit well if moved south a zone, but the apples themselves may have no shelf life. David Bar-Zvi recognizes that people who move to the South have sentimental reasons for wanting to take the plants they love—like lilacs, daffodils, and wisteria—along with them, but he cautions that these plants, with the exception of some cultivars, rarely do well in warm climates.

EXTENDING SUMMER

For Douglas Owens-Pike of Minneapolis's EnergyScapes, Inc., the real secret of season-extending is to use native diversity to find both early- and late-blooming plants—ornamentals and edibles—that are naturally hardy in your area. Cindy Reed of Great Plains Native Plant Society agrees: "We do use floating row covers and various tomato protectors to foil the frost, but our most successful technique lies in variety and species selection favoring those hardy plants that thrive in the cold."

In particularly cold areas, buy plants bred in and for your own region. And as a final season-extender, says Douglas, choose plants such as those with attractive seedheads and plumes that look good even after they've been hit by a hard frost.

The tropics are recreated in Wave Hill, in the Bronx, New York. Most of these plants—aloes, agaves, and palms—are brought indoors in winter. The colorful annuals are planted each year.

THE GROUND WORK

Once you've explored your landscape, learned its lessons, dreamed and thought through your backyard design, you can begin preparing the ground for planting. And though you may be eager to get your plants in the soil immediately, experts recommend that you take time to prepare the ground properly. Your patience will be rewarded with a healthy, lush garden.

Allow a Fallow Season

Is waiting worth it? • *Jumping right in* • *For every plant, a season*

Wherever you live, say the experts, your new garden may benefit from a fallow period, a season during which the newly prepared ground sits empty and unplanted. Kris Bachtell of the Morton Arboretum in Illinois suggests turning the soil over and adding organic matter a season ahead of planting (in cold climates, such as his native Illinois, that would most likely be in fall). "Don't smooth out the soil, leave it mounded," he says. "This allows the winter temperatures and moisture to break up the clods and help the soil dry more quickly in the spring, making it easier to start your planting earlier." Other experts also recommend a fallow period.

• Alan Branhagen, director of Powell Garden in Missouri, recommends letting the soil sit for an entire growing season. "Evidence is mounting that doing so lets beneficial organisms that attach themselves to plant roots (microrhizal fungi) grow and multiply, allowing for the best possible exchange of water and nutrients between the new plants and the soil," he says.

• Norman Schwartz, owner of Virginia's Edgewood Farm and Nursery, likes to prepare new ground in fall because he finds his amendments mix and break down better if left over winter. He notes that farmers usually plow in the fall and plant in the spring. However, he often can't find the time to do it in fall and still achieves good results with spring preparation.

• Debby Kavakos, owner of Stoneledge Farm in New York, always starts her vegetable beds the fall before she plans to plant them. She plants a cover crop that she turns under in the spring, right before

Part of a field at the Santa Cruz Botanic Garden in California is allowed to lie fallow through an entire season, while other fields are planted. The soil is mounded, not smoothed out, to keep it from becoming compacted.

planting. She also advises any gardener whose site needs additional lime to raise the pH level to do so a year before planting because it takes about a year for the lime to become available to plants.

STARTING IMMEDIATELY Impatient gardeners, take heart. Depending on what you want to grow, you may not have to wait an entire season. "If you're planting strawberries or potatoes, then it makes sense to wait because these plants need very loose, well-worked soil," says Carl Thuesen, a landscape architect in Montana, "but with woody plants and ornamentals, I don't think it makes any difference." Strong-rooted perennials will have no trouble penetrating compact soils.

John Jeavons, author of the legendary *How to Grow More Vegetables Than You Ever Thought Possible on Less Land than You Can Imagine* (Ten Speed Press, 1982) argues against leaving a well-prepared vegetable plot unplanted: "It should be planted as soon as convenient to take advantage of the new surge of life you've created by preparing," he says.

WHEN SEASONS DICTATE THE TIMING If you live where winters are harsh, experts generally recommend planting a new garden in spring.

From infancy (above) to luscious beauty in less than a year (below): Horticulturists at Queens Botanic Garden created an almost instant garden by planting fast-growing plants like chaste tree and garden phlox from 5-gallon containers in early fall. By the following summer, the garden was glorious.

Because their shoots emerge so early in spring, peonies do best when planted in fall. Irises and spring-blooming bulbs are also candidates for fall planting.

In the Berkshire Mountains, "it starts getting cold so early in the fall that new plants don't have time to become established and put out new roots before they go dormant," says Dorthe Hviid of the Berkshire Botanical Garden in Massachusetts. "This makes them more prone to winter damage."

However, if you live in a part of the country where brutal summers are more of a menace than severe winters, fall planting makes more sense. "Growth is more gradual, and fall-started plants are just easier to establish," says Mike Shoup, owner of the Antique Rose Emporium in Texas. Some plants, like bulbs or peonies, require fall planting; others, like dogwoods, prefer to be dug in the spring. Oriental poppies and bearded irises should be planted in early summer, right after they bloom.

If you need to plant in a specific season, allowing a fallow season might not be practical. Galen Gates of Chicago Botanic Garden agrees that preparing a new garden in fall and letting the freeze-drying effect of winter improve the soil is best. But he will often plant perennials or trees right after preparation if he can do it early enough in fall (by September 15 in Chicago) so that they will be somewhat established before frost. "The bottom line is to prepare the soil well at any time that it is workable (not wet or frozen), plant, mulch with organic matter, and water it in well," he says.

Removing Weeds

A whole world of weeds • Backsaving weed barriers • Plowing them under • Solar solutions

Weeding is a never-ending task. Your best opportunity to keep weeds at bay is to yank them out of the ground before you plant anything else. It's also the easiest time to do it because you don't have to worry about removing the plants you want.

WHAT IS A WEED? Any plant you don't want in your garden is a weed. But when most gardeners talk about weeds, they're speaking not just of unwanted plants but of rampant self-seeders like crab grass, plantain, and the aptly named speedwell. These weeds are not only unsightly, but they also steal water and nutrients from the plants you do want in your yard.

One person's weed, however, may be another's welcome guest. Some gardeners consider clover a lawn weed, while others see it as an attractive plant that draws beneficial insects and helps the grass grow by fixing nitrogen in the soil. If you're planning to leave a site unplanted for a few years, let the weeds grow, suggests Fairman Jayne of North Carolina's Sandy Mush Herb Farm. "Weeds keep the soil loose, and some of them look very nice," he says.

SMOTHERING If the ground you're preparing has only a scattering of weeds, you can simply pull them up by hand or with a hoe. However, if you need to clear a large area of thick weeds, you'll need a solution that's easier on the back. You could turn the weeds under with a rotary tiller, but then you'd only be readying the ground for a new and lusher crop of weeds by mixing the seeds into newly turned earth. Instead, the experts recommend an entirely nontoxic weapon to help you triumph in the weed wars: black plastic mulch. Frederick Held, a nursery owner in Oregon, suggests covering the entire site with plastic for as long as it takes to completely smother the weeds below. This could take a year, but it often takes less. Once the weeds are dead, you can pull them easily or turn them under by hand or with a rotary tiller. If black plastic is too unsightly for you, you can purchase weed barriers and agricultural fabrics that work just as well. These are available at garden centers and through mail order. An added benefit of smothering weeds is that it does not destroy soil texture, as tilling can.

KILL WEEDS A "NEWS" WAY This method of weed eradication, suggested by Douglas Owens-Pike of Minneapolis's EnergyScapes, Inc., takes about six weeks (more on an established lawn). In early spring or fall, layer sections of newspaper over an area you want to plant. Overlap each section by half. Do this on a calm day, so you don't spend half your time chasing down wind-blown paper. You can also wet the paper slightly to keep it in place. Next, pile 2 to 3 inches of shredded wood chips on top of the newsprint, and then sit back and wait. Be patient. Avoid poking holes in the newsprint to check if the site is ready before the six weeks are up. Once the grass and weeds are dead, you can start planting. The newspaper will decompose on its own, and the chips can be tilled under or treated as mulch.

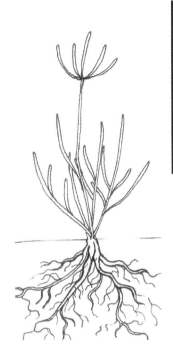

The weed you see is only part of the problem. Most aggressive perennial weeds have elaborate root systems that allow the unwanted plants to grow back unless you pull up every bit of root.

SOLARIZATION

This method uses the heat of the sun to destroy soil-borne weed seeds, diseases, and insects. You can use it only in summer. To solarize your garden site, prepare the bed, water it deeply (to create humidity), and rake it smooth. Then cover it with a 3- to 6-millimeter-thick layer of clear plastic and dig the edges of the plastic into the ground. In a few days, the sun will have warmed the soil to over 100°F. After six weeks the ground will be fully pasteurized and ready to plant.

REPEAT PLOWING Chicago landscape architect Janet Shen likes to cut and mow the existing weeds, plow them under in early spring, then allow the weed seeds to germinate, which takes three to four weeks. As soon as the second crop of weeds has sprouted, she plows them under again before they go to seed. Because a fair number of seeds will still remain in the soil, it's best to repeat the entire process again before planting. Or, suggests Neil Diboll of Wisconsin's Prairie Nursery, till the soil 1 inch deep five to seven days after the first good rain to kill weeds after they germinate but before they come up.

If your soil has good texture—not too loose not too compact—you probably shouldn't use this method, advises Sean Hogan, an Oregon designer and horticulturist. He points out that repeat plowing can ruin soil texture. Niles Kinerk, a garden supply expert from Indiana, recommends that instead you try a product called WOW (<u>W</u>ith<u>o</u>ut <u>W</u>eeds), a safe, corn-based compound that kills weeds before they emerge. WOW is available through Kinerk's catalog, Gardens Alive!

HOT WATER Stephen Breyer of Tripplebrook Farms in Vermont has had great success killing weeds with near-boiling water. A few quarts of very hot water poured over the weeds once a day for a few days will totally eradicate them.

Several experts swear by smothering weeds with newspapers. It's so easy that some gardeners call them lazy beds. With lazy beds, you avoid tilling, which destroys delicate surface roots and soil structure, and the newsprint decomposes and attracts earthworms—another benefit to a new bed.

Removing Sod

Small-scale simplifiers • Timesaving tools • Ideas for big jobs

Chances are you'll need to remove at least some grass when starting a garden. And if the grasses in your yard have strong roots that spread rapidly, you must eradicate them before you plant your new garden, advise the experts. If you don't, you'll have to contend with grass weeds later. The secret to successful sod removal, say the experts, is simply the right tool for the job.

STRIPPING SMALL SITES In areas of 100 square feet or less, most experts recommend removing grass by hand. San Francisco landscape architect Marta Fry suggests using a flat shovel rather than a spade. This allows you to strip only the upper layer of turf, which you can then throw onto the compost heap. (If you can get hold of a zop—a hoelike implement designed for removing sod—so much the better.)

"I don't like to incorporate the old sod into a new garden," Marta says, "because it tends to take away nutrients from the new plants." If you plan to let the plot lie fallow for a season, however, you can simply turn the sod under.

EXTENSIVE SOD REMOVAL For larger plots, Gene Banks of Connecticut's Catnip Acres uses a rotary tiller, which turns everything under with relative ease. (You may still have to hand-pull bits of deep-rooted grass.) California landscape architect John Buchholz also recommends a rotary tiller for areas where the grass is patchy or thin, but uses a sod stripper for thicker grown areas. However, Gail Haggard of Plants of the Southwest in New Mexico disagrees with tilling sod. She doesn't use a rotary tiller unless the soil is packed as hard as a parking lot, and she never uses one in old farm land that is full of weed seed. If you do till in sod, see "Removing Weeds" on page 44, for ways to kill weeds before they grow.

TIMING SOD REMOVAL To make sod removal easier, says Gene Banks, try to do it when the grass is dormant (usually in late winter or early spring). And sod is always easier to remove when the ground is wet. If nature doesn't accommodate you with some rainfall, you can wet the area with a sprinkler or garden hose an hour or two before you plan to clear the area for your garden.

A sod stripper, available at most garden rental centers, has blades that cut about 6 inches under the surface of the ground, neatly removing a 2-foot strip of sod.

Rocks and Stumps

Tools and gadgets • Divide and conquer • Creative camouflage

Rocks seem so abundant that many gardeners swear they've developed a way to procreate. In other words, be prepared to pick them out of your newly dug garden site. And you may have to remove a stump or two, as well.

GETTING THE ROCKS OUT You have several options when it comes to rock removal:

• Bobbie Holder of Wyoming's Pawnee Greenhouse and Nursery removes small rocks with a hard-toothed rake.

• Carl Thuesen, a landscape architect in Montana, uses a rockpicker or rotary rake, both of which can be rented from landscape contractors.

• You can break up large rocks by drilling deep holes in them and leaving them over a winter or two.

Once you remove rocks, incorporate them back into the landscape as steps, terraces, and focal points. In this garden, roses and astilbes are set off by a stone border.

ROCK YOUR GARDEN

Before you remove rocks from your garden, think about how you might make them work for you.

❧ Montana landscape architect Carl Thuesen covers rocks with 3 to 4 inches of imported topsoil.

❧ "In a heather garden, smaller rocks can improve drainage, and larger ones can be placed to add visual interest or even to protect plants from adverse weather or winter heaving," says Alice Knight of Washington's Heather Acres.

❧ Debby Kavakos of Stoneledge Farm in New York leaves some rocks in herb gardens because the rocks absorb heat, contribute valuable minerals to the soil, and help anchor roots in windy locations.

Crocosmia, coreopsis, and lilies were tucked among rocks on this inclined site.

Some plants will grow any-where, even in the rockiest, poorest soil. *Canbyii paxystimia*, also known as rat-stripper, is one such plant.

You can easily turn tree stumps into child-size seating with a can of paint and some sealer. Sand the stump first to avoid splinters.

STUMP REMOVAL Tree stumps present a greater challenge. Many of the experts recommend hiring a professional to remove them. Robert Caughlan of Caughlan & Son Landscapes in California and his colleagues leave the job to experienced contractors: "We have them dig out the stumps or grind them up," he says, "depending on the size of the stump and the size of the contractor." If you're a determined do-it-yourselfer, you can rent a stump grinder from a tree removal company, says Sue Moss. "If the stump is easily accessible, the grinder can be truck-mounted, which will save you a little money over the portable grinders used for out-of-the-way locations," she says.

An old-fashioned method for speeding up the decomposition is to drill holes in tree trunks and pour buttermilk into the holes. The buttermilk attracts organisms that help decompose the wood. The disadvantage is that it will take two to three years.

Let the area rest for six to eight weeks after the stump has been removed, as the soil tends to settle, advises Kim Hawks of North Carolina's Niche Gardens. Then build it up with amended top soil.

DESIGNING WITH STUMPS Of course, you don't have to remove the stump. Bobbie Schwartz of Bobbie's Green Thumb in Ohio suggests drilling a hole in the center and inserting a potted plant there until the stump rots naturally. Kim Hawks drills a hole in the stump, fills it with composted topsoil, and then plants directly in the soil. In some cases, she camouflages the stump with a cascading plant. Other times, she

accentuates the stump's height with an upright plant. Hawks has also brought amended soil up and around stumps, adding a subtle grade change to a flat bed. In an informal landscape, a stump can be a pretty focal point and offers an environmental plus, as well. "Old rotted stumps and logs, become 'nurse logs' as they decompose—micro-environments that give nutrients and protection to other plants," says Bobbie Schwartz.

Rather than removing a tree stump, an ingenious gardener incorporated it into a terrace wall. He makes sure to check it every year for decomposition; if it begins to crumble, he'll shore it up with stone.

Amending Your Soil
Tilth and texture • Fertility and pH • Starting from scratch

Experts from every region, including Norman Schwartz, owner of Virginia's Edgewood Farm and Nursery; Maine plantswoman Claire Ackroyd; Mike Shoup of the Antique Rose Emporium in Texas; and Bill Bruneau from California's Bountiful Gardens agree on the importance of building and maintaining healthy soil. "Failure to fix the soil," says Claire, "is by far the worst problem in most home gardens," especially for vegetables, which require plenty of nutrients and adequate water to grow their best. Moreover, as you harvest your vegetables, herbs, or flowers, you take a lot out of the soil. So build good soil before you start your garden, and tend to its health every year thereafter.

TILTH AND TEXTURE Tilth refers to the condition of the top layer of soil, the layer in which your plants grow. Soil with good tilth is crumbly but not powdery (friable), and easily workable. Texture refers to the space between particles: soil can be clay, sand, or loam (see "Soil" on page 30). Though it's easier to achieve good tilth with loam, clay and sand can become friable if properly worked over a number of years. Tilth and texture affect the ability of water, air, and nutrients to move through the soil to your plants, and they affect drainage.

CHANGING SOIL TEXTURE You can change the texture of your soil by double or triple digging, planting crops to loosen the soil, or manually breaking up the clods in the top layers. Fairman Jayne of North Carolina's Sandy Mush Herb Farm finds that even weeds keep the soil loose. He will let weeds take over a bed a year or two before he plans to plant it. You need to be careful not to overwork soil or you'll damage its texture.

ADJUSTING pH

Most plants grow best in neutral to slightly alkaline soil. If a soil test reveals that your soil is very acid or alkaline, you can find plants that thrive in your conditions, or you can adjust the pH level.

To lower pH: Some experts recommend mulching with pine needles. Galen Gates of Chicago Botanic Garden finds that incorporating 1 pound of 90 percent granular sulfur per 100 square feet is more effective and less costly.

To raise pH: Most experts recommend lime. Scatter it on the surface of the soil, and then water it. Or, use ground eggshells or oyster shells, says Peter Borchard of Companion Plants in Ohio. Tom Butterworth of Butterbrook Farms in Connecticut likes wood ashes. Apply them liberally and water them, or let rain or snow soak them into the ground. These amendments work in a natural time-release fashion, so there's little danger of over-application.

You can also improve soil texture by adding organic matter, such as compost. This increases drainage and workability of clay soils by lightening the texture, and it raises the water-holding capacity and enriches the texture of sandy soils. Peat moss, bark chips, and well-rotted manure or leaves work the same way that compost does, but they are less effective. Adding sharp sand or gravel to clay soil helps drainage, but Galen Gates of Chicago Botanic Garden finds that so much sand must be added that it's easier to use compost. If you use compost to improve soil texture, use lots and lots. "People talk about adding 'bagfuls' of organic matter. I tell them to add truckfuls," says Claire Ackroyd.

ENRICHING THE SOIL When soil tests reveal a nutrient deficiency, your first inclination might be to grab a bag of fertilizer, but the experts advise against it. Go for organic matter instead, they say. Make sure it's well composted, and apply it as a mulch on top of the soil or mix it in deeply. Organic mulches break down slowly over time, incorporating themselves gradually into the soil. Not only does this make your job easier, says Tom Butterworth of Connecticut's Butterbrook Farms, it also avoids the danger of overfertilizing or burning. Peter Borchard of

Nelson Sterner, director of horticulture at Old Westbury Gardens, amended the soil in a new rose garden in his backyard with half a pickup truck's worth of well-rotted leaves. Here is the first season result.

Companion Plants in Ohio also endorses the use of an organic mulch—manure, straw, hay, grass clippings, compost, wood chips—which he tills under in fall or early spring. The one disadvantage to using noncomposted amendments, says Borchard, is that as they decompose, they can tie up nitrogen in the soil. To compensate, he adds a high-nitrogen organic fertilizer. Other experts offer different tips:

• New Jersey nurseryman Don Ledden adds "as much good home-produced compost as I can get my hands on," and also works in composted manure, bone meal, blood meal, crab meal, and fish meal.

• When working amendments into the soil, dig them in 10 to 12 inches deep, advises Tory Galloway of Seattle's Victoria Gardens.

• If you're planning a radical amendment of the soil—say with topsoil, compost, manure, and fertilizer—it's best to let everything settle for the first year, says Richard Boonstra. "You can grow a few annuals or even vegetables in the bed the first year," he suggests. "If they do well, go ahead and add the permanent perennials."

• Not everyone relies on soil fixes. Douglas Owens-Pike of Minneapolis's EnergyScapes, Inc., chooses plants that can tolerate poor soil, achieving "the right mix of native species for a spectacular garden of colorful blooms."

STARTING SOIL FROM SCRATCH If the soil you've been dealt is less than perfect, why not replace it all? Most experts recommend against this extreme approach, mainly because it's time-consuming, expensive, and rarely necessary. Exceptions are when the soil has been contaminated with drywall compound or paint solvents, as on a new construction site, or if you find evidence of fuel oil contamination, says North Carolina landscape architect Rick Boggs. In cases like these, replace the old soil with an organic soil mix, advises Seattle garden designer Sue Moss. Mixes higher in organic matter are best for beds, while those lower in organic material are suitable for lawns.

Sue has also worked on new construction sites where all the topsoil has been scraped away. In these situations she recommends spreading new topsoil 12 inches deep over the entire site. Kim Hawks of North Carolina's Niche Gardens likes a thicker layer—18 to 24 inches. She tills the first 4 inches into the base soil so that the layers bond and the soil drains well.

Although soil amendments can enrich most gardens, sometimes it's best to find plants that will grow in the soil you have. Purple coneflower and barberry are not fussy; they'll thrive in even the poorest soil.

Terracing a Slope

A solution to slopes • Terracing tactics • Choosing materials

Slopes present the gardener with a challenge. You can cover a slope with grass, but then you have to mow it. You can plant groundcovers or low-growing shrubs, but you'll have to deal with dry soil and erosion since water runs off so readily. What to do? Create a terrace, suggests Kim Hawks of North Carolina's Niche Gardens. And if you follow the experts' tips, it won't be as difficult as it might seem.

Use low stone and timber walls, set at different levels, to create a terrace for annuals and perennials.

START AT THE BOTTOM You can save yourself time and energy by not excavating the entire slope at once. Instead, build the lowest wall first, says Nebraska plantswoman Gail Korn. Then remove only enough dirt to form a level terrace, and build the next wall at the back of that terrace. Continue upward until you reach the top of the slope. Use the topsoil you've taken from the slope to increase the depth of the soil in each terrace, says Montana landscape architect Carl Thuesen.

MAKING WALLS Think small. "Terracing is quite doable by home gardeners," says San Francisco landscape architect Marta Fry, "as long as walls are no higher than about 18 inches." "If you want retaining walls higher than 3 feet, you'll need to call in professionals," cautions John Buchholz.

THINK DRAINAGE "If you don't provide proper drainage," adds John, "the pressure of waterlogged soil could knock down your wall." He recommends adding gravel to soil that does not drain well, but sand would work well also. Or you can install seep holes or drainage pipes in the walls and terraces to give water a safe path. (See "Drainage" on page 28, for information on improving drainage.)

MATERIALS You could build your walls from bricks, concrete blocks, landscape timbers, logs, sandstone blocks, even boards. To this list, Seattle garden designer Sue Moss adds broken concrete, split-faced block, and block faced with brick or stone. Your choice depends on what you like and what you're willing to spend. Here are a few other suggestions:

• If you like the look of stone but can't use it because your grade is too steep, Mary Harrison of Mary's Plant Farm suggests using formed cement stones, which mimic the real thing quite effectively.

• Marta Fry recommends using materials that are appropriate to the landscape and the general area, such as native stone or wood, granite in the Northeast, or adobe in the Southwest.

• Mary Irish of Phoenix's Desert Botanical Garden worries that adobe, though strong, might slump and crumble. She recommends drystack rock walls (see the photograph on page 56).

Built on a steeply sloped site, the terrace shown here consists of three levels, each built of uniformly sized small stones. The soil in the terraced beds drains beautifully, making the site perfect for a wide variety of annuals, perennials, and shrubs.

RAISED BEDS AND CONTAINERS

For gardeners who face difficult environmental conditions, raised beds and containers offer an excellent way to garden. Even fortunate gardeners who have access to fertile, well-drained garden soil use raised beds and containers because they like to be able to control the environment in which their plants grow.

Reasons for Raised Beds

Reasons for raising • Weighing the pros and cons • Aesthetic elevation

To create a raised bed, you simply build a layer of soil and organic matter above ground level. Raised beds offer good aeration and drainage, and they can enrich the soil below depending on the mix of topsoil and organic matter they contain.

THE ADVANTAGES Raised beds are absolutely essential in areas with heavy clay soil, says Tom Butterworth of Connecticut's Butterbrook Farms. Though double-digging offers many of the same benefits, raising the soil is a lot easier, says Pennsylvania nurseryman Marc Stoecklein.

In addition to fixing poor soil, raised beds cure a host of garden ills. They help prevent soil erosion on a slope, says Jim Becker of Oregon's Goodwin Creek Gardens. Tom Butterworth points out that raised beds are a godsend in areas that receive heavy rainfall—in Hawaii, for instance, or in the Pacific Northwest. And, he adds, since the soil in raised beds dries out quickly, it warms faster in spring, giving you a jump on planting.

THE DISADVANTAGES Of course, the tendency of raised beds to dry out means they have to be watered more frequently. And it's hard to rotary till the weeds that grow alongside a raised bed, says Jim Becker. Small beds can freeze in winter, warns Rob Layton of Colorado's Design Concepts. Cathy Wilson of Washington, D.C.'s, The Landscape Group thinks that gardeners are too quick to raise beds, especially since the work often has to be done again after a storm or years of natural erosion. "Good clay soil is very fertile; why not use it?" she asks. "Double-dig properly and amend it heavily, and your bed will be

A drystack wall is used to edge this raised bed of carrots and lettuces at the University of Santa Cruz Botanical Garden. The stones are stacked so that they balance each other; their weight keeps them in place without any cement or other fixative.

as loose and well-drained as any raised bed."

A few of the experts object to raised beds on aesthetic grounds. Marc Stoecklein comments that beds raised too high can end up looking like anthills scattered through the landscape. Kim Hawks of North Carolina's Niche Gardens thinks that "often, they are too sharp and look forced in the landscape." She recommends tapering them at the edges down to the ground.

Yet, others find distinct stylistic advantages. Andrea Sessions of Tennessee's Sunlight Gardens considers a little bit of height "aesthetically pleasing." And Ontario nurseryman Robert Anderson suggests raising certain gardens specifically to accent them.

Constructing Raised Beds

Raised bed basics • How high? • The edge on elevations

To create a raised bed, you simply pile a mixture of soil and compost directly on top of existing soil. Whether or not you work the soil beneath the bed depends on what you plan to grow: shallow-rooted annuals don't need more than a foot or so of soil, but most vegetables and perennials like to sink their roots deep. Some experts recommend double-digging the soil beneath raised beds. Others suggest that you simply loosen it up with a spading fork or rotary tiller. But do

The easiest way to edge a raised bed is not at all; the soil is simply mounded.

Cedar planks create permanent containers for raised beds. They look great and provide perfect anchors for row covers.

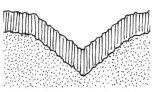

Linda Gay edges her raised beds with a simple v-shape trench, 3 to 4 inches deep, made with a shovel edge. It's quick and easy, and it keeps the soil in its place.

something: If you don't mix the soils at all, water won't pass from one layer to another easily.

HEIGHT Although there's no hard-and-fast rule about the height of raised beds, Andrea Sessions of Tennessee's Sunlight Gardens advises that "the larger the bed, the higher you should raise it." You can go as low as 6 to 8 inches, says Marc Stoecklein of Stoecklein's Nursery in Pennsylvania, and as high as 3 feet, according to Robert Anderson of

Each container in this grouping is planted with a single plant (including herbs, geraniums, alternanthera, and lilies). In combination, they form an interesting pattern that is effective even when none is flowering.

Anderson Nursery and Garden Centre in Ontario. What's most important is making sure the soil contains ample amounts of organic matter—"truckloads," says Linda Gay of Mercer Arboretum in Texas.

MAKING THE BED If you plan on edging your bed with a hard material like wood, brick, or stacked stone, put that in place first, then unload the soil directly into the cavity. Otherwise, says Linda, pile new soil onto your site and firm it with the straight side of a rake. To define a soft-edged bed and keep it in place, Linda takes a shovel edge and creates a 3- to 4-inch V-shape trench all around the bed. (Don't go deeper than 4 inches, says Galen Gates of Chicago Botanic Garden, or soil will erode into the grass or pathway.) Marc Stoecklein forms his edge with a tractor. For a more artistic look, San Francisco landscape architect Marta Fry suggests edging the beds with small shrubs. Some of the raised beds she's created even include seating around the edges.

Container Gardening

Above-ground advantages • Movable design
• Container cautions • Optimal choices

Gardening with containers offers unique benefits. It allows you to place plants on patios, porches, decks, balconies, and pool surrounds. You can move potted plants around the garden for variety and bring them indoors when severe weather threatens. For the urban dweller, it may be the only option. But container gardening presents challenges, too.

THE PLUSES Garden experts can find a dozen wonderful ways to use container plantings.
• Charles Sandifer, a Memphis landscape architect, likes to use containers for unusual plant groupings: perennials and vegetables, for example, or roses and herbs.
• Galen Gates of Chicago Botanic Garden appreciates the fact that containers allow him to grow plants that won't survive the winter in his Chicago garden. When the temperature drops, he brings his potted plants into the garage.
• Bobbie Schwartz of Bobbie's Green Thumb in Ohio appreciates the fact that container plantings can be changed easily for special purposes.

Here's a traditional mixed container planting that's always effective. A tall, spiky plant (in this case, wheat celosia) is placed in the center, surrounded by mid-height flowering and foliage plants (zinnias, salvia, and dusty miller). Edging lobelia and cranesbill complete the arrangement.

One great advantage of containers is that they are easily moved. In early spring, a pot of miniature roses was placed on a pillar at Old Westbury Gardens. After blooming, the roses were replaced with a container of garden verbena, salvia, and lantana.

• Nancy Rose of Minnesota Landscape Arboretum finds that large containers of annuals, perennials, vines, or grasses can make an elegant transition from a naturalized yard to the more structured areas such as decks, porches, or patios around a house.

• Matt Horn of New York's Matterhorn Nursery points out that container gardening allows for total control of the growing conditions.

• And, says Chicago landscape architect Janet Shen, the planting mixes often used in containers keep down the incidence of soil-borne pests and diseases.

THE MINUSES Plants in pots need more frequent watering and feeding, and not every plant is suited to life in a container. Those with large root systems do better in the ground where roots can spread out, says Charles Sandifer.

THE CONTAINERS With the boom in container gardening, the variety of containers seems to increase yearly. In addition to the traditional terra-cotta and wood, you can find fiberglass, plastic, concrete, cast stone, and even a man-made structural foam that insulates against sudden temperature fluctuations. While some experts have strict preferences as to materials, others are more open to experimentation.

• Byron Martin of Logee's Greenhouse in Connecticut uses whatever is available and convenient. This could include a recycled feeding trough, a discarded bathtub, or a weathered watering can.

• Many gardening experts, including Byron Martin and Rhode Island landscape architect Diane Kostial McGuire, prefer terra-cotta over plastic. Diane praises its durability (as long as you take it indoors during the coldest winter months, it will last for years), while Byron likes its ability to allow air and water to penetrate to the root zone. "Our experience," he says, "has been that over the long haul, root systems remain healthier in terra-cotta."

• If you're planning on growing vegetables, however, most of the experts recommend plastic for its water-retaining qualities. "In the dry Southwest, plastic is the only way to go for anything but very well-adapted desert plants," says Mary Irish of Phoenix's Desert Botanical Garden. She uses clay or terra-cotta pots for succulent plants because they do dry out, which is good for succulents.

• Oregon designer and horticulturist Sean Hogan uses a double-container: a plastic liner inside a more decorative clay pot. This way, he can grow seasonal plants in the liners and move them in and out of view as they bloom. Hogan also likes tall, narrow pots, since they provide the best drainage.

• Each material offers its own advantage. "Plastic containers are lightweight, retain moisture well, and are easy to move," says Matt Horn. "Clay containers are porous, reducing the likelihood of root rot. Fiberglass is lightweight and won't freeze and crack in cold weather. Cedar and redwood will last many years and can also be left outside." Be careful when using a wood container, however, to make sure it hasn't been treated with creosote, which can harm plants. And be particularly careful if you're growing edibles.

This textured stone planter is filled with tender succulents, Siberian dragon's head (*Dracocephalum ruvshianum*), and *Sedum caudicolum* 'Lidacense'. They blend beautifully with the surrounding hardy fountain grass during the summer, but will be taken indoors before the first frost.

SOIL FOR CONTAINERS

For success in container gardening, start with the best possible planting medium.

Soilless mixes: Not only is a soilless growing medium sterile, it's lightweight and drains well, making it an excellent choice for hanging containers. Soil becomes heavy when watered and could pull your container out of its mount, says Matt Horn of New York's Matterhorn Nursery. Some mixes contain water-retaining gel, which can also be purchased separately at garden centers.

Homemade potting mixes: If you plan to keep your plants in the container for more than one season, make your own soil-based mix (see "Seed-Starting Mixes" on page 343 for some recipes). Don't use topsoil, either prepackaged or from the garden. It's not sterile, it's heavy, and it may contain weed seed.

GARDEN ACCENTS

A well-designed and planted landscape is beautiful in itself. However, you can enhance the beauty of your backyard with lighting and garden accents like birdbaths, small ponds, unusual pieces of wood, or rocks. And adding pathways and seating can make your garden experience more enjoyable.

Pathways

Leading the way through the garden • *Good measures*
• *High-performance materials*

Pathways perform a few functions. They allow you easy access to your gardens and prevent you from pounding delicate grasses or ground-covers. They also connect the various areas of your yard physically and visually and are an integral part of your garden's design. In addition, a path can be an invitation to you and your guests to come and enjoy your garden.

PUTTING IN A PATHWAY Before choosing materials for your path, map out its width and figure its length so you can determine what materials to use and how much they'll cost. Pennsylvania nurseryman Marc Stoecklein recommends a width of 3 to 4 feet, which allows two people to walk side by side, but if you're pressed for space, 30 inches will do.

For an easy and inexpensive pathway, use cedar or pine bark mulch or needles, suggests Andrea Sessions of Tennessee's Sunlight Gardens. Gravel and other loose material can sink into the soil, but David Bar-Zvi of Fairchild Tropical Garden in Miami finds that a layer of weed cloth under the gravel holds the gravel up. Here are some other expert suggestions:

• For a longer-lasting and more easily maintained path, Inez Berg of the Washington Park Botanic Garden in Illinois recommends using log rounds (although in rainy regions like the Northwest, these stepping stones have a short life).

• Long Island landscaper Gisela Schaeffer uses flat, gray Japanese-style stepping stones, placing them to create an undulating "river" effect. She also suggests pine needles for a woodland garden (though, she warns, they require frequent refreshing).

A brick pathway is a bit more expensive to install than other types, but nothing beats it for durabilty. Bricks are available in many colors and shapes; they can be used to edge a bed as well as to form a pathway.

- Marc Stoecklein recommends using whatever fits your area. In an urban setting, he says, that might be brick or concrete. In his own rural garden he chooses flagstone, fieldstone, or grass.
- Grass pathways look terrific, says Gene Banks of Connecticut's Catnip Acres, but they require a fair amount of maintenance and simply don't work in high-traffic areas. She prefers pea-stone or smooth pebbles. They need to be relaid every four or five years, but they can be spread easily with a shovel and wheelbarrow.
- San Francisco landscape architect Marta Fry likes the look of crushed stone, available in an array of colors from blue-gray to yellow-gold.

Pine needles create a natural effect. They need to be replaced more often than more permanent and expensive pathways. At the New York Botanical Garden, they are combined with a basketry fence and cascading fountain grass.

Flagstones, set in a packed dirt path, form a pattern that is attractive and easy to navigate.

starting your garden

Lighting

Let there be light! • *Do-it-yourself dos and don'ts*
• *Some practical points*

If you plan to take an after-hours stroll through the moonflowers, or if you've planted a pond with night-blooming lilies, or even if you have a large window that looks out on the yard, you may want to install some permanent lighting fixtures. "Night is a magical time in southern gardens, after the blistering heat of day has passed," says Kim Hawks of North Carolina's Niche Gardens.

THE USES OF LIGHT Lighting has both practical and aesthetic uses in the garden. You may need to shed some light on pathways or on outdoor dining areas. Or you can use it to highlight vistas and plantings. In either case, the most effective lighting is achieved with subtlety, say the experts. "We like to see light, not lighting," says California landscape architect John Buchholz. He places lights on stakes that have been hidden among the plantings in a particular area, creating uplighting for dramatic effect.

• Nancy Goldstein, a lighting designer in Massachusetts, usually chooses black fixtures that "disappear into the mulch. Your eye is drawn to the brightest object in its field," she explains. "If you light your garden with a large glass globe on a post, that's what people will see. Wouldn't you rather have them see your trees, shrubs, and plants?"

• San Francisco landscape architect Marta Fry likes "moonlighting": light fixtures buried in trees cast fluid pools of light very much like that created by the moon.

• Most experts recommend that you avoid spotlighting, which can be dramatic but also harsh.

DOING IT YOURSELF According to Nancy Goldstein, most home gardeners can install basic lighting, as long as they work with low-voltage systems (usually 12-volt). Safe to set up and operate, these systems don't need to be deep underground but can simply be buried several inches under the mulch. That way, if you happen to accidentally run over a cable with your lawnmower, you won't harm yourself or the overall system. High-voltage lighting, on the other hand, should be installed by a licensed electrician and usually requires a permit.

Luminous gray stone, fallen leaves, dark brown bark, and deep evergreen needles combine to form an oasis for meditation.

Whether you install your own lighting or depend on a reputable contractor, you'll need a dedicated circuit (an outside outlet, independent of other lines but connected to your circuit breakers). If you have an automatic sprinkling system, says John Buchholz, consider installing two dedicated circuits, one for lighting and one for the irrigation clock. That way, you won't have to continually stop one to work the other.

Garden Ornaments

Complements or competition for plants? • Emphasizing simplicity • Whose taste is it anyway?

Ornamenting your garden is like choosing the jewels to wear with a dress. You want something attractive but not gaudy, a few pieces but not too many, and they should complement not clash.

MAKING A MATCH Most experts agree that garden statuary—containers, furniture, and functional pieces such as birdbaths and lanterns—should bear some relation to the architectural style of the

Seating can be more than merely functional. These chairs in Chanticleer Gardens feature simple construction. The chair above creates a rustic mood; the ones below are starkly modern.

WOOD FOR OUTDOOR FURNITURE

Wooden furniture has natural appeal and blends beautifully into most land-scapes. However, it can require a lot of care.
Choosing wood Teak and mahogany are the most durable woods. They're also the most expensive and often come from endangered rainforests. Redwood and cedar are also good choices. Experts most often recommend western red cedar; eastern white cedar doesn't last as long. Much of the outdoor lumber on the market is pressure-treated pine. It's very durable, but toxic chemicals are used to treat it. Avoid using treated lumber in the garden, since you don't want the toxins contaminating your food, pets, or kids.
Treating wood If you paint or stain wood, you'll have to keep doing so—a problem around plants. Consider the weathered, silver look.

house. "Family resemblance is the key to taste," says Robert Caughlan of Caughlan & Son Landscapes in California. If you fall in love with a piece whose style is at odds with your house's architecture, set it at a distance, in a place where it can be seen from the house but is not next to it. In general, he adds, garden ornaments work best when they're stylistically simpler than the house.

Simplicity is also central to the aesthetic philosophy of Frederick Held, a nurseryman in Oregon. "Fine statuary enhances an estate," he says, "but for a small garden, consider a few well-placed rocks, a small pond with koi, a stone lantern, a birdbath, or a sundial." Dorthe Hviid of The Berkshire Botanical Garden also advises erring on the side of understatement. "Intense colors and loud design in statuary or garden furniture demand a lot of attention," she says. "Statuary or furniture should never compete with plants."

An archway pulls you through this garden; it's a focal point that adds height as well as structure.

DISPLAYING A MIX Kim Hawks of North Carolina's Niche Gardens works a rather eclectic collection of garden accents into her backyard. "In my garden, I use driftwood from the beach to create interesting nooks for plants," she says. I look for dead eastern red cedars in the woods, remove any dried foliage, and 'plant' them as natural trellises." Large stones provide niches for plants that need shelter from prevailing winds, and small stones are scattered here and there as garden accents. Among Kim's favorite items are her yard's many bluebird houses, painted a rainbow of colors by neighborhood children. She also uses metal sculptures, gazing globes, and clay figures. Sounds like a visual cacophony, but Kim averts that by making sure each piece is displayed alone and given its own special focus. "Every time you turn a corner in my garden," she says, "you discover a different piece of sculpture, softened by lots of plants."

Gazebos and pergolas are not as expensive as they look. Many can be built from reasonably priced kits available at garden centers or through the mail.

New Jersey garden designer Leigh Sorenson created this sculpture by bolting together old garden tools and painting them a uniform gray to match the house shingles. An archway built over the banisters completes the picture—a very dramatic but easy-to-create tableau.

Compost piles are rarely attractive. Make space for your compost pile or bin in a spot that's easy to get to, but out of the way.

SPECIAL CONSIDERATIONS

No matter how well you've thought through your garden design, prepared the ground, and planted your flowers, vegetables, and trees, circumstances arise that create challenges. Here you'll find advice from the experts on how to solve some of the problems that come up as your garden grows.

Common Oversights

Room for the future • Making maintenance easy • Preparing for the unexpected

Growing a garden is like planning a wedding. Between your glorious vision of the end result and the multitude of arrangements needed to achieve that end, it's easy to overlook a few details.

THE MATURE SIZE OF SHRUBS AND TREES Many gardeners forget to consider just how large some plants will get, says Ted Lockwood of Highstead Arboretum in Connecticut. We've all seen a beautiful house whose entire facade is obscured by huge evergreens. Once those giants were small, neat shrubs—perhaps the very same shrubs you're planning to grow in the front of your home. Unless you like the "Honey, I shrunk the house" look, always determine a plant's mature size before planting. And don't forget that plants grow sideways as well as up, says Burpee's Sharon Kaszan. Or that roots take up space, too, says Angela Fabbri, a San Francisco garden designer. "People often plant deep-rooted trees next to the house," she says. "They're beautiful, but costly when they get into the sewer system or under the foundation of your house."

AN AREA FOR COMPOSTING Even the best-designed compost bins are less than decorative, points out Robert Caughlan of Caughlan & Son Landscapes in California. Try to find an out-of-the-way nook for composting, or include some kind of screen—living or structural—in your garden plans.

OVERHEAD POWER LINES To save yourself the hassle of constant—and sometimes unsightly—pruning, plant trees away from any overhead power lines, or choose dwarf trees that won't overgrow their bounds.

A PATHWAY FOR MAINTENANCE In our rush to create lush, attractive beds and borders, we often forget that the plants that fill those beds will require maintenance, say Peter and Jean Ruh, garden experts from the Homestead Division of Sunnybrook Farms in Ohio. Leave yourself enough space for weeding, watering, fertilizing, and mulching. The Ruhs recommend a pathway at least 18 inches wide. You'll need that much or more if you plan on using a wheelbarrow.

PLANT REQUIREMENTS "Gardeners often overlook sun and shade requirements," says Diane Kostial McGuire, a Rhode Island-based landscape architect. "It's not unusual to see things planted where they can't flourish because a large tree nearby is casting too much shade or its roots are taking up too much moisture," she says. Charles Sandifer, a Memphis landscape architect, recommends going beyond the glossy catalog pages to get the real lowdown on the plants you're considering. In addition to light and moisture requirements, find out what kind of soil each plant needs, whether it will tolerate weather extremes, and how susceptible it is to pests and diseases.

DESIGN PLANNING CHECKLIST

Make sure you don't forget the obvious when planning a new garden design. Keep this checklist handy to make sure you've allowed for everything you need.

☙ Space for pathways—for garden visitors and for handling maintenance tasks.

☙ Room for a compost center.

☙ Screens to block eyesores beyond your property.

☙ Privacy screens to keep features such as pools, hot tubs, or decks secluded from neighbors' views.

☙ Protection from uninvited animals who may like to dine on your vegetables or ornamental plants.

If your garden is deeper than an arm's length from either side, you'll need a way to get into it for maintenance without disturbing the plantings. A maintenance path can be as simple as a few stepping stones.

WHEN TO CALL A PRO

You can do pretty much everything your garden requires, but here are a few jobs best left to pros:

❖ Pros can sometimes prepare a site or soil more efficiently than a home gardener can, says Kim Hawks of North Carolina's Niche Gardens. "They have the equipment and manpower to remove weeds and prepare beds," she explains, "and skimping on soil preparation isn't wise."

❖ Serious drainage and grading problems, and any job (like certain electrical work) that has to be done according to local code requirements is best done by pros. Long Island landscaper Gisela Schaeffer suggests you consider hiring a pro for all major jobs, like irrigation systems, lighting, and construction. "The pros have the right equipment and experience; they do it once and they do it right," she says. "Why reinvent the wheel for every project?"

SAFETY Some plants aren't visitor friendly, points out David Bar-Zvi of Fairchild Tropical Garden in Miami. Don't place spiny or thorny plants near paths or at eye level, and plants that drop fruit should be kept away from paths where the fruit could make the ground slippery. If you share your backyard with pets or young children, keep all poisonous plants out of the garden or beyond the reach of little hands (and paws), advise Peter and Jean Ruh.

UNINVITED GUESTS As development continues to encroach on once-wild places, animal pests are becoming one of the gardener's greatest challenges, explains Ainie Busse of Busse Gardens in Minnesota. Find out from neighbors and your local cooperative agent which critters are most common in your area, and use plants that will be least appealing (or install protective fencing). If you intend to put in a stocked water garden, don't overlook the fact that a raccoon's favorite food is fish.

Consulting Experts

Where the experts go for information • Developing relationships • The most reliable sources

When asked who they look to for advice and inspiration, experts say each other. Nursery owners turn to cooperative agents and botanical gardens. Cooperative agents query nurseries and botanical gardens. Landscape architects and garden designers seek out nurseries.

SOURCES OF INFORMATION Marc Stoecklein of Stoecklein's Nursery in Pennsylvania suggests that you go to more than one source for advice, since even the experts are likely to disagree on any given subject. Andrea Sessions of Tennessee's Sunlight Gardens recommends garden magazines and, if you have the time, conferences. Other sources of information include books, local garden clubs and horticultural societies (which often have specialized libraries of their own), as well as other gardeners in the area. The key word is "local," since gardening techniques and requirements vary markedly from region to region.

FINDING EXPERTS If you buy your plants from a local nursery, start there. The owners can give you advice and then refer you to other sources. In addition, each state has at least one land-grant university (usually the state university) that sponsors a cooperative extension. You can locate your cooperative agent by calling the state university or looking in your local telephone directory under the listings for county government. Both cooperative agents and nurseries can steer you to nearby botanical gardens, all of which are fertile sources of gardening information.

Your local botanic garden is a great place to find out about your gardening community. Institutions like the Missouri Botanic Garden, in St. Louis (above) have spent decades or even centuries figuring out the best way to garden in your region.

PROS FOR TREE TASKS

Professionals are often better equipped to handle large tree jobs.

❧ Connecticut cooperative agent Dr. Sharon Douglas recommends calling a tree surgeon if you think you might have a problem with girdling roots. She also recommends professional pruning of large trees; too many beautiful trees are botched by amateur pruning.

❧ If you have a tree that needs to come down, don't do it yourself, advises Inez Berg of the Washington Park Botanic Garden. And make sure whoever is doing it has insurance.

❧ If you're planting a tree with a trunk larger than 2 inches in diameter, call a pro and ask for a guarantee, says Rob Layton of Colorado's Design Concepts.

❧ If you have a tree near your house or a playground, think about having it inspected on a regular basis.

Sharing Your Garden with Others

Safety for all • Accessibility counts • Kid stuff

Gardening cuts across lines of class, race, gender, age, and physical ability. Children in particular are at home in the garden, no doubt because of their affinity for playing in the dirt. And older people find gardening relaxing and recreational. When planning your garden, consider the people who will use it and their needs, especially children and those who are physically disabled. If you are disabled, you'll need to take special steps to make the garden safer, more accessible, and easier to work in. "All gardens, public and private, should be accessible and safe for everyone," says Inez Berg of the Washington Park Botanic Garden in Illinois.

THE LITTLEST GARDENERS If you have children or grandchildren, or if you expect kids to be visiting your backyard regularly, make sure they have their own special areas for play and for gardening. It's best to locate these areas away from your prize peonies—or anything else that

Kids love gardens, but sometimes you need to attract their attention. Potmen, whimsically dressed scarecrows, and gaily painted furniture will usually do the trick.

can't take the trampling of little feet. Jerry Kay of California's Let's Get Growing educational catalog suggests letting kids in on the planning. "Show them pictures of plants they might like to grow," he says, "and let them choose." Pumpkins, corn (children love its height), and sunflowers are among kids' favorites. If your children will do any hands-on gardening, make sure that beds are a manageable size, says Lisa Glick of the Life Lab Science Program in Santa Cruz—no more than 3 feet wide, so they can reach into the center from either side.

Here are some imaginative suggestions your children might enjoy.

• "The garden itself can become a playground," suggests Jerry Kay. It just takes a little planning. Consider building a sunflower "room" or a teepee clothed in pole-bean vines.

• Pick a sunny area and plant a butterfly garden, says Cathy Wilson of The Landscape Group in Washington, D.C.

• Most kids love worms; see "Working with Earthworms" on page 286 for information on how to set up your own worm farm.

• Ellen Talmage of Long Island's Horticultural Goddess, Inc., recommends using unusual containers for planting, such as gaily painted pots, old bathtubs, and even old sneakers.

Older gardeners and those with physical disabilities find it easier to work in narrow raised beds like the ones below at Colonial Park in New Jersey. Wide pathways make navigation easy.

2

VEGETABLE &
HERB GARDENING
SECRETS

*"Eating food you've grown yourself is an experience
no one should live without."*
DEBBY KAVAKOS, STONELEDGE FARM

Unlike our ancestors, who grew produce out of necessity, we grow vege-tables and herbs because we enjoy them. We grow them because we like fresh produce that's full of flavor and free of pesticides. We grow them because we want our children to know that vegetables come from the soil and the sun and the rain. Or we grow them because we love to scatter seeds and watch them come up, and then to taste the fruits of our labor.

For our forebears, vegetable gardening was as natural and daily an activity as waking in the morning. But we've traveled a long way from our agricultural origins, and many gardeners today consider vegetable gardening difficult and mysterious.

The truth? It's surprisingly simple—especially when you have the advice of experts to help you with the basics, from plotting out the garden and choosing plants and seeds to enriching the soil, conserving water, and harvesting your bounty. The experts reveal their secrets about heirloom varieties, starting seeds indoors, gardening in containers, how and with what to fertilize, plus many more secrets of successful vegetable gardening.

HERE'S WHAT YOU'LL FIND IN CHAPTER 2

PLANS AND JOURNALS

Some elements to include in your records:

- ✺ Nearby structures, which can cast shade
- ✺ Trees and other permanent plants which may cast shade in the future
- ✺ Paths for maintenance
- ✺ Water sources
- ✺ Wind directions
- ✺ Large rocks
- ✺ Decorative elements
- ✺ Structures on which you can create trellises or lean supports.

Julie Marks of Kentucky's Sleepy Hollow Herb Farm records her garden plans in a five-year journal. That way, she has room for information on successful companions and rotations; pest problems; soil amendments; sources for plants, seeds, and equipment; weather conditions; and yields from specific cultivars.

John Lee of Allandale Farm in Massachusetts, who plots his own 35-acre property "down to the square foot," suggests including microclimate factors, insect and disease problems, seasonal changes, and planned crop rotation.

MAKING PLANS

In gardening, as in the rest of life, some people make plans first and others just dig right in. They may have a general picture in their minds and then begin digging and planting, working out the details along the way. Many gardeners, though, find it helpful—and find their efforts are more successful—if they take the time to create a careful plan first.

Putting It on Paper

Plan pros and cons • How to draw a plan that works • Strategic planning

TO WHAT DETAIL? Many experts couldn't imagine putting in a vegetable or herb garden without plotting it out first. "It's easier to rearrange things on paper than in the garden," says Gene Banks of Connecticut's Catnip Acres Herb Farm. Others consider paper planning a waste of time that could be spent in the garden. "Gardening isn't space shuttle technology," says Dennis McGlynn, vice president of the New England Seed Company. And William Hall of Michigan's Country Carriage Nursery cautions that a garden that's planned on paper will look planned. He recommends working it out on paper only if you have limited space.

One advantage of creating a plan on paper is that you can use it to track the garden's progress from year to year, which is particularly helpful if you intend to rotate your vegetables. Pam Allenstein of Philadelphia's historic John Bartram Garden relies on a long-term plan for recording pest and disease problems. If she sees that a plant has done poorly for several years, she'll try it in a new location.

For Julie Marks of Kentucky's Sleepy Hollow Herb Farm, planning is definitely a long-term affair. Because she switches from herbs to vegetables and back again, she keeps meticulous track of each bed over time, sketching in all the plants in the garden and noting where pests have attacked. This helps her find the best sites for all her crops. If you intend to garden intensively (see "Intensive Gardening" on page 80), planning on paper is a critical step.

WORKING UP A PLAN For an average-size plot, Gene Banks uses graph paper and a scale of 1 inch = 1 foot. You could also use a computer program to help you map your beds; see "Sources" on page 362.

This vegetable garden at Longwood Gardens pumps out delicious produce from April to November. Gardeners follow a plan for each bed that allows them to keep the crops coming.

Trellises, raised beds, and row covers allow this small garden to yield maximum results from minimum space.

Rows or Beds?

Aethestics versus ease • Suggested sizes • Mixing it up

To decide on the right approach for your garden, you need to first determine your priorities, the experts say. Is the look of your garden important to you, or do you most need easy access?

GOING WITH ROWS You can plant in straight rows, or you can place your vegetables and herbs in mixed beds the way you'd plant a perennial border. What difference does it make?

"Rows are easier," says Flora Hackimer of West Virginia's Wrenwood of Berkeley Springs. They allow you easy access to your plants and they keep design worries to a minimum. She finds that rows make the most efficient use of space, offering you greater yield per plant. She does, however, plant in beds for display purposes.

Another plus of planting in rows is that it's easier to distinguish between weeds and crops—an important consideration if your seeds are costly, says Pennsylvania horticulturist Dr. Michael Orzolek.

How big should your rows be? Expert opinions vary. Julie Marks of Kentucky's Sleepy Hollow Herb Farm recommends using 12 × 4-foot rows. These are large, she says, but not overwhelming. Rose Marie

This small, circular garden at Barton-Pell Gardens in New York is filled with culinary herbs. A pathway between the circles makes maintenance easy.

In the vegetable garden at George Washington's Mount Vernon estate near Washington, D.C., decorative beds in unusual shapes are edged with lavender cotton.

McGee of Oregon's Nichols Garden Nursery likes 15 × 2-foot rows, separated by a 2-foot maintenance strip, while William Hall of Michigan's Country Carriage Nursery plants strawberries in 3- to 4-foot-wide beds, giving these perennials plenty of room to grow to their full size and send out "daughter" plants.

All the experts agree that what's most important is that you can reach the center of the row from both sides.

PLANTING IN BEDS If you're aiming for commercial production or maximum harvest, says John Lee of Allandale Farm in Massachusetts, then rows are the way to go. But he recommends beds for most home gardeners, preferably beds planted with a mix of herbs, vegetables, perennials, and shrubs. "It's important for a garden to be beautiful. That way you'll spend more time in it, and the more time you spend, the greater the chance that you'll notice important, useful things," he says.

An avid gardener, George Washington was deeply involved in the creation of this vegetable garden at Mount Vernon. He used beds of different shapes and sizes to create an attractive, easy to maintain garden that produced all the vegetables needed for his large household.

HOW TO GARDEN INTENSIVELY

To get maximum yield from your space, try some—or all—of the following:

❧ Double- or triple-dig soil (see "Double-Digging for Vegetables" on page 104) and enrich it heavily with compost and other organic matter.

❧ Start plants indoors so they're ready to go into the ground as soon as the soil is warm.

❧ Keep indoor plants going so you can plant succession crops.

❧ Use mulch and other methods to warm the soil as early as possible.

❧ Space transplants twice as close as recommended. Place several small plants across each row horizontally as well as spacing them vertically.

❧ Plant a variety of vegetables to use up every inch of soil.

❧ Garden vertically with trellises, arbors, and other supports.

❧ Keep your garden going with cold-season crops such as kale, brussels sprouts, and cabbage.

And while rows may be efficient, they can also be weedier, points out Dennis McGlynn, vice president of the New England Seed Company. Using ornamental beds allows you to plant more densely and keep weeds down. But Niles Kinerk of the Gardens Alive! catalog warns beginners that mixed plantings can be confusing. You could, he says, end up yanking out your vegetable seedlings instead of the weeds they sometimes resemble. Labeling can help you avoid this, says Kim Hawks of North Carolina's Niche Gardens.

Many experts believe that tight planting in beds, also called intensive gardening, yields more vegetables.

Intensive Gardening

What is it? • Intensive methods • Intensive intelligence

Intensive gardening refers to methods designed to help you get the highest possible yield from your vegetable plot, no matter what its size. It originated in eighteenth-century France outside of Paris, where a group of farmers experimented with alternative methods of farming. They planted their crops close together in highly fertile beds, used soil-warming methods to extend the season, and grew vegetables in succession. The most recent turn on intensive gardening is the biointensive method developed by Englishman Alan Chadwick and put into practice in America in the 1960s at the University of California's Santa Cruz Student Garden.

THE BENEFITS OF INTENSIVE METHODS John Schneeberger of Montana's Garden City Seeds believes that intensive gardening is the way to go. "It's anachronistic to use big rows with wide spaces between them," he says. Not only can intensive gardening give you greater yields, it cuts down on weeds. Tightly planted vegetables form a canopy that prevents the sun from penetrating to the soil and encouraging weeds to germinate. It also reduces the need for watering since there are no bare spots to dry out quickly.

Stephen Garrison of the Rutgers Cooperative Extension also recommends the intensive approach, especially for gardeners who have limited space. However, he points out that intensive gardening yields more per square foot, not necessarily more per plant. And Janet

Whippo, a horticulturist at the New York Botanical Garden, uses intensive methods in small gardens. Her favorite techniques—and the ones she recommends to backyard gardeners—include enriching the soil with compost, choosing relatively small plants, planting in all directions (including up), and harvesting and replanting immediately.

Kansas horticulturist Ward Upham is less enthusiastic about intensive methods, given the wide-open spaces in which he gardens. However, he agrees it's a good idea for those who have little space.

vegetable & herb gardening secrets

"Square-foot" gardens produce maximum yield from a limited space. Groups of 1 × 1-foot blocks are laid out and interplanted with companion plants. Every part of the bed can be reached from the outside, which reduces soil compaction from foot traffic. In this square-foot garden, cabbages, lettuces, Swiss chard, chives, and fennel are combined; tomatoes will climb the trellises.

Ward suggests that you keep replacing plants with new seedlings after harvest and that you build structures for vertical planting. The experts label their crops carefully so that they don't confuse different vegetables and herbs in mixed plantings.

THE CONS Packing plants close together can encourage fungal diseases due to reduced air circulation. And for crops that need space, intensive planting simply won't work. For instance, asparagus and strawberries won't grow well if spaced closer than 36 to 48 inches, says William Hall of Michigan's Country Carriage Nursery.

Interplanting

Advantages • Happy companions • Plants that don't get along

Interplanting—also called companion planting—is the practice of growing different crops in the same bed or row. If you've decided to try intensive gardening, you'll probably be interplanting.

THE BENEFITS In addition to making the most out of the space you have, interplanting adds color and visual interest to your vegetable beds and can attract beneficial insects. Here are some expert suggestions on specific plantings that may reduce the pests in your garden.

• Because bronze fennel attracts praying mantises, Illinois horticulturist Diane Nolang interplants it with many of her vegetables and finds its striking color a visual bonus.

• Conrad Richter of Ontario's Richter's Herbs plants herbs among his vegetables for their pest-repellent qualities. Though science has yet to prove that such qualities exist, Conrad and many other gardeners believe in them.

• Alice Krinsky, trial garden manager at Shepherd's Garden Seeds, plants marigolds to reduce root-feeding nematodes (microscopic worms that can stunt root growth). Nematodes enter the roots of marigolds, and when you pull the plants in the fall, the pests come up with them. Don't compost the marigolds; throw them in the trash.

• Tom Eickenberg of Johnny's Selected Seeds has found marigolds useful for keeping the slugs out of his lettuce. The slugs find the marigolds so tasty, he says, that they tend to leave the lettuce alone. Tom says nasturtiums will lure aphids away from your crops the same way. (To get

At the New York Botanical Garden, leaf lettuce is interplanted with beets. The fast-growing, shallow-rooted lettuce shades the emerging beet greens and doesn't harm the developing roots.

Savory herbs, such as sage and thyme, deter cabbage moths. Marigolds attract pollinating insects and, according to some sources, reduce nematode attacks on nearby vegetables.

them off your nasturtiums, spray them with a little soapy water.)

• Recent studies indicate that garlic contains fungicidal and antibacterial substances, which may explain why farmers have long planted garlic in companion with their cabbage.

• According to common gardening wisdom, mint repels ants, basil deters bean beetles, rosemary chases away slugs, and tomatoes keep diamondback moths out of cabbages.

COMPANIONS

Some plants seem to do better or worse because of what's growing nearby. Here are a few combinations that work and a few that don't.

❧ Basil with peppers, cabbages, tomatoes, or beans.

❧ Beets with cabbages or onions; not with pole beans.

❧ Bush beans with corn, beets, or petunias; not with onions.

❧ Corn with potatoes, peas, beans, cucumbers, squash, melons, or sunflowers; not with tomatoes.

❧ Broccoli, cabbage, or cauliflower with potatoes, beets, or onions, but not with tomatoes, pole beans, or strawberries. (Savory herbs such as sage, thyme, and oregano deter cabbage moths.)

❧ Peas with carrots, turnips, radishes, cucumbers, corn, beans, or tomatoes; not with broccoli, cabbage, or cauliflower.

❧ Squash with nasturtium, mint, tansy, radishes, or beans; not with potatoes.

vegetable & herb gardening secrets

In this bed, chives, mustard greens, and Swiss chard are planted in sections. The greens are close enough to benefit from the insect-repelling effect of the chives, but the gardener will have less trouble identifying his plants in their early stages.

Companion planting offers other benefits as well as insect control:

• Tall plants like tomatoes can help shield cool-season crops like lettuce from intense heat and sunlight. For years, farmers have planted seedlings of spinach, lettuce, and cabbage beneath the sheltering foliage of early-season peas.

• Beans set nitrogen into the soil.

• Peanuts increase the yields of corn and squash plants.

• Janet Whippo, a horticulturist at the New York Botanical Garden, follows the Native-American custom of interplanting the "three sisters": corn, squash, and beans. She says this seems to enhance both the plants' health and yield.

• For sheer good looks, Janet suggests planting chives among vegetables. Bronze fennel is another useful and ornamental herb that can be interplanted among vegetable beds.

• One of Diane Nolang's favorite combinations was an interplanting of broccoli, cauliflower, cabbage, and a red globe amaranth that originally moved into the bed uninvited.

Another benefit of interplanting with flowers, says Pennsylvania horticulturist Dr. Michael Orzolek, is the pollinators they attract. If the puritan in you quails at the thought of mixing all those frivolous flowers in among your hardworking crops, remember that lots of blooms—including nasturtium, violet, and impatiens—are edible.

DOS AND DON'TS Try to group plants that have similar cultural requirements, advises Lynn Hartmann of Hartmann's Herb Farm in Massachusetts. Don't, for example, interplant thirsty tomatoes with lavender, which grows best when soil is slightly dry.

To increase air circulation, Janet Whippo recommends staggering tall, medium, and short plants (bush-type peas next to tomatoes next to bronze fennel, for example). And she says you'll make the most of your space by planting herbs next to vegetables. Janet likes to plant dill among her cabbages.

SOME REASONS FOR SEGREGATION Though most experts recommend interplanting, some see good reason to segregate plants. Lynn Hartmann groups different species of mints, basils, and parsleys but doesn't mix them because it's easier to provide the conditions that each one needs if they're not mixed. Niles Kinerk of the Gardens

Alive! catalog in Indiana points out that it's easy to mistake mixed plants for weeds and pull up your crops accidentally. And Barbara Bridges of Southern Perennials and Herbs in Mississippi says she's tried interplanting and segregated planting and has found little difference in disease prevention or yield.

Succession Planting

Keeping the garden planted all season • The experts' successions
• Successful soil from succession planting

Because most crops don't produce over an entire season, it makes sense to replace them when yields slow down. There are several ways to plant in succession: You can stagger plantings of the same crop by sowing seed at two-week intervals throughout the season, or you can plant early-, mid-, and late-season varieties of the same vegetable. You can also, of course, plant different crops in succession, replacing a cool-season crop like peas with a high-summer crop like beans, followed by another cool-season vegetable such as broccoli.

WHAT TO PLANT The experts have their favorite succession crops—those that have worked well for them year-in and year-out.
• Donald Ledden of New Jersey's Ledden Brothers follows leaf lettuce with bush beans, corn, and squash.
• Gary Coull of Johnny's Selected Seeds plants bush snap beans followed by lettuce, radishes, greens, basil, and cilantro.
• The radishes in Kansas horticulturist Ward Upham's garden are eventually supplanted by cucumbers.
• Stephen Garrison of the Rutgers Cooperative Extension likes to follow his cabbages (or other members of the Brassica family) with snap beans, cucumbers, or squash, replanting the same space with fall lettuces at the end of the season.

SPECIAL CONSIDERATIONS Because succession planting requires highly fertile soil, Stephen Garrison recommends an addition of organic mulch, spaded into the soil, or fertilizer between each planting. "If you're using black plastic and a drip irrigation system," says Stephen, "you won't be able to make these amendments, but you probably won't have to because the mulch will keep the soil fertile." Just start a new

A spring crop of spinach is ready for harvest in early summer. After picking, you can replant the bed with a succession crop of beans or squash.

Swaths of chives and sweet marjoram, accented by purple sage, fill this bed that is totally edible and absolutely beautiful.

hole, he says, and keep going. Galen Gates of Chicago Botanic Garden avoids using wood chips in his mulch because wood can deplete nitrogen as it decomposes.

Start your succession plantings with long-season vegetables (those that take 70 or more days to produce). These will stay in the ground for most of the season. Around them, sow or transplant cool-season crops followed by warm-season vegetables followed by crops that flourish in fall. Good cool-season vegetables include artichokes, beets, brussels sprouts, cauliflower, greens, and parsnips. For a high-summer harvest in temperate climates, try corn, cucumber, eggplant, melons, peppers, tomatoes, and squash.

Beautifying Beds

Fashion and function • *Ornamental edibles*
• *Herbs everywhere!*

For many home gardeners—especially those with limited space—appearances matter, even among the radishes and radicchio. By interplanting, you can have your vegetables and a beautiful backyard, too. The garden should be a beautiful, peaceful place, says John Lee of Allandale Farm in Massachusetts. Its psychological benefit can be just as important as its crop yield.

GO FOR THE MIX The notion of combining flowers and vegetables isn't new. In Colonial kitchen gardens like the one that belonged to Philadelphia's John Bartram, vegetables, herbs, and ornamentals happily coexisted. "In Bartram's day, there was no distinction between plants used for medicine, cooking, and eating, so there were a lot of very ornamental plants in the kitchen garden," says Pam Allenstein of Philadelphia's historic John Bartram Garden. Planting ornamentals among your vegetables may benefit your garden because you'll spend more time working in it. "Anything that gives pleasure makes the gardener more likely to want to spend time in the garden," says Louise Hyde of New Jersey's Well-Sweep Herb Farm.

PLANT FLOWERS THAT LIKE VEGETABLES When combining ornamentals and vegetables, plant easy-to-grow annuals, advises Pennsylvania horticulturist Dr. Michael Orzolek. That way, you won't have to

provide much more care than you would for an all-vegetable garden. Here are some flower-vegetable combinations recommended by the experts:

• At Georgia's Callaway Gardens, cosmos, pansies, petunias, and marigolds brighten the edible beds.

• At the New York Botanical Garden, a few pansies tuck in among the transplants in early spring, followed by mums and ornamental cabbages in the fall.

• James Wooten of Virginia's historic Ashlawn-Highland plants some early-spring-blooming bulbs among the perennial herbs, which don't appear until later in the season.

VARIETY IN VEGETABLES You don't have to rely on flowers to dress up the vegetable bed, say the experts. "Edibles offer enough variety of form, texture, and color to accomplish that," says Rose Marie McGee of Oregon's Nichols Garden Nursery.

Start with a design before you put in your vegetables, advises Pam Allenstein. "If you plan with an eye for beauty, you don't have to make yield secondary," she says. Among her favorite vegetables that do double duty as ornamentals are rhubarb, Swiss chard, and scarlet runner beans.

At the experimental garden at University of California at Santa Cruz, gardeners combine proper planting practices with visual appeal. Climbing squash vines create a backdrop to groomed rows of greens, while a hop-covered arbor provides vertical interest and shade.

'Ruby Red' Swiss chard, with its bright red midribs, is every bit as ornamental as the flowering annuals (celosia, canna, and begonias) used in this bed.

Or, says Julie Marks of Kentucky's Sleepy Hollow Herb Farm, combine broccoli and kale with lemon and cinnamon basil, which have highly attractive flowers.

Rose Marie McGee grows a cornucopia of beautiful edibles, including deep red perillas, stately cardoons, hot peppers like 'Super Cayenne' and bright red 'Jingle Bells', and 'Bright Lights' Swiss chard, which combines yellow, orange, and red all on the same plant. She also recommends artichokes, 'Jack Be Little' pumpkins (grow them up a trellis for a vertical accent), vivid yellow 'Gold Nugget' tomatoes, chives and Japanese bunching or Welsh onions (for their pretty spring flowers), and great foliage plants like tricolor sage and pineapple mint.

Sean Hogan, a garden designer and horticulturist from Oregon, uses edibles in his ornamental beds. One of his favorite combinations is purple eggplant and bronze flax lilies.

The architectural qualities of vegetables are evident in this raised bed. The rosette form of purple cabbages contrasts with vertical corn and rambling squash. The dark purple cabbages and bright gold squash flowers are as vivid as the ornamental marigolds.

Rivaling the prettiest flowers: 'Giant Red' mustard greens and 'Selma-Wisa' lettuce.

Swiss chard and lettuce adapt well to containers because they grow quickly and have relatively small root systems. Perk up your containers with annuals, such as the pinks shown below.

Container Gardening

Growing good food in pots • Caring for potted plants

If you have limited space or sun, or if your soil is less than fertile, consider growing vegetables and herbs in containers. For gardeners in cool climates, containers allow you to grow herbs like rosemary, which won't survive the winter outdoors.

However, container gardening has some disadvantages. The soil dries out quickly and needs more frequent watering, points out Peter Borchard of Ohio's Companion Plants. Container plants also require more fertilizer than plants grown in the ground, and they have a tendency to become rootbound. But if you know a few simple secrets, you can grow a lush crop of vegetables and herbs right on your patio or deck.

WHAT TO GROW According to Peter, most culinary herbs do well in containers. Jim Becker of Oregon's Goodwin Creek Gardens recommends starting with container naturals like sage, thyme, and chives. Watch out for the mints, though, warns Gene Banks of Connecticut's Catnip Acres Herb Farm. Known for their vigor, they can easily overrun even a spacious container. Other gardeners, including Kim Hawks of North Carolina's Niche Gardens, like to grow mints in containers because they keep mints from invading the rest of the garden. When necessary, she divides the mints and gives the excess to friends. In Chicago, Galen Gates grows aloes, rosemary, and lavender in pots; they are too tender for Midwestern winters but are fine if they are brought indoors before frost hits.

As long as you choose the right variety, you can grow almost any vegetable in containers, says Shane Smith, director of Wyoming's Cheyenne Botanic Garden. Stick to smaller varieties, choosing plants that are bushy rather than vining and determinate rather than indeterminate. (Determinate plants have stems that stop growing after flowers form at the vine tips. The stems of indeterminate plants continue to grow and produce additional blossoms after flowering.) If you're growing tomatoes, stick to dwarf types, such as 'Patio' and 'Tiny Tim', or cherry tomatoes.

Tender bananas can be grown in containers on sunporches and brought outdoors in summer. This banana bush shares its container with kale.

Containers don't have to be boring: Lettuces planted in an old wheelbarrow add a whimsical touch to your vegetable garden. Just be sure you provide drainage holes in any container you choose.

This container of spinach is set into a bed of Swiss chard at Wave Hill Garden in the Bronx, New York.

SUN AND WATER Nearly all vegetables and many herbs require sun—and lots of it. But those in containers, says Flora Hackimer of West Virginia's Wrenwood of Berkeley Springs, should be shielded from the sun during the hottest part of the day, if possible. Shane Smith advises putting pots on wheels or rollers so that you can easily move them out of bad weather—a plus if summer hailstorms are a problem in your area. Otherwise, just make sure that plants are well watered, especially during hot, dry spells, when you'll probably need to water at least twice a day. If summers in your area tend to be very hot, try potting vegetables and herbs in plastic containers, which retain water better than terra cotta or wood.

POTS AND SOIL Make sure that the containers you use provide enough room for the plants you want to grow. Most vegetables will thrive in a 5-gallon container with a 12-inch depth. When potting them, don't use garden soil, which is too heavy for containers. Instead, use an equal mix of topsoil, peat moss, and a soil lightener like vermiculite (you can also use a commercial potting mix). Make sure containers have ample drainage. (For more information on caring for container plants, see "Container Gardening," page 59.)

INDOOR HERBS

If you have a reliably sunny exposure, says Gene Banks of Connecticut's Catnip Acres Herb Farm, you can grow parsley, chives, cilantro, and other herbs right in your kitchen. The secret is to provide ample humidity and good air circulation. Place plants on very large saucers filled with water and pebbles (setting plants directly in the water can lead to rot), advises Gene, and stagger their height by placing every other plant on an overturned pot.

Make sure your herbs don't become rootbound (one of the first things to look for if you notice a decline in vigor), says Peter Borchard of Companion Plants in Ohio. Fix root-bound plants by repotting or by using this method: Cut off the bottom one-quarter to one-third of the root mass, add new soil to the container, loosen the remaining roots, replace the plant, and water it well.

vegetable & herb gardening secrets

SHOPPING FOR PLANTS

Endless varieties of vegetables and herbs spill from the pages of catalogs. Nurseries and garden centers beckon around every bend. Where's the best place to buy plants and how do you decide what to grow and which plants are healthiest? Turn to the experts for advice.

Sources for Plants and Seeds

Local versus mail order • Using several sources • Specialty nurseries • Decisions at discount chains

You can find seeds and plants in nurseries, garden centers, catalogs, home-building stores, and even some supermarkets. And quality does vary from source to source, warn the experts.

WHEN IN DOUBT, GO LOCAL Nearly all the experts believe in supporting local growers and nurseries, who know not only their plants but also the area and its growing conditions. If you buy at least some of your plants locally, you can be sure they're well adapted to your climate and terrain. When buying through the mail, it's important to find out where the source is located, says Sarah Gallant of Maine's Pinetree Garden Seeds. "If you live in Tennessee, for example, and order seed potatoes from New England, they may not be able to ship early enough for your area," she points out. Conversely, she adds, "If you live in New England and order from the South, you could end up getting your seed potatoes too early and having to store them in your garage."

"I prefer to buy plants grown in Richmond," says Peggy Singlemann of the Maymount Foundation in Virginia. "Sure, I'll buy from Oregon if it's a plant I can't get here, but those plants always need a little extra TLC. Even if the USDA hardiness zone is the same as mine, weather patterns will be different, and that changes the genetic makeup of the plant." For appropriate catalog sources, ask neighboring botanic gardens where they buy their plants, says John Lee of Allandale Farm in Massachusetts. It's also easier to replace a plant from a local vendor if it does poorly.

GO FOR VARIETY Don't buy from a single source, advises John. If you're ordering from catalogs, use two or three, including one from a local

READING CATALOGS

Nursery owners put a great deal of time and effort into providing you with everything you need to know to decide whether or not to buy a particular plant. A good catalog will list the mature size of the plant, water, light, and soil requirements, and usually the plant's Latin and common names. It should also tell you the age and pot size of the plant you'll be receiving (you should not have to pay as much for a young plant as you would for one that's been growing for several seasons).

Keep in mind that every catalog tries to convince you to buy its goods. A plant described as vigorous may be weedy. One that's said to be rare may also be unknown or difficult to grow. If you want more information about a particular offering, call the nursery.

Ordering plants from specialty nurseries allows you to obtain interesting varieties that are often not available from your local nursery. From left to right: 'Purple Ruffles' basil; borage; 'Chioggia' beets.

grower. This will allow you to sample all that's new, tried-and-true, and special, not just one seller's specialty. And don't limit yourself to the big-name sellers. Order from some of the specialty seed purveyors who deal in heirloom and rare varieties, suggests Craig Dremann of the Redwood City Seed Company in California.

Craig also points out that you don't need to limit yourself to commercial sources. "You can breed and cross-pollinate what you like best, the same way the Navajos did," he says. "When you eat a melon you like, save the seeds and mix them with some seeds of disease-resistant varieties. Plant the whole bunch and you'll eventually come up with your own hybrids."

GO FOR SELECTION If you want the best selection, say the experts, order from specialty nurseries. These growers deal in particular types of plants, whether peppers, potatoes, high-altitude vegetables, or heirloom lettuces, and they offer plants and seeds you're not likely to find at your local garden center. The superior selection they offer far outweighs the handful of disadvantages (including waiting for your plants to arrive and the inability to select the size and quality of the plants you're buying), says Michael Cady of the Jackson Perkins catalog. Another disadvantage, according to Peter Borchard of Ohio's Companion Plants, is higher prices. But with the specialty nurseries who really know what they're selling, you generally get what you pay for.

CHAIN SHOPPING

Large chain stores offer an increasing selection of plants at attractive prices. The experts suggest caution in buying plants from these stores. Though the chains may get many of their plants from the same sources as your local nursery or garden center, says Joseph Oppe of the Des Moines Botanical Center, "nursery people are much more knowledgeable and can give better advice."

In addition, says Tom Brooks of Massachusetts's Wilson Farms, "you don't know how the plant you buy from a chain was treated. It could have been in the supermarket for a week, cared for by inexperienced staff." If you must buy from a chain, he says, try to get the plants as they're coming off the truck. And make sure that they look healthy and well tended. (For tips on choosing plants, see "Shopping for Plants," pages 92–100.)

Selecting Varieties

The right plant for your site • *Flavor first!*
• *Experimenting with new varieties*

Of course, you can begin narrowing your choices by considering which vegetables and herbs you'll be able to grow in your backyard.

CONSIDER YOUR SITE A plant that isn't naturally adapted to your site and climate begins life with a major disadvantage. When choosing new plants for his farm in Canada's Saskatchewan province, Joe Bloski of Early's Farm and Garden Center always considers days to maturity. "We're in a short-season region, and we don't plant out until mid-May," he says. Joe needs vegetables that mature quickly.

John Lee of Allandale Farm in Massachusetts looks for cold-tolerance, and, because his soil is rocky, chooses appropriate plants— a 6-inch carrot, for example, rather than a 12-inch variety. He recommends that you look for resistant varieties—plants that are the least susceptible to pests and diseases. And if you know a particular problem is endemic to your area, make sure to choose a variety that isn't likely to succumb to it.

DON'T FORGET FLAVOR For the past several decades, bigger, in the realm of vegetables, has generally meant better. Gardeners and hybridizers alike have gone for the monster pumpkin, the scale-tipping tomato, the zucchini as big as the Ritz. In our rush to breed super-vegetables, we appear to have forgotten that the essential point of growing them is to eat them. Fortunately that's changing. Gardeners and professional growers have rediscovered older "heirloom" varieties (see "How about Heirlooms?" on page 96). They may be smaller than their modern-day descendants, but they're often far more flavorful and sometimes prettier, as well.

"Taste is the key," says Craig Dremann of the Redwood City Seed Company in California. He advises gardeners to look for companies (including his own) that sell rare and heirloom plants and seeds. "Once you've tasted heirloom Italian zucchini," says Craig, "you'll never go back to bitter American hybrids."

When reading catalogs, check the plant descriptions for mentions of flavor, says Shannon Singletary of The Gourmet Gardener in

Kansas. "I'm definitely planning to try the green bean that has a butterbean flavor," she says.

EXPERIMENT While the bulk of your garden should probably contain herbs and vegetables that have worked well in the past—either for you or for the gardening world at large—allow a little room for experimentation. Every year, Joseph Oppe and his colleagues at the Des Moines Botanical Center try 6 to 12 new cultivars. "We go right for those little symbols and starbursts in the catalogs that mark the new stuff," he says. Though some of these experiments may fail or falter in your garden, at least one or two will probably surprise you with their vigor, beauty, or good flavor.

Vivid 'Bright Lights' Swiss chard, lime green broccoflower, deep orange peppers, orange and yellow cherry tomatoes, hot peppers, red potatoes, baby carrots, deep burgundy radicchio, and baby squash brighten your vegetable garden as well as your dinner plate.

LIVING HISTORY

Besides taste, hardiness, and ease of maintenance, growing heirlooms confers a spiritual pleasure. "Every time you plant an heirloom, you get a real sense of history," says Joseph Oppe of the Des Moines Botanical Center. Many heirlooms are the same species that have been used for centuries by the indigenous peoples of a given area, says Peter Borchard of Ohio's Companion Plants. And, adds Joseph, there's a very practical reason to plant heirlooms—preservation of a dwindling gene pool. Each time you grow an heirloom, you're saving a plant, and all future hybrids that it could be used to produce, from extinction.

How about Heirlooms?

What are heirlooms? • *Hardy plants with hearty tastes*
• *In defense of hybrids*

Before the advent of modern hybridizing techniques, plants were mostly propagated by seed collected from the plants of a previous season. Hybrids—new varieties created when pollen from one plant falls or is placed on the surface of another—occurred naturally, through the action of birds, insects, and wind, in a process called open pollination. Over the last half-century, plant propagation became big business. Super-hybrids, touted for their disease-resistance and high yields, overtook the old favorites, which often seemed paltry in comparison. The plants of our ancestors slowly began to disappear from cultivation.

Gardeners are now rediscovering these "heirloom" varieties, bringing them back into cultivation and saving them from extinction. Independent companies, dedicated to heirloom preservation and propagation, have sprung up and prospered. Today, heirloom vegetables represent a growing segment of the commercial plant industry. Are they as good as the hybrids and cultivars we've come to depend on? And if so, what are their advantages?

THE HARDINESS OF HEIRLOOMS Plants become heirlooms through the process of natural selection. The most fertile and disease-resistant survive beyond the weak and vulnerable. "When you see a 100-year-old heirloom, you know that it's able to survive, particularly in its own backyard," says Bill Bruneau of California's Bountiful Gardens. For best results, choose heirloom plants and seeds that grow naturally in your area. Most heirlooms are open-pollinated (pollinated by wind or animals, not by humans), so each plant is slightly different. "Thus the chances are higher that they will develop resistance to a pest or disease, as opposed to hybrids, which are genetic twins of each other," says Bill. If an unexpected problem comes up, at least some of your heirlooms will survive.

LOW MAINTENANCE Hybrids may be more productive, but they often require more care, fertilizer, and water than their heirloom cousins, and they are less tolerant of climatic variation, says Bill. "Hybrids generally work for agribusiness, where everything is sprayed, but in your backyard, open-pollinated varieties are more adaptable," he says. Many heirlooms are also smaller and less aggressive, says James Wooten of Virginia's historic Ashlawn-Highlands.

An endless source of seeds If you want to save your own seeds, go for heirlooms, says Sarah Gallant of Maine's Pinetree Garden Seeds. Although they may not give you exact replicas of the parent plant (a hazard of open pollination if you don't follow the recommended distances between varieties), they will be plentiful.

Every year, hybridizers introduce new cultivars, bred to be more vigorous, ornamental, tasty, or disease-resistant. 'Bright Lights' Swiss chard, for instance, was an instant success because of its bright color and robust taste.

Add a historical context to your garden and dinner plate by planting heirlooms like scarlet runner beans— a favorite of Thomas Jefferson—in your garden.

HEIRLOOM CHOICES

As nice as it is to plant vegetables with interesting histories, we also want them to produce. Here are some heirlooms that work:

❧ 'Jacob's Cattle' dry beans; speckled beans that store for many months.

❧ 'Vermont Cranberry' beans; late-season favorite, does well in both cool and hot climates.

❧ 'Hopi' beans; best varieties for Southwest.

❧ 'Cylindra' beets are carrot-shaped; 'Chiogga' are striped red and white. Both are prolific as well as unusual.

❧ 'Romanesco' broccoli, brought here by Italian immigrants, has a wonderful nutty taste.

❧ 'Early Jersey Wakefield' cabbage withstands both hot and cold spells.

❧ Black-seeded 'Simpson' lettuce resists bolting and grows over a long season.

❧ 'Tall Telephone' peas produce over a long period if continually picked.

❧ 'Cherries Jubilee' potatoes are bite-size, red-skinned, and easy to grow.

❧ 'Brandywine' tomatoes are reputed to be the best-tasting around.

And you could end up with a wonderful hybrid unavailable from any commercial source. Many hybrids, on the other hand, are essentially sterile, the end of their genetic line. By growing heirlooms, gardeners keep the door open for future breeding, says David Bar-Zvi of Fairchild Tropical Garden in Florida.

BETTER TASTE Many of the experts, including Pam Allenstein of Philadelphia's historic John Bartram Garden, point out that heirloom plants taste better than hybrids. While plant scientists busied themselves with breeding vegetables that commercial farmers could harvest, pack, and ship easily and efficiently, they often forgot about flavor. We all know only too well the hothouse tomato—large, long-lived, and with all the flavor of cotton batting. For Pam, heirloom tomatoes like 'Brandywine' "still taste the best."

WHEN TO CONSIDER HYBRIDS Some experts prefer newer varieties over heirlooms. Donald Ledden of New Jersey's Ledden Brothers looks for plants specifically bred for disease resistance and greater productivity. "If you choose properly, you can find new varieties that taste just as good as the heirlooms," he says. "Some of my favorite tomatoes were bred in the 1950s by Joseph Harris in upstate New York," says John Lee of Allandale Farm in Massachusetts. "They have thin skins, good flavor, good texture—better than 'Brandywine'," which in his opinion is a scraggly, difficult-to-manage plant.

Pam Allenstein agrees that not all hybrids should necessarily be ignored. "It depends on what they were bred for," she says. "If a plant was bred for easy picking or transportability, you probably don't want it. But others were bred for disease-resistance, high yield, and even better taste."

Louise Hyde of Well-Sweep Herb Farm in New Jersey also respects hybrids. "Many new hybrid culinary herbs are excellent," she says. Taste being subjective, it would be wise to sample a number of different varieties, old and new, before settling on your favorites. And when it comes to weighing heirlooms against the newer hybrids, Sarah Gallant of Maine's Pinetree Garden Seeds concludes that, "there's room in the garden for both."

Choosing Healthy Plants

Signs of health • Acceptable defects • Inspecting for insects • Diagnosing diseases

So there you are at the local garden center, surrounded by rows and rows of plants. Maybe you've brought a list (as you would at the supermarket, to avoid expensive impulse purchases). At first glance, everything looks wonderful. But before you begin filling your flats, examine plants closely.

CHECK FOLIAGE FIRST The most obvious indicator of a plant's overall health is its foliage. Rose Marie McGee of Oregon's Nichols Garden Nursery looks for uniform color—no yellowed leaves or brown tips. Healthy plants are green and vibrant. (However, if you're buying perennial herbs at the end of the season, expect some foliage discoloration, even on healthy plants, says Canadian herb grower Joyce

Wilted, curled, or yellowed leaves are signs of poor health. It's better to pass up plants that look like this.

Check your plant from top to bottom. This plant's strong white roots—obviously vigorous but not yet forming a dense mat—make it a good candidate for success. Strong, firm foliage is another indication that this plant has been well cared for and will continue to grow.

vegetable & herb gardening secrets

PERUSE FOR PESTS AND DISEASES

You certainly don't want a plant that has already succumbed to disease. Here's how to check for good health:

❞ Look for signs of rust (reddish spots) on mint and powdery mildew (white, powdery film) on perennial herbs.

❞ Check the foliage for spots—a sure-fire indicator of ill health.

❞ Beware of brown or curled leaves; they often indicate that aphids have taken up residence.

❞ Watch for holes in the leaves, which may mean that beetles or caterpillars have been feasting.

❞ Check for damage at the base of a plant, which is usually a sign of cutworms.

❞ Don't forget to look under the leaves, where pests like to hide.

Belyea.) Rose Marie also checks for new growth. You should see new sprouts as well as established foliage.

Gene Banks of Connecticut's Catnip Acres Herb Farm looks at the overall shape of the plant, and "the bushier the better" is her advice. Both she and Rose Marie prefer to buy plants in bud but not in flower. "I want the best flowering to be in my garden, not in the nursery," says Rose Marie.

WATCH FOR WATERING A plant that's been watered infrequently or unevenly has been stressed, no matter what its appearance at the moment, and that stress, say the experts, can result in poor growth and susceptibility to disease. But how do you know what's gone on in the days and even weeks before you arrived? Check the lower leaves, says Dexter Merritt of Vermont's Green Mountain Transplants. If plants have wilted in the past, the lower leaves will be deteriorated or yellowed. Then stick your finger about an inch or two into the soil, says Pam Allenstein of Philadelphia's historic John Bartram Garden. If the soil at that depth is dry, it indicates that the plant hasn't been watered regularly.

GET TO THE ROOT Healthy plants have healthy, well-established root systems. To check the roots, tip the plant gently out of its container. Make sure the plant feels nice and solid, and look for white, not beige, roots, says Canadian herb grower Joyce Belyea. Pam Allenstein avoids any plant that seems poorly rooted. Don't let a large pot fool you, she warns—it could contain an immature plant that has only recently put out roots.

"If you're not comfortable taking the plant out of the container, at least tug on it gently," says Peggy Singlemann of the Maymount Foundation in Virginia. If the whole thing pulls out of the pot without much pressure, it's not well rooted.

While rootbound plants (those whose root systems have grown too large for their containers) can sometimes be stressed, don't pass up a plant simply because you see a large mass of roots. Scented geraniums, for example, are one of several plants that are happiest when rootbound, says Gene Banks of Connecticut's Catnip Acres Herb Farm. So if a plant is somewhat rootbound but otherwise healthy, it's probably fine. Just make sure you loosen the roots before transplanting.

GETTING THE GROUND READY

Vegetables pull nutrients from the soil at an astonishing rate, and with their long roots and a seemingly unquenchable thirst for water, they require porous, well-turned soil. For a prosperous vegetable or herb garden, prepare the ground well.

Preparing and Amending Soil

The best way to prepare a new plot • Different soil for different crops • Annual amendments

Getting the ground ready for vegetables or herbs can be more critical to their success than buying the healthiest plants. Develop rich soil with good texture, and the time, effort, and money you spend to do so will be repaid in a plentiful harvest.

MAKING THE BED Though double-digging has traditionally been re-commended for vegetable beds (see "Digging and Double-Digging" on page 288), many experts consider it unnecessary, and some believe it can be detrimental.

Craig Dremann of the Redwood City Seed Company in California never double-digs in his backyard. "Double-digging was developed for tight clay soil in France, in areas where they get 40 inches of rain a

If your soil is poor, and the idea of large-scale amend-ments is not appealing to you, try raised beds. You can move the best soil into enclosed beds, which provide great drainage, as well.

vegetable & herb gardening secrets

When incorporating a soil amendment into your garden, use a lot of it. Pile the amendment over the whole area, then mix it in the top 6 to 12 inches of soil with a rake or tiller.

year, he says. In our part of North America, where the soil is naturally sandy, you actually make the soil desertlike by double-digging."

Even with clay soil and wet weather, you can still get superb results without double-digging, says Seattle garden designer Sue Moss. Vegetables will do just fine in soil that's been heavily amended with organic matter and tilled (turned over) to a depth of 12 inches, she explains. Simply till the ground, spread a 6-inch layer of organic matter over top, and turn it under. Repeat this process once more, and you'll have a bed that's as good as double-dug.

Unless he starts with very hard, compacted soil, Fairman Jayne of Sandy Mush Herb Farm in North Carolina just stabs a heavy garden fork or shovel into the ground, wiggles it around a little, and considers his soil ready. And Sean Hogan, a horticulturist and garden designer from Oregon, doesn't double-dig because he finds that overtilling can increase soil compaction. He compares his lightly tilled soil to chunky peanut butter and says that roots move between the clods in it more easily than they would in a smoothly blended mix.

GIVING SOIL A GOOD START "Feed the soil and the soil will feed the plants," says Niles Kinerk of the Gardens Alive! catalog in Indiana, quoting an adage familiar to organic farmers everywhere. The experts agree that the best food for soil is organic matter—plant material or animal manure. In the soil, earthworms and beneficial bacteria digest this material, speeding its decay. As it breaks down, its nutrients become available to plants.

Organic matter also helps the soil retain moisture and improves drainage (the ability of water to pass through the soil). Some gardeners add up to one-third of the soil volume of their beds in organic matter. Debby Kavakos, owner of Stoneledge Farm in New York, finds that a 1-inch layer of compost is sufficient. More wouldn't hurt, she says, but "I don't want to use any more of my valuable compost than I need to."

For his own new beds, Craig Dremann uses composted chicken manure, which he spreads over the entire garden at a thickness of ⅛ inch. He then works the manure into the top 2 inches of soil, which is where, he says, plants do most of their feeding. If you can't round up chicken manure, almost any well-composted manure will do.

Canadian herb grower Joyce Belyea likes to add ground oyster shells (available commercially by the bag), which she says provide several benefits to the garden: they're reflective, so they warm the bottom of the plant; they give plants all the calcium they need (especially beneficial for tomatoes); and they inhibit blossom-end rot (a general deterioration of the blossom end of the fruit, usually caused by calcium deficiency or uneven water uptake) in all crops. You can also add simple garden compost.

The amendments that improve your soil can also harm it, though. Adding sand to clay soil can turn it into concrete. All the experts recommend improving soil over a period of a few years, watching what works and what doesn't. (For more information on improving soil, see "Chapter 5: Soil-Building Secrets," on pages 262–89.)

YEARLY MAINTENANCE If you use the same bed year after year, you can't

An easy way to improve your soil is to plant a cover crop such as clover in fall or early spring. Till the cover crop into the soil as soon as the ground is workable.

DOUBLE-DIGGING SHORTCUTS

Frederick Held of Nature's Garden in Oregon shares his secret for "easy" double-digging. "Turn over the upper layer of soil only," he says, "and merely loosen the ground beneath." Richard Boonstra of Ohio's Bluestone Perennials does this by driving a pick or crowbar into the subsoil at regular, short intervals and working it back and forth.

If you use this method, keep your crowbar moving quickly to avoid compacting the soil. Not only is this method easier than double-digging, it also eliminates one of the main drawbacks of double-digging: bringing poorer subsoil up, which isn't as good for your plants as topsoil.

Conventional methods of double-digging move soil around so much that they invariably mix subsoil and topsoil. Simply poking the ground underneath keeps everything where it's supposed to be.

rely on a single application of organic matter in the first year. The vegetables you grew last summer will have depleted the soil of many of its nutrients. To guarantee another healthy harvest, you'll have to amend the soil again. But don't wait for spring, say the experts. Begin in late fall, after you've harvested your crops. Shannon Singletary of The Gourmet Gardener in Kansas rakes up fallen leaves and piles them on her beds. In spring, after the leaves have decomposed, she works them in with a stiff rake.

Rose Marie McGee of Oregon's Nichols Garden Nursery mulches her beds in fall with mint straw (a distillery by-product available in her area) and mushroom compost (a by-product of mushroom farming). In spring, she turns the soil over and lets it stand for two weeks to allow any weed seeds to sprout, which she then pulls up. Next she drops a wheelbarrow of compost on the bed and turns the soil over again. If you can't find mint straw and mushroom compost, look around for soybean waste (from tofu production) and apple pomace (from cider pressing), or use garden compost or well-composted manure. (See "Compost—From Scraps to Soil" on page 278 for more on compost.)

COVER CROPS An excellent way to enrich depleted vegetable beds, says Niles Kinerk of the Gardens Alive! catalog in Indiana, is to use cover crops (plants grown during a fallow season to keep down weeds and to add nutrients to the soil). Kinerk sows a crop of buckwheat in the fall, which helps to release nutrients from the soil. You can also grow clover, winter rye, annual ryegrass, and hairy crown vetch. "Before we put in a cover crop," says Niles, "the soil was so hard that hoes bounced off it. After planting buckwheat, the soil became loose and the hoe went in like a hot knife through butter." (For more on cover crops, see "Going for Cover" on page 283.)

Double-Digging for Vegetables
What it is • What it does • Do you have to do it?

Double-digging is a method of soil preparation that involves turning the soil over to a depth of two spades (roughly 16 to 24 inches). Some experts find it an indispensable way of loosening and improving the soil. Others, like Mary Harrison of Mary's Plant Farm, say, "it's a waste of good time—unless the soil needs a lot of additional sand or

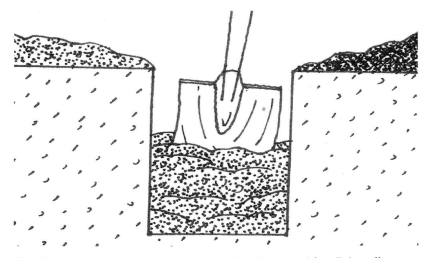

Double-digging is hard work and takes time, but the reward for all that effort is loose, well-drained soil.

compost." Flora Hackimer of Wrenwood of Berkley Springs, West Virginia, agrees. "Plants sometimes grow through concrete. I don't have to double-dig for them," she says.

Whether you choose to double-dig will probably depend on the quality of your soil, the plants you intend to grow, and your overall energy level. (For information about double-digging for roses and other ornamental plants, see "Digging and Double-Digging" on page 288.)

THE BENEFITS Double-digging lightens the soil, so if you have sandy soil, which naturally has a light texture, you can avoid the process altogether. If your backyard is mostly clay, however, or if your soil is compacted, consider double-digging. If it's done right, you only have to do it once, says Tom Butterworth of Connecticut's Butterbrook Farms. And results are long-lived, says Nelson Sterner, who was pleased with the results of double-dug beds at Old Westbury Gardens in Long Island.

Gail Korn of Nebraska's Garden Perennials double-dug her 8 × 8-foot perennial border 20 years ago. "I developed 2 feet of topsoil," she says, "and a terrific waistline." By double-digging and incorporating copious amounts of organic matter into her soil, she also raised the soil level, creating superior drainage and raised beds that haven't sunk in two decades.

DOUBLE-DIGGING HOW-TO

If you decide that double-digging is for you, Seattle garden designer Sue Moss recommends the following method:

Mark off a section of garden about 3 feet wide and as long as you like. In a strip of soil 15 inches long by 3 feet wide, remove 8 to 10 inches of topsoil and carry it (in a tarp or wheelbarrow) to the far end of the section. Loosen the soil you've just uncovered as deep as your garden fork will allow.

Proceed to the next 15-inch strip and, again, remove 8 to 10 inches of topsoil, this time simply emptying it on top of the first 15-inch strip. Continue in this manner until you've dug the entire section, adding the initial topsoil to the final strip. Next, mix organic matter into the upper 8 to 10 inches—a cinch now that the soil is light and loose. Or, mix in organic matter before returning each batch of topsoil to the trench.

PREPARING THE SOIL FOR HERBS

Most experts start their new herb beds by adding a 1-inch layer of organic matter. Fresh compost, oak leaf mold, and well-rotted manure are all excellent sources of nutrients, as are mushroom soil, apple pomace, and mint straw.

Rose Marie McGee of Oregon's Nichol's Garden Nursery and Louise Hyde of Well-Sweep Herb Farm in New Jersey both find that if they start their herb gardens with a mixture of organic matter that includes these ingredients in whatever combinations they can find, and they continue to add organic matter at the beginning of each year, their herb beds produce beautifully with no additional fertilizer during the growing season.

Other herb gardeners add very little organic matter to herb beds. "Herbs like it tough, that's what they're used to," says Debby Kavakos, owner of Stoneledge Farm in New York. "They'll do fine in a rocky, unamended site."

Even experts who don't generally double-dig often acknowledge its benefits. Norman Schwartz, owner of Virginia's Edgewood Farm and Nursery, who usually designs gardens on a fairly grand scale, finds the process too labor-intensive. "But double-digging does make it easier for plants to send their roots deeper," he admits, "giving them access to more nutrients and moisture. This allows you to plant more densely without worrying about competition for moisture, nutrients, and root space."

DEFER TO YOUR CROPS Your decision to double-dig should take into account what you plan to grow in your soil. Sarah Gallant of Maine's Pinetree Garden Seeds recommends double-digging for root crops, since it allows for straighter growth of the edible part of the plant. Vegetables in general, says Seattle garden designer Sue Moss, benefit from the loose soil produced by double-digging. On the other hand, she says, most annual herbs are shallow-rooted and simply don't need access to all that soil. Even perennial herbs will do fine in soil heavily amended with organic matter and tilled to a depth of just 12 inches. (See page 105 for how to double-dig your garden.)

Sandy, rocky soil is inhospitable to many crops. It is perfect, however, for the Mediterranean herbs—sage, rosemary, lavender, and lovage—in this garden.

STARTING FROM SEED

No matter how many times you've done it before, starting vegetables and herbs from seed always brings a thrill. Every time you see that tiny burst of green emerge from bare brown soil it seems a miracle. Fortunately that miracle occurs rather readily if you follow the right seed-starting steps.

Inside or Out?

An indoor head start • Safety inside • Plants that prefer the outdoors • Benefits of exposure

Whether you start your plants indoors or out depends on a number of factors, including the type of crops you plan to grow and the climate in which you'll be growing them. And there are advantages and disadvantages to both indoor seed-starting and outdoor sowing.

GETTING A HEAD START Some growers, like Flora Hackimer of West Virginia's Wrenwood of Berkeley Springs, start all of their seeds indoors. "You lose too much time waiting for the soil to warm," she says, echoing the sentiments of impatient gardeners everywhere. By starting your seeds indoors you get an earlier harvest—an important consideration for plants that take their time growing to maturity. In addition, if you have a short growing season, a head start guarantees that your crops won't be nipped by frost, says Rose Marie McGee of Oregon's Nichols Garden Nursery. Vegetables and herbs that like a lot of warmth, such as tomatoes, eggplant, and basil, are usually happier if started indoors.

PROTECTION FROM THE ELEMENTS Though Peter Borchard of Ohio's Companion Plants prefers to sow most of his herbs in the ground, he recommends starting extremely small seeds (including chamomile, thyme, and oregano) indoors. "That way," he says, "you don't have to worry about losing them to heavy showers, which can easily wash them away." Indoor sowing also protects seeds and young seedlings from animals, birds, and bugs.

BRAVING THE GREAT OUTDOORS Perhaps you don't have the space to start seeds indoors, or you simply find it a bother. Shannon Singletary, who manages The Gourmet Gardener in Kansas, is a great proponent

---

SEED PREFERENCES

Some seeds have distinct preferences about where they are sown.

❧ Beans, peas, rutabaga, and salsify are notoriously fussy about being moved.

❧ Most root crops can be sown in a coldframe, but do best when direct-sown.

❧ Broccoli, cabbage, cauliflower, and brussels sprouts can be planted inside or out; indoor planting saves time.

❧ Lettuce and most greens transplant easily, but they grow quickly and are usually direct-sown.

❧ Corn, which has an extensive root system, is best planted outdoors.

❧ Heat-loving crops like tomatoes, eggplant, squash, and melons are usually planted indoors; they transplant easily and can't be direct-sown until late in the season.

❧ Most herbs can be sown inside or out. Chervil, cilantro, and perilla do not transplant easily and should be sown outdoors; heat-lovers like lemongrass, rosemary, and oregano are best started indoors.

TIPS FOR TOUGH SPOTS

The quintessential growing space for vegetables and herbs is a well-drained bed in a protected area with full sun. However, if you know the secrets of tough-spot gardening, you, too, can grow vegetables and herbs in wind, damp, cold, and shade.

Louise Hyde of New Jersey's Well-Sweep Herb Farm grows many of her herbs in partial shade. But, she warns, you'll need to promote good air circulation because shady spots stay wetter, and dampness tends to promote fungal problems. Her secret for a healthy shade garden: space plants generously.

Steve Whitcher of Washington State University chooses shade-tolerant crops (see chart at right) and teases extra bloom out of them with the application of phosphorus-rich fertilizers like fish emulsion, kelp, and blood-meal.

Most herbs, because they grow naturally in wind-swept sites, tend to do well in windy conditions, says Louise Hyde.

of direct-seeding. "If you work on your soil, rotate your crops, and wait until the soil is warm," she says, "you can direct-sow everything—even crops like tomatoes that take a long time to mature."

Galen Gates of the Chicago Botanic Garden disagrees. He finds that long-season crops yield very little fruit if not started indoors.

However, some plants, including corn, chervil, dill, and fennel, do better when direct-sown. (For a list of other plants to direct-sow, see "Seed Preferences" on page 107.) Certain seed species benefit from stratification (exposure to cold, which breaks their dormancy) and should be sown outdoors in the fall, says Peter Borchard.

According to Tom Butterworth of Connecticut's Butterbrook Farms, direct-seeding toughens up your crops. Seedlings started indoors are generally coddled with optimum light, warmth, and air circulation. This benefits the young plant, of course, but when it comes time to move out into the real world, with its heat waves and cold snaps and flash floods and dry spells, transplant shock can set in, and some vegetables, like peas and beans, never seem to get over it. Plants sown where they'll grow develop street-smarts. By the time they're seedlings, they know the turf and all its abuses.

CROPS FOR TOUGH SPOTS

The real secret to growing crops in tricky sites, of course, is to plant varieties that will thrive under adverse conditions. Here are some of the experts' choices.

LIGHT SHADE				COLD CLIMATES
Angelica	Kohlrabi	Thyme, creeping, not upright	Lovage	Catnip
Arugula	Lettuce		Mint	Fennel
Broccoli	Lovage		Nettle	Lemon balm
Brussels	Mint	POOR SOIL	Watercress	Mint
sprouts	Onions	Anise		Oregano
Cabbage	Oregano	Chicory		Sage
Catnip	Parsley	Dill	DRY SPOTS	Thyme
Chervil	Peas	Mint	Artemesia	Many short-
Endive	Pole beans (in	St. John's-wort	Chamomile	season vege-
Fennel	hot climates)	Thyme	Fennel	table cultivars
Ginseng	Radishes		Hyssop	Fast-growing
Horseradish	Rhubarb		Lavender	greens
Jerusalem	Sage	WET SPOTS	Oregano	Cole crops,
artichoke	Sorrel, French	Chervil	Rosemary	such as
Kale	Spinach	Horseradish	Sage	broccoli,
	Swiss chard	Lemon balm	Thyme	and cabbage
		Lemon verbena	Winter savory	

Treating Seeds

Is it necessary? • *Soaking seeds* • *Fungicides and inoculants*

Seeds are a model of nature's efficiency, carrying within their hulls nearly everything a plant needs to grow, except warmth and water. The process of planting, then, should be a simple one: Cover the seed with soil, water it, warm it, and voilà, a new plant. But it's not always that simple. Some seeds need a little preparation before they're put in the soil.

SCARIFICATION AND STRATIFICATION These techniques sound rather daunting to most beginning gardeners. Stratification involves exposing a seed to moist cold before sowing to break its dormancy. Scarification is the nicking or notching of a seed to hasten germination. Fortunately, most of the seeds you buy from reputable sources will have already been pre-treated, says Paul Taylor of Vermont's Le Jardin du Gourmet. All you have to do is plant and water them—most vegetable seeds are naturally easy to grow. "We eliminated plants that don't germinate well from our cuisine thousands of years ago," says Craig Dremannn of the Redwood City Seed Company in California. If you collect seeds from your own garden, you may not want to bother with varieties that require complicated pretreatment.

SOAKING Some seeds benefit from a little pretreatment. Larger seeds like peas and beans germinate faster if you soak them in water overnight before planting, says Sarah Gallant of Maine's Pinetree Garden Seeds. Justine Mapstone of Crosman Seed Company finds that most seeds, other than morning glory, nasturtium, and peas, do just as well if given constant moisture as if they are soaked.

Craig Dremann recommends mixing parsley and carrot seeds with damp sand, storing them in the refrigerator for two weeks, and then planting them—sand and all. And here's his secret to speeding the germination of hot pepper seeds and increasing the number of seeds per packet that actually sprout: Soak the seeds in a quart of water mixed with a teaspoon of saltpeter for 4 to 12 hours. During the day, maintain the temperature of the water at about 85°F, which you can do with a heating mat if necessary. You can let the temperature fall to 70°F at night.

SPECIAL TREATMENT

Some seeds are fussy and won't germinate or perform well unless they get special treatment.

Seeds that need darkness
Borage
Cilantro
Fennel

Seeds that need light
Dill
Peppers
Lettuce
Perilla

Seeds that germinate better if soaked
Asparagus
Beans
Melon
Okra
Peas
Squash

vegetable & herb gardening secrets

PELLETED SEED

Because some herbs and vegetables produce tiny seeds that are often difficult to handle, growers sometimes use pelleted seeds coated with a special substance that makes them easier to handle.

Tom Brooks of Wilson Farms in Massachusetts recommends buying pelleted seeds if you're planting oregano and thyme, both of which are extremely small. Justine Mapstone of East Rochester's Crosman Seed Company, on the other hand, considers pelleting useful only for commercial growers, whose machinery requires seeds of a uniform size. Most home gardeners, she says, won't really benefit from it. If you suffer from arthritis, however, or have trouble handling very fine seeds, you might find the pelleted versions a real boon.

If you'll be planting in very moist soil, you probably don't need to soak your seeds at all, points out Justine Mapstone of East Rochester's Crosman Seed Company. Most seeds can simply be planted as the packet instructs, says Pennsylvania horticulturist Dr. Michael Orzolek. Nelson Sterner always reads the packet, even if he knows how to plant the seeds without it.

FUNGICIDES Some companies pretreat seeds with fungicide to help prevent damping-off (a common fungal disease of seedlings). Check with the seed company to make sure the seeds you're buying have not been treated, especially if you plan to eat your sprouts.

To discourage damping-off in untreated seeds, try to keep them from becoming damp or wet before planting, and maintain proper air circulation around seedlings, says Dr. Orzolek. Or soak the seeds in a strong chamomile tea, says Bertha Reppert of Pennsylvania's Rosemary House. Chamomile contains a natural fungicide that prevents damping-off.

INOCULATED SEEDS Inoculation is a process whereby seeds are injected or treated with beneficial bacteria that supposedly allow the seedlings to fix nitrogen (absorb it from the surrounding air) more efficiently. Tom Brooks of Massachusetts's Wilson Farms recommends that you try inoculated seeds if your soil is poor and you've had trouble getting seeds to germinate in the past, but he adds that in his experience, inoculation never seemed to have any great effect. Craig Dremann of the Redwood City Seed Company in California finds inoculants useful with beans that are being planted in soil that hasn't been used for beans before. The inoculant supplies "a life-giving bacteria," he says.

Caring for Seedlings

*Providing warmth, water, and light • Dodging fungal diseases
• When to start fertilizing • Toughening up seedlings*

Some gardeners tremble at the thought of starting seeds indoors. All the materials, all that special care, all that money and time invested. But armed with the experts' seed-starting secrets, you'll find it as simple as any other garden routine. For Sharon Kaszan of W. Atlee Burpee & Co., successful seed-starting boils down to one simple rule: "Germinate in warm; grow in cool." The rest is just window dressing.

WARMTH Just as they would in your garden, seeds respond to warmth by germinating—sending out roots and then leaves. To keep seeds warm, you can place commercial heating mats under your seedling trays and hot-air systems under the benches where your trays sit, as Dexter Merritt of Vermont's Green Mountain Transplants does. Or you can harness the sun's warmth, as Bertha Reppert of Pennsylvania's Rosemary House does, by placing your seeds on mirror tiles set on sunny windowsills. The tiles supply extra heat, and later, when seeds have germinated, extra light. Davy Dabney of Kentucky's Dabney Herbs has an even easier way of keeping her seeds properly toasty— she waters them with warm water.

WATER Seeds need water in two forms: humidity in the air and water in the soil. Many experts, including James Arnold of Clemson Botanic Garden in South Carolina, use commercial domes or other plastic covers to create humidity. But you can do just as well with plastic bags or plastic wrap, says Rolfe Hagen of Thyme Garden Seeds. Just make sure you remove them—or any other cover you use—as soon as the seedlings appear.

While it's necessary to keep your growing medium moist, you don't want it soggy, says Alice Krinsky, trial garden manager at Shepherd's Garden Seeds. During and after germination, she waters with a mister,

Place growing seedlings on different-size pots to promote good air circulation. Place a mirror under them to reflect light their way, and run a small fan occasionally to ruffle them up and make them tough.

FIGHTING FUNGUS

The greatest threat to seedlings is damping-off, a fungal disease that attacks the stems at soil level and can stunt or destroy young plants. To avoid it, make sure that your growing medium and your containers are sterile. After seedlings have sprouted, keep the soil moist but not soggy.

To promote air circulation, Bertha Reppert of Pennsylvania's Rosemary House staggers the height of her containers, elevating them on inverted pots at a variety of different levels. Or try her secret fungus deterrent: chamomile tea. "It's a natural fungicide, and I spritz like crazy with it," she says. Steep a tea bag until the water is intensely yellow. Let it cool, then dribble or mist on the soil until true leaves appear. Tessa Gowans of Abundant Life Seed Foundation in California uses a similar tea made from horsetail fern.

Experts also suggest that you remove yellowed or dead leaves and any seedlings that don't survive.

using a light spray but making sure it thoroughly wets the growing medium. To keep seeds from floating to the surface, she covers them with one and a half to two times their height with soil, tamping it down with a small trowel. Or, she plants seeds in soil and covers them with either sand or vermiculite. "It keeps the top dry and the bottom moist," she says. John Schneeberger of Montana's Garden City Seeds is a little harder on his plants, using a water wand instead of a mister. "Misting is too easy on the seedlings," he says. "I want to knock them around a little, toughen them up."

LIGHT Some seeds require light to germinate, while others need darkness. (See "Special Treatment" on page 109.) But once they've sprouted, all seedlings need light, and lots of it. You can choose one of any number of commercial lighting systems, or, says Bertha Reppert, you can simply place your seedlings on a sunny windowsill. To boost the light, set the containers on mirror tiles or a length of aluminum foil, shiny side up. Most seedlings will do well on a cool, well-lighted sill, but if you're growing peppers, says Sharon Kaszan manager of Burpee Seeds Trial Gardens, make sure you keep their bottoms warm. Sharon uses a heating mat to do this, but just until the seeds germinate.

FEEDING SEEDLINGS Conventional wisdom has gardeners applying fertilizer as soon as the first set of leaves appears, but Rolfe Hagen has devised a nifty way to put off that chore for three to four weeks. He has his soil do the fertilizing for him, by planting his seeds in a rich mixture of kelp, pumice, bloodmeal, perlite, and worm castings.

If you've started your seeds in an organic seed-starter mixture, like the one that Johnny's Selected Seeds sells, you probably won't need to fertilize for three to four weeks (read the bag for content). However, if you've chosen plain soil or an unfertilized, soilless mixture (see "Seed-Starting Mixes" on page 343), you'll need to fertilize regularly—preferably when you water. As soon as the first true leaves appear (these are the leaves that look like smaller versions of the plant's adult foliage), water with a solution of 1 tablespoon of liquid kelp to 1 gallon of water, advises Rolfe Hagen. "This hastens growth," he says. At the next watering, he switches to diluted Epsom salts (1 tablespoon Epsom salts to 1 gallon of water). John Schneeberger fertilizes his plants with a mixture of fish emulsion, liquid kelp, and compost tea.

TOUGH LOVE Don't coddle your seedlings too much, say the experts. Before long, you'll be setting them out in the real world of scorching sun, drying wind, and flooding downpours (not to mention occasionally forgetful gardeners). Sharon Kaszan sets a fan near her seedlings and runs it continually at the lowest setting. Not only does it help circulate the air, says Sharon, but rustling the leaves stimulates growth hormones, just as it would outdoors.

Hardening-Off Seedlings

The principle behind the process • Heading for the great outdoors • How slow to go

Seedlings started indoors live a pampered life of optimal warmth, moisture, and air circulation. Life outside is a lot harsher. Temperatures can plunge, especially at night, and midday sun and strong winds can burn tender plants. Hardening off is the process of gradually exposing plants to the conditions they'll have to contend with in the great

vegetable & herb gardening secrets

SEVEN DAYS TO PLANTING

Burpee's Sharon Kaszan hardens-off seedlings with the following procedure, which she finds works for most plants:

Days 1 and 2: Put plants out in full shade, when temperatures are above 55°F, for 2 hours.

Day 3: Put plants in a slightly less shady spot and leave them out around the clock if temperatures remain above 58–60°F.

Day 4: Expose plants to a bit more sun.

Days 5 and 6: Move plants into full sun.

Day 7: Set plants in the ground.

Remember to keep your transplants well-watered during this hardening-off period, says Sharon.

Commercial miniature greenhouses are more expensive than homemade versions, but they add an elegant touch to the vegetable garden and protect tender lettuces from sudden frost.

John Schneeberger of Montana's Garden City Seeds suggests constructing a walk-in coldframe, consisting of a wood or PVC frame covered with Reemay, a lightweight spunbonded fabric that's light- and water-permeable.

outdoors—and not only the cool temperatures, but also the light and wind. "Even shade outdoors is much brighter than light indoors," says Burpee's Sharon Kaszan.

START INDOORS Even before she sets out her transplants, Peggy Singlemann of the Maymount Foundation in Virginia gets them ready by dropping the house temperature for a few days and exposing seedlings, indoors, to increasing sun. Rolfe Hagen of Thyme Garden Seeds takes his transplants on a nightly trip into the unheated greenhouse. Ohio State University's Janet Oberleisen moves plants to the garage.

If you're planting celery, cut back on water just before moving it into the garden, advises John Schneeberger of Montana's Garden City Seeds, who also lowers the nighttime temperature in his house for a few days before transplanting. Galen Gates of Chicago Botanic Garden covers the heat vents in one room for a few days and puts ready-to-plant transplants there.

COLDFRAMES One of the most basic of all garden devices, a coldframe is simply a box that rests on the ground with a cover, either glass or plastic, that allows light to pass through. The coldframe acts as a sort of miniature greenhouse, focusing light and heat on the plants inside. On warm days, you can lift the cover and expose the plants to the elements, and when frost or high winds threaten, you can close it.

A coldframe offers excellent protection for seedlings during the hardening-off process, says Bill McDorman of Idaho's High Altitude Gardens. When frost threatens, he generally chooses one of three options to protect young plants:
- place transplants in a closed coldframe
- move them to the south side of a building where the sun's heat can radiate back to the plants
- cover them with kelp or seaweed, which raises the surrounding air temperature by 2 or 3 degrees.

WATCH THE WEATHER The best day to introduce your seedlings to the elements is any day when conditions are mild. Flora Hackimer of West Virginia's Wrenwood of Berkeley Springs chooses a day without wind. Bill McDorman scans the forecast for two successive days without sun. An ideal first day would be overcast, still, and cool, but free of frost. A light misty rain won't hurt your transplants (and might, in fact, benefit them), but don't set seedlings out in a driving torrent or other harsh weather conditions.

TAKE IT SLOW Most experts recommend a gradual hardening off. For some, this means babying plants for two days and then plunking them into the ground. Others, like Peggy Singlemann, increase their seedlings exposure to the outdoors over a period of two weeks.

MAKESHIFT COLDFRAMES

If you don't own a cold-frame, here are some alternatives:

✥ Janet Oberleisen, editor of The Herbalist and a horticulturist at Ohio State University, uses cardboard boxes lined with Styrofoam, which she covers with Plexiglas, scrap wood, or old windows.

✥ If you have an inflatable swimming pool, you can line it with old towels or Styrofoam pellets and cover it with plastic or Styrofoam. It will be easy to pull into a garage or onto a patio if the weather turns very cold. You could also fill the air chamber with water, which will warm during the day and provide some heat at night.

✥ Construct a walk-in coldframe (see page 114).

✥ A floating row cover stretched over bent pipe can serve the purpose.

A dime-store toy wading pool, lined with towels or Styrofoam, can protect your young seedlings. If a cold snap hits, just pull the whole thing inside.

vegetable & herb gardening secrets

A COOL TEST

John Schneeberger of Montana's Garden City Seeds performed a little test to see if using coldframes really does help extend the growing season. He separated his seedlings into two identical groups. He planted one group in coldframes or under cloches, and the other group he planted out three weeks later in warmer soil. The result? "The early plants didn't die," he says, "but they didn't get any further along than the later ones." That's because roots don't grow in cold soil, John explains, even if the tops of plants are insulated.

TRANSPLANTING SEEDLINGS

For some of us, bringing a tray of transplants out into the garden is a bit like sending our children off to kindergarten. You've been able to watch over them carefully at home, but now they're on their own in an environment that you know can be harsh. Yes, you'll still be there for them, but not all the time. The experts offer several secrets to ease your mind and ensure healthy, happy plants.

Timing It Right

Frost-free dates • Consider microclimates • Different times for different plants • Prepare for weird weather

The United States Department of Agriculture (USDA) offers a city-by-city list of frost-free dates, which provides a fairly dependable marker for the end of frost and length of growing season in a given area. However, like all things weather-related, frost-free dates aren't 100 percent reliable. You'll need to consider a few other factors to determine when transplanting is safe.

KNOW YOUR OWN BACKYARD Just because the USDA says your frost-free date is May 15 doesn't mean you won't experience a frost after Mother's Day. That's because, in addition to the considerable vagaries of the weather, the chart can't account for the individual microclimates that occur from site to site, which are created by the grade of the land, drainage, and the effect of manmade structures.

Sleepy Hollow Herb Farm in Kentucky sits in a shallow valley near a creek, making it susceptible to late frosts. "We try to plant out two weeks after the frost-free date, but even so we watch the weather carefully," Julie Marks says. Paul Taylor of Vermont's Le Jardin du Gourmet finds that his area's frost-free date is inaccurate roughly 10 percent of the time.

More important than frost, says Dennis McGlynn, vice president of the New England Seed Company, is soil temperature. If the soil hasn't warmed sufficiently, most seedlings will do poorly, frost or no frost. Bean seeds germinate best in 60° to 85°F soil; tomatoes prefer 75° to 90°F; lettuce will germinate in soil with a temperature as low as 40°F. Check soil temperature with a soil thermometer, available at garden centers or through catalogs, and check seed catalogs for preferred soil temperatures.

KNOW YOUR PLANTS Like people, some plants do better in the cold than others.

• "Onions and leeks don't mind the cold and can be risked earlier," says Dexter Merritt of Vermont's Green Mountain Transplants.

• The same is true of strawberries, says Maryland grower Richard Allen. Virtually impervious to frost, they can be planted out as soon as you can dig the ground.

• Oregon nursery owner Rose Marie McGee of Nichols Garden Nursery plants her peas, lettuce, greens, and brassicas (the family that includes cabbage, broccoli, cauliflower, and brussels sprouts) in February; beans and corn in March; and tomatoes and peppers only when the soil is quite warm, usually around late April.

• Dennis McGlynn recommends taking a cue from your seedlings as well as from the weather: if they're getting leggy or buggy, it may be worth risking some frost to get them into the ground quickly.

BE PREPARED You can plant outside with more confidence if you have a backup system. Flora Hackimer of West Virginia's Wrenwood of Berkeley Springs plants on her frost-free date but keeps a cover ready to protect frost-sensitive seedlings. (For more about covers, see "Protecting Crops from Cold" on page 134.) Paul Taylor recommends that you let your seedlings harden off for a week or two rather than the two or three days that most people recommend. At Chicago Botanic Garden, plants are always hardened off for a full week in the spring.

WARMING STRATEGIES

Plants know that spring has arrived when the soil thaws out and begins to warm up. You can jump-start the warming process, says David Graper of the University of South Dakota, by using black plastic mulch, which can raise soil temperature an additional few degrees. If you find black plastic unsightly, other dark-color mulches are nearly as effective.

Tender young plants need warm air as well as toasty roots. The experts suggest using any of several protective coverings designed to heat up the air that surrounds your plants, including floating row covers and cloches.

vegetable & herb gardening secrets

Gardeners at Chanticleer Gardens in Pennsylvania use cloches (bell-shaped covers of plastic, fiberglass, terra-cotta, or glass) that can easily be slipped over individual plants when frost threatens.

PLANTS THAT EXTEND THE SEASON

Protecting plants isn't the only way to coax some extra time out of your growing season. For Douglas Owens-Pike of Minnesota's EnergyScapes, Inc., the real secret of season-extending is to "use native diversity" to find both early- and late-blooming plants that are naturally hardy in your area. This strategy applies to ornamentals as well as vegetables. Cindy Reed of the Great Plains Native Plant Society agrees: "We do use floating row covers and various tomato protectors to foil the frost, but our most successful technique lies in variety and species selection favoring those hardy plants that thrive in the cold."

MINIATURE GREENHOUSES To protect plants from sudden frost, Bill McKentley advises building a simple teepee over small plants and then wrapping the teepee in burlap. In northern climates, gardeners regularly wrap entire fig trees in burlap to help the trees overwinter. Peter and Jean Ruh suggest covering plants with a wooden box large enough to provide adequate air circulation, "to prevent breakage and protect the plants from sweeping winds."

Planting Peat Pots

Pros of peat pots ● *A couple of cautions*

Peat pots are small containers formed from peat. They're usually used for starting seedlings indoors. Nurseries and garden centers use them, too, so some of the plants you purchase may come to you in peat pots. Seedlings in peat pots can be planted, pot and all, directly in the soil.

WHY CHOOSE PEAT? Many of the experts start their own seedlings in peat pots. Dexter Merritt of Vermont's Green Mountain Transplants finds them invaluable for brittle-rooted plants like rosemary and cucurbits (pumpkins, gourds, and squashes). Entirely biodegradable, the pots allow Merritt to transplant without handling the seedlings' delicate root systems.

HOW TO PLANT The whole point of peat pots, says Dexter Merritt, is to plant them along with the seedlings. You'll know a plant is ready to go into the ground when you see fine roots growing right through the peat. If you plant before the roots appear and your crops are hit by a surprise frost, the roots may be very slow to establish themselves, warns Pennsylvania horticulturist Dr. Michael Orzalek. When putting potted seedlings in the ground, make sure the pots don't stick up out of the soil, says Merritt. If they do, they will act like a wick, drawing moisture away from the plant. Jim Becker of Oregon's Goodwin Creek Gardens removes the bottom of the pot to speed root growth into the soil and peels the pot's upper rim to the level of the soil.

June Hutson of the Missouri Botanic Gardens advises that you make sure peat pots are very wet before placing them in the ground. Peat is notoriously difficult to wet, she explains, especially when planted, and roots have difficulty penetrating dry peat.

A DOUBTING VOICE Not everyone enthusiastically endorses peat pots. "I just don't find peat-potted transplants any better than soil-planted seedlings," says Flora Hackimer of West Virginia's Wrenwood of Berkeley Springs. And, says Bertha Reppert, peat can retain too much moisture for herbs, which rot if wet.

The Right Space

Plant preferences • Room to grow • Ensuring an air supply • Planting in close quarters

The temptation to plant things too close together is enormous, especially among novice gardeners, but even the experts feel it. Despite her best intentions, Burpee's Sharon Kaszan plants her transplants too tightly every year. "At the end of the season, when I see how big the plants have grown, I tell myself to give them more room the following year," she says. Is there an ideal way to space herbs and vegetables for highest yield and healthiest plants?

When onions and squash are tightly interplanted, each will shade the other and repel pests.

vegetable & herb gardening secrets

In the Alan Chadwick garden at University of California (Santa Cruz), tomato plants are spaced carefully to provide ample room for growth and air circulation.

LET YOUR CROPS GUIDE YOU Plants, like people, grow to different heights and widths. As obvious as this sounds, you might overlook the importance of this at planting time, when all your transplants are more or less the same size. Tomatoes and beans, for example, are notoriously vigorous and need lots of space, says Washington horticulturist Steve Whitcher. Plant them farther apart than you would, say, small cabbages or compact bush beans.

In addition to mature size, consider air circulation. This is a must for basil and sage, says Rolfe Hagen of Thyme Garden Seeds. Thyme, on the other hand, can be packed tightly without suffering. If you place lavender plants too closely, says Virginia Frazier of North Carolina's Adventures in Herbs, they will damp off (succumb to fungus) and die. Certain vegetables require proper circulation to keep them producing. Sharon Kaszan gives her lettuces lots of room. "When they're tight," she says, "they hold in moisture and humidity, and that causes them to rot." If plants have a vertical habit, however, they can get by in close groupings. "Things that grow up, like fennel and dill, get their air circulation on top," says Rolfe Hagen.

WHEN SPACE IS LIMITED Most experts agree that if you have the room, you should space your crops openly. "More room encourages greater vigor and better plants," says James Arnold of Clemson Botanic Gardens in South Carolina.

If you've got a small plot or limited space, try to plant more compactly. Tight spacing doesn't seem to hurt most of Sharon Kaszan's plants. If necessary, you can position transplants so that the leaves are barely touching, says Steve Whitcher. "It's not optimal, but it's the best use of space."

Mike Ruggerio of the New York Botanical Garden advises that home gardeners go for the midpoint in any recommended range of spacing. If the instruction says to space plants 12 to 16 inches apart, he'll use 14 inches. (For information on intensive planting practices, see "Intensive Gardening" on page 80.)

SPACING HERBS Three or four plants of each herb you want to grow should provide all the fresh herbs you need. With that in mind, many experts recommend giving each plant plenty of room to grow to its full size. "Some people want instant results," says Flora Hackimer of West

Virginia's Wrenwood of Berkeley Springs. "They cram two plants in a space intended for one and end up with two small, ugly plants instead of one big, beautiful one." With perennial herbs, tight spacing might work the first year, but fast-multiplying types like mint and oregano will quickly overrun their space and turn into unwieldy mats, warns Flora—which is fine if you have the time and energy to keep pulling them. She suggests you leave at least 18 inches between plants, and if you don't like the bare spots in the first year, throw in some annuals.

At New Jersey's Well-Sweep Herb Farm, Louise Hyde spaces everything 1 to 2 feet apart. The garden may look a little bare for the first year or so, but it will fill in nicely, she says. Gene Banks of Connecticut's Catnip Acres Herb Farm agrees, noting that tight spacing cuts off air circulation and sometimes causes fungal problems. Herbs like a little space, she says. They don't like being stuffed close together.

On the other hand, Fairman and Kate Jayne of Sandy Mush Herb Farm in North Carolina see no harm in close planting for most herbs, especially if you keep harvesting leaves to keep them from becoming too crowded. "If the weather becomes too humid, or if we see some

EASY, ACCURATE SPACING

To space seedlings quickly and easily in your garden, use a spacing board. Any scrap of wood about 18 inches long and a few inches wide will do.

Using a ruler, mark inches with small notches, and make larger notches at 6-, 9-, 12-, 15-, and 18-inch distances, since those are most often used in spacing transplants. When planting, position the spacing board and make holes in the ground with a stick or dibble. Then plant your seedlings.

For seeds or very small transplants, buy chicken wire with the appropriate number of holes per inch. Lay the chicken wire on the ground, make your planting hole in each square, then lift the chicken wire off the ground.

In plantings at Old Westbury Gardens, lettuces are given just enough room to form heads, with little space between mature plants. Tight spacing helps control weeds.

WATER TIPS FOR DESERT GARDENERS

Mary Irish of Arizona's Desert Botanical Garden has discovered that in very dry climates most crops—even sun-lovers like tomatoes and peppers—do better and need less water if you give them a little shade. Mary builds a frame around her vegetable bed and attaches shade cloth (available at garden centers, shade cloth is graded by the amount of light it allows to filter through it). Of course one of the best ways to grow a successful garden in dry climates is to plant varieties that don't need much water, such as black-eyed peas, black mission figs, tomatillos, fava beans, lentils, chiles, 'Tam Mayan Sweet' melons, and 'Tohono O'odham' flour corn.

signs of fungal disease, we just take out the middle plant," they say. When it comes to rosemary and thyme, however, they allow plenty of room, because these plants branch out, and the more space they have the more foliage they will produce.

Caring for Transplants
Essential watering • Protection priorities • Fertilizing wisely

Even healthy, well-acclimated transplants need a little extra attention during their first weeks outside. If they get over their transplant shock without weakening, they'll do better all season.

WATER THEM WELL The most crucial requirement of new transplants, say experts, is water. You need to water them well when you plant them, and make sure they don't dry out during their first few weeks outdoors. For Gene Banks of Connecticut's Catnip Acres Herb Farm, the secret to giving her transplants the best possible start is to water before planting. After digging the holes, she floods them with water. "When we put in the plants," she says, "we're actually working with mud." To keep subsequent watering chores to a minimum, Louise Hyde of New Jersey's Well-Sweep Herb Farm—a self-professed "lazy gardener"—prepares her beds meticulously, adding manure, sand, compost, and necessary nutrients. At planting time, she waters her transplants and lets them sit for two days; then she mulches them with wood chips, waters them again if necessary, and after that they fend for themselves.

PROVIDE PROTECTION Because transplants require time to toughen up, they may need protection, depending on the site. If your bed is exposed to wind, or if you know that flying insects will be a problem, cover them for the first few weeks with floating row covers (lengths of lightweight, porous cloth, sometimes held above the plants with hoops made of PVC pipe or metal; see page 123), suggests Pennsylvania horticulturist Dr. Michael Orzolek. Rose Marie McGee of Oregon's Nichols Garden Nursery uses row covers to protect her early transplants (including brassicas and Chinese radishes) from maggots.

SHOULD YOU FERTILIZE? Most experts agree that well-prepared soil rich in organic matter is preferable to doses of chemical fertilizer. "If the ground has been prepared properly, you don't need to fertilize," says Gene Banks. Only if her plants grow poorly does she add fertilizer. Dr. Orzolek "spoon-feeds" his transplants, applying only minimal amounts of fertilizer to start with. "You can always add nitrogen," he says, "but you can't take it out."

A tunnel of shade cloth stretched over bent PVC pipes will shield young transplants from sun, wind, and garden pests.

DEPTH DECISIONS

On seed packets, you'll find reliable information on how deep to plant seeds. "Years of research have gone into those recommendations," says Mark Willis of New York's Harris Seeds. But many experts have also developed their own rules of thumb for determining proper depth:

🦢 To plant small seeds, Bertha Reppert of Pennsylvania's Rosemary House simply scratches the soil, scatters the seed, and covers them with a board or damp cloth. "I pick up the covering occasionally to check for germination and to look for snails or other marauders," she says. If the seeds are very large, like nasturtiums, she presses them in deeper and covers them with soil.

🦢 Conrad Richter of Ontario's Richter's Herbs sows his seeds at a depth of three to four times their thickness. "Fewer make it through than if planted more shallowly," he admits, "but those that do don't dry out."

DIRECT SEEDING

With all the information you're likely to encounter on starting seeds indoors, it's easy to feel like less than a gardener if you decide to sow seeds directly in the ground. But many of the experts prefer to do it exactly that way, working with nature and following her guidelines, as Tom Butterworth of Connecticut's Butterbrook Farms puts it.

Planting in Hills

Which plants do well in hills • How to hill • Mixed hills

Thousands of years before Europeans set foot on American soil, native people sowed their seeds in hills, a technique that helps warm the soil to hasten and improve germination. In addition, the hills act like miniature raised beds, says University of Nebraska horticulturist Amy Greving, allowing good drainage that in turn benefits germination. And Burpee's Sharon Kaszan hills her seeds not for productivity but to mark the space where seedlings will emerge.

MOUNDING THE SOIL In general, build hills 2 to 5 inches high over a 12- to 18-inch area. Mark Willis of New York's Harris Seeds recommends planting three or four seeds in each hill and eventually

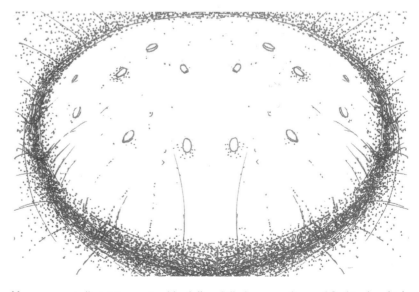

You can create "miniature raised beds," or hills, by mounding soil 3–4 inches high and sowing seeds on top. Hills drain beautifully and make thinning easy.

thinning seedlings so that only two remain. For extra warmth, Bill McDorman of Idaho's High Altitude Gardens covers the soil with black plastic, making holes in the plastic to allow seedlings to come through easily.

WHAT TO HILL Like most experts who hill their seeds, Janet Oberleisen, editor of *The Herbalist* and a horticulturist at Ohio State University, follows the Native American practice of mounding the "three sisters"—corn, squash, and beans. "We get very good germination from at least one seed in each hill," she says, "and then we transplant thinnings when necessary." In addition to squash, you can hill most of the cucurbit family, including cucumbers, zucchini, winter and summer squash, and melons.

You can also hill potatoes (which are planted not from seeds but from tubers). Alice Krinsky, trial garden manager at Shepherd's Garden Seeds, plants her potatoes in indentations, then hills the earth up around the growing plants. This encourages the plants to produce fewer leaves and more potatoes. To make the job easier, you can cut the bottom off a plastic berry basket and place the basket, upended, over the seedlings. As they grow, keep adding soil to the basket until you reach the top.

Plant onions in trenches to protect the seeds and shade the young plants.

MORE DEPTH TIPS

❧ Lynn Hartmann of Massachusetts sets her seeds in holes that are twice as deep as the seed is wide. She simply presses tiny mint seeds into the soil.

❧ Alice Krinsky of Shepherd's Garden Seeds plants one and a half to two times the depth of the seed, a little deeper in hot weather, to keep the seeds from drying out.

❧ The plant's method of rooting can help you determine the proper depth for its seeds, says Burpee's Sharon Kaszan. Peppers, tomatoes, and other vining crops root from the sides of the stems, so Sharon plants them deeper than other vegetables. For bottom rooters like beans, she makes a $2\frac{1}{2}$-inch hole, drops in the seed, and covers it with soil. (Bean seeds are about 1 inch long, so she's planting about $1\frac{1}{2}$ inches deep.)

❧ For lettuce, Justine Mapstone of Crosman Seed Company prepares the soil, broadcasts the seed, and waters it in; she doesn't cover the seed at all.

EFFICIENT IRRIGATION

To make sure that all the water you apply gets to the roots of your plants, experts recommend using soaker hoses or drip irrigation systems.

Soaker hoses are simply lengths of rubber hosing perforated at regular intervals to allow water to seep out. A drip irrigation system does much the same thing, using a series of supply and feeder lines equipped with emitters (small attachments that deliver the water where it's needed). Both are vastly more efficient than over-head sprinklers, which lose much of their water to evaporation, or watering with a garden hose, which can waste water in runoff.

For maximum efficiency, cover your irrigation system with plastic mulch, topped with a layer of organic mulch, suggests Jim Becker of Oregon's Goodwin Creek Gardens.

TENDING TO YOUR VEGETABLES

Okay, your seeds and transplants are all in the ground, they've recovered from transplant shock, and they're growing nicely. Though most of your work is done, a few minutes spent in the garden every day will keep it looking good and growing right.

Watering

When • How • How much

Each year, gardeners expend millions of gallons of water on their vegetable crops, much of it unnecessarily and sometimes harmfully. But by following a few clever strategies, you can keep irrigating chores to a minimum.

WATER ON DEMAND Experts agree that you should water only when your crops require it. To do this, you need to pay attention to your plants, points out Burpee's Sharon Kaszan. If they show any signs of drought stress, such as the wilting of leaves and stem tops, premature fruit drop, yellowing or browning of foliage along the bottom third of the stem, or an inability to set blossoms or fruit, check the soil for dryness. And watch the weather, too, advises Rolfe Hagen of Thyme Garden Seeds. Most vegetables require an inch of water a week. If nature is providing you with less than that, you may need to supplement. Sharon Kaszan waters well early in the season when plants' root systems aren't fully developed. "By July, I don't have to water anymore," she says.

WATER RIGHT Peggy Singlemann of the Maymount Foundation in Virginia waters many of her beds as infrequently as every other week, but when she does take out the hose, she waters deeply. "Good soakings are better than frequent sprinklings," she says. She uses a garden hose with a standard breaker (a nozzle that breaks and softens the flow of water) and holds it on each plant, "for a slow count of five." If fungus diseases are rampant in your area, try to wet only the ground, not the foliage. "Keep the hose down," says Peggy, and keep your plants well thinned so the soil is easily accessible.

WATER EARLY Most of the experts advise watering your crops in the morning. That way the plant has water available to it throughout the day, says Sharon Kaszan. At New Jersey's Well-Sweep Herb Farm, Louise Hyde waters early so that foliage has time to dry. "Otherwise, fungus sets in," she warns. This is especially important with plants that have lots of foliage, says John Lee of Allandale Farm in Massachusetts. If you must water late in the day, keep the water source close to the ground and try not to let water splash onto the leaves above.

CONSERVING WATER By mixing generous amounts of organic matter into the soil, you'll increase its ability to hold water. Because she enriches her herb beds so generously, Louise Hyde rarely waters except in times of drought.

The best system for saving water is mulching. "In a year of normal rainfall, you won't need to water at all if you use enough mulch," says Tom Butterworth of Connecticut's Butterbrook Farms. Most experts recommend 2 to 4 inches of mulch for maximum water conservation. In addition to using mulches and drip irrigation systems, Mary Irish of

In this drip irrigation system, semipermeable pipe is snaked through the garden and attached to a central water source. Such systems aren't easy to install, but they provide excellent irrigation for years.

TROUBLESHOOTING IN THE VEGETABLE GARDEN

No vegetable garden is trouble-free. Here's how to prevent some common problems, and how to deal with them when they surface. For more information on controlling pests and diseases, see "Chapter 6: Expert Answers on Organic Pest & Disease Control" on page 290.

VEGETABLE	PROBLEM	PREVENTION	SOLUTION
Beans	Rust	Select resistant varieties.	Remove affected plants.
	Mexican bean beetles	Plant early (early plantings are rarely infested), plant resistant varieties such as 'Wade' or 'Logan', use row covers, plant a trap crop.	Hand-pick the yellowish-orange grubs and crush the bright yellow egg masses on the underside of the leaves. If infestation is strong, spray with organic controls such as pyrethrin.
Broccoli, Brussels sprouts, cabbage, and cauliflower	Cabbage loopers	Use floating row covers.	Treat with BTK.
	Cutworms	Place cardboard collars around young plants, or plant in paper cups.	Treat with BT. Destroy larvae by digging around damaged plants.
	Mildew, black rot, yellows	Plant resistant varieties. Practice crop rotation.	Remove infected plants.
	Cracked heads on cabbage	Keep plants evenly moist.	Early varieties may split from rapid new growth if rain follows a dry spell. Twisting the heads will break off some roots, which will slow maturity.
	Broccoli going to seed	Keep center heads picked as soon as they begin to loosen, even if they are small.	—
Carrots	Cracking	Plant in loose, well-tilled soil.	—
	Mildew	Keep carrots thinned; avoid overwatering or overfertilizing.	—
	Carrot rustfly	Use row covers. Delay planting until early summer.	Apply parasitic nematodes when preparing soil before planting.
Corn	European corn borer, corn earworm	Plant resistant varieties; attract beneficial insects. Remove old stalks after harvest.	Apply BTK. For earworms, apply mineral oil to top of each ear after corn silks wilt.
	Undeveloped ears	Make sure site is getting enough sun and water.	—

VEGETABLE	PROBLEM	PREVENTION	SOLUTION
Eggplant	Flea beetles	Use row covers.	—
Greens and lettuce	Flea beetles	Use row covers. Plant and harvest early.	—
	Bolting	Plant heat-tolerant varieties. Plant early in season.	Provide some shade with shade cloth.
	Chipmunks, rabbits, and deer	Use wire barriers.	—
Squash, melon, and cucumber	Cucumber beetles	Use row covers, rotate crops. and keep area free of debris.	—
	White flies	Keep well-picked. Attract beneficial insects.	Spray with water or insect-icidal soap. Use sticky traps.
	Squash bugs	Use row covers (remove covers for pollination after blooming). Plant resistant varieties.	Monitor and hand-pick as soon as infestation begins.
	Squash vine borer	Use row covers. Plant resistant, vigorous varieties.	Remove infested stems.
Tomatoes, potatoes, and peppers	Blossom end rot	Keep well watered. Do not overfertilize.	Add calcium to soil in the form of crushed seashells or by spraying with seaweed extract. Do not cultivate around roots.
	Early blight	Buy healthy seed and seed potatoes. Practice crop rotation. Keep area well-weeded and free of debris.	Monitor carefully. Spray with copper fungicide at first sign of infestation.
	Late blight	Keep area free of weeds, especially over winter. Keep air circulation good by weeding and spacing well. Rotate crops regularly.	Cut out and remove affected vines. Spray with copper fungicide.
	Tomato hornworm	Attract beneficial insects.	Monitor and hand-pick. Apply BTK as soon as caterpillars appear.
	Colorado potato beetles	Plant resistant varieties, such as 'Katandin' and 'Sequoia'. Lay a 1-foot layer of mulch.	Hand-pick beetles and larvae. Spray with BTSD.
	Soilborne diseases	Use resistant cultivars. Rotate.	—

At the Desert Botanical Garden in Phoenix, vegetable beds are slightly sunken and water is conserved in "ponds."

Arizona's Desert Botanical Garden suggests trying vegetable ponds— beds that are slightly sunken to minimize water loss. Or you can go the opposite route and raise your beds, amending them with lots of organic matter to hold water in.

Fertilizing

Choosing the right fertilizer • *Timing tips*
• *Testing plants for nutrient deficiencies*

Broadly defined, a fertilizer is anything added to the soil that increases its fertility. Organic fertilizers break down slowly, releasing nutrients to plants as they need them. They also encourage the growth of beneficial microorganisms. The best fertilizers improve soil steadily.

Organic fertilizers come from a wide variety of sources, including fish meal and bloodmeal (high in nitrogen), kelp and liquid seaweed (high in potassium), and composted cow manure (fairly evenly balanced in nitrogen, phosphorus, and potassium). In addition, most fertilizers supply traces of other necessary nutrients like calcium, zinc, and magnesium. Some organic fertilizers, like gypsum and ground oyster shells, are especially heavy in calcium and help combat such calcium-deficiency ills as blossom-end rot on tomatoes.

TO FERTILIZE OR NOT Until recently, guidelines for fertilizing recommended applying heavy doses of fertilizer throughout the growing season. While this approach yielded short-term gains such as a flush of new growth, in the long run it led to poorer soils, more disease-susceptible plants, and pollution of ground water as excess fertilizer leached through the soil. Today, most experts apply fertilizer only as a backup, and many, like Tom Butterworth of Connecticut's Butterbrook Farms, believe it's entirely unnecessary. Instead, Tom relies on the use of organic mulches. "They break down the way leaves break down in a forest, and everything in a forest grows quite well without chemical fertilizer," he points out.

Peter Borchard of Ohio's Companion Plants follows the same philosophy in his own extensive garden. "Even though we raise 150 varieties of seed crops, we give them all the same treatment, which boils down to incorporating organic matter into the soil by the constant use of mulch," he says. During the growing season, Peter and his colleagues apply a variety of mulches to their beds, including hay, leaves, wood chips, grass clippings, and other garden debris (all well-composted or aged), which they till under before the following growing season. The only fertilizers they use are mushroom compost (a byproduct of mushroom farming) and composted horse and cow manure. They use these every two years, along with occasional dustings of agricultural lime for specific crops that require a higher pH (see "Acid Lovers" on page 268).

James Wooten, whose garden domain is Virginia's Ashlawn-Highland, historic home of President James Monroe, plants cover crops (see "Going for Cover" on page 283) and mulches with oakleaf mold at the end of every season. "By doing this," he says, "we make our soil very fertile and we don't need to add any fertilizer during the season."

WHEN TO FERTILIZE Even with well-worked soil, your crops may occasionally benefit from the application of fertilizer. Heavy rainfall, for instance, can wash nitrogen out of the soil. If you live in a rainy climate, you may need to apply a high-nitrogen fertilizer, such as fish meal, two or three times in each growing season.

Soil tests (see "Put It to the Test" on page 264) can help you determine which nutrients are lacking in your garden, but if you want to know exactly what your plants need, Pennsylvania horticulturist Dr.

Plant some annuals near your vegetables. When the flowers begin to look sickly, you'll know that they need fertilizer, and your vegetables probably could use some, as well.

Mulching allows some crops, like the corn salad above, to overwinter, providing early spring salads.

Michael Orzolek recommends tissue analysis. Most cooperative agents can perform the analysis for a minimal cost, which involves testing actual plant matter rather than soil. The results should include a list of whatever nutrients your plants need. Dr. Orzolek, who has his plants tested 20 days after transplanting and then again in July, considers it a terrific money-saver: "You can avoid spending money on things your plants don't really need. Instead of a balanced fertilizer, your crops may only require urea, say, or magnesium."

Mulching

The purpose of mulch • *Synthetic mulches* • *Organic options*

Almost all the experts recommend using some kind of mulch in the vegetable garden, especially with crops like strawberries and squashes whose fruits lie on the ground and might rot when they're in direct contact with the soil. You should also mulch any vegetables that will grow for three months or longer. The kind of mulch you choose and whether you apply it before, during, or after the growing season will depend on your needs and your aesthetic preferences.

Mulching between rows cuts down on weeds and keeps the roots of young plants cool and moist. After the season, an organic mulch can be tilled into the soil. It will decompose and add nutrients for the next season.

Whatever material you choose, the purpose of mulch is the same: to retain moisture, retard the growth of weeds, maintain an even soil temperature, and prevent the soil from compacting. The synthetic, or inorganic, mulches include black and clear plastic, paper-backed foil, and geotextiles (porous materials that allow air, water, and soluble fertilizers to penetrate to the soil below). Organic mulches include bark, leaves, compost, straw, hay, and agricultural byproducts such as cocoa and peanut hulls.

PLASTIC MULCHES Black plastic is by far the most familiar of the synthetic mulches. Inexpensive, widely available, and easy to apply, it's popular with some, but not all, of the experts.

• John Lee of Allandale Farm in Massachusetts likes to use it with his peppers because it warms the soil and allows him to get a jump on the season by at least two or three weeks.

• At the New York Botanical Garden, horticulturist Janet Whippo mulches sweet potatoes and squash with black plastic. She praises it for its exceptional ability to heat the soil, retain moisture, and keep down weeds, but she's not wild about the stuff. "Because it's so unattractive, I have to use another mulch on top of it (after the soil warms), and then I can't see what's going on underneath. Plus, I can only use it for one season because it tears easily when I try to reroll it," she says.

• Louise Hyde of New Jersey's Well-Sweep Herb Farm prefers geotextiles over black plastic. The plastic can be unsightly even when covered with another mulch because over the course of a season, she says, the plastic inevitably starts to peek through. And Mary Irish of Arizona's Desert Botanical Garden points out that black plastic can raise soil temperatures so much that root growth is actually inhibited, especially in warm climates.

• Washington horticulturist Steve Whitcher finds clear plastic a better alternative than black. He uses it to prevent splashing (which can encourage the spread of disease) under melons, grapes, and tomatoes. However, clear plastic allows light as well as heat to penetrate the soil, and some experts, such as Debby Kavakos, owner of Stoneledge Farm in New York, find that it warms the soil too quickly.

• Galen Gates of Chicago Botanic Garden warns that no plastic of any color should be used on permanent plantings. The roots of plants

WEEDING

The best way to keep weeds under control is to get them out before the season begins. (For methods of pre-season weed removal, see "Removing Weeds" on page 44.) Here are the experts' methods for battling weeds as the season progresses.

✺ According to Rosie Lerner, Purdue University's extension specialist in consumer horticulture, "the best way to control weeds is to prevent them from going to seed. A single plant can produce hundreds of thousands of seeds." If you can't get all your weeds out, at least take out those in full flower.

✺ Get the whole weed. You've got to get the root, says San Francisco landscape designer Angela Fabbri. If the root comes up broken, dig deeper until you get the entire thing.

✺ Coreen Schilling's secret: weed when it's wet. Plants are easier to pull in moist ground, and you're far more likely to get all of the root.

vegetable & herb gardening secrets

Experiments are underway at Longwood Gardens in Kennett Square, Pennsylvania, to see if a red plastic mulch that blocks some of the sun's rays is a good compromise between clear and black plastic.

covered by plastic tend to stay near the surface where moisture condenses, making the plants more susceptible to extreme heat and cold, explains Galen.

ORGANIC MULCHES In addition to a variety of synthetic mulches, Washington horticulturist Steve Whitcher uses compost, bark dust, and sawdust. Peggy Singleman of the Maymount Foundation in Virginia mulches her vegetable beds with shredded bark, but chooses peanut and coconut hulls for her herbs. To discourage slugs and snails, both of which find shredded organic mulch an ideal hiding place, she recommends watering as lightly as possible. In addition, she says, make sure that the mulch doesn't knit together and become thatchlike, which will keep water out of the soil rather than conserve it.

To avoid problems associated with shredded mulch, John Lee chooses orange sheathing paper. It smothers weeds, disintegrates in a single season, and can be rotary tilled into the ground in the fall. And Davy Dabney of Kentucky's Dabney Herbs recommends EUE, a material made from sheep shearings that decomposes in two to three years. Easy to lay down, EUE effectively controls weeds without attracting slugs and snails. To plant in either material, make small slits or holes in the mulch and insert transplants in the openings.

Another organic alternative is to plant living mulches. Lettuces and other low-growing crops, interplanted with taller vegetables like broccoli, work well as weed deterrents. (For more, see "Interplanting" on page 82.)

Galen Gates advises gardeners to use only well-composted organic mulches during the growing season because some mulches, like bark chips and sawdust, tie up nitrogen as they decompose.

Protecting Crops from Cold

Crop shelters • Chasing chills with row covers • Anchored protectors • Extending the season with protection

While you can't do too much to save your crops from a hard frost (when temperatures drop below 28°F), there's plenty you can do to shield tender vegetables and herbs from the kind of light frost that often visits unexpectedly in early spring and fall.

GIVE THEM SHELTER The most reliable way to protect your crops from a light frost, say the experts, is to cover them up.

• At New Jersey's Well-Sweep Herb Farm, Louise Hyde covers her rows with old blankets and bedspreads. "It looks funny," she says, "but it saves the plants."

• Mark Willis of New York's Harris Seeds lays down black plastic or newspapers.

• Shane Smith, director of Wyoming's Cheyenne Botanic Garden, sometimes uses burlap in addition to plastic and blankets to cover his vegetable plants.

• In early spring, Paul Taylor of Vermont's Le Jardin du Gourmet shelters his crops under a cover of EUE.

Whether or not you need to protect your plants from light frost depends on what you grow. "I cover squashes, tomatoes, and other fruit crops," says Shane Smith. "But cole and root crops like a light frost and don't need any protection." Most herbs are hardy perennials,

Row covers protect young plants from sudden cold snaps.

BLACK PLASTIC BENEFITS

It's cheap, you can buy it almost anywhere, and it's highly efficient at retaining moisture and suppressing weeds. Many of the experts recommend it.

❧ John Lee of Allandale Farm in Massachusetts jump-starts the pepper season by two or three weeks with black plastic, which warms the soil more efficiently than organic mulch.

❧ Rosie B. Lerner, extension specialist in consumer horticulture at Purdue University, recommends it for warm-season crops grown from transplants: "Transplants suffer more from shock than seedlings do, so keeping the soil warm is more important for them."

But black plastic has its detractors: "It's unattractive, and it creates a lot of nonrecyclable garbage," says Janet Whippo of the New York Botanical Garden. And it can warm the soil too much, warns Rosie Lerner, who advises against using it in very warm climates or during very hot summers.

says Rolfe Hagen of Thyme Garden Seeds, and don't require protection—though he sometimes blankets his basil with straw during an unexpected frost. Other gardeners cover tender perennial herbs with boughs from Christmas trees.

USE ROW COVERS FOR ALL-AROUND PROTECTION They may be a little more expensive than your old bedspreads, but row covers offer excellent protection against light frosts. Lightweight and easy to use, they allow sunlight, water, and air to get to your plants while keeping frost out. As a result, they extend the growing season by several weeks in spring and fall, says Niles Kinerk of the Gardens Alive! catalog in Indiana. He recommends polypropylene covers over polyester, since they're less abrasive and easier on tender crops. "They're so light you don't need hoops to raise them up," he says.

Pennsylvania horticulturist Dr. Michael Orzolek routinely lays row covers on his zucchini plants "until the first large leaves come out." At that point, if frost still threatens, he supports the covers with hoops to protect the leaves.

In addition to providing frost protection, row covers shield crops from insects and cross-pollination (a potential problem only if you plan to collect seed), says Gary Coull of Johnny's Selected Seeds. And they protect young plants from strong sun, adds Dr. Orzolek.

THE CONS OF COVERS Not all the experts love row covers, however. Burpee's Sharon Kaszan considers them "too much trouble." And if you like to cultivate around your plants, warns Virginia Frazier of North Carolina's Adventures in Herbs, you'll have to wait until the covers are up. Furthermore, says Gary Coull, covers make it difficult to check plants for pests, diseases, and nutritional deficiencies. David Bar-Zvi of Fairchild Tropical Garden in Miami finds that leaves become damaged if they touch the polypropylene during a freeze unless a layer of newspaper or cloth is used in between.

And, depending on where you live, covers may not be practical. In Wyoming, the wind blows too hard for covers to stay in place, no matter how well they're anchored, says Shane Smith. Instead, he and his colleagues protect their plants with rock- or dirt-pile windbreaks.

Trellising

Types of trellises • Gardening up • Vertical vegetables

Designed to support vining plants, trellises come in a variety of forms and materials. The most common trellis is a wooden frame with crisscrossing strips, but any number of supports can do the job. Teepees made with three or more long poles leaning together and lashed at the top provide excellent support for pole beans, tomatoes, and other tall or climbing crops. Even a piece of lattice or some leftover wire fencing can work as a trellis, as long as it's strong enough and anchored sufficiently to support the weight of a mature plant.

Gary Coull of Johnny's Selected Seeds places 7-foot metal poles in the ground at 10-foot intervals and runs a wire between them at the top and the bottom. Then he hangs netting or twine from the top wire and anchors the bottom wire with tent stakes. Whatever form of trellising you decide to use, you'll find it offers several benefits.

SPACE The primary reason for trellising crops, says Donald Ledden of New Jersey's Ledden Brothers, is to save space in the garden. Vining plants like cucumbers and tomatoes tend to sprawl over a large area. You can fit more plants into your vegetable bed by trellising them, which will double or even triple your yield.

Trellises can be as simple as two poles connected with twine, or they can be wooden structures like the ones shown. Height and complexity depend on the needs of the crop being grown.

Teepee trellises are easily constructed and save space in the garden. Their shape allows several plants to grow in just a few feet of space, with plenty of air circulating between them.

PROTECTION Trellising promotes better air circulation around plants, which allows fruit to dry more quickly and prevents rot and fungal infection. In addition, says Gary Coull, fruit that's trellised is out of the reach of slugs and other crawling pests.

EASE OF MAINTENANCE Because trellising keeps plants off the ground, soil cultivation is easier, says Gary Coull. And, he adds, you can spot disease and insect problems at an early stage, when there's still time to save the plant.

Trellised plants, however, may need more water than those on the ground. The same airiness that protects against fungal infection also

Cherry tomatoes climb this arched trellis at Longwood Gardens. This planting makes use of vertical space, providing pounds of luscious, easy-to-harvest fruits while using very little of the garden's space.

exposes stems and leaves to drying winds, points out Pennsylvania horticulturist Dr. Michael Orzolek.

ORNAMENTATION In addition to their functional advantages, trellised plants add interest to your garden design, providing a vertical note to an otherwise low-growing vegetable plot and showcasing vining plants, many of which would be worth growing for their flowers and foliage alone. Trellises add a kind of sculptural quality usually absent from the vegetable garden.

In Philadelphia's historic John Bartram Garden, Pam Allenstein grows her beans on branches lashed together with heavy twine—an interesting and historically accurate touch. Though most herbs aren't climbers, Louise Hyde of New Jersey's Well-Sweep Herb Farm allows her hops to attach themselves to a thick rope suspended from an old oak tree.

CROPS FOR TRELLISING Anything that naturally vines or sprawls can be grown on a trellis. Vining plants like pole beans and cucumbers climb by twining, and they'll scramble up a structure without any assistance at all. Sprawling plants, like tomatoes, on the other hand, need to be tied or otherwise secured to the trellis. Other plants you can trellis in your backyard include cucumbers, hops, and peas. (See also "Staking Crops," below.)

Trellises can be easily constructed from wooden poles and branches lashed together with stout rope. Even under harsh conditions, these trellises will last for several years.

Staking Crops

When it's worth the time and trouble • When staking is a necessity • Shrewd stakes • Avoiding mis-stakes

Like trellising, staking gets your vegetables off the ground. Some experts do it routinely and swear to its effectiveness. Others find it of little value. If you have limited space and you want to grow lots of vegetables, however, staking is the way to go.

WHY STAKE? Bill McDorman of Idaho's High Altitude Gardens experimented with 15,000 tomato plants, half of which he staked and half of which he allowed to sprawl on the ground. "I found little difference in either the yield or the size of the tomatoes," he says. Nevertheless, he recommends staking because it makes harvesting easier and it looks nicer—a staked tomato plant is just plain prettier than an ungainly tangle of stems.

Spiral stakes, available at garden centers, provide excellent air circulation as well as extra space for growing plants.

Like trellising, staking makes routine maintenance around your plants easier, points out Donald Ledden of New Jersey's Ledden Brothers. Virginia Frazier of North Carolina's Adventures in Herbs finds that staking her tomatoes protects against blight, and Sharon Kaszan of Burpee gets fewer broken branches on her staked pepper plants (which is only a problem when plants produce a lot of fruit, as Sharon's do).

WHAT TO STAKE As a rule, heirloom or open-pollinated varieties need staking more than modern hybrids, many of which have been bred for compactness, explains Sharon Kaszan. She provides support, "for all the big stuff, including peppers and tomatoes." Most experts advise staking indeterminate varieties of tomato—those whose stems continue to grow after producing a blossom.

HOW TO DO IT You can simply stick a piece of wood or metal into the ground and tie plants to it, however, most gardeners use slightly more sophisticated stakes such as tomato cages (wire hoops through

This gazebo-trellis at Chanticleer Gardens in Pennsylvania is a boon to both plants and gardeners. The structure provides support for the plants that grow up its sides, plus it provides filtered shade and a place for the gardener to sit.

The most natural-looking stakes are fallen twigs and branches from nearby trees. And, of course, they're free for the gathering!

vegetable & herb gardening secrets

The simplest, neatest stakes are lengths of wood stuck into the ground at planting time.

which the plants climb) and post-and-wire trellises. Donald Ledden sets tall metal or wooden posts at 10- to 12-foot intervals and stretches 2-inch mesh poultry netting from post to post. He makes sure that the netting is at least a foot off the ground so that he can cultivate and weed with ease. Attach plants to your stakes with cloth or coated wire, but don't tie them too tightly, or the branches can snap. Virginia Frazier waits for a hot day when plants will be soft, and she winds string loosely around the stems, keeping the spirals about a foot apart.

HARVESTING

Now comes the best part. Oh sure, planting and caring for herbs and vegetables is fun, but the real reward of gardening is harvesting and enjoying what you've grown. Keep in mind that harvesting isn't done in a day; it's an ongoing process. Some plants continue to produce after the first harvest but will stop producing unless you continue to pick them.

When the Time Is Ripe

Plant cycles • Morning harvest • Getting the heat out

The joy of growing your own vegetables and herbs is that you can pick them and eat them at their peak. You should, of course, harvest crops when they're ripe, but is there an ideal time of day to pick them? Experts disagree on this subject.

PICK THEM EARLY Louise Hyde of New Jersey's Well-Sweep Herb Farm says you'll ensure the freshest possible produce by harvesting late in the morning, just after the dew dries but before the sun heats up. Tender herbs and leaf crops, especially, can deteriorate quickly after picking, so it's best to pluck them when they're dry.

PICK THEM LATE Many experts, including William Hall of Michigan's Country Carriage Nursery and Virginia Frazier of North Carolina's

Harvesting beans and other vining vegetables is a breeze when they are grown on a two-sided trellis. Place supports about every 3 feet and don't make them higher than you can easily reach. Tie or nail twine horizontally and vertically, or attach mesh fabric.

Adventures in Herbs, believe that late afternoon or early evening is as good a time to harvest as morning. For William, the condition of the gardener is at least as important as that of the vegetables. "It's just more comfortable to harvest during the cooler parts of the day."

John Lee of Allandale Farm in Massachusetts offers another reason to harvest in the evening: "Plants accumulate sugar during the day through photosynthesis," he says, "and are sweetest just before they close down for the evening." Regardless, he suggests you not worry too much about the time of day. "It's more important to harvest vegetables right before you eat them, because sugar starts converting to starch immediately after picking," he says. To maintain freshness and sweetness, don't let newly harvested vegetables sit out in the sun, advises John. As soon as you pick them, move them into a shady spot. But don't put them into the refrigerator if you don't have to, he warns. Refrigerators dehydrate even freshly harvested produce. If you must store vegetables for a short time in the fridge, he says, put them in water.

Gathering Greens and Herbs

Whole-head harvesting • *Cut and come again*
• *Herbal harvest hints*

When you grow your own greens, you can harvest the leaves as you use them, at their peak of freshness and flavor. But is this "cut and come again" method the best?

A HEAD AT A TIME Bill McDorman of Idaho's High Altitude Gardens harvests their greens every two weeks, taking the whole plant. "With lettuces and most other plants, you lose quality after the first cutting. The plant is different from others in that it's trying to produce seed, not fruit or leaves," says Bill. According to Alice Krinsky, trial garden manager at Shepherd's Garden Seeds, "If you keep cutting, you will get usable salad leaves, but you won't get a big head." When you harvest the whole head, you will have room to replant a new crop.

REPEAT HARVESTING If you don't mind sacrificing yield for freshness, you may do better to harvest greens as you use them. Remember though, says Alice Krinksy, that lettuce leaves get crisper as they mature. She recommends leaving 1 to 2 inches of the plant above the heart so

STORAGE SUGGESTIONS

You can store most vegetables in the fridge for several days. Stephen Garrison harvests high-sugar vegetables like corn and peas, and vegetables that metabolize quickly like broccoli and cauliflower, early in the day to lock in natural sweetness. He doesn't wash them (because moisture can cause decay) and puts them into the refrigerator immediately after picking.

Tomatoes, however, should never be stored in the refrigerator, because low temperatures render them permanently tasteless. If you can't eat your tomatoes as they ripen, pick them just before they're fully colored and store them in a cool, shady spot. Under those conditions, you can expect them to keep for two or three days.

STORING IN OIL

Though some cooks preserve their herbs in oil, the experts advise against it—unless you're planning to use the herbs in salves, says Janet Whippo, a horticulturist at the New York Botanical Garden. You can store garlic in oil, says Bertha Reppert, but most herbs develop anaerobic bacteria—potentially harmful microorganisms that thrive in the absence of oxygen—when preserved this way. To be safe, use oil for preserving only if you plan to freeze the mixture.

If you do store your garlic in oil, make sure it is completely covered and keep it refrigerated. It will keep for several months, and the garlic-flavored oil will be quite tasty, too.

that it can regenerate. Take whole leaves, though, since individual leaves won't regenerate. Janet Whippo of the New York Botanical Garden uses this method on her salad greens and gets two or three excellent harvests per plant. Donald Ledden of New Jersey's Ledden Brothers is more conservative, never removing more than half a plant at a time.

CUTTING HERBS Unlike salad greens, herbs can be snipped anytime, says Alice Krinsky. She makes sure to cut her herbs before they flower, since flowering can cause leaves to toughen. "In oregano and thyme, oils are best just before flowering," she says. According to Bertha Reppert of Pennsylvania's Rosemary House, many herbs do best with frequent cuttings. Comfrey and chives, for example, will get too large if you don't cut them, sprawling over surrounding plants and robbing them of light and air. While it's best to harvest chives piecemeal, taking the leaves as you need them, Bertha sometimes cuts the entire plant down to about 2 inches so that it can regenerate.

Be judicious, however, about cutting back woody herbs like lavender and santolina. "If you cut back too much in fall, the plants may be too weak to get through the winter," says Bertha. She advises taking no more than a third of the plant off after summer's end. Fairman and Kate Jayne of Sandy Mush Herb Farm in North Carolina cut their mint plant down

Plastic rope stapled to porch rafters provides an excellent spot for curing garlic. Hang garlic to dry away from sun and wind for several weeks to mellow its flavor and improve its storability.

to about 1 inch high in midsummer. By fall, the new growth is strong enough to last right through frost, and they can harvest fresh mint in the middle of winter.

Storing Vegetables

Refrigerators and root cellars • A few wise words on washing •Tips for tomatoes

One of the great rewards of growing your own vegetables is enjoying them at their freshest and most flavorful, but since you can't eat everything right off the vine, here are some storage secrets.

GREENS Lettuces and other salad greens won't last forever, but most will keep for at least a few days without losing much flavor or texture. Greens are delicate, so wash them right after picking. Rutgers cooperative agent Stephen Garrison recommends removing the outside leaves (where you'll find most of the garden dirt and moisture) and, after rinsing, drying them quickly and completely. Janet Oberleisen, editor of *The Herbalist* and a horticulturist at Ohio State University, wraps her greens in paper towels and puts them in the crisper. Or you can follow the lead of John Schneeberger of Montana's Garden City Seeds and simply store them in plastic bags.

ROOT CROPS Of all the vegetables you grow, your root crops—potatoes, onions, radishes, carrots, and anything else that grows under the ground—will store best and keep the longest. That's because the sugar in root vegetables doesn't change to starch immediately, as it does in most other crops, explains Stephen Garrison. Before they make their trip down to the root cellar, John Schneeberger's vegetables sit for a few minutes in the shade "to get the heat out." Though root crops prefer darkness and cool temperatures, don't store them in the refrigerator, warns Stephen. "Your fridge has high humidity," he says, "and most root crops, like onions, need a low-humidity environment." Other experts find that refrigeration dries vegetables because cold air can't hold as much moisture as warm. Many refrigerators have both humid and dry sections; the environment in your refrigerator will depend on how new it is, what's in it, and how it was built. Look at the manufacturer's instructions or experiment to find out how it works.

STORING DRIED HERBS

Unless you use the freezer method, you'll need to store your herbs in some kind of container. Lynn Hartmann of Hartmann's Herb Farm in Massachusetts likes to keep hers on paper towels in cardboard boxes. "If you store your herbs in plastic or glass, any moisture left in the plant will cause it to rot," she explains. "But cardboard will absorb excess moisture."

Amy Greving, on the other hand, thinks herbs stored this way might absorb the taste of the cardboard. She prefers to store hers in glass containers, first making sure that they're completely dry. Whichever method you choose, check dried herbs before using them. They should be aromatic and retain some of their original color. Never use herbs that have become moldy, warns Davy Dabney of Kentucky's Dabney Herbs. In addition to being unappetizing, they may be harmful.

PESTO

A great way to keep enjoying your basil after fall frost is to make pesto with it, says Janet Whippo of the New York Botanical Garden. Finely chop or mash your basil leaves, mix with olive oil, and freeze. (You can add the cheese and pine nuts either before freezing or when it's time to cook the pesto sauce.) Janet doesn't limit herself to basil, either. She makes pestos with cilantro, chives, and thyme, as well. Pesto tastes great over pasta, but you can also use it as a pizza topping or add it to soups, stews, and sauces for a burst of fresh flavor.

If you don't have a root or wine cellar, any cool, dark, dry area will do. Potatoes store best at about 60° to 65°F, says Stephen Garrison (though temperatures can go as low as 40°F for regular potatoes and 55°F for sweets (after curing at 85 to 90°F for 10 to 15 days). Don't, however, let your potatoes freeze, since freezing triggers the conversion of starch to sugar and yields vegetables that are mushy, discolored, and oversweet.

Most experts recommend not washing your root crops before storage, since moisture can lead to deterioration.

Preserving Herbs

Drying, microwaving, freezing • Storing dried herbs

Herbs bring so many pleasures beyond their fresh flavors in foods. You can use them to make teas, balms, and everlasting arrangements, and of course you can save culinary herbs for seasonings. For long-term use of the herbs you've harvested, take care to preserve them correctly so they retain maximum flavor and fragrance.

AIR-DRYING To air-dry herbs, which is the traditional method of preservation, bundle them with twine and hang them upside down until they've dried out. If you plan to use your herbs in potpourri and dried arrangements, you can hang them uncovered all over the house as University of Nebraska horticulturist Amy Greving does. "They become part of the decor," says Amy. Those herbs you want to dry for cooking should be hung in a paper bag with a hole for ventilation, she advises. "It's not attractive, but your herbs stay clean," she says.

Whatever method you use to hang your herbs, keep them away from excessive heat, which can rob them of taste, advises Davy Dabney of Kentucky's Dabney Herbs. If possible, hang them near an air-conditioning vent or other source of cool air. Sage and rosemary are two herbs that air-dry well, says Davy. Basil, on the other hand, shouldn't be dried at all, since it becomes virtually tasteless. And Bertha Reppert of Pennsylvania's Rosemary House warns against air-drying parsley, which can lose both flavor and color.

DEHYDRATORS AND MICROWAVES A dehydrator is a dandy little machine that takes the moisture out of herbs and vegetables. It works well for many herbs, including sage, basil, and parsley. However, a good one is

Hanging herbs from the rafters to dry can add a decorative touch to a room, as at Louise Hyde's Well-Sweep Herb Farm in New Jersey.

pricey and will take up space in your kitchen. You can get similar results, say the experts, from an appliance you already own—the microwave oven. Notorious for its tendency to rob foods of moisture, the microwave does an excellent job of drying herbs.

Place your herbs between two layers of paper towels. Using the medium setting, turn the microwave on for 15 to 20 seconds, check your herbs, and continue to zap them until they are dry. Bertha has had great success drying parsley, fennel, and dill this way, but she warns never to stray far from the machine when it's on. "If you go away," she says, "you could return to a pile of ashes."

Davy Dabney has come up with a simple but successful method of preserving chives. After washing and chopping them, she places them on a cookie sheet, wraps the sheet with clear plastic, and puts it in the freezer. Amy Greving freezes mint, pineapple sage, and parsley. They retain their flavor, she says, but not necessarily their texture. This doesn't matter if you plan to cook with them, but you won't want to use them as garnishes. They'll be mush, says Amy.

Basil freezes well also, says Bertha Reppert, who simply chops it up, mixes it with water, and pours it into an ice cube tray (a process she sometimes uses with mixed herbs). "The basil darkens," she says, "but the flavor remains."

3

FLOWER GARDENING SECRETS

"A beautiful garden is a journey, not a destination"
CLAIRE ACKROYD, MAINE

For many of us, flowers don't just dress the garden; they are the garden. Flowers add color, form, and fragrance to the landscape; they attract brilliant and beneficial pollinators; they brighten shady spots; and they help disguise backyard flaws. Whatever your reason for growing flowers, the experts can make the job easier and more rewarding with advice on designing beds and borders, buying plants, and more.

In this chapter you'll discover the secrets of producing beautiful, healthy, productive flowering plants—plus lots more. Want to grow a garden that's at its best after the sun goes down? Bring birds, bees, and butterflies into the yard? Make a small bed look expansive? Plant antique flowers and ornamental grasses like a pro? Let the experts show you how to tame invasive plants, use groundcovers in the flower bed, design a garden that "blooms" even in winter, and grow brighter and more beautiful bulbs (the secret's so simple, you'll be amazed you never thought of it yourself). If your backyard plans include flowers, the experts will show you how to get the best blooms and the most beautiful beds and borders.

Here's what you'll find in Chapter 3

GOAL DIGGING

Every garden has a purpose, even if it's simply to please the eye. Perhaps you yearn for summer color or a late-blooming fall garden. Maybe you'd like to grow a diversity of flowers for cutting or drying, a vivid butterfly garden, a bed that can provide food for the birds, or a combination of all of these.

Once you've decided on your dream garden, you should choose an appropriate site, says Kim Hawks of North Carolina's Niche Gardens. For example, if you hope to bring butterflies to your backyard, you'll need to locate the bed in a sunny spot, since nearly all the nectar-rich flowers that butterflies feed on require six to eight hours of full sun daily.

GARDEN DESIGN

Occasionally, we come upon a scene in nature so perfect we couldn't improve on it with all the planning and experience in the world. And sometimes we create our best gardens through luck or accident. But more often, a beautiful garden grows out of a good design.

Think Before You Dig

Style • Color • Texture • Height • Composition

When planning a flower garden, most of us think about color, and it's certainly an important feature of any flowerbed. But if you don't also give some consideration to the sizes, textures, and foliage of plants and the overall look you're trying to create, you could end up with disappointing results.

STYLE Do you want a garden that's formal, or maybe even geometric? Or perhaps a cottage garden where annuals and perennials grow together in profusion? Maybe you'd like to plant an elegant single-color flowerbed (like a white garden) or one that looks natural and untamed.

Before you choose your plants, advises Ellen Talmage of Long Island's Horticultural Goddess, Inc., think about style—your own style, the style of your house, and the style of the bed you're designing. Then choose the plants that naturally suit that style. Rambling roses and old-fashioned hollyhocks work well together for a cottage look. Clippable shrubs like boxwood and yew bring geometry to a classic landscape. And dramatic cannas and twining trumpet vine create a tropical feel.

FLOWER COLOR Do you like bright, hot colors like orange, red, and yellow, or are you partial to the cool end of the spectrum—the blues and the violets? Perhaps you're fond of pastels or passionate about pinks or drawn to the serenity of an all-white palette. Plant what you like. But whatever you choose, don't forget the single most important color in the garden: green.

FOLIAGE COLOR In Chesterland, Ohio, home to Peter and Jean Ruh of the Homestead Division of Sunnybrook Farms, most perennial blooms last little more than two weeks, so foliage color is essential to the lasting beauty of the garden. Even in a bed composed mainly of

Old-fashioned yarrow and veronica are allowed to sprawl casually in this informal garden.

The carefully arranged plantings in this bed—including lambs' ears, catmint, and coreopsis—along with the brick walk lend a formal, yet inviting air to the garden.

annuals, foliage shows. And it doesn't have to be green. You can grow plants with silver, gray, red, or maroon leaves, or ones with variegated or multicolor foliage.

TEXTURE The texture of foliage can also help carry a flowerbed when blooms have faded. When choosing plants, think about how the leaves will blend with and complement one another. "The eye is drawn to texture combinations," says Linda Gay of Mercer Arboretum in Texas. "Place large-leaved plants with smaller-leaved plants, feathery foliage with broad, and use swordlike foliage to fill the need for 'vertical green.'"

HEIGHT AND SHAPE Unless you're going for a Victorian bedding-out effect, where low-growing, colorful annuals are planted in masses to create dramatic patterns, use plants of varying heights and shapes. Keep in mind that your tallest plants will form the backbones of the bed, points out Linda.

Combine a variety of shapes, sizes, and plant types for contrast and texture in the garden. Notice how the bold foliage of *Iris pallida* becomes a focal point with its spiky form and intense yellow-green color.

COMPOSITION Cynthia Rice, a landscape architect in North Carolina, looks at her prospective beds with a painterly eye. Think about the overall look of the finished bed just as an artist would the entire effect of a painting. Consider the way color, perspective, texture, rhythm, and repetition all work together.

For North Carolina landscape architect Richard Boggs, a key aspect of composition is the angle (or angles) from which you're likely to view your garden. Even if you plan to "float" your bed in the middle of a lawn, you'll probably look at it most often from a particular spot—the patio, for instance, or a large picture window at the back of the house.

Another crucial element of composition, according to Kim Hawks of North Carolina's Niche Gardens, is repetition. She likes to choose "signature" plants that she places at intervals throughout the garden. In

In this garden, glowing golden torch lilies and purple-leafed cannas add vertical accents to set off the mounded shapes of dahlias and sea lavender.

MEASURE FOR MEASURE

Experts agree that depth from front to back is the most critical measurement in a flower garden.

✦ According to Memphis landscape architect Charles Sandifer, the perfect depth is one that allows you to reach over halfway across the bed from both sides.

✦ If your garden will be viewed from both sides, 6 feet is a good depth, says Cleveland garden designer Bobbie Schwartz. But go a little shallower—5 feet—if the bed is backed by shrubs. Free-standing beds, in which large plants can be massed in the center, can go as deep as 8 feet.

✦ Consider the size of the plants you intend to grow, says North Carolina landscape architect Richard Boggs. A border of rhododendrons, for instance, might be as deep as 30 feet (with a maintenance path). In a bed of bachelor's buttons, though, you wouldn't want to go much deeper than 2 feet.

A tightly clipped boxwood hedge gives a formal feeling to a garden that reflects the look of the wall behind it. Within the confines of the hedge, arching, flowing plants (roses, daisies, and daylilies) provide a contrast to the stiffness of the boxwood border.

her own backyard, a red-hued pygmy barberry and the ornamental grass *Miscanthus sinensis* 'Morning Light' play signature roles, carrying the eye through the landscape and giving the garden a sense of continuity.

SEASON OF BLOOM When Mary Harrison of Mary's Plant Farm in Ohio plans a flowerbed, her single most important consideration is nonstop flower color. She chooses her plants so that she'll have continuous bloom "from the first hellebore to the last berried shrub." Whatever your zone, you should be able to find a selection of plants with staggered seasons of bloom so there's always something flowering, from last to first frost (and perhaps beyond).

POINT OF VIEW If the garden will be viewed from the window of a second or third story, Kim Hawks of North Carolina's Niche Gardens always goes upstairs and looks at it from that perspective. She finds that awkward or off-balance lines will pop out from the bird's-eye perspective.

What's Your Style?

Formal or casual? • *Architectual matching* • *Style mixing*

Broadly speaking, gardens have either a formal or an informal style. Symmetry and geometry reign in the formal garden, and the plants that work best in such designs are those that grow slowly and lend themselves to being shaped easily.

Informal gardens have a wilder look. Beds and borders often curve, taking their cue from the natural landscape. Plants may sprawl or twine or shoot out all over. Informal, however, doesn't mean formless. The same principles that govern the formal garden—balance, repetition, and perspective—also apply to a more natural bed or border.

YOUR BACKYARD SETTING When deciding which way to go, consider the garden's setting, defined by Alan Burke of Seattle's Preview Landscape Architecture as "the architecture of your home and the character of your neighborhood."

Design your garden to complement the style of your home. Here, the garden fits neatly beneath the wide eaves, hugging the contours of the modern architecture.

flower gardening secrets

Bright colors, like the oranges and reds in cinquefoil and marigolds, are energizing.

An unusual color scheme can be dramatic: tall, brown, New Zealand flax; deep purple heliotrope; and pinks.

A cottage garden, for example, would look out of place behind a classic Federal-style house, but would be perfect nestled up against a bungalow. For a modern geometric house, you might consider a Japanese garden for its simplicity and understatement.

Think about the lay of the land, says Ellen Talmage of Long Island's Horticultural Goddess, Inc., If your backyard abuts a forested area, a woodland or bog garden might work best. If you're surrounded by farmland or meadow, consider prairie-garden plantings.

MIXING STYLES What if you like elements of both formal and informal styles? Can you mix the two without aesthetic disaster?

Suzanne Biaggi of California's Sculptured Landscapes, whose own preference is for "understated elegance," cautions against mixing styles, which, she says, "can result in a disjointed and confusing look." Ellen Talmadge, on the other hand, believes that you can get away with a mix by using garden "rooms"—areas of the yard that are separated from one another by plantings or structures. In general, though, she also feels that "style should be consistent."

If you're really drawn to more than one style, Montana landscape architect Carl Thuesen recommends separating gardens of very different styles and creating an area of transition between them. Diane Kostial McGuire, a landscape architect in Rhode Island, offers the following simple rule to mixing styles: "The closer to the house, the more formal the design," she says. "If your bed is set far from the house, it can be quite naturalistic."

David Bar-Zvi of Fairchild Tropical Garden in Miami suggests that formal elements may work well in informal gardens, but not the other way around. "Informal gardens in formal settings tend to look unkempt," he says.

A NOD TO NATURE For most backyards, the experts suggest free-form beds and borders. "In nature, everything meanders," says Angela Fabbri, a San Francisco landscape designer. She finds curves easier on the eye than severe geometric shapes. Ellen Talmage agrees: "Truly straight lines are appropriate in formal gardening, but most people should use gentle curves." Nevertheless, she points out that curves can be overdone. "For example, too many tiny, kidney-shaped beds to match the shape of a pool can look distinctly unnatural," she says.

Color Coordinating

Color wheel wonders • Crafty combinations • Is one color enough?

Colors go in and out of style in the garden just as they do on Paris runways. For years, everyone planted pastels. If your taste ran to bright orange or hot pink, you were out of luck or out of touch. But just as fashion has come to allow for more variety in style, so has gardening. Few gardeners feel compelled to follow the trends. They mix the colors that they like best. However, there are a few guidelines that can help you combine colors that complement rather than clash.

flower gardening secrets

Brilliant red, orange, and gold celosia; magenta impatiens; and red, blue, and white salvia combine to create an eye-popping effect at Queens Botanic Garden. If you think you'd like this type of color scheme, try it first with annuals, as shown here, and live with it for a year or so before investing in perennials.

Color wheels show the relationships between colors. They're useful in planning color combinations, but you don't need to follow them slavishly.

Garden designer Leslie Scott uses purples and blues (catmint, verbena, lobelia, and purple-leaved perilla), colors that are adjacent on the color wheel.

COLOR COMPANIONS One sure way to arrive at companionable colors, according to Virginia nurseryman Andre Viette, is to use a color wheel. Here's how:

• Choose colors directly across the wheel from one another—orange and blue, for example.

• Combine a primary color (red, blue, or yellow) with the colors on either side of its opposite—yellows, for instance, with blues and reds.

• Use three adjacent colors, such as blue, purple, and red.

   Ken Miller of Missouri's Horticultural Consultants is much more straightforward in his approach to color. "If you like a color or a combination, go with it," he says. Barry Glick of West Virginia's Sunshine Farm and Gardens agrees. "I've arrived at some of the best garden combinations through sheer accident," Barry says.

   When you're choosing plants at the garden center, bunch them together and see if you like the result. If you must have two plants whose colors don't blend, use them at different ends of the garden, gradually blending in more harmonious colors until you reach the center. "Don't attempt to 'glue' them together with white," advises Alan Summers of Maryland's Carroll Gardens. "People think white is a great harmonizer of color, but it's not. Instead, whites tend to break up colors," he says.

Silver soothes and blends. The silvery foliage of *Yucca filamentosa* and *Festuca ovina* 'Elijah Blue' can sustain the brightest colors or stand alone.

MASS APPEAL One way to avoid the hassle of color combining, advises Gene Dickson of Prentiss Court Ground Covers, is to use only a few colors in the garden. "Sometimes a solid mass of one type of plant is your best bet," he says.

You can take this concept a step further and plant a single-color garden, in which all the blooms share the same color. To make sure the color doesn't become monotonous, take a tip from Aileen Lubin, director of Maine's Merryspring Park, and mix plants with contrasting foliage textures. She also recommends using bold-looking plants as accents throughout the bed—towering meadow rue in an all-blue garden, for example, or sculptural *Digitalis purpurea* 'Alba' in an all-white border.

Getting an Edge

The best plants for edgings • Proper plantings • Edgings that last forever

If you think of your bed or border as a kind of landscape painting, then an edging is the frame that surrounds it. Like a good frame, edgings should emphasize your plantings but never overwhelm them. Some gardeners use wood, brick, or stone edgings (see also "Pathways" on page 62). They require little or no maintenance and help keep grass

Not every edging comes at the edge of the bed! Here, a whimsical bed is defined by a snaking row of lambs'-ears, alternating with brightly colored annuals.

Easy to find and easy to use, lilyturf creates a soft but uniform border (in this case, to a bed of multicolor ornamental sages). Lilyturf needs little care and looks good from early spring through frost.

out of the flowerbed. But many gardeners prefer the softer look of flowering or foliage plants.

FLOWERY EDGINGS Edging plants should be small and neat, vivid and eye-catching, but they shouldn't steal the floral show from the rest of the planting.

To frame beds and borders effectively with flowers, plant them close enough to give the impression of a single, continuous line, but not so close that they compete with one another for water and nutrients or grow into an unappealing tangle. Ainie Busse of Busse Gardens in Minnesota spaces edging plants so that the spaces between their centers is equal to their mature height.

How far you place edging plants from the rim of the bed or border depends on where you want the plants to end up. If you're using, say, both flowers and stone as edgings, plant right along the outer rim of the soil, says Angela Fabbri, a San Francisco landscape designer. This will allow the flowers to spill over the edging material.

EDGING PLANTS

Among the qualities the experts seek in edging plants is the ability to either stay small and restrained or cascade gracefully over the edge of a bed. The following plants qualify.

EDGINGS FOR SUN			EDGINGS FOR SHADE	
Alyssum	Dwarf sedge	Sanvitalia	Ajuga	Japanese painted fern
Baby blue eyes	Germander	Sedum (especially	Begonia	Lamiastrum 'Herman's Pride'
Begonia	Heliotrope	S. kamtsha-	Candytuft (especially 'Purity')	Lily-of-the-valley
Candytuft	Lamb's-ears	ticum,		Lilyturf
Catmint (especially 'Dropmore Hybrid', 'Blue Wonder')	Marigolds	'Dragon's Blood'	Coral bells	Lobelia 'Aureo-Variegata'
	Mountain sandwort	Sempervivum (hens and chicks)	Fringed bleeding heart	Japanese sedge
	Oregano (especially 'Herren-hausen')	Speedwell, veronica	Dwarf astilbe	Primrose
Cranesbill (hardy geranium)	Parsley	Zinnia (especially Zinnia angustifolia 'Classic White')	Dwarf daylily	Lamium, especially 'Chequers'
	Pinks (especially 'Tiny Rubies')		Dwarf hosta	
Dwarf boxwood	Santolina		Impatiens	

BENDER BOARD Available in redwood, cedar, and plastic, bender board is made from a series of thin blocks strung together loosely so that it will flex around curves. Wood bender board is very flexible, but it tends to rot over time, says Seattle garden designer Sue Moss. If you don't want to replace your edging every couple of years, Angela Fabbri advises using a plastic variety, which has the additional advantage of visually blending into the surrounding landscape.

BRICKS AND TERRA-COTTA Many gardeners use bricks to edge their flowerbeds. Sue Moss likes to place them on end for smoother curves along borders and round beds. (You'll need to sink them slightly into the soil to keep them standing.)

Terra-cotta tiles come in a variety of pretty patterns and work well in either square or curved beds. They were used during the Victorian era and therefore make appropriate edgings for period gardens.

STONE For a natural look, consider stone. You can place it in a single row along the edge of a bed or border, or you can stack it to edge a

Bender board solves edging problems permanently, and at little expense. It's easy to install—just press it into the ground—and it stays where it's put. Use cascading plants to disguise it.

flower gardening secrets

Lavender cotton is rigid and upright, qualities that make it an excellent edging plant for a formal garden, as in this bed at Old Westbury Gardens in Long Island, New York.

DOWNSIZE YOUR PLANTS

As much as you might love towering shrubs and big, bushy perennials, large plants can dwarf a small space. Choose small plants that make big impressions. Richard Boonstra of Ohio's Bluestone Perennials recommends any of the following: 'Dazzler', 'Dotti', 'Tiny Rubies', and 'Spotlight' pinks (Dianthus spp.); 'Tinkerbelle' Shasta daisy (Chrysanthemum leucanthemum), 'Nana' cinquefoil (Potentilla verna); foamflower (Tiarella wherryi); and 'Stella de Oro' daylily (Hemerocallis sp.). Carl Thuesen, a landscape designer in Montana, likes to use tulips, daffodils, and grape hyacinths in smaller gardens, along with hens-and-chicks and periwinkle.

raised bed (see "Raised Beds and Containers" on page 56). Montana landscape architect Carl Thuesen recommends using random pieces of hard sandstone fitted up together and set flush with the ground. "You can run the power mower around them and you'll only need to weed between them once or twice a season," he says. If you're not a fan of weeding, you can set the stones in mortar or concrete, but keep in mind that if you do that, you won't be able to change the contours of your beds.

Ellen Talmage of Long Island's Horticultural Goddess, Inc., likes to use Pennsylvania fieldstone. "It looks natural, especially with plants growing between and on top of the stones to create a cascading look," she says. Kim Hawks of North Carolina's Niche Gardens uses native stone as often as she can.

If your garden is small, don't go too heavy on the stone, says Linda Gay of Mercer Arboretum in Texas. "It can be overpowering if there isn't enough green to offset and balance it," she says.

LANDSCAPE TIMBERS Landscape timbers work best for straight-edged beds. One advantage is that you can use them to create raised beds of virtually any height, says Linda.

METAL Linda also recommends Ryerson steel or prosteel. This 4-inch-high edging, held in place by metal stakes, is a cinch to install and bends easily around curving beds and borders.

PLASTIC EDGING Plastic edging is inexpensive, widely available, and creates an instant edge, but some experts caution against it. "Plastic edgings don't cooperate and can be very frustrating to use—like a telephone cord that's always getting tangled up," says Linda.

"EDGELESS" BEDS You don't have to create an edging at all. Some of the prettiest beds simply have a border of mulched soil. You can define your beds with what Carl Thuesen calls "a clean-cut spade edge." Using a sharp spade or a metal edger, simply dig into the turf at a slight angle all the way around the rim of the bed. You'll probably need to repeat this procedure once or twice during the season and again the following spring, and you'll undoubtedly need to do a little hand-weeding to keep the flowerbed from meandering into the grass (and vice versa).

Even in just 7 feet from end to end, you can make a big impact. Here, a brick pathway divides the space, allowing small, fine-leaved plants—gomphrena, 'Homestead Purple' verbena, and 'Victoria' sage—to share center space with some taller ones, including peacock orchids.

Big Things from Small Spaces

Tricking the eye • Simply does it • Best plants for small spaces

Most of us garden in less space than we'd like, and beds and borders, while enlivening the landscape, tend to make that space look even smaller. To open up your backyard, the experts offer a cache of secrets that don't involve buying up the property next door.

GO FOR CURVES Since a straight line is the shortest distance between two points, it makes sense to eliminate straight lines from your design if you want to make your yard look larger. According to Rhode Island landscape architect Diane Kostial McGuire, rounded shapes and curved lines fool the eye into believing a small space is larger than it really is.

Garden designer Bobbie Schwartz of Bobbie's Green Thumb in Ohio suggests using curved beds and borders to "hide" portions of the yard, pointing out that when we can't see everything at once, we tend to envision the space as larger than it is.

flower gardening secrets

The layered look: Artemisia, feverfew, and chaste tree in just a few feet of space.

Ellen Talmage of Long Island's Horticultural Goddess, Inc., has a neat trick for making the most of a small space: put in a curved path that ends somewhere out of sight. It will look like your garden continues, even if the path ends at your compost pile just around the bend.

LAYER YOUR PLANTS You can make your flowerbeds look deeper by layering your plants, say Philip Steiner of Mellinger's Nursery in Ohio and architect Alan Burke of Seattle's Preview Landscape Architecture. They recommend at least three layers, one in front of another. The secret is to place coarse-leaved plants, such as bearded iris, up front, and then to put taller plants with progressively finer foliage, such as peonies and then Russian sage, behind them. This creates an illusion of a receding plane of vision, says Alan.

To make the whole yard look deeper, plant masses of small-leaved plants like periwinkle in open areas of your property, suggests Ellen Talmage.

This small bed looks fresh and colorful from early spring, when bulbs, catmint, and columbines bloom to late fall, when grasses and 'Autumn Joy' sedum take over. In midsummer, bright gold black-eyed Susans take center stage.

SIMPLIFY Resist the urge to pack as much as possible into a small space, whether that space is a bed, a border, or the whole backyard. Like a tiny living room furnished with overstuffed easy chairs, a small garden planted too intensively can feel claustrophobic.

When you yearn for more but don't have the room, work with "borrowed" scenery—incorporating your neighbor's trees and shrubs into your backyard design, suggests North Carolina landscape architect Cynthia Rice. For example, if an attractive tree stands just outside a corner of your backyard, you could place a bench beneath it and plant a curved border of shade-loving flowers around the bench.

GO VERTICAL To avoid that "overcrowded" look, Tory Galloway of Seattle's Victoria Gardens suggests mixing in a few tall, narrow perennials such as meadow rues (*Thalictrum* spp.) or a columnar holly or boxwood. Vines, too, draw the eye upward, enlarging the space in a different dimension without overwhelming it. Ainee Busse of Minnesota's Busse Gardens recommends any of the clematis vines, with their vivid flowers and delicate foliage. Obelisks and arbors add a great deal to the garden for the little space they take up, too.

Put It in Writing

The power of positive planning • The joys of spontaneity
• The rewards of plant research

Some experts carefully plan their flower gardens on paper, but others find it a bother. "Whether your beds and borders will benefit from a paper plan depends on how your brain works," says Ken Miller of Missouri's Horticultural Consultants.

TO PLOT OR NOT If you're designing a large landscape that will include garden structures, trees, and large shrubs, a paper plan is indispensable. It's less so if you're putting in a flower garden, says Kris Bachtell of Morton Arboretum in Illinois. "Because the plants are small, it's easy to move them around to different locations after they've been planted," he says.

Seattle garden designer Sue Moss always graphs out her flower gardens, marking down everything down to the finest detail. This can be very helpful if you're the sort of person who can mentally translate

---

A PAPER PLAN

To plot the designs of your beds and borders, get some graph paper. In most cases, use the standard scale of 1 inch=1 foot. (To include greater detail, Seattle garden designer Sue Moss advises using a scale between 1 to 4 inches per foot.)

☙ Mark down all the plants you intend to grow, but don't make the mistake of graphing them at their present size. "The most common error in most landscapes is that too many plants are planted in the allotted space," says Kris Bachtell of the Morton Arboretum in Illinois. He suggests you estimate the size of the plants in four to five years' time.

☙ Don't forget to include long- and short-distance views and any walkways, paths, arbors, and fences. Donald Buma of Wichita's Botanica even marks the trash cans in his layout.

flower gardening secrets

TRACING TIP

To make creating a graph-paper plan as painless as possible, Virginia nurseryman Andre Viette suggests using tracing paper as an overlay. Once you've achieved the right effect on your overlay, you can transfer it to your final plan. You may want to use several sheets of tracing paper, says Andre, so that you can color the garden plants as they'll look in the various seasons.

a graph into a garden. "Some people can see a finished space in their heads, but it takes practice," says Ken Miller.

If you like the idea of starting with a plan, but you aren't the plotting kind, consider Ken's approach. Instead of graphing the design, he sits in front of the projected garden space and makes a sketch of the finished garden. "I'm not making a plan. I'm drawing it as if it were art," he says.

Nelson Sterner of Old Westbury Gardens in New York adds another layer to his planning: he researches plant material before he starts sketching his designs. "All too often we draw our dream gardens and then find we can't get the plants we planned on using," he says.

WINGING IT There are those gardeners—you may be among them—who just don't like to plan at all. "Take heart—the flowerbed is the best place to try out new ideas and not get too focused on a fixed plan," says Alan Burke of Seattle's Preview Landscape Architecture. Alan suggests that home gardeners start out by planting whatever catches their eye, then removing rampant growers and anything that doesn't thrive. It may take you a little longer to achieve a finished look this way, but you're bound to enjoy the journey.

Though Ken Twombley of Connecticut's Twombley Nursery draws up plans if his customers insist, he prefers not to. "Our own five acres were created as we went along," he says. "Garden design is an art form. You keep adding as you see it developing."

KNOW YOUR PLANTS Alan Summers of Maryland's Carroll Gardens thinks mapping out your design on paper can be helpful, but he believes that the most important thing you can do to plan for a successful flower garden is to research each plant you're considering before buying anything. "A lot of people follow the 'little red wagon' method of landscaping. They walk around a garden center and plop whatever looks good that day into the wagon," he says. The problem with this approach, says Allan, is that no effort is made to use plants that look good the whole summer or fill in each other's gaps, so the finished garden is likely to be a jumble. You don't need to spend a day at the library researching plants—a good garden center can give you nearly all the information you'll need, and most are happy to do so.

Making Your Mark

Ways to outline your garden • Hoses and how to use them

Once you've decided on the size and overall shape of your bed or border, you'll need to trace its final outline in the yard before you start digging. Any one of the following methods can make tracing a bed as simple as connecting the dots.

STAKES AND TWINE You can use twine to trace the bed and then place stakes at regular intervals to hold the twine in place. Or try one of these variations:

•North Carolina landscape architect Richard Boggs prefers wire flags to stakes for their visibility.

•On straight-edge beds, Robert Caughlan of Caughlan & Son Landscapes in California uses thick twine, which he stakes only once, at either end.

•Tory Galloway of Seattle's Victoria Gardens says parachute cord is extremely easy to use. It's thin, flexible, and doesn't break.

Garden designer Bobbie Schwartz plants late-blooming daisies, asters, and fountain grass (*Miscanthus sinensis* 'Adagio') to keep her border looking fresh and colorful well into fall.

Straight lines and symmetrical beds may look rigid when they're first dug, but when they're filled with annuals, the strict geometric forms will be softened by the plant life.

Curvaceousness is easy to achieve in flowerbeds. Form your curve with garden hoses, stakes and twine, lime, or special spray paint, then plant along your marks.

GARDEN HOSE One of the most popular tracing tools—probably because every backyard has one—is the garden hose. You can easily bend it to the form and shape you desire, and you don't have to stake it. "When you use a hose, you can change your mind several times without having to make repairs or apologies," says Linda Gay of Mercer Arboretum in Texas. Plus, the bright color of the hose makes it easy to see what the final bed will look like, says David Graper of the University of South Dakota. After he's satisfied with the bed shape, he uses a hoe to follow the contours of the hose.

To make the hose even easier to work with, Kris Bachtell of the Morton Arboretum in Illinois lets it warm for an hour or so in the sun. Here's his secret for creating a natural, easy-to-maintain outline: "Run your lawn mower (power off) along the hose's edge to see if you can easily maneuver around curves. If they're too tight, reposition the hose and do the test again."

LIME Ellen Talmage of Long Island's Horticultural Goddess, Inc., likes to trace her beds with lime—it's inexpensive and easily correctable. Philip Steiner of Mellinger's Nursery in Ohio simply sprinkles his lime from a pot.

SPRAY PAINT Spray paint is a very easy and effective tool for marking off bed and border outlines, but it's devilish to erase. The experts advise using it only after you've achieved a satisfactory outline with any of the methods mentioned above. After making her initial contours with a hose, Linda Gay sprays just outside the hose for a final outline. Make sure that the paint can has an inverted spray tip for ease of aiming, says Alan Burke of Seattle's Preview Landscape Architecture. And only use special turf paint; other paint will damage plant material.

BLOOMING BEDS AND BORDERS

You only have to look at a few catalogs or visit a garden center or two to realize the spectacular array of flowers and foliage plants that are available. There are blooms of every hue and leaves of every texture. Each year, new plants are introduced. Some that have fallen into obscurity return to the limelight. It's exciting to explore the many options. As you do so, consider how you plan to use your garden and what sorts of effects you hope to achieve.

Beauty That Lasts

Long-term bloomers • Foliage plants • Bloom after bloom

Every flower garden seems to have a peak month, when annuals and perennials push their way into bloom and the foliage on every plant looks crisp and fresh. How you wish you could keep that busting-out-all-over look going through spring, summer, and fall! The experts say you can, if you choose the right plants.

Here are two perennials that bloom profusely from early summer to frost: purple *Veronica alpina* 'Goodness Grows' (far left) and pale yellow *Coreopsis verticillata* 'Moonbeam'.

LONG-BLOOMERS

Most perennials produce flowers for only two to three weeks. Matt Horn, owner of New York's Matterhorn Nursery, recommends the following sun-loving beauties for their longer bloom time.

Frickart's aster
Black-eyed Susan
Carpathian harebell
Checkerblooms
Purple coneflowers
Ozark sundrops
False sunflower
Garden phlox
Gaura
Obedient plant
Painted daisy
Pincushion flower
Plumbago
Russian sage
Shasta daisy
Tickseed
Veronica

Many perennials, including pinks, columbines, and phlox, will rebloom if they are pruned back after their first blossoms fade.

CHOOSE LONG-SEASON PLANTS Many perennial flowers perform dramatically for a very short period—usually two to three weeks—and then fade into the general green. Even foliage plants may have a relatively short period of glory. But some perennials produce heavy bloom and vibrant greenery for months.

Donald Buma of Wichita's Botanica relies on a few long-term beauties to keep his flower garden looking good all season. He likes Siberian irises (especially 'Caesar's Brother') and peonies for their good spring color and wonderful all-season foliage. (Peony foliage doesn't stay beautiful in the South, though.) If you're a fan of daylilies but don't like the sad-looking leaves after they bloom, Donald has an inspired suggestion: Since daylily foliage tends to look terrific before blooming, simply plant the late-blooming varieties. He also recommends Siam tulip (not a tulip at all, in fact, but a member of the ginger family), which blooms from spring to fall. And if you live in a dry region where blackspot isn't a problem, roses that repeat-bloom offer brilliant color from June through frost.

Alan Summers of Maryland's Carroll Gardens says his favorite long-season perennials are candytuft ("It looks good all summer except for the brief period when you cut it back," he says), and some of the perennial geraniums, including *Geranium macrorrizum* and *G.* × *cantabrigiense*. Robert Herman of White Flower Farm recommends 'Coronation Gold' yarrow and 'Moonbeam' coreopsis for both their reliability and extended period of bloom. (For more perennials that keep on blooming, see "Long Bloomers" at left.)

USE FOLIAGE PLANTS "Blooms come and go. For long-term beauty, rely on foliage plants," says Frank Peterson of Tennessee's Good Hollow Greenhouse and Herbarium. His favorites are pampas grass and lamb's ears, but in your own garden (depending on zone and light exposure), you might want to try ferns, hostas, dusty miller, or wild ginger. Or seek out your own green, silver, red, or variegated beauties.

CHOOSE SUCCESSIVE BLOOMERS "If you want long-term bloom, it's better to link plants that will form a longer bloom pattern than to rely on one plant for a long season," advises Don L. Jacobs of Eco-Gardens in Georgia. In his own garden, a scutelaria called 'Eco Blue-Blaze' blooms in late August and fills in for earlier-blooming daisies. A popular combination for long-season interest, says Steve Frowine, is daffodils followed by daylilies, and if you choose a selection of daylilies with staggered bloom periods, you can actually have flowers from April through August. (For more on plant combining, see "Plant Partners," below.)

Plant Partners

Considering color, texture, and shape • Clever combinations for multiseason magic

A successful garden is more than a collection of plants. No matter how pretty they may be individually, the plants that make up your garden must work together as a harmonious whole, or the effect will be disjointed and confusing.

Sometimes, great combinations are made up of dozens of plants, artfully juxtaposed and intertwined, but that's not always necessary. Dale Hendricks of Pennsylvania's North Creek Perennials recommends choosing a few favorite flowers and planting them in masses.

Sometimes, one or two plants are all you need. Here, a row of daylilies is accentuated by balloon flowers—the similar shapes of the two plants blend well, but the balloon flowers add a touch of blue, a color not available in daylilies.

Soft, feathery *Pennisetum setaceum* 'Rubrum' provides color and texture contrast to the bright, tight blossoms of French marigolds. Both are annuals, so this combination can be achieved with only a few weeks lead-time.

"Don't create 'collections' (beds made up of one each of a great many plants)," he says. They look cluttered and unplanned.

COLOR COMBINATIONS You can easily create an effective combination based on flower or foliage color. For example, you could plant flowers of varying hues of a particular color. Illinois horticulturist Diane Noland achieves a harmonious mix with pale lavender chives and dark purple Siberian iris. Or look for color "echoes." Kim Hawks of North Carolina's Niche Gardens has brought together Japanese painted ferns with burgundy-foliaged 'Pewter Veil' heuchera. The rosy highlights in the painted ferns subtly echo the burgundy in the leaves of the heuchera.

For a really dramatic combination, choose flowering plants of contrasting or complementary colors. Gail Korn of Nebraska's Garden Perennials likes to interplant red-and-yellow 'Goblin' gaillardias, yellow 'Sunray' coreopsis, scarlet-bloomed maltese cross, and 'Sunny Border Blue' veronica for a spectacular patchwork of primary colors.

Kim Hawks likes the selective use of silver-foliaged plants, which she places throughout the garden. "Silver makes anything beside it look brighter and better," she says.

TEXTURE COMBINATIONS In addition to color, consider the texture of foliage when combining plants. You can create the greatest effect with contrast. A nearly foolproof combination, according to North Carolina landscape architect Richard Boggs, is a mix of plants with coarse- and fine-textured foliage. Aileen Lubin, director of Maine's Merryspring Park, plants bluebells and snowdrop anemone in her shady spring garden. Even without the pretty blue-and-white blooms, the bluebells' fleshy, grasslike foliage looks dramatic next to the finely cut leaves of the anemone.

SHAPE COMBINATIONS Think, too, about the shapes of plants. Again, go for contrast. Ellen Talmage of New York's Horticultural Goddess, Inc., plants black-eyed Susans with *Pennisetum setaceum* 'Rubrum' (red fountain grass). The black-eyed Susans have a rounded shape overall, which creates a dramatic counterpoint to the narrow arching foliage of the grass.

It lasts as long as spring or summer: Why shouldn't your garden be attractive throughout fall? Holly, fountain grass, and *Sedum* 'Autumn Joy' combine to keep your garden looking beautiful until hard frost, and even after it.

OLDIES BUT GOODIES

Bring back the beauty of long-ago gardens with some of these antique flowers.

Bleeding heart
Bells-of-Ireland
Christmas rose (hellebore)
Columbines
Corn-cockle
English primrose
Gillyflower (stock)
Hollyhock
Lady's-mantle
Lungwort
Lupine
Nicotiana
Pulmonaria
Rugosa rose

MULTISEASON COMBINATIONS To keep your perennial garden colorful for a full season, you'll need to combine plants of varying bloom times. And because many perennials don't look their best all season long, it's important to find plants that will hide their neighbors' shortcomings. Kim Hawks recommends combining hostas with 'Pictum' arum. Both plants have large, broad leaves but different peak seasons. "Hostas take center stage midspring through frost," explains Kim. "In the fall, when the hostas die down, the arum comes up and stays up all winter."

Blasts from the Past

Not just for nostalgia • Antiques vs. hybrids

Old-fashioned flowers—those that graced our grandmothers' gardens, and their grandmothers' before them—are experiencing a resurgence in the American landscape. Planting them in your garden will bring back their ancient beauty, but it may revive some old problems, as well.

Hollyhocks form the backbone of an old-fashioned bed at Old Westbury Gardens in Long Island, New York. Other antique flowers in the bed include culver's root, pinks, and catmint.

ANTIQUE VIRTUES Nostalgia alone would be reason enough to grow antique flowers. Hollyhock, lupine, primrose, and poppy inhabited our parents' childhoods and twined through our fairy tales. "Antique flowers allow people to see and smell things from the past," says Ellen Talmage of New York's Horticultural Goddess, Inc., But old-fashioned flowers offer more tangible benefits, as well.

Alan Branhagen, director of Missouri's Powell Garden, likes antique flowers for their hardiness, insect- and disease-resistance, and general substance. Some new varieties, he points out, have been overbred, so that their huge, sometimes ungainly flowers sit on top of flimsy stems that can barely hold them up. Another advantage to antique flowers, says Bobbie Holder of Wyoming's Pawnee Greenhouse and Nursery, is that they tend to be true to seed (producing flowers of the same color and general type as the parent plant). And Frederick Held of Nature's Garden in Oregon likes them for their fragrance, a property often bred out of modern hybrids.

A FEW FLAWS Among the disadvantages of antique flowers, according to Bobbie Holder, are aggressiveness, legginess, and a short period of bloom, "qualities that have been engineered away in modern hybrids,"

Billowing drifts of poppies, catmint, and other old-fashioned flowers in soft shades of pink and purple are planted along an unpaved pathway to create an informal garden style.

Choose groundcovers to fit your site and your needs. *Euphorbia dulcis* 'Chameleon' (top) needs full sun; its deep purple foliage keeps its color through the winter. Sweet woodruff is invaluable in shady spots with dainty leaves that provide coverage and interest, and tiny white flowers in early spring.

she says. Though it might not be wise to plant your garden exclusively with antique flowers, a few favorites make a lovely addition to the landscape.

Covering Ground

Choosing appropriately • Planting in sun and shade • Groundcovers for large spaces

Groundcovers grow low, spread quickly, and do an excellent job of covering large areas or difficult sites, such as dry banks where little else will grow. Some, however, bring a nice touch to the flower garden. They're especially useful if you have large beds or borders, but a few work well even in smaller gardens, as edgings or front-of-the-border plants. Ken Twombley of Connecticut's Twombley Nursery uses groundcovers instead of mulch to fill in holes in his flowerbeds and borders. Be wary, though—some groundcovers will take over a garden, and others aren't sufficiently ornamental.

FOR SUNNY BEDS If you have a sunny site to cover, Donald Buma of Wichita's Botanica recommends golden creeping Jenny (*Lysimachia nummularia* 'Aurea') and waterperry speedwell (*Veronica* × 'Waterperry'). "They stay low and aren't aggressive," he says. Gene Dickson of Prentiss Court Ground Covers likes lily turf for its dramatic striped, grasslike foliage and pretty purple flowerstalks.

FOR SHADY BEDS Many groundcovers perform beautifully in shade. Barry Glick of West Virginia's Sunshine Farm and Gardens recommends *Meehania cordata*. "It has nice 1-inch green leaves, trumpet-shaped pink flowers in spring, it stays low, and it's evergreen," he says. "And not only will it grow in dry shade, it will grow in the dark." Ken Twombley's picks for shade include spotted dead nettle (an offputting name for a very pretty plant, *Lamium maculatum*), Allegheny pachysandra (*Pachysandra procumbens*), vinca (periwinkle), and ajuga (bugleweed). In Southern Florida, mondo grass, peperomia, and wandering Jew are used.

FOR LARGE BEDS AND BORDERS Aggressiveness can be a virtue if you have lots of ground to cover. Ken Miller of Missouri's Horticultural Consultants recommends the following quick-spreading groundcovers for large gardens: monkey grass, green stachys, fernleaf tansy, stephanandra, lady's-mantle, and the ajugas (the giant ones, he says, are easier to keep in bounds because they pull easily). Another choice for quick coverage, says Donald Buma, is 'Siskiyou' evening primrose.

Night Life

Colors you can see in the dark • *Perfuming the night air*

Do you wish you had more time to enjoy the flower garden? Take a cue from the experts, and plant an evening garden that you can enjoy after the sun has set. You'll probably want to install some garden lighting (see "Lighting" on page 64), but there are other ways to make your beds and borders "shine" after dark.

REFLECTION Dark colors absorb light and pale colors reflect it, which is why you need to consider color first when choosing flowers for a night garden. "Whites and pastels, either in flowers or foliage, always read better in the night landscape," says Kim Hawks of North Carolina's Niche Gardens. Bobbie Schwartz of Bobbie's Green Thumb in Ohio agrees and recommends white and pale pink flowers. She suggests growing a pale rose such as 'Climbing Iceberg' on an arch that you and your guests can walk through. She also likes to use plants with silvery foliage such as 'Powis Castle' artemisia.

White tulips and sweet alyssum light up the spring night.

Here's a garden that is as inviting at night as it is during the day. White petunias and double feverfew sparkle in the moonlight and the scent of the white roses in the back-ground fills the air.

THE NIGHT GARDEN

To help you plant an evening garden, the experts offer a selection of their top choices.

Plants that reflect light
Cardoon
Clematis (white and pastel)
Daphne
Evening primrose
Four-o'clocks (yellow)
Globeflower
Hostas (white- and yellow-variegated)
Lacecap hydrangea
Lilies (especially madonna lily, regal lily, 'Bright Star', 'Gold Band', 'Casa Blanca', and Easter lily)
Lily-of-the-valley
Scotch thistle
Shasta daisy
Verbena canadensis (white)
'The Pearl' yarrow

Fragrant plants
Daturas
Flowering tobacco (especially Nicotiana alata and Nicotiana sylvestris)
Hostas (especially 'So Sweet' and Hosta plantaginea)
Lantana
Lily-of-the-valley
Night phlox
Roses
Tuberose

If you want to surprise your friends and dazzle them with some silver-leaved plants, do as Alan Branhagen, director of Missouri's Powell Garden. does—plant a few artichokes. "Even where the growing season isn't long enough for them to produce their edible, thistlelike flowers, artichokes are well worth growing as foliage annuals," he says.

Yellow is another color that jumps out of the evening landscape. Peter and Jean Ruh of the Homestead division of Sunnybrook Farm in Chesterland, Ohio, recommend yellow hostas—especially *Hosta* 'Fragrant Moon' and *Hosta* 'Moonglow'. And for optimum drama, Ken Twombley of Connecticut's Twombley Nursery likes anything with white variegation, especially caladiums.

FRAGRANCE The second most important consideration in the evening garden, says Kim Hawks, is fragrance. If you can't see the flowers, at least you can smell them. In fact, there's a whole group of plants whose flowers don't open until late afternoon or early evening, and most of these—like climbing moonflower—use pale or pastel colors and intense fragrance to attract the moths that pollinate them. Jasmine, night-bloom cactus, and datura offer intoxicating aromas.

"I plant low herbs such as rosemary and salvias along the edge of a path so that if you happen to brush against them, they'll emit their wonderful fragrances," says Kim. Another plant that's highly aromatic when brushed or touched, says Richard Boonstra of Ohio's Bluestone Perennials, is calamint, which has lavender flowers in early summer that are reflective, as well.

Winter Wonders

Evergreens for every season • Stems and berries in the snow • Hardy flowers

If your flowerbeds and borders look a bit forlorn in winter, take heart. There are ways to keep your gardens bright during the year's dark days.

ADD EVERGREENS If you have the room, try using some small evergreen plants, such as dwarf boxwoods or hollies, in the flower garden. Gene Dickson of Prentiss Court Ground Covers suggests evergreen groundcovers, including pachysandra ("It's often denigrated, but it's a great plant," he says), and English ivy.

THINK STEMS AND BERRIES Many plants have handsome stems and produce beautiful berries in winter, says Frank Peterson of Good Hollow Greenhouse and Herbarium in Tennessee. Alan Summers of Maryland's Carroll Gardens likes winterberry—a small holly that loses its leaves but keeps its brilliant red berries all through the winter.

Donald Buma of Wichita's Botanica recommends any of the ornamental grasses, 'Autumn Joy' sedum (the snow looks stunning on the flat dried flowerheads), and black-eyed Susan ("the centers stay black all winter," says Donald). Red-osier dogwood (*Cornus sericea*), with bright red twigs, and and gold-twigged *Cornus serecia* 'Flavirama' brighten any winter landscape.

PICK COLD-HARDY PLANTS For a flower garden that's interesting year round, Alan Summers suggests winter heaths. In the right spot, these low-growing, shrubby plants are never out of season, he says. Donald Buma's cold-season favorite is pansies. "If you plant them in a protected area, they'll bloom right through winter. If the temperature goes down to 10°F they'll flop over, but they'll come back up when it gets warmer," he says.

For late-winter and very early-spring color, Alan Summers recommends bulbs. He plants his perennial beds with a multitude of Thomasiana crocus (*C. Tomasinianus*, a species crocus) and gets a carpet of brilliant color in early spring. "If I dig in the perennial beds, I sometimes accidentally slice the crocus bulbs right in half, and they still grow," he says.

Cotoneaster berries are a feast for the eyes and for visiting wildlife all through winter.

Design a garden with winter in mind. Evergreens, red-twigged dogwood, and gold-twigged willow add color through the colder months.

BEAUTY AND THE BULB

For sheer drama, nothing beats the showiness of bulbs. You'll also find that they're easy to plant, require little maintenance, and there's a wide selection to choose from beyond the old standbys like tulips, daffodils, and dahlias.

For Every Bulb a Season

How important is soil temperature? • Shelf life • Overeager fall bloomers

The timing of bulb plantings can be a bit worrisome, especially when the bulbs are spring bloomers and need to go into the ground in fall. Is August too early? November too late? What if you don't get your bulbs into the ground exactly when recommended? Here's what to do.

Tulips add height and excitement to low-growing spring bloomers like creeping phlox.

If you haven't discovered ornamental alliums yet, perhaps the time has come. Dozens of different species, such as the flamboyant blue, burgundy, and lavender ones shown here, provide accents from early to late summer. Many alliums are tall and perfectly round—perfect foils for a reflective gazing ball.

SPRING BLOOMERS For bulbs that bloom in spring—including daffodils, tulips, crocuses, and hyacinths—fall is the time to plant. But fall officially lasts three months, and can be longer or shorter depending on where you live. So when, exactly, is the right time to plant?

"It depends on your zone," says Jan Ohms of Van Engelen, one of the country's largest bulb importers. Shane Smith, director of Wyoming's Cheyenne Botanic Garden, starts planting daffodils at the end of August. In San Francisco, on the other hand, Anthony Skittone of Greenlady Gardens doesn't even begin until October and is still putting in the last of his bulbs when his neighbors are decorating for the holidays.

Don't be in a rush to plant, the experts agree. It's important to let the ground cool before the bulbs go in. "If the soil isn't cool enough, the bulbs won't make roots, but they will make topgrowth that can be damaged in severe winter weather," says Anthony. Damaged topgrowth can leave bulbs susceptible to fungal and other diseases later in the growing cycle.

In addition, different bulbs require different planting times. Scott Kunst of Michigan's Old House Gardens hierloom bulbs catalog recommends the following method of staggered planting. Start by putting in smaller bulbs, such as crocuses, snowdrops, and grape hyacinths. Not only do these bulbs dry out more quickly, but because they require shallow planting, you want to get them in the ground and give them a chance to send out roots before a cold snap freezes the top layer of soil and stops root growth. After the small bulbs, plant daffodils and hyacinths. "They like a longer rooting time than tulips," says Scott. End your staggered planting with tulips, which prefer cooler soil. (A preplanting tip from Maryland bulb grower Kitty Washburne: If any of your smaller bulbs appear dry after shipping, soak them in tepid water overnight before planting. This will plump them up, and it won't hurt the bulbs. Sometimes, though, very dry bulbs are really dead, and soaking won't bring them back to life.)

SUMMER BLOOMERS Most summer-blooming bulbs, including lilies, can be planted in either spring or fall, but make sure the soil is not frozen, says Dianna Gibson. On the other hand, it shouldn't be too warm; if planted in warm ground, bulbs will begin to put out top

Some of the most beautiful bulbs wait for the end of the season to bloom. *Colchicum* 'Waterlily' has large, double flowers and is just one of several autumn crocuses that can perk up a fading garden. The trick is to plant them in late summer.

flower gardening secrets

Mike Ruggiero has perfected a method of planting the tulips that make up the New York Botanical Garden's spring display. In late fall, staff members string ribbons across the prepared beds, separating colors and shapes. Bulbs are planted according to the desired pattern within each ribboned-off section.

growth, when you really want them to put down roots. In warm climates, most bulbs are best planted in spring. In cold climates, tender bulbs, like glads, cannas, and dahlias, must be planted in spring. Scott Kunst doesn't plant his tender bulbs outdoors until June, but he sometimes starts them inside. Plants ordered from a reputable catalog should arrive more or less at the right time for planting. If you're putting in lilies, try to plant them as soon after they arrive as possible, since lily bulbs are never really dormant, says Dianna Gibson of B & D Lilies.

What if your bulbs arrive and you just don't have time to plant them? Dianna advises keeping the bulbs in their poly shipping bags in a cool but not frozen area of your garage or basement, or in your refrigerator. (The ideal storage temperature ranges from 34 to 40°F.) They'll keep this way for two to three weeks.

FALL BLOOMERS Fall-blooming bulbs, such as saffron crocuses and autumn crocuses, create a wonderful splash of bright color in an otherwise waning season. But make sure you get these temperamental bulbs in the ground right away. "Their shelf life is extremely short, and they should be planted as soon as they arrive," says Jan Ohms. They're so anxious to begin flowering, he says, that they'll often bloom right in the shipping box. If you're buying fall bloomers at the garden center, Jan recommends that you avoid any that show topgrowth.

How Low Should a Bulb Go?

The proper depth • Methods of planting • Some special techniques • Intelligent interplanting

To cut hours off your planting time and get the healthiest, showiest blooms, you need only a follow a few expert tips and one very basic formula.

THE RIGHT DEPTH Not sure how deep to plant a given bulb? Scott Kunst says to set the bottom of the bulb at a depth two to three times the bulb's height; use the two-times ratio for larger bulbs, the three times for small ones. For instance, if you're planting a 1-inch crocus bulb, set the bottom of the bulb at a depth of 3 inches. The bottom of a 2½-inch tulip bulb would sit 6 to 8 inches below the soil. According to Anthony Skittone of San Francisco's Greenlady Gardens, the appropriate depth for most small bulbs averages about 3 to 4 inches, with some very small bulbs going down only an inch or so and a few extra-large bulbs sitting as deep as 9 inches.

This formula works best in average soils. In heavy soil, plant slightly shallower, and in sandy soil, plant slightly deeper. (If you're not sure about your soil type, err slightly on the deep side.)

PLANTING METHODS You can plant spring-flowering bulbs in one of two ways. The first involves digging a large area, setting the bulbs in place, and covering them with soil. The second is to dig individual holes for each bulb—a better method if you want to create a natural effect in a lawn or open woodland (see "Bountiful Bulbs" on page 184).

flower gardening secrets

The payoff: When the bulbs at the New York Botanical Garden bloom, they are neatly arranged; their colors and patterns form a spectacular display. This works just as well with 50 or 100 bulbs in your home garden.

BOUNTIFUL BULBS

"Naturalizing" is the ability of bulbs to multiply and spread on their own, with no help from the gardener. Bulbs naturalize by producing offshoots—"baby" bulbs that grow from the base of the parent bulb—or by casting seed. Some bulbs naturalize readily, while others never multiply.

Of all the spring-blooming bulbs, says Anthony Skittone of San Francisco's Greenlady Gardens, the easiest to naturalize are daffodils. Make sure that the variety you choose is reliably hardy in your zone.

You can do this with a bulb planter (a tool specially designed for planting individual bulbs) or with a spade. An auger also works well.

The most enjoyable way to plant a large number of bulbs, says Dotti Schultz of McClure & Zimmerman, is to enlist the assistance of a gardening friend. One person steps on a spade to the desired depth and rocks it back and forth a few times; this creates a "half-moon" hole. While that person pushes the spade forward to open the hole, the other person presses a bulb into the hole. If you're planting smaller bulbs, says Maryland bulb grower Kitty Washburne, you can plant more than one in a single hole. After pulling the spade out of the hole, simply firm the soil with your foot (don't do this if you have heavy clay soil). You'll be amazed at the speed with which you can cover a large expanse of lawn this way.

Make sure you don't set your bulbs in the ground upside down, says

This small bed will remain attractive even when the tulips are just a memory because the bulbs are interplanted with colorful annuals and perennials.

Kitty, or they may not grow. The bottom of the bulb is generally flatter than the top and will often bear the remnants of last year's roots. If you can't reliably determine which end is up, she suggests planting the bulb on its side. A bulb will right itself from a sideways position, but not from completely upside down.

Jan Ohms of Van Engelen says his secret for spectacular spring bloom is to plant all bulbs in filtered shade. "Because the temperatures stay cooler, the flowers last longer and the colors are much more vibrant." he says.

TENDER LILIES Certain bulbs require more careful handling when you plant them—lilies, in particular. If you've prepared new raised beds in the fall, don't plant them with lilies until the following spring. "The soil will be too fluffy, with too many air pockets," says Dianna Gibson of B & D Lilies. "If you get a really deep freeze, the lily bulbs will die."

Lily bulbs also don't like to be pierced, which can easily happen when staking taller varieties. Dianna suggests placing a short stake in the ground next to each lily bulb as you plant it. If you find later that you need to stake the plant, you can pull out the old, short stake and insert a new, taller one in the same hole without any danger of cracking the bulb.

TEMPERAMENTAL TULIPS Among the spring bloomers, tulips are the least reliable, often refusing to bloom after their first year in the ground, and almost certainly losing their luster after two or three seasons. Winter cold isn't the culprit; it's our desire for bigger, brighter, flashier blooms. To get those spectacular flowers, hybridizers have had to sacrifice rebloom. It may be a decent enough tradeoff, but you don't have to settle for it. Many experts, including Alice Hosford of Bulb Crate in Illinois, have found that deep planting encourages rebloom. The trick, says Kitty Washburne, is to choose the hardier tulips— either Emperor or Darwin—plant them deep, and provide them with good drainage and lots of sun. Kitty plants her tulips at least 8 to 12 inches deep ("the further north you live, the deeper you should plant"), and they continue to bloom for 10 to 15 years. Deep planting also discourages squirrels. Here's Kitty's secret for growing extra-showy tulips: "Plant the flat side of the bulb forward. The stem will be covered by the main leaf, and you'll get a much prettier effect," she

THE HARDY ONES

"There's a wide range of hardiness among daffs," says Scott Kunst of Michigan's Old House Gardens catalog, who warns that catalogs and garden centers can be overly optimistic in their definitions of hardiness. "Lots of plants are sold that can't, in fact, overwinter in the zones listed," says Scott. "Take 'Pencrobar'. It's a daffodil with jonquil blood, and jonquils aren't hardy."

Linda Gay of Mercer Arboretum in Texas recommends 'Fortune', 'Ice Follies', 'Liberty Bells' 'Soleil d'Or', 'Erlicheer' daffodils.

Other reliable naturalizers include alliums, crocuses, Dutch iris, grape hyacinths, Siberian squill, summer snowflake, and the species tulips Tulipa clusiana and T. chrysantha.

says. This is especially effective in pots because it makes the large leaf cascade over the pot's edge.

There is, however, a limit to how deep you can plant. Scott Kunst of Michigan's Old House Gardens catalog remembers a customer who bought a large number of tulip bulbs from him and, having heard that deep planting could perennialize tulips, proceeded to set them all at 18 inches in the ground. Not a single one came up. Eight inches down is deep enough, says Scott

COMBINING BULBS If you love the colorful look of an interplanting of several bulb varieties, or if you want to extend the season of bloom, plant bulbs in layers, advises Kitty Washburne. Most spring bloomers grow quite beautifully from layered plantings. Plant the largest ones (daffodils, for example) 10 to 12 inches deep. Cover them with a few inches of soil, and then place medium-size bulbs, such as hyacinths and tulips, on top. Cover those with soil, and plant your smallest bulbs—crocuses, glory-of-the-snow, grape hyacinths—on the very top. Spread the final layer of soil over them.

Though most bulbs grow well in groups, not all take well to crowding. Lilies, says Kitty, like their space. Plant them at least a foot apart. A few bulbs are, as Linda Gay of Mercer Arboretum in Texas puts it, "space hogs." They tend to quickly take over a site, given conditions that suit them. These include Siberian squill, freesias, and tuberoses.

Weathering Winter

Bulbs for northern and southern climates • Storing bulbs during the winter

Most of the commonly grown spring bulbs overwinter successfully in the ground. In fact, nearly all require a period of cold in order to bloom again the following year. For this reason, southern gardeners need to choose their bulbs (including lilies) carefully, making sure that they're zone-appropriate. Tender bulbs, such as cannas, tuberous begonias, glads, and caladiums, don't tolerate freezing temperatures. They can stay in the ground year-round in southern gardens, but they'll need to be dug up before winter in northern climates.

DIG OR DISCARD? Even if you live in the North, a little winter cold shouldn't deter you from growing tender bulbs. If you don't want to go

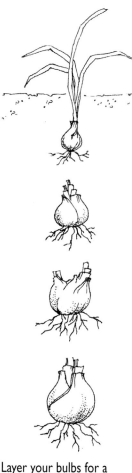

Layer your bulbs for a profusion of blossoms through spring. Plant the biggest ones deepest—up to 12 inches deep for big tulips and daffodils—and leave about an inch between bulbs, with the smallest ones planted just below the surface.

Store tender bulbs over winter by letting them dry completely and covering them in sand or perlite.

to the trouble of storing them over the winter, most are inexpensive enough that you can throw them onto the compost pile without too much guilt. "You don't dig up and save your annuals in the fall, and you probably spend as much on them as you would on tender bulbs," points out Scott Kunst of Michigan's Old House Gardens catalog. (The same logic applies to cold-hardy bulbs in southern climates.)

However, if you can't stand the thought of discarding bulbs, plant tender bulbs that store easily. Scott suggests starting with glads. "Glads are so easy to store, any basement would be fine." he says. "Simply dig up the corms, either when the foliage turns brown or before a hard freeze, cut off the tops, and let the corms dry out for a week or so. Then remove any old, dry corms from the bunch, and store the rest in paper bags at a temperature of between 40 and 50°F." You can store tuberous begonias in much the same way, says California grower Skip Antonelli.

Caladiums, which dry out easily, can be difficult to move and store, but Linda Gay of Mercer Arboretum in Texas has a solution. At planting time, pot them up, three to a pot, in 6-inch containers. Then sink the plants, pots and all, into the ground. When October comes, just pull out the containers, move them into a garage, greenhouse, or shed, and give them a monthly watering. In the spring, they'll be ready to plop back into the ground.

flower gardening secrets

A DRINK BEFORE WINTER

Water your bulbs well after planting—unless you've planted late or you know that a hard freeze is predicted. "Bulbs that are freshly planted and watered can be quickly destroyed by a heavy freeze during the night," says Dotti Schultz of McClure & Zimmerman. Instead of watering, he recommends mulching the bulbs with leaves, straw, pine branches, or some other protective covering.

Dahlias have to be handled cautiously, since the tubers break easily at the neck, and they're more susceptible to damage from moisture loss and cold than either glads or begonias. If you want to save your dahlias, wash them gently to remove any excess soil, let them dry out for a week or so, and store them in sand or vermiculite at about 40°F.

Plants for Pots

Container comfort for bulbs • Soil and watering tips

Don't have room in the garden or yard? Many spring- and summer-blooming bulbs grow well in containers.

BEST BULBS FOR CONTAINERS Choose low-growing plants, says Anthony Skittone of San Francisco's Greenlady Gardens. Taller plants generally have more extensive root systems that won't feel at home in the tight space of a pot or planter. Good spring bloomers for pot culture include miniature daffodils, species tulips, crocuses, grape hyacinths, and *Iris reticulata*, but any modest-size hardy bulb is worth trying as a container plant.

According to Jan Ohms of Van Engelen, the greatest risk to growing bulbs in containers is that they're more susceptible to extreme temperature fluctuations. "Any bulb you grow in a container has to be extremely hardy," he says. Select those that survive winters a zone or even two zones to the north of you. For summer containers, Jan likes any of the new varieties of low-growing dahlias. The smaller lilies, too, are perfect for potting. Dianna Gibson's picks include the new 'Pixie' hybrids, the Oriental 'Mona Lisa', with blooms that face up, and 'Sans Souci', with blooms that face out and make them an especially decorative plant for patios and terraces. Avoid the species lilies, warns Dianna. "They take great offense at being moved, and because they like their bulbs cool, they find container life to be extremely stressful," she says. Lilies that like pot-growing, says Alice Hosford, include the reliable and striking 'Stargazer' and 'White Ruffles', a new cultivar that grows only 2 feet tall on strong, compact stems.

CONTAINER HOW-TOS Layering (see page 186) is a great way to plant bulbs in containers. It gives you a spectacular effect and a prolonged bloom period that can brighten a sunny porch for weeks. Don't use heavy garden soil in your containers. Instead, choose a soilless blend, available at garden centers and through mail-order, says bulb importer Howard French of Vermont. Water the bulbs well after planting.

Because you can't rely on snow or the surrounding ground to keep temperatures even during winter, insulate your container well. If you have lots of space in the yard, says Howard, you can sink the container into a deep pit covered by a glass frame, or place it in a sheltered spot and insulate it with burlap or bubble wrap. Maryland bulb grower Kitty Washburne suggests surrounding containers with baled hay and placing dried grasses on top. It isn't a good idea to water bulbs, says Howard, since they're dormant and watering can cause rot.

AN EASY LONG-TERM GROWER Want a long-lived plant that you can keep going with a minimum of fuss? Try potting some tuberous begonias in conventional containers or hanging baskets. California grower and begonia specialist Skip Antonelli recommends letting the plants die back at the end of the summer, then storing them on their side, pot and all, in a protected area. Don't water them, he says— they'll sprout on their own. When new growth appears—weather permitting—you can bring them back into the open.

'Merry Christmas' tulips and 'Paperwhite' narcissus are grouped in a cheerful display at Filoli Gardens in Woodside, California.

flower gardening secrets

THE NATURAL GARDEN

Gardening is always a collaboration with nature, but some gardens are more "natural" than others. We're not talking just about meadows or informal flowerbeds. A natural garden is one that includes native plants, encourages wildlife, and follows nature's rhythms rather than fighting them.

Native Americans

What is a native plant? • Why grow them? • Natives versus exotics

Native plants are those that originated in a specific region—*Trillium albidum* is native to the West Coast, for example; foamflower is native to the Allegheny Mountain Region; switchgrass is a native of the Midwestern prairie; and yucca originated in the desert of the Southwest. Most of the plants found in American gardens are not natives but exotics, imported from other regions or other continents. The ubiquitous daylily, for example, hails from Asia, while yarrow is of European descent. Only recently have native plants begun to gain popularity in American gardens. How can you decide if they belong in your backyard?

WHY GROW NATIVES? For Cindy Reed, president of the Great Plains Native Plant Society, growing natives is a hobby and a passion. "Native plants have the advantage of being able to thrive with the least assistance—no watering, no covering, no soil amending," she says. Many are also hardier than the exotics, adds Loretta Spilker of Living Landscapes, who goes on to point out that native plants "blend naturally with nature's backdrop." That's an aesthetic plus if your yard abuts a woodland, bog, desert, or meadow.

When you plant natives, says Alan Branhagen, director of Missouri's Powell Garden, you do more than enhance your landscape, you give a boost to the local ecosystem. "The local fauna rely on native plants for their livelihood," he says. And by planting natives you preserve them for the future. With so much land under development and so few gardeners using natives in their backyards, the very existence of these plants is threatened. Grow a native and you just may help rescue it from extinction, says Neil Diboll of Wisconsin's Prairie Nursery.

Butterflies, birds, and other fauna add to the health of our gardens and our enjoyment of them. Planting to attract and sustain wildlife is easy and satisfying.

A CHANGED HABITAT You can fill your yard with native plants only to find that they don't thrive in what's supposed to be their natural habitat. "In many instances, the soil and the site no longer resemble what was originally there," explains Kim Hawks of North Carolina's Niche Gardens. This is especially true in areas that have been heavily farmed or on new construction sites where much of the topsoil has been stripped away and what's left has been badly compacted. More important than choosing natives, says Kim, is to find the right plant for the site you have now.

NATIVES AND EXOTICS While the experts encourage gardeners to grow natives, most believe there's a place in the garden for exotics, as well. "Human evolution revolves around the use of plants whose seeds were carried great distances—it's part of our heritage," says Ken Asmus of Michigan's Oikos Tree Crops. And Dr. Richard Lighty, director of the Mount Cuba Center in Delaware, grows both natives and exotics, though not side-by-side, on his own 7½-acre Delaware property that is neatly divided by a small stream. On one half of his acreage he's planted only natives, while on the other he grows plants from Korea, China, and Japan. "The soils, climate, exposure, and so on are the same on both sides of the stream," he says, "and all the plants are doing well."

Black-eyed Susans and purple coneflowers, native to much of North America, are among the most popular and easy to maintain of all perennials.

Native plants usually look best in an informal setting, as in this San Francisco garden where mallow, meadow foam, and *Iris douglasiana* are allowed to sprawl naturally.

FOR THE BIRDS

Plant this dynamic dozen, and you're sure to have a regular roster of songbirds lining up at your back fence:

Juniper
Dogwood
Firethorn
Flowering quince
Forsythia
Fruiting cherry and crabapple
Holly
Purple coneflower
Privet
Sunflower
Trumpet creeper

Because the flora of Southeast Asia mirrors much of our own, says Bob Stewart of Arrowhead Alpines in Michigan, many plants from that region thrive in American gardens. "I freely mix native plants with 'outsiders' as long as their general requirements are compatible," says Cindy Reed. And Kim Hawks agrees: "Why not use the largest plant palette available to you?"

PLANTS TO AVOID Nearly all the experts agree that some exotics should never be planted in American gardens. "I strongly discourage the use of invasive exotic plants such as loosestrife and Japanese honeysuckle, which threaten to take over large expanses of our wildlands, and in many cases already have," says Alan Branhagen. Because these plants lack their normal environmental checks, they often run rampant over the landscape. (For more on invasive plants, see "Made to Invade" on page 200.)

Creatures' Comforts

Friends not foes • Plants that persuade • Wildlife-friendly gardening

Until recently, most of us barred wildlife from our gardens—or tried to as best we could. We banished native plant species; cut down trees, shrubs, and meadows to create rolling lawns; and generally manicured the wildness out of our landscapes. And then we wondered where all the birds, bees, and butterflies had gone.

These days, however, a growing number of gardeners are wooing wildlife back to their yards and gardens, not just because we enjoy the visits of these creatures but because they benefit the garden. Butterflies, bees, bats, and birds are essential pollinators. Without them, we'd be unable to grow most flowering plants. Birds and bats—and many beneficial insects—control insect pests far more effectively than bug zappers and bait traps.

Together, the landscape and the animals that inhabit it create a whole system that works best with minimal interference. When you load your roses with pesticides, you kill not just the aphids but also the ladybugs that eat the aphids and the bees that pollinate the roses and the birds that eat the poisoned ladybugs (and might have formerly eaten your mosquitoes, as well).

Of course, you don't want an open-door policy, where you invite moles to dig up your lawn, rabbits to gobble leafy greens, and hungry deer to devour anything that grows. Instead, the ideal is to create a healthy garden to help sustain the wildlife that will benefit your plants. You'll end up with a complete ecosystem, which offers physical and spiritual sustenance to you as well as to the plants and critters.

A WILDLIFE FRIENDLY GARDEN By keeping your yard free of toxic herbicides and pesticides, you've taken the first step toward creating a wildlife-friendly environment, but don't overlook other hazards. "In California, the polypropylene netting that's placed over fruit trees to protect the fruit from birds has killed many small insect-eating birds, which tend to get tangled in it," says Celeste Wilson of California's Las Pilitas Nursery. And if the netting is allowed to drape on or near the ground, she adds, it can strangle garden snakes or ensnare them so that

Bright flowers—gayfeather, Russian sage, and yarrow among them—a small pond of water, and sheltering shrubs. What more could a butterfly ask for?

they die of overheating. "Nonpoisonous snakes are a great asset to the garden, and this is such a sad thing to see," adds Celeste.

Once you've cleared your yard of hazards, you're ready to make it more welcoming to wildlife. Provide the same things you need: food, water, shelter, and a place to live (or nest). Put up bird, butterfly, and bat houses. Keep in mind that not all birds like to hole up in enclosures. Most, in fact, make their nests on the ground. Sparrows prefer small areas of tall grass, so consider letting an out-of-the-way corner of your lawn go unmowed. Ducks and other birds will nest happily among fallen leaves. If you have the room, make a leaf or brush pile. And keep in mind that a wide selection of plants—including annuals, perennials, and shrubs—is a sure invitation to wildlife. "I don't go out of my way to attract birds, bees, and butterflies, but I find that growing a large variety of crops pretty much does the job," says Tom Butterworth of Connecticut's Butterbrooke Farm.

Tall grasses provide shelter for visiting wildlife and viburnum berries provide food. The bright blossoms of Japanese anemones attract pollinating bees and butterflies.

FEED THEM AND THEY WILL COME Every animal in the wild needs to eat. If you provide food, animals will follow. Though you can hang bird and butterfly feeders to attract pollinators, why not grow plants that will produce the food they like?

FOR THE BIRDS Birds need three things: food, water, and shelter. In addition to insects, birds love seeds and berries. If you want to bring birds to your backyard, grow plants that fruit heavily or produce seed in abundance, says Memphis landscape architect Charles Sandifer. To attract an even wider range of birds, Charles suggests planting flowers that attract butterflies and caterpillars (see "Butterfly Beacons," below). "Since birds eat butterflies and caterpillars, plants that attract butterflies ultimately attract birds, as well," he says. Birds also need a source of water and some kind of coverage for nesting.

FAST FOOD FOR HUMMERS Unique in the avian world, hummingbirds feed on nectar, rather than seeds, insects, or fruits. And because they're nearly always in motion, they need lots of nectar. Hummingbirds are fondest of bright red and orange flowers, says Loretta Spilker of Living Landscapes in Indianapolis—especially those flowers with trumpet-shaped blooms, like trumpetvine and honeysuckle.

BUTTERFLY BEACONS To create a garden that's beneficial to butterflies, you'll want to do more than simply plant their favorite flowers. "Though flowers in shades of purple, pink, and yellow will draw butterflies to your yard, you also want to cater to caterpillars," says Loretta. For the past several decades, development has destroyed many of the meadow plants that sustain caterpillars—and without caterpillars, there are no butterflies. "Both caterpillars and butterflies are finicky eaters," says Loretta. Some varieties, in fact, dine only on one particular plant. To nourish a range of caterpillars, try planting cabbage, viburnums, artemisia (for painted-lady caterpillars), milkweed (for monarchs), and fennel, rue, dill, and nettle (for swallowtails).

Matt Horn of New York's Matterhorn Nursery suggests that you also provide a source of water. Butterflies need salt, which they absorb by sipping water at the edge of a pool or puddle. They also prefer full sun, which helps them raise their body temperature

HUMMINGBIRD FAVORITES

Charmed by the sight of these hovering hummers? Plant one or more of these favorite nectar flowers in a bed or border:

Azalea
Bee balm
Blue-flowered morning glory
Bougainvillea
Columbine
Honeysuckle
Impatiens
Jasmine
Passion flower
Penstemon
Salvia (especially pineapple sage)

flower gardening secrets

FOOD FOR BUTTERFLIES

Many trees, shrubs, flowers, and herbs provide nourishment for caterpillars and the butterflies they become. Here are some favorites.

Asters
Bee balm
Black-eyed Susan
Butterfly bush
Butterfly weed
Cardinal flower
Catmint
Common thrift
Cosmos
Daylily
Dill
Globe amaranth
Goldenrod
Heliotrope
Honeysuckle
Joe pye weed
Lantana
Lavender
Marigold
Nasturtium
Parsley
Pincushion flower
Primrose
Purple coneflower
Thyme
Viburnum
Yarrow
Yoshino cherry
Zinnia

(essential for flight), and they like protection from the wind. Keep existing native trees on site when possible, says Kim Hawks, as this is one of the areas where eggs are laid.

FOOD FOR BEES "I've never had a client ask me to attract bees to their property, but bees seem to come naturally when you plant flowers that attract hummingbirds and butterflies," says Loretta Spilker. Jim Becker of Oregon's Goodwin Creek Gardens, and Boston landscape architect Diane Kostial McGuire both bring bees into their gardens with flowering herbs. Diane also suggests planting wild-flowers. "I have a meadow next to my vegetable garden, and it's full of wild plants. I call it my 'singing meadow' because it attracts so many bees," she says.

Great Grasses

Their beauty and benefits • Grassy aggression • Maintenance

Not that long ago, the only grass growing in most gardens was the kind you mow, but a burgeoning interest in ornamental grasses has changed all that. More and more gardeners use these showy perennials in their foundation plantings, as focal points in the landscape, in mass plantings, and in flowerbeds and borders.

THE GRATIFICATION OF GRASSES How many plants offer four-season beauty, ease of maintenance, and drought resistance, while packing a dramatic punch? When you consider all their good points, it's not surprising that ornamental grasses have invaded American gardens.

Kim Hawks of North Carolina's Niche Gardens plants them throughout her garden. She likes them for the interest they provide in fall and winter and for the wonderful sound they make when the wind blows through them. Gail Korn of Nebraska's Garden Perennials likes the movement they add to the garden as they toss their seedheads in a light breeze or gracefully arch their stems in a strong wind. San Francisco landscape designer Angela Fabbri praises grasses for their height and their usefulness as focal points. If you need a quick and dramatic landscape effect, many of the ornamental grasses will grow almost to mature size in a single season. Do you have a large area to landscape? Consider using evergreen grasses such as sedge, which makes a terrific low-maintenance groundcover, suggests Ursula Herz of South Carolina's Coastal Gardens and Nursery.

Ornamental grasses offer many benefits beyond their beauty. Loretta Spilker of Living Landscapes in Indianapolis points out that they are "environmentally friendly, sending down long root systems that hold water, control erosion, and improve soil quality." Grasses like big bluestem have roots that reach down as far as 10 feet, says Douglas Owens-Pike of Minneapolis's Evergreen EnergyScapes, Inc., and can handle his region's worst droughts. Unlike their lawn-bound cousins, most ornamental grasses require no more maintenance than an annual pruning. Let them brighten the winter garden, then cut them 3 to 6 inches from the ground in late winter or early spring. One more advantage: deer don't like ornamental grasses.

CHECKING OVERZEALOUSNESS Do some research on the particular species of grass you're considering, advises Alan Branhagen, director of Missouri's Powell Garden. Many grasses, such as *Miscanthus sacchariflorus*,

Not all grasses are green. Bright red Japanese bloodgrass, blue-green fescue, and the golden flower-stalks of fountain grass and feather reed grass provide as much color as any conventional flowers.

flower gardening secrets

SEEDS FOR A MEADOW

After soil preparation, the secret of a successful meadow lies in the selection of good-quality seeds. Be wary of "meadow" mixes, says Alan Burke of Seattle's Preview Landscape Architecture, since the gardens they create often revert to a "monoculture" consisting of only one or two of the dominant plants in the mix.

In addition, David Graper of the University of South Dakota warns that some seed mixes contain undesirable weeds like creeping Jenny and thistle. A reliable dealer will sell seeds of individual plants or well-balanced mixes for your region (see "Sources" on page 362).

spread by underground root systems called stolons, and they can be highly invasive. Others self-seed so successfully that they make themselves a nuisance. You can plant self-seeders, says Ellen Talmage of New York State's Horticultural Goddess, Inc., just make sure you deadhead them (remove spent blossoms) before seedheads can form. "I've never experienced a takeover by any variety that I've grown because I keep them in check," she says.

MAINTAINING GRASSES Although ornamental grasses are largely low-maintenance, you'll have to divide some of them after several years to ensure tight growth and good flower production, and this can be a chore for tall grasses, says Kim Hawks. "Rather than risk pulling a muscle or breaking your prized gardening tools, consider hiring a pro to do the job," she says. Some of the smaller grasses, like bloodgrass and fescue, can be divided easily by the home gardener.

Prairie Home Companions

Defining a prairie garden • Pros and cons • Site preparation

In a meadow or prairie garden, native flowers and grasses grow in a loose, almost random fashion to look as if nature alone were responsible for the design. The inspiration for these gardens comes from "the beautiful flowers and grasses of the North American prairie," says Neil Diboll, director of Wisconsin's Prairie Nursery.

Prairie gardens aren't for everyone, and they don't grow well in certain soils and climates. However, if you like their lush, informal look, and you live in an area where such plants grow naturally, a prairie garden can offer unique benefits.

WHY PLANT A PRAIRIE? Prairie meadows, as Neil calls them, look good year-round. After the spring and summer flowers have faded, the grasses take over, glowing golden in fall and flashing spectacular plumes and seedheads even in winter.

Once established, a prairie garden is virtually self-sufficient—it needs no watering, no fertilizing, and no toxic pesticides, says Neil. And by planting a meadow or prairie garden, you help preserve native plants and support birds, butterflies, and other animals whose habitats are threatened by development.

SELECTING AND PREPARING THE SITE If you want to have a go at prairie gardening, choose your site carefully. "Prairies and meadows require sunny, open, level sites with good air circulation," says Neil. Your garden should receive at least a half-day of full sun.

After choosing the site, remove the vegetation (for a variety of methods, see "Removing Weeds" on page 44) and prepare the soil. Soil preparation is "the single most important factor in the success of any prairie planting," says Neil. He advises cultivating the soil with a sod-cutter, rotary tiller, tractor-mounted rotary tiller, or plow. (See "Amending Your Soil" on page 51 for more information on preparing soil.)

GETTING GOOD SOIL Amending the soil with organic matter may or may not be necessary. In South Dakota, where David Graper of the University of South Dakota gardens, much of the soil is naturally

A blazing display of wildflowers was carefully planted and watered in its first year. Later, the plants will reseed themselves. The most vigorous species will sometimes need to be pulled up so that they do not overtake the garden.

PERVASIVE PLANTS

There's no real consensus on which plants to avoid growing, since a plant can be invasive under some conditions and a valuable addition to the garden in other situations. The following plants turned up on most of the experts' lists of invasive plants. Also, check with your local cooperative extension agent to determine which plants are illegal to grow in your state.

Artemisia 'Silver King'

Bamboo

Bishop's weed (Goutweed)

Common buckthorn

Fernleaf tansy

Kudzu

Mints

Multiflora rose

Purple loosestrife

Sumacs

Water hyacinth

Japanese and Chinese
    wisteria

suited to prairie plants. Nonetheless, he recommends having the soil tested for proper pH—tell the lab or cooperative extension agent that you plan to put in a prairie garden.

To enrich soil that's been depleted of its fertility, Alan Burke of Seattle's Preview Landscape Architecture recommends the following: Add 1 cubic yard of well-composted organic matter (see "Shovel It On" on page 280) for every 300 square feet, digging it in to a depth of 12 inches.

Made to Invade

What's an invasive plant? • To grow or not to grow • How to control them

Invasive plants fall into one of two categories: Plants that spread aggressively using runners or underground stems (known as stolons), and those that self-seed so abundantly that they threaten not just the backyard but the wild environment, as well. "Most self-seeders aren't native to North America but have been introduced from other parts of the world," says Peter van der Linden, curator of plant collections at the Morton Arboretum in Illinois. "Common buckthorn and purple loosestrife have been particular nuisances, but each region has its own complement of weeds that 'escaped' from gardens."

No subject generates more heat among the experts than the use of invasive plants in the garden. Even deciding which plants to call invasive causes controversy. To some gardeners, English ivy is an attractive, quick-spreading groundcover; to others, it's a green blanket with feet, smothering everything in its path. Climate can help to determine a plant's degree of invasiveness. In areas north of Zone 5, for example, red fountain grass is a showy annual, but in states like Arizona, where it easily overwinters, it's become a public nuisance. Some plants seem to be on everyone's invasive list, including loosestrife, that plague of the wetlands across North America; kudzu, the strangler of the South; and the freely seeding multiflora rose.

SHOULD YOU PLANT THEM? Given the risks, why would anyone consider planting invasives? "Because some of them can be useful in places where their rapid growth rate is an advantage, such as difficult landscape locations like confined parking-lot islands, spaces between sidewalks and buildings, and even in patio containers." says Kris

Fountain grass can become invasive in some areas because it reseeds prolifically. If you want to keep your fountain grass in its place, cut off its seedheads as soon as they dry.

Bachtell of the Morton Arboretum in Illinois. Among the invasives that would do well in these and similar situations, Kris lists dwarf Japanese fleeceflower, wormwood, wild blue rye, and bamboo.

Kim Hawks of North Carolina's Niche Gardens believes that every plant has its place. The trick with invasives is to find a site where they can be themselves without threatening the environment. "A vigorously growing plant is considered invasive when sited in the wrong spot, such as a tiny, defined area," she says. "However, the same 'invasive' plant becomes useful in other settings," such as a slope that's difficult to mow, a large expanse of ground where nothing seems to grow, and other hard-to-landscape areas.

Most of the experts agree, however, that you should avoid growing aggressive self-seeders, especially if they've become a threat to

Black-eyed Susan can be invasive in a small garden. Plant it where it will have room to spread.

How do you control an invasive plant like Japanese silver grass? Plant it with perennials that can hold their own, like Joe-Pye weed and artemisia.

flower gardening secrets

wetlands. "Gardeners have an ethical responsibility to become informed about this problem," says Peter van der Linden. In fact, in some areas, it's illegal to plant certain invasives. To find out about the laws in your region, contact your local cooperative extension agent.

CONTAINMENT POLICY If you do choose to plant invasives, Dr. Richard Lighty, director of the Mount Cuba Center in Delaware, stresses the importance of keeping them in bounds—something that's easier to accomplish with the stolon-spreaders than the seeders. The simplest way to restrain invasives is to plant them in containers or in an area of the ground surrounded by bricks or pavement.

Another way to contain invasives is to maintain them scrupulously. Nurserywoman Loleta Powell loves mums, yarrow, and Stokes' aster, but in her neck of North Carolina they spread with unrestrained enthusiasm. "To keep them from taking over the garden, I put a shovel down straight around the part I want to keep and remove every stolon beyond that line," she says. Ken Miller of Missouri's Horticultural Consultants offers his secret for taming invasives: "If you want to make a plant less aggressive, weaken it by putting it in less-than-perfect conditions." Artemisia, for example, spreads rapidly in full sun but is more restrained in shade.

GROWING GREAT GARDENS

Once you've decided on the look and feel of your garden, mulled over all the plant possibilities and combinations, and sketched your design in your mind or plotted it on paper, you're ready to begin planting.

Ground Prep

Soil savvy • Digging in • Getting ready to plant

Getting a bed ready for flowers isn't much different from preparing a vegetable garden or shrub border. You'll need to till the soil (loosen it, so that roots can spread out), add amendments to enrich it, and if necessary, improve drainage.

If you're going to be planting annuals exclusively, you can probably get away with a little less work—even if the garden doesn't perform to your expectations, you've only lost a season. Perennials, on the other hand, are in it for the long haul. You don't want to dig them up the following season because you didn't prepare the ground right the first time around.

KNOW YOUR SOIL Before you do any real digging, have your soil tested (see "Put It to the Test" on page 264). A soil test will tell you if your site needs any key nutrients, and it will give you a reading on pH (the degree of acidity or alkalinity). You'll also need to assess your soil's makeup—whether it's mostly clay, sand, or loam. Don't assume that because your neighbor down the road can grow anything, your soil must be equally rich. "Soil can be very different a short distance away," warns Alan Summers of Maryland's Carroll Gardens. Plus, your neighbors may have done a lot to enrich their soil. Once you've determined what your soil needs, you can start to dig and amend your garden plot. (For more on soil types, soil tests, and amendments, see "Soil" on page 30, "Put It to the Test" on page 264, and "Making Super Soil" on page 266.) When you send your soil sample, tell the testers what you'll be planting; they'll be able to give you more specific information on what you need.

DIG IN No matter what the quality of your soil is, loosen and aerate it before planting. You should till annual beds each year before planting. When preparing a bed for perennials—a chore you should only have

---

SCRUMPTIOUS SOIL

Your plants will love their soil if you enrich it with a little organic matter. The experts share their favorite amendments.

❧ In Alan Summers's Maryland garden, the soil is mostly clay. To improve it he adds "lots of compost, coarse sand, and kelp meal—all to encourage earthworms, which are nature's fertilizers."

❧ New Jersey garden designer Cassie Brown prefers well-rotted cow manure, but says any well-composted organic material will improve the quality of your soil.

❧ Gail Korn of Nebraska's Garden Perennials swears by alfalfa meal. "I've mulched with it when I could get it easily," she says. "Now I like to add a cupful to mix with the soil as I put in each plant. It adds organic matter plus vitamins, minerals, and trace elements, and it releases them slowly so you can't overdo it." You can find alfalfa meal at feed stores.

flower gardening secrets

HOW THICKLY TO LAY IT ON

When it comes to organic matter, most experts agree with Dr. Richard Lighty, director of the Mount Cuba Center in Delaware. He recommends to add "as much as possible." But not everyone agrees.

❧ Ken Twombley of Connecticut's Twombley Nursery believes that, "in a reasonably adequate location, plants should be able to stand alone." If your soil is sandy, however, Ken suggests adding organic matter to make up about 10 percent of the overall soil volume.

❧ Ken Miller of Missouri's Horticultural Consultants mixes in 1.8 cubic feet of organic matter for every 100 square feet of soil.

❧ Less mathematically inclined gardeners may want to go with Seattle garden designer Sue Moss's suggestion and spread 4 inches of organic matter over the entire bed, then dig or till it in well.

to do once in the bed's lifetime—dig deep, the experts concur. Dr. Richard Lighty, director of the Mount Cuba Center in Delaware, recommends tilling the soil "to the greatest depth practicable." In most gardens, that would be anywhere from 8 inches to 2 feet. You can either use a rotary tiller or a spade and garden fork, and you may want to consider double-digging the bed (see "Digging and Double-Digging" on page 288). If you don't want to dig the ground, consider constructing a raised bed, (see "Constructing Raised Beds" on page 57).

You will probably want to remove most of the large rocks you come across (see page "Rocks and Stumps" on page 48), but both Ken Twombley of the Twombley Nursery in Connecticut and Frank Peterson of Good Hollow Greenhouse and Herbarium in Tennessee recommend leaving at least some of the small ones in place to help hold in moisture and warmth.

FIRM UP? While old-time gardening lore suggests that you "walk down" the bed after digging to firm up the soil, most experts share Seattle garden designer Sue Moss's opinion: "The soil in a flowerbed should be as fluffy as possible. The only time you should compact the soil is just before seeding or sodding a lawn." Instead of walking the bed, says Dr. Lighty, "let it rest through several rains." Or you can water the bed several times before planting to help it settle.

Annual Beginnings

Starting from seed • Indoors or outdoors?

Starting annuals from seed offers several advantages: It's cheaper than buying "starts" from the garden center; you can choose among a wide variety of plants, including exotic and so-called heirloom annuals; and it's personally satisfying to see your seeds sprout.

You can start seeds indoors or sow them directly in the soil (called direct-seeding). Many experts choose to start all of their seeds indoors so they can control conditions (for more information on indoor seed-starting, see "Starting Seeds Indoors" on page 333). But to save time and trouble, nothing beats direct-seeding.

STARTING INSIDE OR OUT? Plants that grow rapidly and aren't fussy about growing conditions are the best candidates for direct-seeding. If

Finicky delphinium is difficult to overwinter; start it from seeds or cuttings each year. *Nicotiana sylvestris* grows 4 feet tall from seed in a few months. In this planting, it's mixed with perennial catmint, tansy, and lady's-mantle.

flower gardening secrets

you have a long growing season, you'll have a wider choice of annuals to direct-seed than gardeners in colder climates do. Starting seeds indoors, on the other hand, lets you get your garden going earlier in the season.

To decide if a plant needs to be started indoors, read the seed packet and determine the number of weeks from planting to flowering. Then figure out your frost-free date and do some basic arithmetic. Pansies, for example, generally take three to four months to flower. If you live in Zone 5 and your frost-free date is May 1, that means the plants won't flower until August or September if you direct-seed them. In most areas though, you can sow seeds outdoors in late summer for early spring bloom. Purple hyacinth bean, on the other hand, is notorious for its rapid growth. It's the only annual Donald Buma of Wichita's Botanica direct-seeds. "I plant in late spring, and it grows to 10 feet tall," he says.

SOWING IN THE SOIL When it comes to direct seeding, it's easiest to simply follow the directions on the seed packet. But here are basic instructions from Ellen Talmage of New York's Horticultural Goddess, Inc.: Rake the soil lightly, spread the seeds on top, then sprinkle them with soil—"the way you'd put powdered sugar on a doughnut," she says—and water lightly. Use a watering can or a hose with a sprinkling attachment so that you don't flood the soil and disperse the seeds.

DEADHEADS

It may sound cruel and painful, but pinching and deadheading annuals and perennials produces bigger and more beautiful plants. When blossoms have faded, remove them (a process called deadheading). If you don't, the plant will begin to set seed and will stop producing flowers.

Pinching means removing a plant's growing tips before it matures. This encourages side shoots to grow, which creates a denser, rounder, fuller plant.

Most annuals benefit from pinching and dead-heading, with some exceptions—stock, sunflowers, and zinnias among them. And there are those plants, like fuchsia and impatiens, that oblige the gardener by self-deadheading. In general, though, a regular grooming of your plants will yield a better-looking garden and keep your annuals going long after nature would have allowed them to fade.

Planting Perennials

Proper depth • *Handling roots* • *Firming the soil*

With perennials, the hole you dig will be their home for years to come, so you'll want to make that home as hospitable as possible. Dig to the right depth, and provide enough space for the roots to grow into the surrounding soil.

HOW DEEP? Because each plant has its own ideal depth, most reputable growers will provide you with information on how deep to dig the hole. If the perennial has come to you in a container, says Douglas Owens-Pike of Minneapolis's EnergyScape, Inc., simply plant it so that the top of the soil in the pot is level with the surface of the surrounding soil in the garden. Bareroot plants will need a little more attention.

If you're not sure what the ideal depth is, you won't go too far wrong if you follow the advice of Celeste Wilson of California's Las Pilitas Nursery. "Each plant is different, but as a general rule, placing the crown slightly above the soil line works well," she says. In colder areas, plant the crown at the soil surface, not higher.

MAKING THE ROOTS COMFORTABLE In addition to planting at the right depth, it's crucial to dig a hole that's wide enough to let the roots expand comfortably. Philip Steiner of Mellinger's Nursery in Ohio always spreads the roots of his perennials manually before covering them with soil. Douglas Owens-Pike simply cuts them on four sides with a sharp knife if the root balls are small enough (roughly 1 × 2 × 1 inches).

If you're planting perennials with large, fleshy roots (such as daylilies), it's easiest to make a small mound of soil and then spread the roots out on top of the mound. One problem you might encounter, especially with container-grown plants, is how to encourage perennial roots to expand into the surrounding soil. One neat way to solve this problem is to add a little soilless mix to the soil you've dug, says Richard Boonstra of Ohio's Bluestone Perennials.

FIRMING THE SOIL Once you've filled the hole with soil, tamp it lightly but firmly. You want to make sure that the soil is packed tightly enough to support the plant, but you don't want to compact it. The best way to firm the soil, says Richard, "is to place your knuckles on each side of the plant and lean your weight on them." Carl

Thuesen, a landscape designer in Montana, suggests that you use the bottom of your fist (but resist the urge to punch down on the soil). Always water in new plantings.

Pampering Your New Plants

Watering • Shading • Looking out for problems

If you've prepared your bed well and chosen healthy plants that are appropriate to your climate, caring for them should be a cinch.

WATERING The major threat to newly planted perennials or annuals is lack of water. Unless you're putting in a desert garden, you can't go too wrong if you follow the advice of Barry Glick of West Virginia's Sunshine Farm and Gardens: "Keep everything good and wet." Here are tips from other experts:

•To give his flowers an extra nutrient boost, Alan Summers of Maryland's Carroll Gardens waters them in with liquid seaweed and kelp (both are available at garden centers and nurseries).

Peonies won't flop if they are staked. Plant them in the fall with grow-hoops around them (above). The plants will grow through the hoops and camouflage them (left).

CAUTIOUS MULCHING

If you apply the right mulch at the correct depth, you can't really hurt your plants. To make sure you mulch healthy, follow these tips from the experts.

Beware of green mulch. "Green, or fresh, mulch probably won't kill your plants, but it can stunt their growth" says Rosie B. Lerner, extension specialist in consumer horticulture at Purdue University. The microorganisms that cause decomposition draw nitrogen from the soil. In addition, the natural deterioration of fresh mulch creates an enormous amount of heat.

If you mulch with farm or industrial byproducts, watch out for possible toxins or pesticide residues. If you choose mulch from a municipal pile, use it only on tough, established plants; it may be in the first stages of decomposition.

Discourage nesting. "Certain pine meadow mice will nest in mulch and can damage bark by grawing it," says Jack Crittenden. Discourage mice by keeping mulch—especially in winter—well away from the base of shrubs and trees.

- Gene Banks of Connecticut's Catnip Acres Herb Farm floods her planting holes after she digs them—she literally plants in mud.
- North Carolina landscape architect Richard Boggs adds a thick layer of mulch to help retain moisture. (For more information on mulches, see "What to Make of Mulch" on page 209.)
- Douglas Owens-Pike of Minneapolis's Energyscapes, Inc., recommends an occasional deep watering during the first several weeks after planting to encourage deep rooting, which will help your plants survive the long, drying summer.

SHADING TRANSPLANTS "If your plants have been out of the sun for any length of time in a shipping box, or if you've held them inside for a day or two, they should be lightly shaded after planting," advises Richard Boonstra of Ohio's Bluestone Perennials. He covers plants with a single sheet of newspaper, which he then anchors with a few handfuls of soil. It's a good idea to provide shade when planting in hot weather, says Alan Summers. He places a sheer window curtain over his plants, or uses shingles or boards stuck in the ground at a slight angle to make a shadow from the southwest. Once the plant begins to put on new growth, which tells you that the roots are established, you can remove the shading.

STAKING Taller plants, such as delphiniums, peonies, and mallows, tend to flop over unless they're staked. Ellen Talmage of Horticultural Goddess, Inc., gathers twigs and short branches and sticks them into beds at regular intervals before she plants her perennials; when the perennials begin to grow, the twigs provide natural support. Hoops that allow plants to grow through them are also useful.

CHECK YOUR GARDEN REGULARLY You should watch over your plants throughout the growing season, but especially during those first few weeks after planting. Bobbie Holder of Wyoming's Pawnee Greenhouse and Nursery regularly checks the color and texture of the foliage. "If the leaves are yellow and moist, you've overwatered. If they're yellow and brown on the ends, they've gotten too little water. If they're yellow but the veins are green, they need iron," she says. Wilting in a new transplant almost always indicates dehydration. Mist and shade wilted plants immediately, says Richard Boonstra, and they should revive by the next morning.

What to Make of Mulch

To mulch or not • Choosing mulches

Mulching helps suppress weeds and retain soil moisture. For much of the country, it reduces work time in the flower garden in addition to helping plants grow.

THE BENEFITS Mulch is especially useful in the first few years of a perennial bed's long life, when plants may not have reached their mature spread and weeds have ample room to grow. Like most experts, Kim Hawks of North Carolina's Niche Gardens prefers organic mulches, both for their soil-enriching qualities and their good looks. She recommends fine-textured materials, such as very small pine nuggets or well-shredded bark, that won't detract from the beauty of your flowers. With plants that prefer dry soil, she uses small pea gravel, which allows for rapid drainage and keeps moisture away from the plants' water-sensitive crowns.

flower gardening secrets

Mulch looks good, providing an even, neutral layer of earth. Annuals and perennials can be mulched right up to their bases, as long as the mulch layer is not more than $\frac{1}{2}$ inch thick.

MIND YOUR P'S AND N'S

If your garden is new or your soil is less than perfect, your beds might benefit from a judicious application of organic fertilizer. Most commercial fertilizers are marked with three numbers (5-10-5, for example) representing the ratio of key nutrients: nitrogen, phosphorus, and potassium. (For more on fertilizer, see "Creating Fertile Ground" on page 273.)

Most flower gardens—especially those planted with perennials—do best with a fertilizer that's high in phosphorous and low in nitrogen. Phosphorus helps plants grow strong roots and stems and produce an abundance of flowers. Nitrogen speeds growth, but too much of it leads to weak, leggy plants and fewer flowers.

Aileen Lubin, director of Maine's Merryspring Park, uses a 5-10-10 fertilizer in her flower beds. South Carolina grower Ursula Herz recommends her own special formula: equal parts cottonseed meal, cow manure, kelp, and bonemeal, mixed with an equal volume of commercial organic fertilizer.

Gail Korn of Nebraska's Garden Perennials likes to use chopped leaves. "They're plentiful and free, and as they rot, they send nutrients into the soil," she says. She also likes the dark brown color, the texture, and the earthy smell. "And with leaf mulch, the soil will turn from brown to black in only a few years," she says—a sign that the soil's rich in nutrients. To chop leaves for the flower garden, spread them in a thin layer on the lawn and run the mower over them. Then rake them up and spread them on your beds. An electric leaf mulcher makes the job even easier. Unlike whole leaves, chopped leaves can remain on your beds throughout the growing season.

Dr. Richard Lighty, director of Delaware's Mount Cuba Center, applies chopped leaves to his own flower garden each fall, right after Thanksgiving. "The leaves are natural, they protect the plants through the winter without stifling their shoots in the spring, yet they suppress weed seedlings. And they rot down into the soil by August of the following year," he says.

The Well-Fed Garden

Do you need it? • Enriching soil the organic way

Manufacturers of fertilizer have been so successful in their advertising that most of us consider fertilizer a necessity. But is it?

FERTILE ADVICE Many of the experts use little or no fertilizer on their flowerbeds and still grow lush, brilliant, healthy flowers. North Carolina landscape architect Cynthia Rice relies on organic mulches to enrich her soil. By applying a mulch of chopped leaves in the fall and a layer of well-rotted horse manure in the spring, she's been able to create a nutrient-rich soil that needs no additional fertilizer.

Neil Diboll of Wisconsin's Prairie Nursery tests his soil (see "Put It to the Test" on page 264) to determine if it's lacking any specific nutrients. He adds fertilizer only if the tests show a deficiency, and even then, he adds only the specific nutrient that's needed. For meadow and prairie gardens, says Neil, fertilizer is completely unnecessary and, in fact, could be harmful, making the plants grow tall and floppy.

Douglas Owens-Pike of Minneapolis's EnergyScapes, Inc., agrees. If you grow plants that are native to your area and well-suited to your

specific soil type, you won't need to fertilize at all, he says. Like Cynthia Rice, Douglas uses an organic mulch to enrich the soil naturally.

Dr. Richard Lighty, director of Mount Cuba Center in Delaware, fertilizes his perennial beds only when slower growth indicates a nitrogen shortage—every five to eight years. "Over-fertilization produces wonderful growth, but makes plants more pest- and disease-prone and shortens the life of many flowers, particularly the weaker perennials and some bulbs," he says. Annuals may need more fertilizer than perennials.

What do these plants—Russian sage, 'Bright Eyes' phlox, catmint, holly, and barberry—have in common? All will thrive with very little fertilizer. In fact, they'll do better without it.

Tasks for Autumn

What to cut back • What to let stand • What goes in the compost pile

Most of us pull up spent annuals before the winter, but what about perennials? Should they be cut to the ground, or is it okay to let them stand? And how do you know what to compost and what to bag and discard? The experts offer some surprising answers.

TO CUT OR LET STAND At Fieldstone Gardens in Maine, winters are long and hard, and fall cleanup is critical. Steve Jones and his colleagues do an extensive cleanup "because we have more time in fall." But there's another reason: "Plants are better off if they don't retain moisture with wet foliage, which can harbor diseases and attract pests," says Jones. He recommends cutting most plants to within a few inches of the ground, although he's found that Russian sage does better if it's left over the winter and cut in spring. Suzanne van Schroeder of Wisconsin's Winter Greenhouse cuts most of her perennials back to 4 or 5 inches—but not all. She leaves plants with large seedheads to feed the birds, "and we leave grasses because they look good."

Most experts don't cut back their gardens until well into fall; it allows an extra season of interest. Fall leaves, when raked, can be used to mulch the flowerbeds.

flower gardening secrets

While most of the experts recommend cutting back perennials, a few prefer to let them overwinter. Bobbie Holder of Wyoming's Pawnee Greenhouse and Nursery does most of her cleanup in spring. "I don't like to see bare ground," she admits. "I like the color and texture of seedheads, and I find that plants hold and protect the soil." At Mary's Plant Farm in Ohio, Mary Harrison leaves her borders alone for the winter. "The plants serve as their own mulch," she says.

DISPOSING OF DEBRIS Most of the experts recommend composting "healthy" debris, but warn against tossing diseased foliage onto the pile. Gail Korn of Nebraska's Garden Perennials discards iris, peony, and phlox foliage, even if it appears healthy, since it can harbor hidden pests or diseases. And Shane Smith, director of the Cheyenne Botanic Garden, recommends disposing of weeds and aggressive perennials, as well.

How do you know what's diseased and what isn't? Steve Jones looks for drying out or hollowing of stems, stems that flop, yellowing or chewed foliage, scarring, and mildew. "If you can, burn the bad stuff. Or make a separate pile and let it rot on its own—never mix it with the rest of the pile," he says.

Winter Mulches

What to mulch • What to use • When to apply

Unlike mulches applied during the growing season, winter mulches have one basic purpose: to protect shrubs and perennials from the cycle of freeze and thaw that can heave plants out of the ground. The experts explain where and when to mulch, and which materials work best in winter.

WHO NEEDS TO MULCH? If the temperature in your area rarely dips below freezing, you don't need a winter mulch. In Wisconsin, where winters can be brutally cold, Suzanne van Schroder of the Winter Greenhouse covers only those plants in very exposed areas. "We have a good snow cover, so we don't have to worry much about winter mulch," she explains. (Not only is snow a natural insulator, but it applies itself, making it the ideal winter mulch.)

WHEN TO MULCH Wait until the first hard freeze, advises Edric Owen of Tennessee's Owen Farms. If you lay your winter mulch too early, it may look like the perfect nest to rodents searching for a winter hideaway.

MULCHING MATERIALS

Winter mulches should be light and fluffy, but not so light that they blow away in January winds. Steve Jones of Maine's Fieldstone Gardens recommends pine or fir boughs. "They're better than bark chips because they allow air to circulate," he says. If you've already dragged your Christmas tree out to the curb, drag it back and put it to good use in the garden.

Another good winter mulch is chopped leaves or leaf mulch, especially on vegetable beds. At Virginia's Ashlawn-Highland, historic home of President James Monroe, James Wooten spreads a winter mulch of oakleaf mold over his beds—not to protect the plants (there aren't any), but to add fertility to the soil. Oakleaf mold is also a great earthworm attractor, says Douglas Owens-Pike of EnergyScapes, Inc.

flower gardening secrets

4

LANDSCAPING WITH TREES, SHRUBS & VINES

"First, get your bones in position."
LEIGH SORENSON, SORENSON DESIGN

Imagine that your backyard is a painting: Flowers and vegetables provide texture, form, and color; structures, statuary, and specimen plants serve as focal points to draw the eye. But it's the landscape elements—the trees, shrubs, vines, lawns, and groundcovers—that tie the whole composition together. Those elements don't just represent the "bones" of the garden; they help to set its tone and mood. If you're planning a new garden, then, or just planning to revamp an old one, the best place to begin is with the landscaping.

In this chapter, the experts pool their knowledge to help you make some of the most critical backyard decisions. Starting with where to shop, they lead you deftly through the landscaping maze, with advice on how to buy healthy plants, when and how to plant trees and shrubs, the secrets of low-maintenance lawns, the most unusual groundcovers, and the best supports for climbing vines. They also share their solutions to some of the stickiest landscaping problems: what to plant under trees, how to deal with the wrapping on balled-and-burlapped plants, and whether or not to amend the soil in your planting holes.

HERE'S WHAT YOU'LL FIND IN CHAPTER 4

Flowering shrubs—lilac, rhododendrons, and weigela—are combined with perennials and annuals for a welcoming display that lasts from spring to fall.

LANDSCAPING

Most landscapes have many elements—sunny spots and shady places, beautiful flowerbeds and productive vegetables plots. A skillful landscape design pulls together every area of your backyard—from the tallest trees to the lowest groundcovers—in a harmonious whole, making it a joy to live in and look at.

The Big Picture

Assessing your yard • Time's on your side • Working in stages

Maybe you've just moved into a new home and want to put your own stamp on the landscape. Or perhaps you've lived with your yard for years and suddenly feel the urge to start ripping things out. As appealing as the end result may be, big landscaping jobs can be daunting. But by following the right steps, you can enjoy the process.

LOOK AT WHAT YOU HAVE Unless you've moved into a new development whose only landscape feature is bulldozed earth, your yard is probably filled with unrecognized treasures. Boston garden designer Philip Hresko suggests that you resist the impulse to do away with every last shrub and perennial. "In the first year, get rid of only the worst plants or those that are diseased, and then live with what you have for a few years," he says. Often, gardeners find that a mild pruning is all it takes to tame existing plants, especially native shrubbery. It's also a good idea to learn everything you can about your yard—soil, climate, existing plants—before you start redoing it. (For information on site analysis, see "Know Your Site" on page 18.)

COLLABORATE WITH TIME Most of the world's great gardens are the result of years of planting, observation, and replanting. Ken Twombley of Connecticut's Twombley Nursery believes that, large or small, a garden should evolve. "If you have a set plan, with everything in place right from the beginning, you might not take advantage of the artistry that can result only after the garden has been started," he says. Even the best plan is only an approximation of the real garden. Furthermore, an overambitious plan can set you up for disappointment—something that Louise Hyde of New Jersey's Well-Sweep Herb Farm has witnessed countless times. "People try to install a huge garden and end

Repeating patterns of perennials are punctuated by evergreen shrubs in this Connecticut garden. The garden borders three sides of a medium-size backyard, leaving ample room at the center for enjoying the view. A bench, created from stones dug from the ground, is a pleasant place to sit.

landscaping: trees, shrubs & vines

up getting discouraged and dropping the whole thing," she says. "Don't try to do it all at once."

WORK IN STEPS Allan Summers of Maryland's Carroll Gardens points out that "most big jobs are done in stages—usually some in the spring and some in the fall." He likes to put trees in first because they take the longest to mature. Then he'll plant climbing or shrub roses because they add instant drama. If you're not putting in trees, he suggests focusing on a single area to begin with—perhaps the front yard.

Seattle landscape architect Peter Harvard recommends starting with all the jobs that require heavy equipment: drainage, irrigation, earth-moving, and so on. "It's usually more efficient to do these jobs for the entire yard all at one time," he says. If you're drawing up a plan on paper (see "Put It in Writing" on page 165), consider breaking it up into several smaller plans, drawing each one on a different layer of tracing paper, and making sure you allow for the inevitable changes of mind and heart that go along with any backyard landscaping.

A rose-covered arch invites viewers into this charming garden and frames the plantings from both sides. The arch also provides vertical interest and balances low-growing annuals and perennials with taller shrubs and trees.

The Lay of the Lawn

Pros and cons of lawns • Reducing lawn space
• Good soil for good grass • Maintenance-saving tips

The American lawn is under attack these days. Gardeners complain that it wastes water, needs fertilizer, and requires lots of money and time to maintain. Of course, there are still many people who love the look of a lush lawn, its soft feel underfoot, and its practicality (have you ever tried to play touch football on a bed of pachysandra?). You can reduce the water and maintenance requirements of your lawn by following a few simple tips from the experts.

CUT YOUR LAWN BACK Tired of mowing, watering, and fertilizing, but don't want to get rid of your lawn? Shrink it instead, say the experts. Seattle landscape architect Deborah Harvard likes to include a bit of traditional lawn in the landscapes she designs, but she says "an acre and a half of it is excessive." She plants some of the yard with grass

The ultimate in easy-care groundcover: a spread of hardy shrubs that is attractive in every season. Once established, they rarely need water or fertilization. With the contrasting foliage of barberry, pine, juniper, and false cypress, just a few bright annuals are needed for color.

landscaping: trees, shrubs & vines

ALTERNATIVE LAWNS

If you choose the right variety of grass and mix it with other low-maintenance plants, you can have an attractive, easy-care lawn.

❧ Seattle landscape architect Deborah Harvard recommends a mix containing fescue (ask for new varieties that need less water and cutting), lemon thyme, veronica, and English daisies.

❧ Christina Hopkins of the lawn care specialists Hobbs & Hopkins shares the secret recipe for their Eco-lawn and Fleur-de-lawn seed mixes: 80 percent dwarf perennial ryegrass and 20 percent flowers—mostly baby blue eyes, English daisies, alyssum, and dwarf yarrows. These mixes yield what she calls "a fragrant, herbal ecology lawn that requires no fertilizer or additional water after establishment."

❧ Boston garden designer Philip Hresko plants several species of grasses, including some that are really weeds. The resulting lawn is strong and healthy and requires very little fertilizer.

and some with groundcovers, and then she creates paths that meander throughout. "I use lots of bulbs like little daffodils, alliums, grape hyacinths, and species tulips," she says. And she's especially fond of shrub roses like Meidiland's 'Carefree', which can cover large areas of ground quickly and which blooms freely all season, even into December in her Seattle backyard.

Ken Twombley of Connecticut's Twombley Nursery suggests putting in a shrub border to reduce the lawn, but does not advocate eliminating the lawn altogether. He believes that "a small lawn accentuates beds and is a big part of the winter landscape." Alan Summers of Carroll Gardens in Maryland agrees, and points out that nothing sets off your house like a lawn—or increases its value if you're selling.

A GOOD START FOR GRASS Whatever you choose to plant, the secret to a successful, low-maintenace lawn is good soil. "If you add new seed to bad soil, you're just putting a Band-Aid on the problem," says Christina Hopkins, of Hobbs & Hopkins in Oregon, who believes that "the better the soil, the lower the maintenance." For the best possible lawn, she advises starting with bare soil and rotary-tilling in compost and other soil amendments (see "Creating Fertile Ground" on page 273).

But Matt Horn of New York's Matterhorn Nursery says not to forget to have soil tested for both nutrients and pH (see "Put It to the Test" on page 264). "Nutrients are more readily available to grass root systems if they're in a soil with the proper pH level," he says.

THATCHING AND AERATING Once you've established your lawn, thatch and aerate it regularly, says Christina Hopkins. Thatching means removing the thatch—the dead grass stems, blades, and roots that bind together into a mat at the surface of the soil and keep water from reaching the living roots below. "Removing thatch allows you to water 50 percent less," she says. The best way is with a dethatcher, but you can also remove a lot of thatch by working the lawn thoroughly with a stiff rake.

To aerate the lawn, rent a core aerator, a machine that removes small cigar-size plugs of earth (or hire someone to do the job for you). Let the plugs decompose and enrich the lawn. Christina recommends backfilling the holes with a porous ceramic like Hobbs & Hopkins'

Profile soil modifier (see "Sources" on page 362) to keep clay soil from compacting underfoot. The best time to thatch and aerate is early spring, when moisture is abundant. Never thatch or aerate a lawn that's under stress from drought.

OTHER MAINTENANCE-SAVING STEPS Matt Horn recommends mowing high—no shorter than 2 inches—since root growth roughly equals blade height, and letting clippings lie where they fall. The clippings decompose quickly and add a burst of natural nitrogen to the lawn.

To keep your lawn healthy, stay away from chemical pesticides, adds Matt. Instead, use lawn seed treated with endophytes—beneficial fungi that live inside plant tissues and offer resistance against many insects and some diseases.

The lawn below is made of vigorous ground-covers such as clover (see closeup above) that are allowed to flourish. They need much less water, weeding, and fertilizer than a traditional lawn does.

landscaping: trees, shrubs & vines

GREAT GROUNDCOVERS

If you think that groundcovers can enhance your backyard, here is a selection of picks from the experts:

For full sun: Asiatic jasmine, ceanothus, creeping juniper, creeping phlox, evergreen heather, goldenstar, sedums

For shade or partial sun: wild gingers, English ivy, foamflower, pachysandra, vinca (periwinkle), lady's-mantle, heucheras

For dense shade: ferns, epimediums, sweet woodruff

Shrubs to use as groundcovers: dwarf spirea, stephanandra, Siberian carpet cypress, daphne (while these aren't evergreen, their twigs look good throughout the winter)

A note of caution: Vigor is a good quality in a groundcover, but some plants are just too aggressive in certain conditions. For example, vinca should not be used in California, where it over-winters and becomes a pest. Ask at local nurseries and botanic gardens.

Going with Groundcovers

What's a groundcover? • *Landscape uses* • *Planting suggestions*

Any low-growing plant that covers the soil is, by definition, a groundcover, including the most popular groundcover of all, turf grass. In general, however, when gardeners speak of groundcovers, they mean grass alternatives—everything from the familiar pachysandra to spreading perennials like hosta and daylily to low-growing shrubs such as prostrate junipers and dwarf spirea. There are many ways to use groundcovers in the yard.

CLOTHE LARGE AREAS Bored by your lawn? Nancy Rose of the Minnesota Landscape Arboretum suggests planting groundcovers as an interesting alternative. "There are a wide range of foliage types and textures, and many have attractive flowers or fruits," she says. Stephen Breyer of Tripplebrook Farm in Massachusetts likes to use ground-covers instead of mulch. "They're an excellent way to control weeds and, unlike mulch, they're permanent and don't move around," he says.

SOLVE BACKYARD PROBLEMS If your yard includes a steep slope where soil continually washes away, Nancy Rose suggests planting one of the deep-rooted groundcovers such as ivy or groundcover roses to stabilize and hold the soil.

Have a difficult area where nothing seems to grow? Try a tough groundcover, advises Celeste Wilson of California's Las Pilitas Nursery. *Ribes viburnifolium* (Catalina perfume) and some species of *Symphoricarpus* (snowberry), such as *S. mollis*, for example, do very well in the kind of dry shade that occurs under mature trees in California.

PULL THE GARDEN TOGETHER "Groundcovers can help unify a landscape by providing transition zones between low features like lawn and pavement areas and taller plants like shrubs and trees," says Nancy Rose. To help pull together and unify a variety of different plantings, use a single species of groundcover in various areas throughout your garden.

INSPIRED SUGGESTIONS Whether you choose to plant a single groundcover or to mix several in close proximity depends largely upon personal preference. Gene Dickson of Prentiss Court Ground Covers

False cypress is used here as a heavy-duty, all-season groundcover. There are many cultivars available that will stay low and spread over a large area. Once established in a sunny site, this woody groundcover needs almost no care at all.

Heather, an old-fashioned groundcover, is particularly attractive when it flowers in early spring, but it also provides near evergreen foliage and great fall color.

likes the look of single plantings. "I think a mass of one plant variety always looks better," he says. Stephen Breyer, on the other hand, prefers variety. He chooses groundcovers with contrasting textures and staggered flowering times. But there's another, more practical reason to go for variety, says Stephen: "Your whole planting is much less likely to be wiped out by disease."

Avoid using highly invasive groundcovers like crown vetch (*Cornilla varia*), bird's-foot trefoil (*Lotus corniculatus*), and variegated bishop's weed (*Aegopodium podagraria* 'Variegatum'), warns Alan Branhagen, director of Missouri's Powell Garden. (For more on invasive plants, see "Made to Invade" on page 200.)

landscaping: trees, shrubs & vines

Ground Patterns

Linear versus "flowing" plantings • Strategic spacing

If you've planted and tended your groundcovers well, in four or five years it won't really matter how you've spaced them—the plants will have grown together so that they resemble a single spreading plant. Until then, though, you'll have to look at the bare spaces between them, so it's worth taking a little time to space them in a pleasing way.

PLANTING CONFIGURATIONS If you're going for a formal, linear design, plant your groundcovers in rows, suggests Alan Branhagen, director of Missouri's Powell Garden. For a more natural feel, place them casually. Alice Knight of Washington's Heather Acres likes to plant in drifts—natural-looking, flowing rows.

To maintain even spacing between plants, North Carolina landscape architect Cynthia Rice recommends triangular planting. Imagine a line of connected Vs, with a plant sitting at the bottom point of each V and at the two outermost points at the top of each of the Vs.

SPACING BETWEEN PLANTS Ideal spacing, according to Stephen Breyer of Tripplebrook Farms in Vermont, would enable your plants to cover the ground completely when the mulch between them deteriorates—usually in a year or two. But that can be expensive, he notes, especially in large areas. If you space them further apart, you can fill in the spaces with annuals for the first few years.

For heathers, Alice Knight recommends planting on 2-foot centers (with the center of one plant sitting 2 feet from the center of the next), but she advises gardeners to consider the mature spread of the individual plant. If the groundcover you're planting will be 3 feet wide at maturity, you should space it on 3-foot centers. Though this saves you planting time and money, you'll have to look at bare ground for a while.

Using Cynthia Rice's formula, you could speed up the fill-in time. She spaces plants in 3-inch pots on 6-inch centers and those in 4-inch pots on 12-inch centers. For larger containers, Chicago landscape architect Janet Shen places 1-gallon pots on 15- to 18-inch centers and 2-gallon pots on 18- to 24-inch centers.

A river of blue turns this shady area into an enchanted forest. You can naturalize many perennials and bulbs, including Virginia bluebells and Siberian squill, to create this effect. Choose your favorite!

Dramatic Touches

Water, statues, and other fun garden features
• *Creating topiary*

Arbors and pergolas, statuary and topiary, ponds and fountains—the stuff of grand estates and sweeping botanic gardens is becoming more common in backyards across America. Still, many gardeners shy away from them. Some people think they'll be too difficult to install and maintain, or they fear that the result, in a small landscape, will look more silly than sublime. But these days, even the experts encourage home gardeners to try at least one or two special features. They're widely available, less expensive than they used to be, and the proliferation of kits has made installing them a lot easier.

A focal point like this stone pedestal, topped with a potted evergreen shrub and surrounded by trailing sweet alyssum, transforms a garden from ordinary to elegant.

Make sure, however, that when it comes to adding a special feature to your backyard, you apply the same principles of planning that you

landscaping: trees, shrubs & vines

One of the experts' favorite tricks is to create a tiny, secret garden tucked into a small corner.

would to the rest of the garden. "All special features are site-specific," says Ken Miller of Missouri's Horticultural Consultants. "You have to build a setting for them, not just dump them in." It's tempting to order a nice bit of statuary that appealed to you in a catalog, but look at your garden first and determine what would work best in it, and where. A small herb garden might include a traditional sundial. A birdbath should be placed under a sheltering tree. Water gardens do best in level, sunny areas away from mature trees. If there's a natural entry-point in the garden, you might consider an arbor planted with wisteria or fragrant roses.

SIZE AND NUMBER Most garden features work best as focal points. Because they naturally draw your eye, you need to use them with restraint. If your property is large enough, you can probably incorporate a number of different items, as long as they don't detract from one another. In a small yard, however, one or two will provide all the drama you need. And keep them in scale. In a modest backyard, a small birdhouse will look better than a towering topiary or a large gazebo.

WATER GARDENS AND FOUNTAINS "Water is fabulous in the garden, even on a small scale," says Boston garden designer Philip Hresko. He especially likes the dimension of sound that water adds to a backyard. "A small fountain can mask the sound of a highway," he says.

Joseph Tomocik, head aquarian at the Denver Botanic Garden, believes that every yard, no matter how large or small, can include water in its design. "You can create a handsome aquatic garden in a very small space with only a modest outlay of money and effort," he says. He has used a remarkable variety of containers for small-scale water gardens, including tubs, troughs, old sinks, and half whiskey barrels. You can find water garden supplies, plants, and advice at nurseries that specialize in aquatic gardens. Several mail-order companies specialize in water gardening (see "Sources" on page 362).

STATUARY For adding four-season color, Seattle landscape architect Deborah Harvard believes that nothing beats statuary. But don't assume that you're limited to human figures. "An Asian-style niche with several large stones and dramatic plants is a great focal point," she

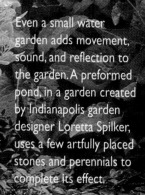

Even a small water garden adds movement, sound, and reflection to the garden. A preformed pond, in a garden created by Indianapolis garden designer Loretta Spilker, uses a few artfully placed stones and perennials to complete its effect.

landscaping: trees, shrubs & vines

says. For smaller yards, Frederick Held of Oregon's Nature's Garden advises sticking to a single, small-scale piece such as a stone lantern or a birdbath.

ROCKS AND ROCK GARDENS If your taste runs to more subtle features, consider adding a rock garden. You can do it with a minimum of labor, says June Hutson of the Missouri Botanic Garden. If you're not blessed with the strength of Hercules and can't quite see yourself hauling boulders, June suggests grouping smaller rocks together. "The groupings look as good as any single boulder," she says. For a more natural (and professional) look, especially in a small rock garden, she advises sticking with a single type of rock rather than risking a hodgepodge of textures and colors.

If you yearn for a rock garden but live in an area where rocks are hard to come by, you can get a similar effect by adding a few "living" rocks—silver-flecked, mounding plants like 'Powis Castle' artemisia.

ARBORS, PERGOLAS, AND TRELLISES Functional as well as decorative, arbors, pergolas, and trellises provide support for climbing plants and can add shade or screening to a small area without the expense of awnings or fences. To find out which support is right for your plant, see "Training Vines to Climb" on page 230.

Model railroads are becoming more and more popular in the garden. They bring new challenges, such as finding miniature plants that work well with the scale of the trains.

Use a rock wall to its best advantage. Perennials like moss pink, candytuft, euphorbia, and basket of gold will thrive in its crevices, creating a look of unmatched opulence without taking up any valuable garden space.

landscaping: trees, shrubs & vines

TOPIARY A garden of clipped or trained plants in geometric or figurative shapes once required an entire staff of gardeners to create and maintain—but no longer. If you've always liked the look of topiary but weren't sure it would work in your yard, Joyce Held of Vermont's Topiaries Unlimited suggests starting with a "portable" topiary—a potted plant that you can move around the garden or set on a porch or patio. Companies like her own Topiaries Unlimited sell a variety of wire frames in shapes that range from simple orbs to fanciful animals.

To create a topiary, all you need to do is choose a twining plant and insert or weave it through the wire. Joyce recommends ivy because it's so vigorous and easy to grow, but morning glories or a combination of ivy and flowering plants also works well. You can stuff the frame with sphagnum moss and insert rooted cuttings. Joyce's favorite method, because it's so easy, is to place a hanging basket of ivy inside the frame, then weave the ivy streamers onto the wiring. In a day or two they'll turn themselves toward the light and begin to grow outward. Wire topiaries are easy to maintain. Just snip off the streamers when they get too long.

A topiary can be as simple as a spiral-shaped evergreen (as shown above), or as whimsical as the elaborately trained ivy figure below.

landscaping: trees, shrubs & vines

Training Vines to Climb

The ways plants climb • Types of support
• Materials for supporting structures • Living "trellises"

Did you know that different vines have different ways of climbing? Some, like wisteria and morning glory, are twiners. They wrap their stems around sturdy supports like trellises, arbors, pipes, and other plants. Others, including clematis and passionflower, climb by means of tendrils, which coil around slender supports such as string, wire, or plant stems. Still others, such as ivy and Japanese hydrangea, climb by clinging to a support with rootlike structures known as holdfasts. And climbing roses aren't really vines at all; they simply have a tendency to grow upward in a vinelike way.

Most vines benefit from training, and some require it. The secret to training a vine easily and successfully is to choose the right structure and to fasten the vine to it safely.

SUPPORT SYSTEMS "The best structures for twiners have horizontal crossbars, placed at 8- to 12-inch intervals, to help support the vine's weight and relieve stress on the anchored branches," says Galen Gates of the Chicago Botanic Garden. For heavy twiners like wisteria, be sure to use a structure that's strong enough to support their considerable weight, says Seattle landscape architect Deborah Harvard.

Tendril climbers don't require superstrong supports, but they do need something to wrap their tendrils around. For relatively small vines, Aileen Lubin, director of Maine's Merryspring Park, likes the look of

To train a vine to a wooden fence, Galen Gates of the Chicago Botanic Garden uses cup hooks threaded with kitchen string. To get his vines to cover an arbor or pergola, he hammers in galvanized nails every 12 to 18 inches and ties the vines to the nails with string (preferably in the same color as the structure).

Don't expect your arbor to be covered in blooms the first year you plant it. But if you find the right plant for your site and train it patiently, you can have a profusion of blooms—such as these 'New Dawn' roses—in two or three years.

Hundreds of clematis cultivars (such as 'General Sikorski', above) are available, but be sure to provide adequate water during establishment of any variety. Sink a pot with a hole in the bottom near a new planting of clematis, and refill the pot daily so the water leaks slowly into the ground to water the roots.

tuteurs (wooden box planters with a pyramidal wooden trellising structure set in them, often topped with a ball or other decorative finial).

If you have a tendril climber and would like it to clamber around a wooden or stone pillar, Galen Gates suggests wrapping the pillar with a thin strip of netting, either wire or plastic. You can also use clear fishing line. To get twiners to climb a pillar, stretch three or four single wires, set about a foot apart, from the top of the pillar to the bottom.

Clinging plants will climb on almost any surface, but they can harm the surface. Holdfasts will eat through brick and mortar and rot wood. Stone walls or trellises set out from the wall are the best bets. Take care when using the most aggressive of these vines; don't let them attach themselves anyplace you don't want them.

BEST MATERIALS FOR SUPPORTS "Roses will pull down weak lumber," warns Mike Shoup of the Antique Rose Emporium in Texas. He recommends using 2 × 4s or 4 × 4s made from any strong, durable

Vines can give a look of timelessness—especially when cloaking a brick wall as shown above right. Or, vines can provide a fleeting spot of color, as does the mandevilla that drapes from a basket atop a post, above left.

wood. Arbor and trellis specialist Tim Brown, owner of New Jersey's Cedar Corps, likes both Western red cedar and Philippine mahogany—the former for its resistance to rot and the latter for its exceptional strength. If your garden is formal enough to demand a finished look, says Tim, you can apply an exterior stain and a clear preservative to postpone the inevitable weathering. If you mind the maintenance, however, don't paint the wood.

More durable than wood are metal alternatives like steel conduit piping, copper, and rebar (a rod used in construction to reinforce concrete). Gunnar Taylor uses all of these materials in the trellises he builds for North Carolina's Taylor Ridge Farm, because he prefers them for their long life in the garden. Metal supports are sturdy, and they look good. And some of them give a surprisingly formal feel to the garden.

Of course, not all vines demand such strong support. Some, like morning glory, thunbergia, and most varieties of clematis, are lightweight enough to grow on almost anything. If you don't mind replacing your supports every 10 years or so, Boston garden designer Philip Hresko recommends his own favorite material—batter-board, a form of rough-sawn spruce. "It's one-third to one-sixth the cost of plain pine, takes stain very well, and holds up for many years. When it falls apart, which can take 10 years or more, I just replace it," he says. Philip also likes to build his own supports with the trunks of "weed" saplings—trees that have seeded themselves uninvited in his or his neighbors' gardens.

LIVING SUPPORTS Want a superstrong support that never needs painting, looks great in the garden, and will last for years? Consider using other plants, especially trees and shrubs. "One of my favorite effects is climbing roses on conifers and broadleaf deciduous and evergreen trees," says Deborah Harvard. "If you train them up the first few feet, they'll seek the light and climb by themselves." John Fairey of Yucca Du Nursery in southern Texas likes to train clematis on spring-flowering shrubs. After the spring flowers fade, the clematis vines begin to bloom.

If you don't want to bother building a trellis, plant goldflame honeysuckle or other vines to spill over an existing wall.

ATTACHING THE VINE

While some vines climb naturally on their own, others need a little coaxing. Many vines need to be attached to a structure, at least for a while, so they know which way to climb.

❧ For roses, Mike Shoup of the Antique Rose Emporium in Texas recommends jute for its strength. You can also use commercial plant ties or stretchy fabrics like pantyhose cut in thin strips. "Don't use metal with roses," he warns. "It can cut into a growing stem and damage it, and some roses will have an adverse reaction."

❧ Seattle landscape architect Deborah Harvard uses strong twine on roses. "It will rot eventually, but by then the roses stay up by themselves," she says.

❧ For weaker vines, John Fairey of Yucca Du Nursery in southern Texas uses string, raffia, or thin wire surrounded by green foam (available at garden centers).

landscaping: trees, shrubs & vines

BUYING THE BIG STUFF

The trees and shrubs in your landscape usually cost more than annual and perennial flowers do. More important, they affect your landscape significantly. Once they're in place, you really don't want to have to replace them. The secret is to plan well and buy well in the first place.

Where to Shop

The pros and cons of local nurseries • Buying from catalogs

Maybe you've bought seeds through the mail or browsed the catalogs for bulbs and perennials. But what about "landscape" plants like shrubs and trees? Does it make sense to order them through the mail, or should you stick to local nurseries and garden centers?

One good reason to shop by mail is the availability of uncommon but valuable shrubs and trees like bluebeard or blue spiraea (left), which flowers in late summer and Japanese stewartia (right), which bears profuse blooms in spring.

WHY TO BUY SMALL

Many experts say smaller plants are the way to go.

❧ Ken Durio of Louisiana Nurseries recommends buying trees and shrubs no larger than 6 feet tall. "In most cases, young trees will outgrow big ones," he says.

❧ Neil Diboll of Wisconsin's Prairie Nursery points out that for each inch of caliper (the diameter of the trunk), a tree will experience a year of transplant shock. "Ten years after planting both a small tree and a mature one, you'll find that the smaller tree is bigger and healthier," he says.

❧ Seattle garden designer Sue Moss advises choosing young pot-grown plants whose roots are just beginning to show at the edge of the container. She's planted 1- and 5-gallon plants of the same variety and found that it takes only three years for smaller plants to catch up.

❧ "With very large, machine-dug trees, you can count on no growth for the first year. All the feeder roots have been cut off and need time to re-establish," says Lucille Whitman of Whitman's Farms in Oregon.

LOCAL ADVANTAGES If you're doing some major landscaping and want a finished look right away, Alan Branhagen of Missouri's Powell Garden recommends using locally grown plants. Tory Galloway of Seattle's Victoria Gardens agrees, pointing out that while you can get some surprisingly large shrubs and trees through mail-order, most catalog plants are, by necessity, relatively small—not so much because of the difficulty of shipping larger plants but because of the expense. Some garden centers will let you take a plant home and try it out in its new surroundings before you commit to it. And Guy Sternberg of Starhill Forest Arboretum in Illinois likes to purchase large plants locally because it allows him to "window shop."

Another advantage to purchasing plants grown close to home, says Memphis landscape architect Charles Sandifer, is the fact that "they're already acclimated to the idiosyncrasies of your particular climate." And, he adds, plants shipped through the mail have a tendency to dry out. Though most survive, it can take them considerable time to bounce back.

Harold Greer of Oregon's Greer Gardens, on the other hand, doesn't worry too much about adaptability. "Buying a plant from a mail-order source in a warmer climate isn't a disadvantage. Though there might be some hardier cultivars in colder areas and a plant grown for a long time in a cold area might develop hardier strains, a well-grown plant from a warmer climate will quickly adapt," says Harold.

HUNTING FOR TREASURES If you're looking for a rhododendron or a red maple, you'd probably do best to buy it from a neighborhood nursery. But if your taste runs to the exotic or you'd like to plant a new variety or cultivar, your only recourse may be catalogs. "Mail-order can offer some hard-to-find gems," says Tory Galloway.

If the plant you want isn't available in your neighborhood, but you don't want to pay a hefty shipping bill or wait years for a mail-order specimen to reach maturity, take a cue from Linda Gay of Mercer Arboretum in Texas and see if your neighborhood garden center will order it for you. "Let them pay the freight," she says. But if you're buying in bulk quantities, catalog shopping can actually save you money, since your local nursery will add a per-item markup to any purchase that may exceed your volume discount from a catalog according to North Carolina landscape architect Richard Boggs.

WHY TO BUY BIG

Some experts choose larger trees and shrubs.

⚜ Older plants are hardier, says Oregon's Harold Greer of Greer Gardens (but notes that younger plants are more resilient and bounce back quickly from the shock of transplanting).

⚜ Buying small means waiting. "If your plant won't fill your landscape, you either have a yard with a hole the first year or the temptation to fill in with other plants that might compete with or shade the new plant," says Wayne Mezitt of Massachusetts's Weston Nurseries.

⚜ Loretta Spilker of Indianapolis's Living Landscapes advises clients to "splurge on their trees and pinch pennies on their shrubs and flowers." When you want your garden to look good fast, buy balled and burlapped trees as large as your budget will bear (generally in the 8- to 18-foot range), she says. This doesn't work with trees that don't transplant well, like tupelo.

landscaping: trees, shrubs & vines

landscaping: trees, shrubs & vines

A SHOPPER'S CHECKLIST

Here are some questions the experts ask when buying trees for their own backyards.

❧ When buying balled-and-burlapped trees, they ask if the rootball is covered in real, not synthetic, burlap. Real burlap does not have to be completely removed before the tree is planted; it will break down and allow roots to grow into the soil. Synthetic burlap, which is sometimes manufactured to look like the real thing, must be removed.

❧ When buying bare-root plants, they ask when the plant was dug. Bare-root plants should only be dug out during dormancy. If the nursery doesn't know for sure, it's best to buy a different plant.

❧ The experts ask to remove a containerized shrub from its pot and check the roots. If the roots have circled the pot and formed a dense, inpenetrable mass, there's a good chance that the tree's growth will be stunted.

The Shape of Things to Come

Balled-and-burlapped, container-grown, or bareroot
• Planting tips

Whether you're buying trees and shrubs from a nursery or through a catalog, they'll come to you in one of three ways: balled-and-burlapped (also known as B&B), container-grown, or bareroot. With balled and burlapped plants, the rootball, including soil, is wrapped in burlap or another material (sometimes the rootball is placed in a wire basket before wrapping). Container-grown trees and shrubs have been grown in the pots they're sold in, usually in a light, soilless planting mix. Bareroot plants have been dug up from the field and the soil has been removed from around their roots in preparation for transplanting.

BALLED-AND-BURLAPPED If you're buying a good-size tree, says Rick Pearson of Ohio's Chadwick Arboretum, it will probably come balled-and-burlapped. The B&B process helps keep the tree and its roots stable. Make sure, though, that the tree has a healthy ball-to-caliper ratio (the caliper is the diameter of the tree trunk). For a tree with a 1-inch caliper, the Nursery Assocation recommends that the rootball measure at least 11 inches in diameter; a tree with a 2-inch caliper should have a 22-inch rootball.

Lee Morrison of North Carolina's Lamtree Farm points out that the B&B process helps keep roots from drying out—a potential problem with plants shipped bareroot. However, he cautions that the rootball should be wrapped in real burlap, not synthetic material. This is both to allow water to pass through readily and so the burlap will break down after planting, allowing roots to grow into the surrounding soil.

PLANTING TIPS The experts differ considerably on the best way to plant a balled-and-burlapped plant. Some, like Robert McCartney of South Carolina's Woodlanders, Inc., believe you should leave the burlap on when planting. "That's what it's there for," he says. (But that's only if it's real burlap; roots simply won't penetrate the synthetic stuff.) Lanny Rawdon of Missouri's Arborvillage Farm Nursery recommends the following method for planting B&B trees and shrubs: Loosen the string, but don't take off the burlap or break up the ball. "There's an integrity to the ball; fine hair roots have already begun to grow through the burlap, and you'll set the plant back if you shear them off," he says. Lee Morrison agrees. "If it's real burlap, just uncover the top, and you're in," he says. If the ball is very hard, water it for a few days to loosen it.

Some experts, however, including Rick Lewandowski of Pennsylvania's Morris Arboretum, recommend removing at least a portion of the burlap. "There's no problem with root penetration if the burlap is left on. However, there can be pest buildup, and the rotting burlap can be a home for fungus," he says. When planting, he positions the tree, fills the soil in halfway, and then peels back the burlap and cuts it away from the top 6 inches of rootball.

Doris Taylor, plant information specialist at the Morton Arboretum in Illinois, recommends the following procedure: If the plant is in a wire basket, remove as much wire as possible. Once the plant is in the

The roots of balled-and-burlapped trees and shrubs are covered by soil and burlap. Although some experts recommend leaving the burlap in place when planting the tree, most agree that peeling it back to expose most of the rootball is a good idea.

When choosing landscape plants, plant for fall and winter color as well as spring and summer flowers: spring-flowering azalea (top); burning bush takes center stage in fall (center); and winterberry, whose red berries brighten the winter landscape (bottom).

hole and positioned, remove the twine and cut away as much burlap as you can. If any burlap is left, loosen and push back most of the top layers so it's not left exposed above the surface—exposed burlap can act like a wick and draw moisture away from the roots.

CONTAINER-GROWN Though container-grown plants can present the gardener with a few problems, most experts prefer them. "They're especially good for difficult-to-transplant trees like nyssa, oak, and some magnolias," says Lanny Rawdon. And they work well for pyracantha and sassafras, "trees with difficult root systems or long taproots," adds Robert McCartney.

"Container plants are intensively grown, which results in a more vigorous condition," points out Ken Asmus of Michigan's Oikos Tree Crops. "This translates into much higher survival and growth rates the first year." Rick Pearson agrees, saying "A container plant will have a good root system because it usually gets more attention, water, and fertilizer." Another benefit of container plants is that you can plant them virtually anytime during the growing season.

PLANTING TIPS The major drawback of container-grown plants is that they can become potbound. With nowhere to stretch out, roots begin to circle the crown—a process that can persist after planting and eventually stunt or even kill a plant, says Lanny Rawdon. "I've lifted plants that have been in the ground for 10 years and found that their roots were still going around in a circle," he says.

However, don't let this stop you from buying container plants, because you can avoid or correct this problem. One way is to buy plants grown in "spin-out" containers—pots fitted with a copper ring at the bottom. When the roots come into contact with the copper, they stop growing. However, you'll still need to check the roots higher up in the pot for circling, warns horticulturist Rick Lewandowski.

If you do find yourself with a potbound plant, John Fairey of Yucca Du Nursery in southern Texas recommends removing all the soil and reorienting the roots outward at planting time. Lee Morrison offers a slightly easier method: "Make a shallow cut in four places around the rootball—north, south, east, and west." Even if the plant isn't severely potbound, you should encourage root development by freeing up the

A well-branched, sturdy specimen will immediately make a statment in your garden. Here are some terms you might encounter when shopping for large trees.

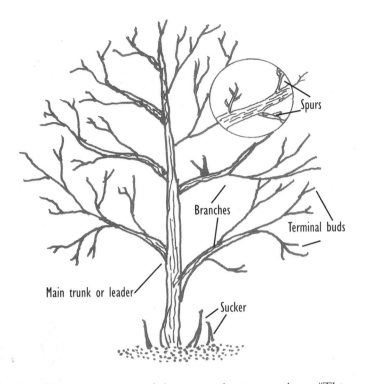

root ends and loosening some of the outer planting medium. "This enables the roots to come into direct contact with the new backfill soil, and that's crucial," says Wayne Mezitt of Massachusetts's Weston Nurseries.

BARE ROOTS Fruit trees are traditionally shipped bareroot. "This also works well with young hardwoods and dormant seedlings," says Robert McCartney. The advantage, according to Rick Pearson, is the fact that newly dug bareroot plants will be "kick-started into root growth the minute they hit the new earth." Make sure, though, that you order your bareroot plants from a reputable source. Improperly prepared roots can dry out before the plant reaches you, warns Lee Morrison. Unlike container plants, bareroot trees and shrubs have a small planting window and do best when planted in spring. "Don't buy them June through August," cautions Rick Pearson.

PLANTING TIPS Bareroot trees are easy to plant. You don't need to worry about cutting off wire or burlap or reorienting potbound roots. For specific planting instructions, see illustrations on pages 244.

landscaping: trees, shrubs & vines

PRUNING YOUNG GROWTH

Traditionally, trees were pruned just after planting to compensate for root loss during the digging-up process. The thinking was that a tree without all its roots couldn't support a full canopy of leaves.

Now, more and more experts recommend against pruning at planting time, and among them is the Morris Arboretum's Rick Lewandowski. "Pruning reduces the vegetation that trees use for photosynthesis. Without enough vegetation, the plant can't produce new growth," he says. Lewandowski advises pruning only if the branches are broken, damaged, or crossing in such a way that they're likely to rub against one another.

Fruit trees are the exception to these pruning rules; see "Fruit and Nut Trees" on page 318 for information on pruning young fruit trees.

The Smart Shopper

What to look for • Signs of poor health

Trees and shrubs are an investment, so choose wisely. Buy only those plants that are vigorous and healthy. It's one thing to lose a flat of marigolds, quite another to replace a tree or hedge.

LOOK FOR VIGOR Wayne Mezitt of Massachusetts's Weston Nurseries says to check for a strong branching pattern. Good color also indicates good growth, but, he adds, "a plant can be off-color for reasons that aren't significant—it might have been recently dug, for instance."

A plant's root system tells a lot about that plant's vigor. "To check the roots of a prospective purchase," says Kris Bachtell of Illinois's Morton Arboretum, "pick up the plant by the pot, place the base of

Although you can't check the roots of these balled-and-burlapped trees, you can look for other indications of their health. Dying branches and limp, yellowed foliage indicate that these trees have gone without water for a while; crowded, crossing branches show that they've been neglected.

the stem (or stems) between your fingers, and position your palm on the soil. Turn the pot over, making sure your hand catches any soil that may fall out, then carefully pull the pot away from the soil—you may need to tug lightly." In a vigorous, healthy plant, you should see viable roots at the surface of the soil. If you don't see any, the plant may have been transplanted too recently; moving it again might cause too much stress. Roots that are so tightly packed that you can hardly see any soil means the plant is potbound. "A potbound plant is often slow to establish, so don't purchase it unless it's something you've just got to have," says Kris.

If you're considering a balled-and-burlapped plant, make sure the roots aren't protruding through the burlap, advises Philadelphia horticulturist Rick Lewandowski. And Bill McKentley of New York State's Potsdam Nurseries cautions against buying plants that are overlarge; he doesn't like to use plants that are more than 5 to 6 feet tall. "If you buy small, you get more of the root system, and roots are everything," he says.

LOOK FOR SIGNS OF TLC If the grower or garden center has tended a plant well, it has a much greater chance of success in your backyard. When buying container-grown plants, make sure that they look as if they've been grown in—not thrown in—the pot, says Dr. Richard Lighty, director of the Mount Cuba Center in Delaware. He's quick to reject newly dug plants masquerading as pot-grown: "those that appear to have been divided with an axe a week before they were put on the sales bench." If you're considering a plant that's balled-and-burlapped, peek underneath the wrapping and make sure the rootball contains real soil, not sand, says Bill McKentley.

REASONS FOR REJECTION Certain signs qualify a plant for instant rejection. Chicago landscape architect Janet Shen avoids any plant that shows scarring, injury, or weakly structured branches. For Bill McKentley, red flags include signs of disease, insect infestation, and drying out, and he won't buy any plant labeled "in deep dormancy." "That's akin to coma," he warns. Celeste Wilson of California's Las Pilitas Nursery cautions against purchasing any plant with roots that are twisted around the trunk at the plant's crown, and she adds, "If a plant is wilted in moist soil, don't buy it."

ROOT CAUSES

The most important part of any plant you buy is its root system. Don't ignore the rest of the plant—look for symptoms of poor care and insect infestation—but pay particular attention to the roots.

❧ Look for roots at the surface of the soil on a containerized plant. If you don't see any, the plant may have been transplanted too recently.

❧ Roots should not be protruding from the burlap of a balled-and-burlapped plant.

❧ It's easiest to check the roots on a bare-root plant, but it's also easiest for those roots to become damaged. If you can't plant them immediately, bury them in soil and keep them well watered.

landscaping: trees, shrubs & vines

PLANTING TREES AND SHRUBS

The most critical day in the life of your tree or shrub is the day it's planted. Then, with a little tender care, your tree or shrub will be off and growing toward a long and healthy life.

Timing It Right

Autumn's advantages • When spring is best

In part, where you live will determine when you plant. If you live in a cold climate with a short fall, spring may be your best time for planting. Spring planting allows roots lots of time to establish themselves before the ground freezes and growth stops. Gardeners in warm climates, on the other hand, will sometimes do better to plant in fall, to avoid the heat stresses of early and overly warm or dry summers that can harm plants during establishment.

THE CASE FOR FALL PLANTING Given a choice between spring and fall, most of the experts choose fall. "It's nature's time for planting," says Lanny Rawdon of Missouri's Arborvillage Farm Nursery, the time when the majority of trees and shrubs drop their seeds, and the soil is still warm so plants can establish their roots without expending energy on topgrowth. Tennessee grower Virginia Pearsall recommends fall planting. "You get a stable root system before the plant has to grow," she says. In most areas of the country, rainfall is likely to be more even and consistent in autumn than spring—an important consideration when planting large trees and shrubs.

If you do plant in fall, Jack Crittenden of Missouri's Stark Brothers Nurseries recommends planting shrubs and trees only after they've gone dormant, unless they've been grown in pots. Container-grown plants can be planted before or during dormancy.

SPRING PLANTING Some plants dislike fall planting. Magnolias, says Lanny Rawdon, have fleshy roots and need to start growing quickly after their roots are cut. Most garden centers and nurseries will offer plants only at appropriate planting times, but if you have any doubt, ask an expert who knows your area.

When you start with small plants, use this simple trick to keep them safe. Drive a stake into the ground a few inches from the tree. You might not see the tree sapling when you're mowing the lawn, but you won't miss the stake.

A ten-dollar hole for a five-dollar plant: dig your hole two to three times the width but no deeper than the rootball, with gently sloping sides. You can use a shovel handle to measure and to steady the plant in the hole.

If you choose to plant shrubs and trees in spring, Jack Crittenden suggests getting them in early, before they've begun to leaf out. "Roots will begin to grow when soil temperatures reach 40° to 42°F," he says. Early planting will also help you avoid the drought stresses that can stunt or kill young shrubs and trees. In his Potsdam, New York, nursery, Bill McKentley planted 1,000 filbert trees in mid-April and 1,000 more two weeks later. He treated both batches identically, but the trees planted later didn't do as well. "The water table begins to recede as it gets warmer," Bill explains.

All the experts agree that the most critical timing is in the digging of trees—never dig up trees while they're actively growing.

ANTICIPATING ENVIRONMENTAL IMPACT One of the most important factors to consider when deciding when to plant is what conditions your tree or shrub will have to contend with once it's in the ground, says Wayne Mezitt of Massachusetts's Weston Nurseries. "If you plant too late in the fall, the plant won't root in time to stabilize itself, so it might need wind protection or staking," he says. "If you choose spring,

landscaping: trees, shrubs & vines

the plant will be putting out topgrowth before its roots get going, so it might need extra water." Know your climate and monitor weather conditions so you can protect plants appropriately and ensure their success.

ROOT CARE Regardless of when you decide to put your trees and shrubs in the ground, don't let the roots dry out before planting, says Wayne Mezitt. If they become too dry, they may not bounce back, even with a good watering.

Digging In

How deep? • How wide?

You get one only opportunity to plant a shrub or tree correctly, so it's important to do it right. Pay special attention to planting depth, advises Wayne Mezitt of Massachusetts's Weston Nurseries. Research has shown that planting too deep is a major cause of tree mortality.

Containerized shrubs should be planted at a depth equal to the height of the container.

GO WITH THE SOIL LEVEL If you're planting a container-grown shrub or tree, figuring out its proper level in the ground is easy. Simply plant it at the depth at which it was growing in its original pot, advises Guy Sternberg of Starhill Forest Arboretum in Illinois. If your plant isn't container-grown, look for root flare, says Dr. Richard Lighty, director of the Mount Cuba Center in Delaware. Root flare is the site at which the roots emerge on a tree and where the main stems originate on a shrub. These should sit level with the top of the soil. If you're unsure where the original soil level was, err on the shallow side. "There's always more settling than you think," says Washington nurseryman Hunter Carleton.

With shallow-rooted shrubs like rhododendrons, it's important to plant high—even in raised beds—says Harold Greer of Oregon's Greer Gardens. He uses a dense mixture of bark, pumice, and other composted organic materials to raise the level of the soil.

HOW WIDE? It's probably the best-known adage in gardening: For a five-dollar tree, dig a ten-dollar hole. But not every gardener interprets this saying in exactly the same way. For Hunter Carleton, it means that a plant with a 5-inch root mass should sit in a 10-inch-wide hole. Seattle garden designer Sue Moss's ten-dollar hole, on the other hand, is three or more times as wide as the rootball. Adages aside, most experts agree that your plants will feel right at home in a hole that's at least twice as wide as the rootball.

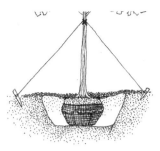

Set your tree in its hole so that the root flare—the place at which the roots emerge on a tree—is level with the top of the soil. The tree will settle, so if you're not sure where the root flare begins, err on the shallow side.

Souped-Up Soil

Enriching the earth • Growing media for container plants

When planting a tree or large shrub, you may be tempted to toss some compost into the backfill (the excavated soil), but is this such a good idea? Opinions vary.

MAKING AMENDMENTS Though the experts aren't of one mind on the subject, they all agree that the soil you plant in should be fairly fertile. Prepare the ground deeply and make sure your soil meets the pH requirements of the plant you're putting in it, says Dr. Richard Lighty, director of the Mount Cuba Center in Delaware. It's especially important to check for adequate drainage, advises Lucille Whitman of

landscaping: trees, shrubs & vines

WHAT'S IN A BERM?

A berm is a doughnut-shaped "shelf" of soil built up around a plant. It allows water to collect at the root zone without running off into the surrounding soil. Most experts are in favor of using berms.

❧ "A berm contains the mulch and keeps water from running off downhill," says Guy Sternberg of Starhill Forest Arboretum in Illinois.

❧ Harold Greer of Oregon's Greer Gardens says that berms help improve drainage—always a boon for new plantings.

❧ Wayne Mezitt of Massachusetts's Weston Nurseries finds that by creating a berm, he can water once a week instead of every day.

❧ And Lanny Rawdon of Missouri's Arborvillage Farm Nursery praises berms for their ability to keep the surrounding area free of grass and weeds.

Whitman's Farms. When a tree in her Oregon yard was felled by the wind, she checked the hole and found standing water. "The hole never drained, so the roots didn't form properly," she says. (See "Drainage" on page 28 for information on assessing drainage.) Here's what other experts have to say:

• Hunter Carleton of Washington's Bear Creek Nursery adds a bit of peat moss mixed with compost to his backfill, but he warns that changing the original soil too much could mean the plant may never adapt.

• When planting shallow-rooted shrubs like rhododendrons, Harold Greer of Oregon's Greer Gardens always adds some humus (composted organic matter).

• John Fairey of Yucca Do Nursery in southern Texas amends the soil around the edge of the hole, adding iron, guano, sulfur, and lime. If he's putting in a container plant, he mixes in a bit of the original soil from the container, as well.

• Jack Crittenden of Missouri's Stark Brothers Nurseries recommends adding peat to loosen heavy clay soils, but only if you can amend the entire planting area. "If peat is placed only in the hole, it creates a bowl that collects water and drowns roots," he says.

• Seattle garden designer Sue Moss agrees, adding amendments only if she can dig the entire planting area.

• Guy Sternberg of Starhill Forest Arboretum in Illinois also advises against amending backfilled soil, but he does crumble the backfill thoroughly.

• North Carolina landscape architect Richard Boggs offers what for him has been a very successful compromise: In good, loamy soil, he digs a relatively small hole and backfills it with the excavated material only; in poor soil, he digs a wider hole and amends the backfilled soil with organic matter. (For information on determining the quality of your soil, see page "Put It to the Test" on page 264.)

• Gerry Donaldson of Michigan's Hilltop Nurseries recommends digging and amending the entire planting area if at all possible, but advises against adding soil amendments into individual planting holes.

SOIL STABILITY The reason many experts leave their backfill alone is that if the difference in quality between the soil in the hole and the surrounding soil is too extreme, the roots of the tree or shrub may never grow beyond the backfill, and the plant may be stunted or killed. Container-grown plants often fail because the soil around their roots is so different from the soil in the ground. To help ease the transition, Lucille Whitman suggests transplanting pot-grown trees and shrubs with only a small amount of the container soil.

TLC for Transplants
Watering • Fertilizing • Checking for signs of stress

"If your tree has been planted correctly, proper watering is 90 percent of its success," says Illinois tree expert Guy Sternberg of Starhill Forest Arboretum in Illinois. (The other 10 percent is protection from rabbits, deer, and string trimmers.) But how do you determine what's proper for your plantings? What, if anything, do they need besides water? And how do you get water to the root zone, where it belongs?

WATERING-IN Immediately after planting, water your tree or shrub deeply "to remove air pockets and allow roots to make contact with the soil," says Jack Crittenden of Missouri's Start Brothers Nurseries. Linda Gay of the Mercer Arboretum in Texas likes to add vitamin B1

Linda Gay of the Mercer Arboretum in Texas builds a water-retaining berm 4 inches high around newly planted trees. She packs it firmly, then top-dresses with mulch.

THE ANTI-BERM BUNCH

Not everyone is enthusiastic about berms.

❧ Lucille Whitman of Whitman's Farms in Oregon prefers to conserve moisture with mulch, which she says acts like a berm, holding in water and directing it to the root zone. She leaves a 1-inch diameter ring of soil around the base of the plant unmulched and mulches the rest of the soil only 2 to 3 inches high to facilitate drainage.

❧ Gerry Donaldson of Michigan's Hilltop Nurseries believes that berms are only necessary on slopes that are so extreme that even a slow trickle from the garden hose runs off.

❧ And some experts, including Jack Crittenden of Missouri's Stark Brothers Nurseries, warn that berms can hold too much water—a problem for plants that dislike "wet feet," such as cherry trees.

landscaping: trees, shrubs & vines

A "GREENHOUSE" FOR TREES

A great way to boost tree growth is to plant the trees in minigreenhouses, says Ken Asmus of Michigan's Oikos Tree Crops. He recommends "supertube tree shelters," made of transparent double-walled polypropylene and available commercially from nurseries and tree specialists. Supertubes create a minigreenhouse environment for young saplings and offer protection from foraging animals. "Because of the higher levels of carbon dioxide and water, trees in supertubes grow two to five times faster than seedlings in an open environment," says Ken.

To install the tube, just slip it over the seedling and drive in a stake for support. There's an additional advantage to using the tubes: Because growth is forced upward, you'll need to do little if any early pruning.

(available in liquid form from nurseries and garden centers) to her initial watering-in. Before planting, she pushes organic fertilizer tablets into the side walls of the hole. The tablets provide nutrition for the first growing season without burning the young roots.

To make sure your soil isn't too firmly packed (which can destroy the fine air spaces roots need to take in water and nutrients), Wayne Mezitt of Massachusetts's Weston Nurseries suggests watering the soil halfway through the backfill process, allowing it to drain, then backfilling and watering again. "To complete the backfilling, smooth the surface soil with your hands or a rake and check that the root flare is completely exposed and that the top of the rootball isn't covered with soil," he says. After this, you may want to construct a berm (see "What's in a Berm?" on page 246) to help retain moisture and prevent runoff.

This enclosure provides some protection for a young tree, but also allows free movement so that it can form strong roots.

WATERING A GROWING TREE OR SHRUB In the first season after transplanting, a tree or shrub expends much of its energy regrowing roots lost or destroyed in the replanting process. And because this root loss affects the plant's ability to take in water, you'll need to water your trees and shrubs frequently, especially during the first month, says Bobbie Holder of Wyoming's Pawnee Greenhouse and Nursery. "Don't wait for symptoms of water stress to appear," advises Jack Crittenden. "If leaves are wilted, your tree is probably dead." Given the competition for moisture from grass, weeds, and larger trees with well-established root systems, Jack recommends ½ inch to 1 inch of water per week, or 2 to 3 gallons of water per tree.

Don't use an overhead sprinkler, which allows much of the water to be lost either to evaporation or on overhanging leaves and branches. "It's important to get the water deep into the ground," says Lanny Rawdon of Arborvillage Farm Nursery in Missouri. He suggests that you position a garden hose near the tree and let it trickle, or pierce a bucket with several nail holes, fill it with water, and leave it near the tree. Don't worry about wetting the entire root system. "Trees have the ability to absorb water from a relatively small area," says Gerry Donaldson of Michigan's Hilltop Nurseries. "A slow trickle from a garden hose placed halfway between the trunk and the tip of the branches can adequately water the tree."

SIGNS OF STRESS Watch carefully for signs of water stress—wilting, lack of vigor, and any changes in the appearance of the leaves. "The leaves of many fruit trees appear less lustrous and may have a gray cast to them when they're water-stressed," says Gerry. If in doubt, check the soil 2 to 3 inches below the surface at a number of locations under the tree canopy. "If you can't feel any residual soil moisture, you need to water," says Gerry. Linda Gay waters more frequently during periods of drought and at the beginning of growth or bloom cycles, and she always adds additional moisture if the plant sits beneath mature native trees.

A 2- to 3-inch layer of mulch helps retain moisture, and diligent weeding cuts down on competition for precious rainwater, points out Hunter Carleton of Washington's Bear Creek Nursery. Mulching is especially important if the plant has been container-grown, says

The "spindle" training system, shown above, trains young trees into cone shapes to improve air circulation. Branches are anchored horizontally with stakes and twine until they can hold their positions without help.

landscaping: trees, shrubs & vines

MULCHING DEPTH

How deep you mulch depends on the material you're using, says Rosie B. Lerner, Purdue University's extension specialist in consumer horticulture. For a light-textured mulch like straw, she recommends a depth of up to 4 inches. "But for materials that compact, like grass clippings, 2 inches is tops," she says.

When Ken Asmus of Oikos Tree Crops mulches with sawdust—another material that can compact easily—he lays down no more than 1 inch. Steve Jones of Maine's Fieldstone Gardens is even more cautious. "With dense materials like cocoa hulls, I keep the mulch very thin—maybe 1/2 inch," he says. Thick mulches suppress weeds and look good but keep air and water from reaching the root zone.

The amount of mulch you lay down also depends on what you're mulching. "Small plants like perennials have a difficult time in a big, thick mulch—they drown or suffocate," says Suzanne van Schoeder of Wisconsin's Winter Greenhouse.

Wayne Mezitt, since water will have a more difficult time moving from the backfill into the soil from the original container. Roots can also dry out when strong winds work the plant loose from its planting hole, so keep a close eye on new plantings, Wayne advises.

FERTILIZING Most experts use little or no fertilizer the first year. The roots of new transplants aren't able to take up fertilizer, and in many cases it's more likely to burn roots than help the tree.

Gerry Donaldson relies on good soil preparation to provide nutrients, and Bobbie Holder of Wyoming's Pawnee Greenhouse and Nursery fertilizes only with vitamin B1 in a light liquid concentrate. "It's a 'soft' fertilizer, and it helps reduce transplant shock," she says. Jack Crittenden relies on light applications of "starter" fertilizers; look for slow-release, organic fertilizers that won't burn or stress new transplants.

Mulch Madness

The advantages • The options

Most experts swear by mulch for its moisture-retaining qualities, its ability to maintain even soil temperatures, and (depending on the type of mulch used) its rugged good looks. Mulch also keeps you and your lawn mower or trimmer at a safe distance from vulnerable tree trunks, and it replaces grass that might otherwise struggle to coexist with thirsty tree roots, resulting in ragged patches of grass and slow establishment of trees.

CHOOSING A MULCH Most of the experts use shredded tree bark. "It can breathe, and it doesn't compact," says Dr. Robert Nuss of Pennsylvania State University. Robert McCartney of Woodlanders in South Carolina mixes pine bark with pine straw. Rick Pearson, of Ohio's Chadwick Arboretum, recommends composted bark. "Avoid anything fresh," says Rick. "It ties up nitrogen, and young trees need nitrogen to grow and leaf out." Kyrnan Harvey, a landscape architect on Long Island, New York, chooses shredded cedar bark for its appealing russet-brown color.

If you have a chipper/shredder, as Kathryn Mathewson of San Francisco's Secret Garden design firm does, you can make your own mulch from shredded leaves. She keeps two piles in her yard: one fresh, one a year old. If possible, she mulches with the year-old material.

Perhaps the easiest way to mulch is with mulch mats—biodegradable geotextiles made from cellulose. Ken Asmus of Michigan's Oikos Tree Crops uses them. "They biodegrade in two to three years, eliminate weeds, and help provide good soil for young trees," he says. "And they're an aesthetically pleasing light brown."

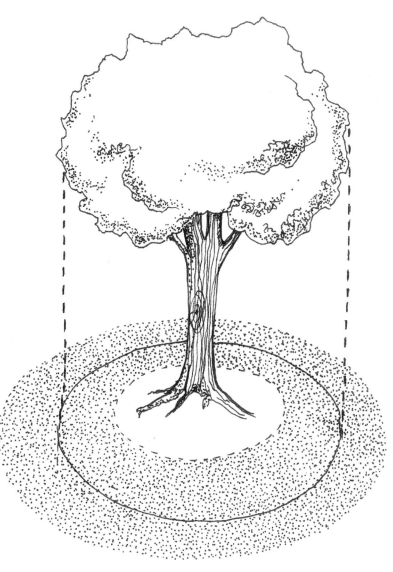

MULCHING FOR SUCCESS

Take care not to mulch above the crown (the juncture of root and stem), says Wayne Mezitt of Massachusetts's Weston Nurseries, or you can "bury" the plant and suffocate it.

Most of the experts recommend keeping mulch away from the base of your plants because mulch can cause fungal diseases. According to Steve Jones, it's important to make sure that the mulch doesn't end up burying the crowns of your perennials. "Always keep mulch at least 3 inches away from the stem," advises Suzanne van Schroeder of Wisconsin's Winter Greenhouse. Jack Crittenden, a fruit tree specialist with Missouri's Stark Brothers Nurseries, maintains a 6-inch distance between mulch and the bases of his trees.

Apply mulch around a tree and extend it several inches beyond the dripline. But keep a 4- to 6-inch ring around the trunk uncovered so that air can circulate around the bark.

landscaping: trees, shrubs & vines

Fast Forward

Ways to encourage quicker growth • A few cautions

Smaller trees eventually catch up to larger ones after transplanting, but the wait can be frustrating to anyone with visions of spreading canopies and sheltering branches. There are ways to stimulate faster growth, but are they safe?

BOOSTING GROWTH Most experts agree that the best way to get your tree off to a quick start is to water it well. John Fairey of Yucca Do Nursery in southern Texas waters frequently for the first two growing seasons, and then tapers off gradually during the third. Fertilizer, judiciously applied, can also help speed early growth, but make sure it's organic. "Synthetic fertilizers are high in salt and destroy the small tree roots," he says.

To strengthen saplings, Lanny Rawdon of Arborvillage Farm Nursery in Missouri recommends staking them, but only for several months. "I've seen trees that have been staked for a year or two flop over flat when the stakes are removed," he says. In fact, recent research suggests that trees need to be shaken by the wind to produce a strong root system. "When you stake a tree, give it some room to flex," says Pennsylvania horticulturist Rick Lewandowski. "We try to position trees perpendicular to prevailing winds and use two or more stakes so that the tree isn't held in a rigid position." He and his colleagues at the Morris Arboretum stake only if the tree is in a windy spot or a site where passersby might damage it.

CAUTIONS Not everyone believes in stimulating growth. "I don't like pushing a tree," says Dr. Robert Nuss of Pennsylvania State University. "You're likely to end up with weak, whippy growth, or you might change the shape of the tree." He advises doing a soil test before planting and adding no fertilizer unless weak growth indicates a need for it. "A tree's roots aren't ready to take up fertilizer until it's been in the ground for several weeks," he says, adding that even at that point, fertilizer can burn young feeder roots. In fact, many experts, including Chicago landscape architect Janet Shen, believe you should wait a full year between transplanting and fertilizing.

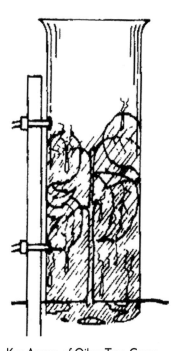

Ken Asmus of Oikos Tree Crops in Michigan recommends planting saplings in "supertube tree shelters." The transparent tubes, he says "create a mini-greenhouse environment around a seedling tree while giving protection from animals." He finds trees grow two to five times faster in the tubes.

landscaping: trees, shrubs & vines

Making It in the Shade

Trees best left undisturbed • Plants that grow well under trees
• The act of underplanting

Trees add so much to the landscape—structure, shade, and a sense of permanence, plus fruits, flowers, and spectacular fall foliage. They also take a lot out in terms of nutrients and water, making it a challenge to plant anything beneath them.

CONSIDER THE TREE Some trees and shrubs, like sassafrass and pyracantha, don't like their roots disturbed, warns Lucille Whitman of Oregon's Whitman's Farms. If you do decide to plant underneath them, do it gradually and observe how the plantings affect the tree. Better yet, spread a 2-inch layer of mulch under the tree and plant only at the outermost edge of the leaf canopy.

Small-leaved hostas, including 'Ginko Craig', fit nicely under a graceful weeping willow. The tree will compete greedily for all moisture, so the site must be watered regularly.

landscaping: trees, shrubs & vines

Then there are the trees that don't like to share their space. These include strong-rooted species like beech and Norway maple, says Long Island, New York, landscape architect Kyrnan Harvey. Trying to plant perennials around them is a losing battle. "It never hurts the trees, but most plants don't do well in dry shade," he says. Kyrnan has had success with plants suited to dry shade, notably vinca (periwinkle), liriope (lilyturf), and *Euphorbia robbii*. You can also try comfrey and epimediums, two favorites of Allan Summers of Maryland's Carroll Gardens, or, suggests Bobbie Schwartz of Bobbie's Green Thumb in Ohio, bigroot geranium, lady's mantle, and Serbian bellflower.

Black walnuts have a notorious reputation for inhibiting the growth of anything planted beneath them. These trees contain juglone in their roots and leaves, which some experts think may be harmful to the growth of other plants. But Lanny Rawdon of Missouri's Arborvillage Farm Nursery and others have had little or no trouble planting under

The open crown of this small beech tree allows some sunlight to peek through. The site is sunny enough for partial-shade plants like columbines; sun-loving annuals grow in the sunnier edges of the bed.

Roses need room; planting close to their bases cuts off air circulation and promotes disease. But you don't need to leave their leggy bottoms showing. Plant a ring of annuals and herbs, such as the salvia and germander shown here, a generous two feet from a group of roses and all the plants will thrive.

black walnuts, with the exception of vegetables (a bad bet under trees in any case, given their need for sun).

In general, though, most mature trees take just fine to under-planting, as long as you plant correctly. In fact, some of the experts believe that underplanting benefits trees. "The thing that hurts trees most is compaction from people walking on surrounding soil. So planting under a tree helps by discouraging people from treading on the root zone," says Boston garden designer Philip Hresko. He carefully monitored street trees in Brookline, Massachusetts, and found that those with planted tree wells grew and looked better than those surrounded with bare soil.

AGE MATTERS Jack Crittenden of Missouri's Stark Brothers Nurseries believes that the majority of trees can be successfully underplanted, but not during the first few years after transplanting. "Beware of competition for nutrients and water during the establishment period,"

landscaping: trees, shrubs & vines

CUT BRAVELY

"When in doubt, take it out," says Gerry Donaldson of Connecticut's Hilltop Nurseries. Jack Crittenden, of Missouri's Stark Brothers Nursery, agrees: "Everyone can prune, but most people are afraid to go far enough," he says.

If you're worried that too much pruning could hurt your fruit trees, Crittenden offers the following extreme examples: "A two-year-old, 6-foot-tall tree is girdled by a rabbit above soil level because of deep snow. Cut the tree off below the girdle, and you'll still have a good tree in a few years," he says. Or imagine that a 12-year-old tree is badly broken in a storm. You can cut that tree to a stump, says Crittenden, graft in a 1/4-inch branch, and in two years you'll have a growing tree.

he warns. Stephen Breyer of Tripplebrook Farm in Vermont recommends planting nothing in a 4- to 6-foot zone around young trees. "After a few growing seasons, put in a few things and make sure the tree is still doing well before you add more," he says.

THE EXPERTS PICKS FOR UNDERPLANTING Philip Hresko's favorite under-tree plants include groundcovers like ivy and vinca (periwinkle). You can also try shallow-rooted shrubs like rhododendron and holly, says Ken Twombley of the Twombley Nursery in Connecticut. And Rick Pearson of Ohio's Chadwick Arboretum has been very successful with hostas, "because they have a very contained root system." However, he and other experts warn against planting annuals, whose yearly installation can disturb tree roots. Avoid grass as well, advises Seattle landscape architect Deborah Harvard. "Lawns hurt trees and vice versa," she says. Grass competes with trees for water and nutrients. The fertilizer grass requires doesn't suit the needs of the tree, and the tree, in any case, is likely to suck up moisture that the grass requires to survive.

PLANTING PROCEDURES The root systems of most mature trees tolerate some disturbance. In fact, according to Chicago horticulturist Galen Gates of the Chicago Botanic Garden, you can rotary-till the entire area under a tree. Afterward, spread a 6- to 8-inch layer of new topsoil and well-composted organic matter and work it in so that old and new soils are combined. Galen advises planting flowers or groundcovers closer together than you would elsewhere in the garden and giving them additional water and fertilizer. Unfortunately, the tree will inevitably reclaim its territory. "In three to five years, the root system will come back up into the plants," he says.

Allan Summers suggests that instead of disturbing the entire area under the tree you should dig a hole for each plant. To make the job easier, he recommends an auger (a large, screwlike tool used for boring holes). Even Galen Gates, whose backyard includes a large Norway maple, decided against the rotary-tiller method. Instead, he built a deck around the tree that included planter boxes for annuals. Not only did this allow him to "plant" under the tree, it made the best possible use of the tree and its shade.

PRUNING

Want to strengthen your trees and shrubs? Promote lush new growth? Encourage bigger and more bountiful blooms? A regular program of pruning can accomplish all this and a great deal more. Pruning opens up your plants to light and air, discouraging disease and insect infestation. It boosts production on fruiting trees and shrubs. And it helps your plants attain a pleasing, natural shape. By limbing up your trees (pruning off the lower branches), you can invite sunlight into your yard. By shearing your shrubs, you can create dense, healthy hedges. And all these tasks are within the grasp of every home gardener—with a little help from the experts.

FINE POINTS OF PRUNING

If you know what you're pruning goals are, it's easier to accomplish them.

Get the dead out According to Dr. Paul Steiner, extension fruit pathologist at the University of Maryland, weak and dead branches attract scale, insects, and numerous diseases. Remove these branches as soon as you see them—no matter what the time of year.

Open up the tree to light and air When looking for places to cut, choose the ones that will allow the most light and air to penetrate the canopy, says Steiner. More light equals greater fruit production, and increased air circulation means less chance of fungal and other diseases.

The goal of pruning is to open the tree to allow light and air to filter through its crown while retaining a graceful shape.

landscaping: trees, shrubs & vines

You can rejuvenate an out-of-shape shrub like forsythia by cutting the whole plant back to the ground. It won't be as big or flower as much in the first year, but by the second year it will be healthier and more graceful looking.

Pruning to Promote New Growth

How and when to prune • *Pruning rosebushes*
• *The best tools for the job*

A tree or shrub responds to the loss of a branch by growing another—often several others—to replace it. By pruning, you're simply prodding your plant to replace old wood with new, vigorous growth. If you suffer from fear of pruning—a common affliction among gardeners—the experts can calm your anxieties and offer you their secrets for producing lush new growth.

CUT TO THE QUICK Renewal pruning is the act of selectively removing a shrub's old wood to encourage new growth. "Most people misunderstand the concept of renewal pruning—they tend to take out the little wood and keep the big," says Jeff Epping, director of horticulture at Wisconsin's Olbrich Botanical Gardens. In fact, Epping advises removing a quarter to a third of the oldest wood every year "so that you'll never have branches that are more than three to four years old." In addition to stimulating new, lusher growth, you'll be removing the wood that's most subject to pest infestation.

HOW DEEP SHOULD YOU CUT? Epping recommends going right down to the soil level. "If you leave a two- to three-inch stub, the new shoots will come off the stub, and that stub will be subject to insect damage," he says. After you've taken off enough of the oldest canes, you can do some tip pruning to shape the shrub. "Take the tip down to a crotch; don't just lop it off," advises Epping. If you don't want to go down that far, prune the tip off to a bud, says Bobby Mottern, curator of South Carolina's Brookgreen Gardens.

REJUVENATION PRUNING Shortly after arriving at the Olbrich Botanical Gardens, Jeff Epping was faced with a badly overgrown planting of spirea. "To renewal-prune them would have been almost impossible," he says. So instead he employed the more drastic technique known as rejuvenation pruning—the act of cutting a shrub down to the soil level. According to Epping, the best time to rejuvenate a shrub is in early spring, while it's still dormant. That way, all the shrub's stored energy will go into the crucial job of creating new, vigorous branches. After cutting back, fertilize the plants well to get them off to a good start. If you've had problems with deer or rabbits, Epping recommends caging the shrubs for the first year—all that tender young growth will be far too tempting to wild foragers.

PRUNING ROSES Louise Clements of Oregon's Heirloom Old Garden Roses recommends pruning twice a year: in spring (when new growth begins) to shape the bush, encourage new growth, and remove dead and spent canes; and in fall, to protect the bush from potential winter wind damage. In fall, prune only the longest canes, shortening them to about 3 to 4 feet. Always prune to an outside-facing bud (to keep the new canes growing outward), cutting the cane at a 45-degree angle so that water doesn't collect on the end. The cut should be between ¼ and ½ inch above the bud eye. If your rosebush blooms only once a season, Clements recommends pruning it immediately after flowering (usually in mid-July). "You can prune once-blooming roses to 15 inches every other year with no damage," she says. She trims and shapes rambling roses after the blooming season, keeping the number of canes between four and eight depending on the area they cover.

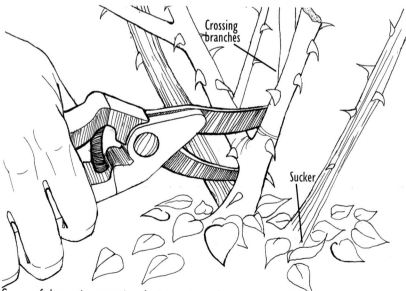

Some of the easiest pruning decisions to make: remove suckers (low-growing branches) and crossing branches.

PRUNING FRUIT TREES

Pruning is essential for fruit trees and it should be started when they are young. Jack Crittenden of Missouri's Stark Brothers Nurseries recommends a hard pruning. "Pruning helps roots develop first and keeps a young tree in balance," he says. For a bareroot tree, remove all but four main branches, then cut these branches down by half. Cut about 12 inches off the top branch.

Because fruit develops better on horizontal limbs, prune fruit trees so that branches can zigzag (this also helps to control size). After you prune, bend the branches and secure them with rope in a close-to-horizontal position.

landscaping: trees, shrubs & vines

Wisteria, usually allowed to ramble as a vine, is easily trained as a small tree. Start early, use stout stakes and heavy twine, and keep the pruning shears handy. This method provides the luxury of wisteria blossoms without the nuisance of its aggressive growth.

landscaping: trees, shrubs & vines

REASONS TO PRUNE DECIDUOUS TREES Most home gardeners are capable of pruning young trees, and according to Mike Stansberry of Tennessee's Beaver Creek Nursery, it's young trees that benefit most from pruning. Prune when the tree's getting started, he says, "and you'll need less help later on." But don't do heavy pruning on newly transplanted trees, warns Oregon arborist Philip Frazee. "Transplants need as much leaf surface devoted to food production as possible," he says.

WHY PRUNE? Prune to remove crossing branches, which can rub and damage one another, and broken limbs, advises Jeff Epping of Wisconsin's Olbrich Botanical Gardens. And to provide headroom, Mike Stansberry advises limbing up young trees (removing their lower branches) as they grow. If the tree has double leaders (trunks), he recommends pruning one out to maintain a pleasing "treelike" shape. In addition, Chuck Flynn, forester at Pennsylvania's Musser Forests, prunes to eliminate branches with narrow crotches—those growing at a 35-degree or smaller angle—since these branches are likely to split in an ice storm. Don't try to force your tree into a shape nature never intended. "When you fight nature, nobody wins—plants don't look natural, and you're continually hacking at them," warns Jeff Epping. And don't top off a young tree. "If you have to top a tree, it's probably the wrong tree in the wrong place," says Mike Stansberry.

PRUNING POINTERS "In general, cut back to a bud or branch," says Stansberry. If you're removing the entire branch, Jeff Epping advises cutting it back to the branch collar—the raised, ridged area where branch meets trunk. "If you cut too flush and remove the collar, the wood will take a long time to heal—and sometimes will never heal," says Epping. He stresses the importance of using the proper tool: "For big branches, use a saw, not a lopper, and don't strip the bark."

WHEN TO PRUNE According to Chuck Flynn, most deciduous hardwoods can be pruned anytime during the year. He prefers to shape them in winter, then prune again in midsummer to retain fullness. Avoid pruning during leaf-out and leaf drop, says Philip Frazee, since these are the times when trees most need their stored carbohydrates.

Pruning Conifers and Hedges

Avoiding mistakes • Going natural • Shearing and spot-pruning • The best tools

Conifers and other evergreens are indispensable in the landscape, adding form and structure to the garden and offering year-round color and interest. Most yards include at least a conifer or two, yet few gardeners are comfortable with the idea of pruning them. How much is too much? Can you under-prune? Clippers or loppers? And when do you prune?

PRUNING CONIFEROUS TREES As with deciduous trees, mature conifers require little in the way of pruning. "If you have to do a lot of pruning on an evergreen tree, it's probably in the wrong place," says Mike Stansberry of Tennessee's Beaver Creek Nursery. Dr. Richard Lighty, director of Delaware's Mount Cuba Center, never prunes hemlocks and cryptomerias, except to remove dead wood. At Indiana's Musser Forests, forester Chuck Flynn prunes only new growth. "If you do more than that on a pine, you're going to end up with a dead stub," he warns. He recommends pruning shortly after the first flush of growth in spring.

PRUNING CONIFEROUS SHRUBS Like most of the experts, San Francisco landscape designer Angela Fabbri prefers conifers with a natural look. She prunes them lightly "so they can breathe," and cuts the lower branches to make it easier to work the ground. Dr. Richard Lighty prunes dwarf conifers to show off, not disguise, their interesting branch structure. At Tennessee's Beaver Creek Nursery, Mike Stansberry never uses shears or electric clippers. Instead, he hand-prunes individual branches to maintain a plant's natural shape. "Don't cut back past where you see evergreen foliage," he warns, or you could end up with a plant that's mostly dead wood.

The best time to prune yews and other coniferous shrubs is in spring. Richard Miller of Pennsylvania's American Arborist Supplies likes to prune after new growth has hardened off—in his West Chester backyard, that's usually sometime in May. Mike Stansberry, on the other time, tries to prune just before growth begins. "The cuts heal up faster, and you get more bud break from beyond the pruning cut," he says.

Jeffrey Kirch, an Indianapolis landscape architect, uses lots of hedges in his designs. He uses hand pruners to prune out only the foliage that's exceeded the general growth of the hedge.

landscaping: trees, shrubs & vines

5

SOIL-BUILDING SECRETS

"Soil is alive. It needs to be fed and cared for."
PEG COOK, NEW YORK

Dig your hands into the earth on a warm spring day and you bring up more than dirt. There, in your upturned palms, is a miniature world, a working environment composed of minerals, air, water, plant matter, and microfragments of rock, where millions of tiny organisms feed on organic matter and turn it into plant nutrients. The experts know that soil, more than anything else, is the key to healthy plants. Which is why soil building should be your number one concern as a gardener.

That doesn't mean that it has to be your life's work. Over decades, in their own backyards, in laboratories, on farms, and in fields, the experts have amassed a harvest of soil-building secrets to make your job easier and more rewarding. In the entries that follow they'll tell you when and how to test your soil, explain the quick route to first-class compost, list the best ways to improve clay and sandy soils, and describe the amazing benefits of crop rotation. If you don't understand the role that pH plays in your backyard—or don't know how to alter your soil's pH—keep reading. You'll also discover the benefits of "green manure," sources of cheap compost, the most effective organic fertilizers, and more. "Feed the soil, and the soil will feed your plants," the old adage goes. The experts share both their soil- and plant-feeding secrets and show you why the most important part of your garden is the part you don't usually see.

HERE'S WHAT YOU'LL FIND IN CHAPTER 5

SECRETS OF YOUR SOIL

The soil in your yard is a magical mix of organic matter, nutrients, moisture, air, rock granules, and microorganisms. Discovering the exact combination of ingredients will help you understand how well your soil will feed the plants you hope to grow in it. This is the first step to creating the best growing environment for your flowers, vegetables, trees, and shrubs.

Put It to the Test

Timely testing • How often? • Testing tricks and tips

To get all of the dirt on the soil in your backyard, you need to do a test. A good one will give you the scoop on the "big three" nutrients—nitrogen, phosphorus, and potassium—as well as key micronutrients such as calcium, iron, and magnesium. You'll also get advice on what to do if any of these nutrients are missing.

One thing you won't learn is how "active" the organic matter is—whether it's just lying around or actually coming in contact with microorganisms that break it down into a form that plants can use, says Dr. Ray Weil of the University of Maryland. If you want to learn more about the activity of your soil, Dr. Weil recommends Maine's Woods End Research Laboratory (see "Sources" on page 362 for more information) as the best place to go for a test of this type.

THE BEST TIME TO TEST

The time of year you do a soil test affects its results.

❧ Dr. Ray Weil of the University of Maryland says that potassium, for example, tends to be higher in the spring.

❧ John Jeavons, author of the legendary How to Grow More Vegetables, recommends testing after the growing season, so you'll know what your soil needs for next year.

❧ Peg Cook, who runs a soil-testing service in New York, says that if you suspect your soil lacks lime, have it checked a season before planting, since lime takes a while to work its way into the ground. Another reason to do your soil test in the fall is that fewer gardeners test then, so you'll get your results faster.

To take soil for a soil test, dig down about 5 inches for flowers and vegetables, 3–4 inches for lawn. It's easy to do with a bulb planter.

SHOULD YOU TEST? Not all experts think soil testing is essential. For instance, Dr. Richard Lighty, director of the Mount Cuba Center in Delaware, recommends it only if you're growing plants with unusual requirements (such as azaleas, which prefer acid soil). Otherwise, he feels that a good, balanced, organic fertilizer will correct most common deficiencies. And Seattle garden designer Sue Moss doesn't bother with testing unless plants show clear signs of trouble. Most of the pros, however, believe that soil tests are a good idea, especially when you're installing a new lawn or garden or putting in rare or expensive plants.

WHEN TO TEST AND HOW OFTEN "Always do a soil test when you start a new garden," advises Patty Kleinberg of New York's Queens Botanical Garden. After that, she retests every three to five years. If plants aren't thriving, consider having your soil checked several years in a row to see how it's changing, advises Larry Ringer of Ohio Earth Food. For gardens full of annual flowers or vegetables, Patty Kleinberg tests more frequently because these plants tend to deplete the soil of nutrients more quickly than perennials do.

DOING THE TEST You can buy a home testing kit and do it yourself, but don't expect to get the detailed results you'd get from a professional lab. If all you're interested in is pH, however, a home test is good enough. (See "Sources" on page 362 for the experts' home test picks.) Use a lab, which you can find by contacting your local cooperative extension agent or a nearby botanic garden, for more detailed information. The lab will probably ask you to gather several soil samples from a variety of areas in your yard. Peg Cook, who runs a soil-testing service in New York, usually asks for five samples, thoroughly mixed, which will give you a good average reading. If you're planting things with very different requirements in separate areas of the yard—rhododendrons in the shrub border and tomatoes in the vegetable garden, for example—Dr. Ray Weil suggests sending separate samples. This will cost a little more, but the results will be more useful. Peg Cook suggests sending along a crop list—a rundown of everything you'll be planting. This way, the lab can be more specific about recommending amendments, since different plants can have very different requirements.

TESTING TIPS

For ease and accuracy, follow these expert hints:

❧ Gather the soil with an iron-free spoon or trowel, says John Jeavons. Even a trace of iron can skew the test results. Be careful not to include debris and residue like mulch, and don't sample for 30 days after adding fertilizer.

❧ To make the job really easy, follow the lead of Patty Kleinberg of New York's Queens Botanical Garden: Use a bulb planter to pull out soil samples.

❧ Don't dig too deep. A deep sample won't indicate the soil your plants roots will be growing in, says Dr. Ray Weil of the University of Maryland.

❧ If you're planting flowers or vegetables, Peg Cook, who runs a soil-testing service in New York, recommends digging down about 5 inches; for lawn areas, you should stick to the top 3 to 4 inches, since grass is relatively short-rooted.

soil-building secrets

MAKING SUPER SOIL

Examine your soil test when it comes back, and if you don't like what you see, change it. Many experts say the biggest mistake home gardeners make is not improving their soil before planting. Good soil can make all the difference in how your garden grows. By taking time to enrich the earth in your backyard, you'll be rewarded with lush lawns, beautiful flowers, and basketfuls of fruits and vegetables.

Fattening the Land

Should you or shouldn't you? • *Favorite soil for flowers and veggies*
• *Amending soil around trees and shrubs*

Most plants thrive in soil that's rich in organic matter—compost, shredded leaves, grass clippings, and the like. Organic material boosts fertility, improves soil texture, and aids drainage. It not only creates a healthier home for plants, but it also creates an ideal environment for the microorganisms that break down decaying matter to make nutrients readily available to growing things. But are soil amendments always a good idea?

PROS AND CONS OF FEEDING THE SOIL For Maine horticulturist Lois Stack, there's simply no debate: "Experienced gardeners know that over half the plant is below the ground, and many of them consider working the soil their main activity," she says. North Carolina landscape architect Richard Boggs agrees that unless your soil is perfect to begin with, all soil benefits from amendments, no matter what you plan to plant. On the other hand, Douglas Owens-Pike of Minneapolis's EnergyScapes, Inc., is against enriching the soil—not because it doesn't work, but because he believes in planting only what the soil will naturally support.

If you do amend the soil, you'll have to keep at it to maintain improved fertility, drainage, and moisture-retention. As long as the environmental conditions that formed your soil in the first place—rainfall, temperature, and so on—continue to prevail, the soil will revert to its natural state unless you maintain it. That means mixing organic matter into a vegetable bed or adding a side-dressing of compost to a perennial garden each year.

PLANT ANALYSIS

When experts are stumped as to why a particular plant isn't doing well, they often have the plant itself analyzed for nutrient deficiencies. Most labs that perform soil tests will also analyze plant tissue, says Pennsylvania horticulturist Dr. Michael Orzolek. It's more expensive than a soil test, but it gives you a more accurate reading of which nutrients are getting to your plants and which aren't, and it can save you money in the long run by preventing you from using soil amendments and fertilizers that you might not need. All you'll need is a few leaves from the failing plant. Call your local cooperative extension agent to find out where you can have this test done.

PLANTS THAT BENEFIT MOST Vegetables are hungry plants that consume a lot of nutrients. They do best in very fertile soil, but if things don't work out, you can always fix the soil next year. The same goes for annual flowers. Perennials, on the other hand, are in the ground for the long haul—decades, for some varieties. "And it's harder to improve the soil once they're in," says Maine horticulturist Lois Stack. So prepare the ground carefully before you plant. The same goes for shrubs, although you can amend the soil around the entire root zone without too much difficulty because shrub roots don't extend very far. Trees are another matter. Their roots tend to extend out at least as far as the leaf canopy, and may reach two or even three times as far in large trees. "It's very difficult to amend the entire root zone," says Lois, who recommends planting trees in native rather than enriched soil to avoid the so-called "bathtub effect," in which roots refuse to go beyond the rich, amended earth into the less-fertile ground beyond. (For more on amending the soil around trees, see "Souped-Up Soil" on page 245.)

Some plants don't need fertilizer and are even harmed by it because it causes them to produce more foliage than flowers. Daylilies, coneflowers, and obedient plant will all thrive in any normal soil without adding fertilizer.

ACID LOVERS

Nutrients such as phosphorus, potassium, calcium, magnesium, and iron don't travel well in acid soil. When the pH level of soil drops below 5.5, even nitrogen is not readily available to plants. It's not impossible to change the pH level of your soil, but it is easier to find plants that will thrive in the soil you have. If your soil is heavily acid try these plants:

Alumroot
Bayberry
Bearberry
Blueberry
Calla lily
Camellia
Carolina silverbell
Crape myrtle
Fir
Fringetree
Heath
Holly
Hydrangea
Magnolia
Mountain laurel
Mugo pine
Oak
Pachysandra
Rhododendron
Serviceberry
Turtlehead
Viburnum

Quick Fixes

Longlasting advantages • Short-term harm • Quick fixes that work

Ah, the lure of the quick fix. In spite of everything we've learned about the benefits of slow and steady soil amendment, most of us are still enticed by instant solutions. A quick fix might help in the short run, but it may do harm in the end. In general, most of the experts agree with Dr. Richard Lighty, director of the Mount Cuba Center in Delaware, when he says "Quick fixes are only for when you're about to sell your property. If you're going to live with your garden, long-term improvement is the only way." Still, there are a few fast solutions to garden problems that can come in handy.

TAKING YOUR TIME Enriching the soil slowly doesn't mean you have to wait forever to grow vibrant, healthy plants. Even poor soil can become first-rate in a couple of years. The secret, says Maine horticulturist Lois Stack, is to start with a soil test to see what problems exist and then to add organic matter to improve them. Then follow the advice of Zach Finger of Nitron Industries: "Treat the soil as if it's a living thing that's constantly feeding." Plants regularly deplete soil of its nutrients. To keep it healthy and well-nourished, you need to supply it with a steady diet of organic matter.

QUICK FIXES THAT WORK While instant cures won't improve your soil overall, there are a few fixes that are fast and effective:
• If a soil test indicates a lack of nitrogen, you can get nearly immediate results by applying a commercial organic fertilizer, says Peg Cook, who runs a soil-testing service in New York. Bloodmeal, chicken manure, cottonseed meal, and guano are all high-nitrogen, as is alfalfa meal.
• Having a modest drainage problem? You can fix it in an afternoon (in an average-size garden) by adding lots of compost, says Lois Stack.
• Iron sulfide added to alkaline soils can lower pH in a matter of days, says Dr. Ray Weil of the University of Maryland, adding that the effects aren't long-lived. You'll need to add other amendments, including elemental sulfur and organic matter to maintain proper pH.

QUICK FIXES THAT FAIL Certain fast solutions to soil problems can harm plants, says Seattle garden designer Sue Moss. In particular, turning your garden soil over too often can lead to compaction. And adding organic matter to the hole in which you're planting trees and shrubs may prevent roots from reaching into the soil beyond. "They'll just circle the planting hole," says Sue, "making it possible for large shrubs and trees to blow over in a big wind."

Playing Around with pH

Defining pH • Sweet and sour soil • Up and down

A soil's pH is its degree of alkalinity or acidity, and the pH scale runs from 0 (highly acidic, or "sour") to 14 (highly alkaline, or "sweet"). Neutral soil, in which acidity and alkalinity are in balance, has a pH of 7.0. Most plants prefer a soil with a pH somewhere between 6.0 and 7.0. The slight acidity makes certain minerals (such as iron) easier for plants to use. In highly alkaline soils, plant roots have more difficulty absorbing minerals.

soil-building secrets

Rhododendrons and other members of the Erica family, like mountain laurel, heath, and blueberry, require acid soil. Most are happy even if pH is a low 4.5, but will falter when the pH is above 5.5.

COMPOST AND pH

Well-composted organic matter, also called humus, has an almost magical effect on pH. It acts as a buffer, helping the soil maintain its pH, says Dr. Ray Weil of the University of Maryland. Whether you've just raised or just lowered the pH of your soil, adding organic matter will help keep it there. Peg Cook, who runs a soil-testing service in New York, also points out that if your soil is alkaline, adding compost can lower the pH. It's a lot cheaper than using sulfur, she adds, especially if you get it from the backyard compost pile.

The pH in your backyard is determined, in part, by where you live. In areas with heavy annual rainfall, like the Northeast and Northwest, the soil is likely to be acid and the pH low, since rain removes calcium from the soil and calcium is highly alkaline. In desert or semi-arid climates, on the other hand, and in areas where limestone and marble are part of the landscape, the soil is more alkaline and the pH higher.

CHANGING pH You can alter the pH in your yard, but you'll probably have to keep at it because soil has a tendency to revert to its original pH. Rick Lewandowski of Pennsylvania's Morris Arboretum suggests that if a soil test turns up a pH appropriate to your area, don't change it. Instead, choose native plants that are naturally suited to that pH. Dr. Richard Lighty, director of Delaware's Mount Cuba Center, fusses with pH only in the lawn and vegetable garden. "Those are the places where we tend to grow plants that evolved elsewhere—Europe and the Mediterranean," he says.

RAISING pH If your soil is too acid, you can raise the pH pretty easily (sometimes called "sweetening the soil"), but it won't happen overnight. "It takes six months to a year, depending on soil moisture, to see results," says Peg Cook, who runs a soil-testing service in New York. Here are some of the products the experts use:

• Peg applies soft rock phosphate, which is 48 percent calcium.

• Another popular soil sweetener is lime, but choose calcitic rather than dolomitic lime, unless your soil has a serious magnesium deficiency. "There's a lot of magnesium in dolomitic lime, and if you have too much magnesium, you suppress calcium and plants don't grow well," says Floyd Ranck of Symo-Life, a soil amendment company in Pennsylvania. Most plants do best in soil with a calcium level that's about seven times its magnesium level.

• Both Floyd Ranck and Dr. Ray Weil of the University of Maryland also recommend wood ashes (never coal) to raise pH. But don't spread wood ash with a heavy hand, warns Peg Cook, since too much can tie up potassium in the soil, making it unavailable to plants. Peg also warns that any pH-altering material you put on your garden should be added slowly; it's a process that can be started over a single gardening season, but significant results will take a few years.

LOWERING pH "To lower pH, use sulfur or sulfur products," says Larry Ringer of Ohio Earth Food, a supplier of natural soil conditioners and amendments. He prefers potassium sulfate. Other forms of sulfur include elemental sulfur and iron sulfide. They can be used separately, but Rick Lewandowski of Pennsylvania's Morris Arboretum recommends combining them for the best effect. Iron sulfide works fast ("I've seen a difference in three days on azaleas," says Dr. Ray Weil), but its effects are short-lived. "To maintain pH over time, you'll need elemental sulfur," says Rick. Even so, he warns, you'll need to monitor your soil's pH regularly, since it will have a tendency to creep back up.

If your compost pile is right in the middle of your garden, it will be easy to add to it and to use it. A store-bought or homemade contraption can enclose it, or, if you don't mind the way it looks, just let it be.

soil-building secrets

FIBROUS FIXES

Dr. Stanley Buol, a professor of soil science at The University of North Carolina, believes the best permanent fix for clay soil is to grow fibrous plants, such as rape, which create channels in the soil through which water and nutrients can move. Rape is a cold-tolerant member of the broccoli family; it adds significant amounts of potassium and calcium to the soil as well as conditioning it. Alfalfa and lupins also help break up clay soil. See "Sources" on page 362 for information on where to buy specialty cover crops.

Dr. Buol isn't a fan of sand. "If you add sand to clay soil, all you get is sandy clay or cement," he says.

Tailoring Soil Texture

The importance of good texture • Loosening clay • Enriching sandy soil

Lucky is the gardener blessed with loam. This fertile soil perfectly combines sand and clay in a texture that allows water and the nutrients it carries to travel to the roots of plants, and it enables excess water to drain away. In soil that's too sandy, water passes through so quickly that plants don't have the chance to soak up any, and they become thirsty and wilt. In soils that contain too much clay, on the other hand, water finds it difficult to work through the dense medium to get to plant roots. Whether you have sandy or clay soil in your backyard, mixing in some organic matter will help it perform like a luscious loam.

CORRECTING CLAY SOILS Because water moves quickly through sand, it would seem like a good idea to mix sand into a heavy clay soil to improve drainage—and to some extent it is. "Sand certainly helps improve clay soil—but you'll need truckloads and truckloads of it," says Patty Kleinberg of the Queens Botanical Garden. And that's the problem. To really fix your soil's drainage problems with sand, you'll need more than you can comfortably handle. "Sand is very, very heavy to move and mix into the soil—a cubic yard of it weighs a ton," warns Maine horticulturist Lois Stack. Her secret for fixing drainage is to add organic matter.

Compost and other organic materials loosen up clay soils and help moisture move more freely. Also, clay is composed of very fine particles, while organic material is made up of much larger particles. Mixing them together creates the overall effect of enlarging the soil particles in your garden, says David Graper of the University of South Dakota, making the soil easier to work. In addition to compost, gypsum will loosen a clay soil, says Lois Stack. A form of calcium sulfate, gypsum improves soil texture and adds calcium without changing soil pH.

IMPROVING SANDY SOILS Sandy soils tend to be dry. There's just not much in them to keep moisture from draining away, and with that moisture go any nutrients that might be in the soil. The solution? Compost. "Compost adds and holds nutrients, and it improves the soil's ability to hold water," says Leslie Cooperband, a waste management specialist at the University of Wisconsin. If you've added compost and it doesn't seem to help, consider Stanley Buol's fix for sandy soil—add organic matter that isn't fully decomposed. "That will give soil fungi something to work on," he says. Zach Finger of Nitron Industries has a secret for turning sand into a super growing medium: Add 25 percent earthworm castings (see "Sources" on page 362) by volume, plus a tablespoon of phosphorus.

Creating Fertile Ground

Fertilizing versus soil conditioning • *What to add and when to add it* • *Side-effects of overfertilization*

Confused about the difference between fertilizing your soil and conditioning it? Not surprising, since both tasks enrich the soil. Conditioning the soil is the more extensive task of improving overall health. We've already read how adding organic matter is one of the best ways to condition the soil. It helps the soil retain water and nutrients, while allowing good drainage. It encourages earthworms and

Professionals use a specialty tool, available at landscape supply firms, to deep-fertilize shrubs; it gets the fertilizer down to root level, right where it's needed.

FERTILIZE CAUTIOUSLY

When choosing a fertilizer, remember: There's no such thing as a magic bullet, says Maine horticulturist Lois Stack. Different fertilizers work well in different situations. It's best to begin with a soil test before adding anything to your garden. Here are some reasons why:

❧ Manure raises nitrogen levels in soil, but it also lowers pH. That's fine if your pH needs lowering, but if your soil is too acid to begin with, adding manure will make the problem worse.

❧ Too much of any single element can mask the benefits of others. If you add too much nitrogen, for example, your plants will produce a great deal of foliage and few flowers, even if you've also added potassium to promote blossoming.

And remember, too much of any fertilizer can burn the roots of young plants that aren't ready to receive nutrients.

soil-building secrets

The key to productive gardens is the soil in which they grow. And the best way to improve that soil is to add copious amounts of compost.

microorganisms that make nutrients available to plants. And organic matter is itself a source of nourishment. To fertilize the soil means to add specific nutrients, such as nitrogen.

WHEN TO FERTILIZE If you've amended your soil well with organic matter, you may not need to add fertilizers at all. But if a soil test or poor plant performance indicates a nutrient deficiency, fertilizing can make a significant difference. Before choosing a fertilizer, it's helpful to have a general idea of the nutrients your plants need and a sense of what those nutrients do.

The "big three" minerals—nitrogen, phosphorus, and potassium—are the most important. Nitrogen nourishes the healthy growth of stems and leaves, phosphorus encourages root development, and potassium increases fruit and flower production and the growth of root crops. Most plants also need the secondary minerals calcium, magnesium, and sulfur, as well as such trace elements (so called because they're needed in small amounts) as boron, iron, and zinc.

SIDE-EFFECTS OF MINERALS In addition to nourishing your plants, the minerals in your soil can affect your plants' ability to absorb other nutrients. If your soil contains too much potassium, for instance, plants will have a harder time taking up calcium and magnesium. Too much magnesium, and they won't get enough calcium. And an excess of phosphorus keeps plants from fully absorbing copper, iron, and zinc. Applying too much of any particular fertilizer, then, can actually lead to decreased fertility.

CHOOSING A FERTILIZER From alfalfa meal to worm castings, you have dozens of organic fertilizers to choose from. The following are the experts' favorites—for both overall soil conditioning and for correcting specific nutritional deficits. (For information on the benefits of compost, see page 278.)

• *Alfalfa meal*, a cattle feed, is an inexpensive source of nitrogen. It takes a year for it to break down, though; use another source while you wait. And it's dusty, so wear a mask when applying.

• An excellent source of nitrogen, *bat guano* also contains smaller amounts of phosphorus, potassium, and calcium (Larry Pozarelli of Cleveland's Guano Company International puts the NPK ratio at

Everyone likes to look at the end result of soil-building: lush flowers and foliage. It takes more experience to appreciate the soil that creates them.

about 13-8-2.) If you're applying fertilizer around seedlings, don't use high-nitrogen guano, which can push young plants too hard. Instead, Larry recommends buying a special high-phosphorus guano, or, even better, seabird guano (see "Sources" on page 362). Whichever type you choose, be judicious in your use—guano is expensive.

• *Blood meal* supplies nitrogen and several trace minerals, including iron. Because it releases nitrogen into the soil quickly, it's a good pick-me-up, and it's great for quick-growing plants. Patrick McGinity of The Ringer Corporation, a gardening supply company in Minnesota, likes to apply it along with a slow-release fertilizer like feather meal and a moderate-release fertilizer such as soybean meal. He and his colleagues have experimented with a wide variety of fertilizer combinations and found that blood meal was indispensable. "Whenever we took out the blood meal, the results were poorer," he says. Zach Finger of Nitron Industries uses it on corn and okra, both of which like lots of nitrogen.

HOLD THE NITROGEN

According to Dr. Stanley Buol, a professor of soil science at The University of North Carolina, many gardeners overuse nitrogen, which presents a problem not just for plants but also for the environment. If you keep putting nitrogen fertilizer into the soil throughout the growing season, it will still be there, decomposing, in the fall, says Dr. Buol. If you live in an area where rainfall is 15 inches or more per month in December through March, much of this nitrogen will leach out into groundwater, which could present health risks to humans.

Dr. Buol recommends boosting the soil's nitrogen content only when necessary, and adds that you can also spray plants with compost tea when they are 8 to 10 inches tall for a quick nitrogen fix. (For more on making compost teas, see the illustration on page 277.)

•A great sources of phosphorus (its NPK ratio is 1-11-0), *bonemeal* also contains significant amounts of calcium. While some of the experts, including Floyd Ranck of Symo-Life in Pennsylvania, recommend it highly, others advise caution. Patrick McGinity praises it as a topnotch phosphorus source, but warns that it can be diluted and is sometimes chemically treated. "It's not what it used to be," he says, "and in diluted state it loses most of its micronutrients." To find out what's in the bonemeal you're buying, Patrick recommends that you read the bag carefully. Maryland bulb grower Kitty Washburne points out that if animals are a problem in your backyard, bonemeal will only attract more of them. "It's like cake and ice cream to them," she says. She has even known animals to dig up daffodil bulbs that have been planted in bonemeal. Though they didn't eat the bulbs (which are toxic), they did lick them clean of the bonemeal before scattering them across the lawn.

•Want the high-phosphorus benefits of bonemeal without the potential hassles? Floyd Rank recommends *colloidal phosphate*, a byproduct of rock phosphate mining. It contains less phosphorus than bonemeal, but the phosphorus is in a form that's more usable to plants.

•Floyd Rank uses *cottonseed meal* on his peas, beans, and corn because of its high nitrogen content. Spread it sparingly, however. "Peas and beans like a nitrogen boost, but if you give them too much, their nitrogen-producing nodules become lazy," says Floyd. Zach Finger likes cottonseed meal for acid-loving plants such as azaleas and blueberries. If you decide to use it in your garden, be forewarned that because cottonseed meal is a byproduct of farming, it may contain pesticide residues, so check your source before you buy.

•Another farming byproduct, *feather meal* is made from, yes, ground poultry feathers. Patrick McGinity chooses it as a good source of slow- release nitrogen. In fact, it contains few significant nutrients other than nitrogen. Because it breaks down slowly, it's a good fertilizer for fall, says Zach Finger.

•Containing nitrogen, phosphorus, and potassium as well as sulfur, *fish emulsion* is a good all-around growth-booster. Zach Finger uses it weekly on all his crops. He admits that the scent is unpleasant and that he has had to chase away neighborhood dogs and raccoons—but the odor usually dissipates in a few hours and only the benefits are left.

•"It's one of the oldest fertilizers, and one of the best," says Zach Finger. *Fish meal* breaks down in 30 to 60 days, slowly releasing nitrogen, phosphorus, and potassium into the soil. It's a good choice for fall fertilizing because it releases nutrients over a long period.

•Originating on the ocean floor, *greensand* is a rich mix of minerals found along stretches of the New Jersey coastline and elsewhere along the Northeast coast. Floyd Rank uses it in conjunction with cottonseed meal and rock phosphate on peas, beans, and corn. It's an excellent source of potassium.

•Sometimes called land plaster, *gypsum* contains lots of calcium and sulfur. Unlike lime, it won't change your soil's pH. But it can help loosen heavy clay soils, says Lois Stack of the University of Maine. It can also help reduce salt in seashore soils.

•Available in liquid and dry forms, *kelp* and *seaweed* fertilizers provide potassium and trace minerals, as well as some nitrogen and phosphorus. Peg Cook, who runs a soil-testing service in New York, likes to apply liquid seaweed at the end of the growing season. "It acts as an antifreeze," she says. Rebecca Reardon of Maine's Saltwater Farms finds it useful for all phases of growth. "It helps seeds germinate, helps seedlings grow faster and stronger, and encourages leafing out," she says. "In addition to adding micronutrients, it feeds and stimulates soil organisms as it breaks down," she adds. At the end of the growing season, Rebecca applies 1 pound of dry kelp per 100 square feet of garden surface. Floyd Rank uses seaweed—sparingly—around young trees. (Once the trees are about 10 years old, he stops fertilizing them altogether.) Patrick McGinity praises kelp highly: "It's like a witches' brew of all kinds of good stuff." His secret for super-healthy plants is to give them a mixture of kelp and compost. And Larry Ringer of Ohio Earth Food also recommends the combination. "Compost contains concentrated humates; if you add seaweed to it, you have everything," he says.

•Both *cow* and *horse manure* are good sources of organic matter. Like compost, they benefit your plants by conditioning the soil (though both supply small amounts of nitrogen, phosphorus, and potassium, plus trace minerals).

When your annuals start to look a little spent, offer them a spot of compost tea. Simply put a few scoops of compost in a burlap bag and soak the bag in water for several hours or until it turns a muddy brown. Water your plants with the tea or spray it on their leaves and they'll perk up quickly.

soil-building secrets

COMPOST—FROM SCRAPS TO SOIL

It's magic. You take everything from kitchen parings to grass clippings to discarded garden plants, toss them together, stir the mix regularly, and in a matter of weeks it begins turning into rich, black humus. Thanks to the work of many mighty microorganisms that decompose all that discarded material, you'll have a valuable pile of organic matter before you know it, ready to spread on your garden.

Creating Compost

Picking a composter • Placing your pile • Making a good mix
• Speeding up the process

You can buy compost, but there are advantages to making your own. "If you do it yourself, you know it will be good," says Floyd Ranck of Symo-Life, a soil amendment company in Pennsylvania. "Store-bought compost may have been made in a hurry." It won't be fully decomposed and nutrients won't be immediately available to your plants.

This compost display at the University of Santa Cruz shows the stages of creation, from raw garden debris through partially decomposed material to "black gold." If you have several compartments in your composter, you can create a steady supply of compost.

If you don't make your own compost, or can't make enough, look for sources other than the local chain store. Ohio garden designer Bobbie Schwartz buys leaf humus, often available from municipalities that do their own composting (and sometimes free to residents). If you live in a rural area, consider buying compost from a local farmer, as New York grower Dana Keiser of Stony Hill Farm does. "If you can find a farmer who uses his own material, you'll often get the best compost," she says.

CHOOSING A COMPOSTER There are as many approaches to composting as there are gardeners, and nearly as many composters. You can buy or make a barrel composter that tumbles the compost so you don't have to turn it regularly. Or, there's the multibin composter that makes mixing easy—you just move part of the compost from one bin to another to turn it. You can also build a simple structure out of staggered cinderblocks or chickenwire, or you can do as Patty Kleinberg of the Queens Botanical Garden does and not use a bin at all. "For me, any enclosure impedes my ability to get into the pile," she says. Her pile is simply that—a mound of organic matter, which she turns on a regular basis—and she says it works fine.

POSITIONING YOUR PILE The best place for a pile, according to Patty Kleinberg, is in full sun and away from cold winter winds. "But it needs to be accessible," she adds. Pick a site that's easy to get to in all seasons. From an aesthetic standpoint, you'll probably want to put your pile in an out-of-the-way corner of the backyard. And you can even do some decorative planting to keep it from being an eyesore. Kleinberg plants vinca and ivy around hers.

THE RECIPE If you don't think your little household generates enough material for a working pile, you'll be surprised once you start. Anything that's 100 percent organic qualifies for the compost pile, although you should avoid throwing meat scraps in because they can create a foul odor and attract animals and other pests. The simplest—and also the slowest—way to make compost is to pile up your scraps and let nature do its work. However, since the center of the pile generates the most activity, experts recommend turning the pile occasionally—once a week is best—to move the uncomposted material into that central hotspot and the finished compost to the outside.

IS IT COMPOST YET?

When your beds are ready for compost, it's hard to be patient while waiting for it to be ready. Here's how the experts know when their compost is cooked:

❧ Zach Finger of Nitron Industries goes by looks. "I start using it when it resembles a sticky soil," he says.

❧ New Jersey garden designer Cassie Brown uses a compost thermometer (see "Sources" on page 362). When the temperature goes down rapidly—when an active compost pile falls under 100°F—she considers it ready.

❧ At the Woods End Research Lab (see "Sources" on page 362), compost is tested to check whether it is decomposing actively; reports indicate whether it is ready to be used.

❧ Tibor Miller at the Fellowship Foundation Farm in New York just waits three years. By that time, it's surely done. She keeps several piles going so there is always one that is ready for use.

soil-building secrets

HOT COMPOST TIP

Want to really dig-in to composting? A compost thermometer will help you mix up high-quality compost fast. These 20- to 30-inch-long thermometers are extra-sturdy and can withstand high heat—an important consideration, given that the center of a good home-compost pile should register between 120° and 130°F.

Knowing how hot your pile is helps you determine when to add more organic material or give the pile a turn to speed things up, says Mike Hughes, whose Reotemp Corporation (see "Sources" on page 362) manufactures compost thermometers. Check the temperature daily by sticking the thermometer directly into the center of the pile. You have good compost when the thermometer reads about 120°F. If you notice a drop in temperature from one day to the next, it's time to turn the pile and add more organic material.

SPEEDING THINGS ALONG Can't wait for your compost? Try these secrets and you'll have a well-rotted supply in weeks instead of months.

• Turn the pile frequently, says Floyd Ranck of Pennsylvania's Symo-Life. "If you keep after it—turning it every few days— you'll have compost in 10 to 12 weeks," he promises.

• Keep the pile wet, adds Floyd. "When you squeeze it, you should just see water between your knuckles."

• Zach Finger, whose Nitron Industries produces organic soil amendments, gets good, fast compost by adding materials high in nitrogen. He recommends feather meal, fish meal, and blood meal.

• Patty Kleinberg and Peg Cook like to add a "bacterial layer"—either fresh manure or organic fertilizer—to activate soil microbes.

• You can also speed things up by eliminating certain materials, says Zach Finger—specifically, leaves and grass, which take longer to "cook." If you do add leaves, make sure they're finely chopped. Or consider two separate piles: a "slow" pile for grass clippings and leaves (the green pile) and a "fast" pile for kitchen debris and already-rotting materials.

Shovel It On

Is more always better? • *Application information*

Nothing improves soil like the addition of well-composted organic matter. Compost evens soil texture so that it's not too fine or too coarse for the most desirable drainage. It balances pH and boosts the soil with essential nutrients in a form that plants can use easily.

TOO MUCH OF A GOOD THING? "You can never have too much compost," says Aileen Lubin, director of Maine's Merryscape Gardens, "but it has to be fully composted." According to Zach Finger of Nitron Industries, "If the compost isn't fully decomposed, its nitrogen and ammonia content can be too high." In addition, fresh organic matter actually consumes oxygen and nitrogen, stealing it from the very plants you're trying to feed. Furthermore, not all compost is equal, warns Leslie Cooperband, a waste management specialist at the University of Wisconsin. "There's a wide variation in quality out there," she says. If you're making your own compost from kitchen waste and adding lots of manure, you can be pretty certain that you've got high-quality compost. But if you have any doubts, Leslie says, have your compost tested just as you would your soil. (See "Sources" on page 362 for companies that will test your compost.)

RATES OF APPLICATION The easiest way to apply compost is to spread a certain thickness on top of the entire garden plot. The thickness depends on the state of the soil you're starting with. North Carolina grower Loleta Powell generally recommends 2 to 3 inches unless the soil is mainly clay or sand. In Binghamton, New York, where clay soil is the norm, Stony Hill Farm's Dana Keiser spreads a full foot of compost on her beds. How much you spread also depends on what you're growing. For vegetable gardens, Seattle garden designer Sue Moss recommends a 6- to 8-inch layer of compost; for flowers, 4 to 8 inches; for shrubs, anywhere from 2 to 8 inches. The higher levels would be used in cases where the soil is very poor.

DIGGING IT IN After spreading compost over his newly prepared beds, Dr. Richard Lighty, director of Delaware's Mount Cuba Center, digs it in to the full depth of his spade, then rakes the bed with a four-tined cultivating tool. If you're adding compost to an existing perennial bed or shrub border, Mary Harrison of Mary's Plant Farm in Ohio suggests piling it around the plants (this is known as side-dressing) in fall and working it into the ground in spring, taking care not to disturb delicate surface roots.

These two compost containers represent the extremes of available products. The huge cylinder (left) allows turning and aeration. The smaller cage (right) is little more than a covered bucket. Both work well.

ROTATION TIPS

Some plants are natural rotation partners.

❧ Potatoes work well as the first crop in a rotation because you'll need to dig deeply and thoroughly for them; future crops will reap the benefits.

❧ Plant heavy feeders after medium to light feeders.

Light feeders:
Onion family (onions, garlic, leeks, and chives).

Light to medium feeders:
Carrot family (carrots, celery, dill, and parsley).

Heavy feeders:
Cole family (broccoli, cabbages, and Brussels sprouts); Nightshade family (tomatoes, peppers, and potatoes); Squash family (cucumbers, melons, and squash); Composite family (lettuce); Goosefoot family (beets, spinach, Swiss chard).

❧ Peas and beans enrich the soil by releasing nitrogen. Use them before and after heavy feeders.

❧ Brassicas, the heaviest feeders, should be last in the rotation. Follow with a fallow season or a cover crop.

MORE WAYS TO BETTER SOIL

Sometimes it's not what you put in your soil, but what you plant that makes great ground: soil that is alive with nutrients and micro-organisms that help your plants grow rather than impeding their progress. Crop rotation and cover crops can condition the soil and help replenish needed nutrients. And the experts have a few other techniques that can transform the soil into a superb growing medium for your vegetables and flowers.

Crop Rotation

Rotating for disease prevention • Rotation for increased fertility • The rules of rotation

For centuries, farmers have rotated crops—usually vegetables—moving them from one area of the garden to another or alternating crops in the same site year after year. Should modern gardeners try it?

A REASON TO ROTATE The main reason to rotate crops, says Peg Cook who runs a soil-testing service in New York, is to prevent the proliferation of soilborne diseases, some of which can live in the garden for years. The key is to plant different families of crops that aren't likely to be susceptible to the same diseases. If you have experienced a soil disease like tomato blight, it's important to keep your next tomato crop as far from the first one as possible. But crop rotation offers other benefits, too.

INCREASING FERTILITY In the vegetable garden especially, rotating crops can help keep the ground fertile. Because most vegetables feed heavily on nutrients, they can quickly deplete the soil. By alternating vegetables with different nutritional requirements— cabbage, for example, which loves nitrogen, with corn, which has a preference for potassium—you allow the soil to rebuild its fertility. It helps to add compost or other organic matter. Or you could throw a cover crop into the rotation. Cover crops are quick-growing plants like buckwheat and rye that add nutrients to the soil when they're plowed under. (See "Going for Cover" on the opposite page.) Consider planting peas and beans as a rotation cover crop; they'll not only benefit the soil but your table as well. For more information, see "Rotation Tips" at left.

Going for Cover

Why the experts love cover crops • *The cover crop calendar* • *Tilling it in* • *Choosing the right crop*

They don't call it green manure for nothing. Growing cover crops is one of the best ways to improve soil, and it dates back to the ancient Greeks. But these days, few gardeners use this soil-improvement technique. Why? Farmers and home gardeners abandoned green manuring when cheap chemical fertilizers appeared on the market just after World War II, says William Brinton of the Woods End Research Laboratory. Why bother sowing seeds and turning under plants when you could get the same effect by sprinkling a little granulated fertilizer on the garden? Four decades later, we know why: The widespread use of synthetic fertilizers has degraded the soil and polluted the groundwater on commercial farms and in backyard vegetable plots alike. Green manuring can bring our depleted soil back to life. Cover crops deliver nutrients naturally and evenly into the soil and condition the soil at the same time. They're often less expensive than soil amendments, and they do their work during the garden's downtime, preventing compaction and erosion during winter.

Winter is not the only season to use cover crops. Cover crops like buckwheat (below) can be grown alongside vegetables. They're a great way to prepare a bed that you don't need this year for future crops.

TILLING TRICKS

You'll get the greatest benefit from your green manure by turning it under while it's still green. "The nutrient value is in the green material," says Peg Cook, who runs a soil-testing service in New York. Before sinking it in the soil, run a rotary mower or rotary tiller over the crop several times. If you have a small plot, you can dig your green manure in by hand. But don't use a rotary tiller if your soil is soggy, since tilling can compact wet soils. In fact, one of the secrets to successful green manuring is to schedule your planting so that you won't have to harvest when the soil is still wet. If spring in your area tends to be cold and rainy, consider a fall crop.

WHAT IS A COVER CROP? Any plant grown specifically to enrich the soil qualifies as a cover crop, but some do the job better than others. Grasses like buckwheat and winter rye or legumes like soybeans and clover make excellent cover crops. All grow quickly and break down easily in the soil. And legumes offer a bonus with their nitrogen-fixing roots, which, with a little help from microorganisms, absorb nitrogen from the air and make it available to other plants in the soil. (That's why clover, a legume, was a traditional mix in the pre-World War II lawn.) You can boost your legumes' nitrogen-fixing capacities, says Gary Coull of Johnny's Selected Seeds, by treating the seeds with an inoculant—an organic, peat-based culture of the bacteria that normally interact with legume roots in the soil.

THE BENEFITS Just growing a cover crop benefits your garden. It suppresses the growth of weeds and prevents soil erosion. And plants with deep roots, such as red clover and radishes, loosen and aerate the soil. At the end of the season, when you turn the crop under, you supply the soil with nitrogen and organic matter. And as we've seen, organic matter improves soil texture and drainage and releases a horde of nutrients to the garden as the organic matter decays.

PLANTING Weather permitting, you can plant mustard, fava beans, and spinach in early spring and turn them under before you sow your main crop. Or try winter rye or winter rape in fall; in a mild climate, they'll keep growing right through the winter. If your growing season isn't long enough to accommodate a cover crop and food crops, consider rotating crops—planting green manure one year and vegetables the next. If you don't want to lose a season's harvest, Minnesota's Patrick McGinity suggests planting a cover crop that's also a food crop—fava beans or peas, for instance. Or try Patrick's secret and plant a cover crop around a cole crop (cabbage, cauliflower, broccoli, or any of their cousins).

DO YOU PLANT CORN? William Brinton suggests underseeding—growing a green manure under the corn. Clover, English rye, hairy vetch, flatpod pea, and birdsfoot trefoil all make good companions for corn. If possible, let the cover crop continue to grow for a month or two after you harvest the corn.

CHOOSING YOUR COVER There are dozens and dozens of cover crops, so how do you decide on the one that's right for your garden? First, consider when you'll be sowing; each crop prefers a particular season. Then, think about how you plan to use it. Will you rotate it with another crop? Make sure the two are compatible. Do you want to boost nitrogen? Think legumes. Are you looking for a harvestable crop? Plant fava beans, peas, or radishes. Do you want something that looks good while it's growing? Consider crimson clover or—despite its unattractive name—hairy vetch. As with anything else you grow, you'll also have to consider zone and climate.

MIXING IT UP William Brinton of the Woods End Research Laboratories recommends a combination of hairy vetch and winter rye for soil regeneration. Or plant a mix of two parts hairy vetch to one part each of crimson clover and ryegrass before putting in late-season carrots. Gerry Coull of Johnny's Selected Seeds has had great success with a mixture of oats, vetch, and field peas, a combination recommended by Dr. Matt Liebman of the University of Maine's Sustainable Agriculture program. (William Brinton is also a fan of this mix; he uses one part vetch to two parts each of peas and oats.)

The experts offer their favorite cover crops in the following chart.

COVER CROPS		
CROP	WHEN TO SOW	ADVANTAGES/COMMENTS
Alfalfa	Late summer	Adds nutrients; roots break up soil.
Buckwheat	Late summer or early spring	Brings up phosphorus from subsoil. Turn it under as soon as it comes up, or it will get too big to turn under easily.
Crimson clover	Spring, summer, or fall	Grows quickly; adds nitrogen to soil; has attractive flowerheads
Lupin	Fall or early spring	Edible beans. Makes phosphorus available to other plants. Lupinus albus is cold-tolerant.
Oats	Late summer or early spring	Fixes nitrogen in soil; doesn't get as tall and fibrous as buckwheat.
Rye	Spring or fall	Easy to till in. Grows quickly, good for short-season area. Don't rotate with lettuce or other small-seeded crops; rye can add toxins to soil, which can keep small seeds from germinating.
Soybeans	Spring or fall	Easy to broadcast; helps condition soil by secreting an organic acid that's broken down by soil fungi.
Summer vetch	Late summer	Withstands early frost; good nitrogen fixer.

soil-building secrets

Working with Earthworms

Burrowing for a better garden • *Attracting worms to your garden*
• *Inviting wigglers into your kitchen*

Earthworms are the world's most efficient garden machines. While innocently going about their business, they voraciously consume organic matter and excrete it in the form of castings—nutrient-rich manure that not only provides food for plants but also helps condition the soil. They secrete calcium carbonate, which helps bring pH close to neutral. And as they tunnel through the ground, they turn and aerate the soil and create channels for roots that can go down 4 feet or more. So put these wrigglers to work for you right away.

FEED THEM AND THEY WILL COME You can order earthworms by mail (see "Sources" on page 362), but earthworms are easily attracted to your garden. "If you add organic matter to the soil, the earthworms will find it," says Leslie Cooperband, waste management specialist at the Univeristy of Wisconsin. Douglas Owens-Pike of Minneapolis's

CASTINGS CALL

Worm manure, called castings, is high in organic matter and rich in nutrients. It has a pleasant earthy smell and a crumbly texture, and many of the experts consider it to be a near-perfect fertilizer. Both Larry Pozarelli of Cleveland's Guano Company International and Zach Finger of Nitron Industries in Arkansas include worm castings in their formulas for perfect soil.

You can buy castings from a variety of sources, (see "Sources" on page 362) but if you have a good working population of earthworms, you probably won't need to. Dig up a trowelful or two of soil from various places in your backyard. If you don't find any wrigglers hanging off the trowel, consider adding worms or castings.

Creepy, crawly, and good as gold: red worms, like those above, speed up compost production. You can keep a large population of worms happy and ready to work in a small bucket.

EnergyScapes, Inc., offers another way to attract earthworms. "I cover bare soil with 2 to 3 inches of unprocessed leaf mulch and leave it there all winter," he says. "Most of it is gone by the end of the season, consumed and digested by an army of earthworms." In fact, decaying leaves are an earthworm's favorite food in the garden and in the compost pile. If you do buy worms, 10 worms per square foot of soil is ideal.

WORMS IN YOUR KITCHEN Another way to put worms to work is to buy or build a worm bin, says Leslie Cooperband. You can order one by mail or simply construct one from an old foam cooler. Poke about 20 air holes in the cooler and fill it with dampened dead leaves, shredded newspaper, or a combination of the two. Then add about half a pound of red wigglers—not earthworms (see "Sources" on page 362). A handful or two of your kitchen vegetable waste weekly should satisfy even the hungriest worms, and they'll reward you with grade-A compost in a matter of months. Leslie puts her worms to work in the kitchen during winter, then moves them to the compost pile in spring.

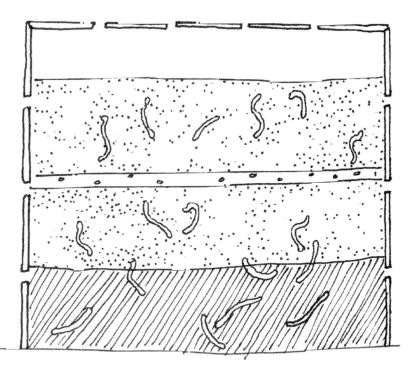

Worms like to burrow through layers of different materials such as soil, paper, and organic matter.

Digging and Double-Digging

The great double-digging debate • Pros and cons
• How deep to dig

To dig or to double-dig? That's a question gardeners face every time they prepare a bed. Double-digging—the process of working the soil to a depth of two spades, or about 16 to 24 inches, depending on your spade and your energy level—is a controversial procedure. Some experts swear by it, based on their own successes, while others consider it a potential danger to the soil. Still others, like Patrick McGinity of Minnesota, dismiss it as simply too much work. "I believe in making gardening fun, and double-digging isn't," he says. (For information on how to double-dig, see "Double-Digging" page 104.)

REASONS TO DOUBLE-DIG In his own backyard, Tom Butterworth of Connecticut's Butterbrook Farms faced soil that had been badly compacted by farm machinery. He decided to double-dig the garden in order to loosen and aerate it. Sarah Gallant of Pinetree Garden Seeds in Maine likes to grow root crops, so she always double-digs. "It allows for straighter growth of the edible part of the plant," she says. And whenever Tessa Gowans of Washington's Abundant Life Seed Foundation prepares a new bed, she double-digs. "It makes the bed a loose, friable environment for the seeds," she says, "and it only has to be done once."

REASONS NOT TO "Double-digging is too much work," says Dr. Philip Helmke, a horticulturist with the University of Wisconsin. He prefers to turn the soil with a small plow or rotary tiller, and he never digs deeper than 8 inches. "When you go down farther, you bring up subsoil that isn't as fertile as the topsoil," he warns. Ohio Earth Food's Larry Ringer agrees: "The most important soil life is in the top few inches," he says. "If you bring up the lower soil, you bring up material that's weaker and may have some toxins in it." University of North Carolina soil scientist Dr. Stanley Buol has had first-hand experience with deep tilling and the problems it sometimes produces. "In the 1960s, we did some experiments with deep plowing in the Midwest, going down 3 feet and bringing up

Double-dug soil is loose and friable. It allows roots to grow freely, water to drain quickly, and water and nutrients to travel through the soil to the roots where they are needed.

soil-building secrets

lime from the subsoil," he explains. "The soil in that area is still a disaster today."

WHAT SHOULD YOU DO? If you don't want to double-dig, don't. And you certainly don't have to do it more than once in your garden's lifetime. "Double-digging by hand one time isn't a problem, but running over your soil five times with a rotary tiller is the worst thing you can do to it," says Maine horticulturist Lois Stack. Overworking the soil can compact it and make it an uninviting environment for beneficial microorganisms. If you do decide to double-dig, don't just bring up the subsoil, says Lois. Mix some organic matter into it, or better yet, consider building raised beds (see "Constructing Raised Beds" on page 57). Working in the heavy clay soil of his backyard, Rick Lewandowski of Philadelphia's Morris Arboretum turns the soil under to a depth of 12 to 15 inches for roses. For perennial flowers, however, he suggests going down only 6 to 8 inches—a depth even the laziest gardener shouldn't mind digging.

Once a bed is double-dug, you shouldn't ever have to do it again (unless the soil is compacted by outside forces). The soil will be easier to work for years to come.

soil-building secrets

6

Expert Answers on Organic Pest & Disease Control

"The time to control pests and diseases is before they start."
PAUL STEINER, UNIVERSITY OF MARYLAND

More and more of us—experts and home gardeners alike—are turning to organic methods to control pests and diseases, as we come to understand the dangers posed by chemical controls. Chemical insecticides and fungicides threaten the health not just of insects and pathogens but of all living creatures; they persist in the environment long after they've stopped being useful; and their abuse has contributed to the growth of resistant insects and disease organisms.

Organic pest and disease control means relying on naturally occurring substances to check infestations and infection, but it also means taking a whole new approach to garden problems. Instead of trying to rescue afflicted plants with sprays and dusts, organic gardeners make an attempt to prevent problems before they start. This means taking preemptive measures like spraying for mildew with baking soda or repelling insects with garllc or hot pepper wax. Even more important, it means creating a garden environment where problems are less likely to occur, by building the soil, planting resistant varieties, allowing for good drainage and air circulation, and cleaning up debris where pests and diseases can hide and multiply.

HERE'S WHAT YOU'LL FIND IN CHAPTER 6

OUNCE OF PREVENTION

The first step in insect control is to cultivate strong, vigorous plants by creating a healthy environment in which they can grow. Here are seven things to do

1. Keep your garden clean.

2. Let the air flow. Good air circulation is the best prevention, says Louise Clements of Oregon's Heirloom Old Garden Roses. This rule holds true for any plant thats vulnerable to fungal diseases. Fungi love moisture, and freely circulating air keeps moisture to a minimum so fungal spores can't germinate.

3. Build good soil.

4. Weed regularly.

5. Mulch your garden beds. It looks good, keeps down weeds, and holds moisture. According to Paul Steiner of the University of Maryland it also acts as a barrier, coming between the fungi in your soil and your plants. Without mulch, rainfall might splash fungal spores onto the leaves and fruits of your plants.

6. Rotate crops.

7. Choose pest- and disease-resistant plants.

SPOTTING PROBLEMS

Are slugs and snails sneaking around beneath your hostas? Have your rosebuds become a haven for aphids? Is that little pile of leaf litter harboring the spores of botrytis blight? One of best things you can do to control pests and diseases is to discover them before they've had a chance to get a foothold in your garden. Then you can get rid of them before they do noticeable damage.

The Search

Scheduling your searches • Tools to increase your effectiveness • Looking in all the right places

Checking for pests and diseases is all part of the process of growing and nurturing a healthy garden. While you're monitoring the progress of young plants and enjoying the beauty of just-opened blossoms and newly unfurled foliage, take a few minutes to look for signs and symptoms that some insatiable insects, fiendish fungi, or bad bacteria may have also found your garden attractive.

BE A FREQUENT FINDER The more often you look, the better your chances are of uncovering pest and disease problems at an early stage. Andy Force of Indiana's Foellinger-Freimann Botanical Conservatory recommends checking the garden at least once a week. And more often is better, he adds. Gary Coull of Johnny's Selected Seeds checks daily. Many of the experts simply make monitoring for pests and diseases a part of every garedning task. "We look for problems routinely as we plant, weed, mulch, and harvest," says Peter Borchard of Ohio's Companion Plants.

TOOLS OF THE TRADE You don't need anything more than a good pair of eyes and the ability to get around the garden, but David Ittel of Illinois's Alternative Garden Supply likes to take along a small magnifying glass. Lots of insects are very tiny, he points out. Dr. Sharon Douglas, a disease control specialist at Connecticut's Agricultural Experiment Station, advises that you carry a notebook into the garden once a week to record what you see so that you can follow up on anything suspicious-looking. For instance, you might note that you saw a pair of aphids on some new rose growth. A look at

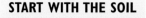

your notebook next week would remind you to check and make sure those aphids hadn't amassed an entire family. Among David's favorite tools are sticky traps, which can provide important clues about insect visitors.

HOW AND WHERE TO LOOK Walk in a zigzag pattern when you're checking your garden for pests and diseases, so you're not looking at the same thing every time, advises Sharon Douglas. Over the course of a week, you should have looked at every plant, or at least one of every variety of plant. To make the best use of his time, Michael Cady of Jackson & Perkins in Oregon determines which plants are the most pest-prone and then gives them extra attention.

Because pests and diseases can attack anywhere, you need to take a good look at the whole plant. Louise Clements of Oregon's Heirloom Old Garden Roses checks around the base of the plant and the lower leaves for blackspot, then looks at the upper leaves for mildew. She's especially watchful of tender new growth, which is irresistible to aphids and provides a haven for mildew. "Gardeners are all too likely to accept the garden at face value," says Gary Coull. He recommends turning over leaves to make sure nothing has taken up residence beneath them. The underside of a perfectly normal-looking leaf can harbor a horde of harmful insects.

START WITH THE SOIL

"Building good soil is an essential defense against pests and diseases," says Virginia Hayes of California's Lotusland. Healthy soil produces healthy plants that can easily fight off infection. Furthermore, soil that drains poorly provides the perfect breeding ground for fungi, bacteria, and viruses. You can improve it by adding organic matter or by building raised beds. Or you can choose plants that don't mind soggy soils—they're generally resistant to fungal infection.

pest & disease control

A hollowed-out rose cane is a sign that cane borers have attacked your roses. Patrol your garden often to look for clues like these to pest problems.

YANK THE WEEDS

You already have good reasons to rid your garden of weeds—they steal water and nutrients from the plants around them, and they're unsightly. Here are a few more:

❧ Many broadleaf weeds harbor diseases that can be moved to garden plants by insects, especially aphids, says Dr. Paul Steiner, professor and extension fruit pathologist at the Univeristy of Maryland.

❧ Weeds impede air circulation around your plants, making them more susceptible to fungal diseases such as black rot and downy mildew.

❧ Weeds attract what Paul calls garbage insects—not major pests but trouble-makers nonetheless. Tree crickets, for instance, like to feed on raspberry plants; the wounds they inflict aren't life-threatening, but they create the perfect opening for fungi and other disease-causing microbes.

When Is a Problem Problematic?

How bad is it? • *The right time to take action* • *Declaring war*

Not all bugs are bad. Some insects benefit the garden by policing the true pests. So know your insects before you try to eradicate every six-legged creature that crawls through the vegetable patch. And even those that do cause harm won't necessarily level your garden. Some problems pass, causing only a minor inconvenience. They're like having a cold—often you don't need to take medication, you just need to wait it out a week, and it'll be gone. It's the same with some garden problems, so you need to weigh whether a particular infestation will devastate your plants or do only minor damage. In the latter case, controls may not be necessary. How will you know? Identifying the pest and keeping records of last year's problems are two effective techniques.

KNOW YOUR ENEMY Before you declare war on the insects in your backyard—even if you're fighting that war with organic controls—make sure there really is an enemy to fight. If you have a strong history of infestation with certain pests, you'd certainly have a reason to begin treatment as early as possible, says Dr. Bastiaan Drees, professor and extension entomologist at Texas A & M University. The same goes for any insects with a history of infestation in your area. But John Jeavons, author of *How to Grow More Vegetables*, suggests that you ask yourself if the damage is extensive enough to warrant a war before you enter into one with pests. He recalls an experience some years ago with bush beans. The primary leaves were almost entirely destroyed by the 12-spotted cucumber beetle. But in most cases the damage wasn't so rapid as to prevent the development of healthy secondary leaves. And even though the beetles destroyed about 20 percent of the secondary leaves, that didn't stop the plants from producing a large harvest of tasty, unblemished beans.

KNOW YOUR GARDEN Knowing your garden is at least as important as knowing your pests. Every year in his central New Jersey nursery, Richard Pillar of New Jersey's Wild Earth Native Plant Nursery gets an

Sometimes, damage to a tree is caused by environmental stress rather than by pests and diseases. This tree was subjected to strong winds, which dried and then broke branches. The tree will be pruned carefully, leaving only the strongest branches.

pest & disease control

infestation of small black aphids on his honeysuckle plants. "But I've discovered that they disappear later in the season, either because of the warm weather or the ladybugs or both," he says. If, like Richard, you grow plants that are native to your area, you'll probably experience a lower incidence of serious pest problems. "Most of my plants have adapted to the local insects," he says.

TIME TO TAKE ACTION If you're reasonably sure that the insects you've found pose a serious problem, begin treatment right away. "Problems are best controlled early on," says David Ittel of Illinois's Alternative Garden Supply. And as Connecticut disease control specialist Dr. Sharon Douglas points out, "Organic controls aren't as fast-acting as chemicals." If an infestation does become severe, most likely you'll still be able to successfully control it, says Kathy Hackim of Oregon's Nature's Control, but it will take longer and require more time, effort, and money.

DO CIRCLES AROUND DISEASES

Crop rotation is by far the best way to control diseases and insects, according to Eric Sideman of the Maine Organic Farmers and Gardeners Association. It prevents the spread of soilborne diseases and pests by removing host plants after a single growing season. Eric encourages home gardeners to consider having two or three gardens located far enough away—50 feet or more, if possible—from one another so that pests and diseases can't spread easily.

You don't need to keep them all full of vegetables. Eric recommends growing a green manure—a crop like hairy vetch or buckwheat, which you plow under at the end of the season to enrich the soil. If your backyard is small and you don't like the idea of staring at buckwheat all summer, Eric suggests planting marigolds. They make a great green manure and a very pretty garden plot, he says.

CHEMICAL-FREE WARFARE

Once you've identified an invasion—of insects or of microbes—and determined it to be serious, you need to decide on a course of action. There are many organic means of fighting pests and diseases. Some are easier to implement than others; some are more effective than others. Of course, the strategy you choose will depend, too, on the problem at hand. What follows is a review of the most popular means of controlling pests and diseases organically, with the experts' comments on which techniques worked best in their gardens and how to use these strategies to your best advantage.

Do It By Hand

Effective hand-to-pest combat • Easy pickings • Removing diseases by hand • Special tips and techniques

You can't get more hands-on than simply picking insect pests off your plants. It won't work with every pest or for every garden, but where hand picking does apply, it can be surprisingly effective.

WHEN IT WORKS "Whether or not hand picking will work for you depends on time and space," says Dr. Bastiaan Drees, professor and extension entomologist at Texas A & M University. It's absolutely wonderful for very small plantings or people with lots of time. If you have a half dozen rose bushes and a 10-foot vegetable plot, or if you have the time to patrol your yard plant by plant, give it a try. If you don't have the time or your garden is simply too large, look for other methods. However, for certain insects, hand picking is the most effective control.

WHICH PESTS TO PICK Hand picking is a good way to deal with a small infestation of any sucking insect—aphids, scale, mites—as well as slugs and snails, says Virginia Hayes of California's Lotusland. Eric Sideman of the Maine Organic Farmers and Gardeners Association recommends it for Colorado potato beetles, and if you time it right, you can entirely eradicate this pest in one thorough sweep of the garden. The Colorado potato beetle overwinters as an adult and can't fly in spring. If you pull them off your plants when they first appear, you might actually rid your garden of the problem, he says.

Other insects that are easily removed by hand include squash bugs, Japanese beetles, tomato hornworms, and other large caterpillars. Richard Pillar of New Jersey's Wild Earth Native Plant Nursery, contends yearly with monarch caterpillars on his milkweed. Because milkweed is the monarch's sole food, and because Richard would like to encourage the butterfly population, he handpicks the caterpillars and transports them to a patch of wild milkweed near the perimeter of the nursery. "At the end of the growing season, I just let them have anything they want," he says. Ursula Herz of South Carolina's Coastal Gardens and Nursery finds hand picking highly effective on bagworms, armyworms, and tent caterpillars. But you have to be consistent, she adds.

PICK THE RIGHT PLANTS

Richard Pillar of New Jersey's Wild Earth Native Plant Nursery has few pest and disease problems because he grows plants that have adapted to the local pests and diseases and have developed clever defenses against them. Choosing native plants is one of the best ways to keep infection and infestation at bay. In addition, if you know that a particular pest or disease runs rampant in your area, grow plants you know are resistant. In the Northeast, anthracnose (a fungal disease) has decimated the dogwood population. But Korean dogwoods are unaffected by the disease and are therefore the best choice for gardeners in that region.

Local plants are usually able to resist local pests. Bowman's root (*Gillenia trifoliata*), native to the Northeast and Midwest, is rarely attacked by insects.

pest & disease control

FALL CLEANING

Sanitation is rule one in the fight against pests and diseases, according to Dr. Paul Steiner, professor and extension fruit pathologist at the University of Maryland. By cleaning up the garden, he says, you eliminate places where germs and pests can breed, multiply, and ultimately infect your plants. At the end of the growing season, toss healthy debris onto the compost heap, and bag and dispose of anything that's diseased or might harbor diseases or pests. Keep in mind that insects can cozy up inside old flower stalks, and fungal spores like to hunker down in leaf debris.

Fall cleanup is great, but don't skip routine cleanup during the season. Dr. Bastiaan Drees, professor and extension entomologist at Texas A & M University, recommends ridding your garden of what he calls sowbug and pillbug condominiums—landscape timbers and piles of leaves that make the perfect homes for these seedling-munching pests.

REMOVING DISEASES On a limited scale, hand picking can help control certain diseases in their early stages, says Dr. Sharon Douglas, a specialist in disease control at Connecticut's Agricultural Experiment Station. It's very effective for powdery mildew and some of the leaf spots, she says. Pick off all the leaves that show signs of disease, then put them directly in a plastic bag, so you're not carrying the diseases to different parts of the garden.

TIPS ON TECHNIQUE Though hand picking is a simple process, here are a few ways to make it easier and more effective:
• One of the easiest ways to dislodge small sucking insects like aphids is to blast them with the garden hose, says Sharon Douglas. But use this only on plants that can stand it.
• Many gardeners, like Oregon rosarian Louise Clements of Oregon's Heirloom Old Garden Roses, simply crush small insects between their fingers. If you're too squeamish to squash, pick insects off and drop them into a can of soapy water. (This is best for anything larger than an aphid, unless you have strong fingers and a stronger stomach.)
• You can shake large insects like Japanese beetles off of plants. Lay a sheet down underneath your plants, and then shake the plants

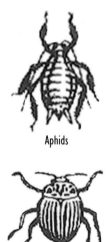

Aphids

Cabbage loopers

Beetles

Cutworms

Knowing your enemy always helps. Here are some common pests that you may find in your garden.

vigorously. Keep watch over the bugs that drop onto your cloth, and before they have a chance to fly away, drop them into a bucket or can of soapy water.

• For culprits that feed at night, such as snails and slugs, go out to the garden after dark with a flashlight and a bucket of soapy water, and plop those suckers right into the drink. John Jeavons, author of *How to Grow More Vegetables*, finds this method extremely effective after a period of heavy rain. Because he and his colleagues use soap that degrades quickly, they simply dump the snails on the compost pile the next day. Three nights are sufficient to catch the vast majority of slugs, he reports. Then over the next two weeks, he goes out occasionally to catch newly hatched slugs or those that were too small to be seen in the first sweep. This kind of concentrated cleanup can be effective for several months.

• If nighttime isn't your best time for collecting pests, place several damp boards in areas of the garden that show signs of slug and snail damage. The next morning, lift up the boards and remove any pests that have taken refuge there.

Corn earworms

Leaf miners

Plant bugs

Spider mites

pest & disease control

SOAP SAFETY

When not used carefully, soap sprays can harm plants and beneficial insects. Follow these precautions:

❧ On days when the temperature soars into the 90s, leave your soap sprays on the shelf. And back off on spraying if you notice any yellowing on your plants, says Eric Vinje of Montana's Planet Natural.

❧ Because soaps only kill on direct contact with pests, there's no reason to leave them on your plants for long periods of time. David Ittel of Illinois's Alternative Garden Supply recommends spraying just after sunset and rinsing first thing in the morning.

❧ Soaps are most effective—but also most harmful—during the heat of the afternoon, says Eric Vinje. Another reason to spray just after sunset; you might have to respray a week later to get the same effect, but at your plants will survive!

Wash Pests Away

Strategic soaping • Commercial versus homemade

In your great-grandmother's day, soapy water was the insecticide of choice. Inexpensive and easy to mix and apply, it also worked—at least on certain problems. Then came powerful chemical pesticides, and soap stayed on the laundry room shelf. Now it's back, working at ridding the garden of soft-bodied insects such as aphids, mealybugs, mites, scale, and whiteflies. But is it as effective as great-granny claimed?

A SLIPPERY ISSUE Among the experts, soap sprays get mixed reviews. Gary Coull of Johnny's Selected Seeds finds that they work well on mites. "Whenever we get an attack of mites in the greenhouse, soap is the only way to get rid of them," he says. Dr. Bastiaan Drees, professor and entomologist at Texas A & M University, finds them highly effective, especially against insects like silver whiteflies that have developed resistance to chemical products.

Other experts have reservations about the use of soaps. Richard Pillar of New Jersey's Wild Earth Native Plant Nursery occasionally sprays the aphids that attack his milkweed plants, but he warns, it sometimes has a detrimental effect on new growth. So Richard uses soaps sparingly. So does Eric Vinje of Montana's Planet Natural, who points out that some herbicides are made from soap but in higher concentrations than you'd find in an insect spray. According to Dr. George Silva of the University of Michigan, soap can strip the waxy surface from certain houseplants and herbaceous annuals if you spray too heavily (soap can actually dissolve ficus foliage). Other plants that are highly susceptible to damage from soap include beans, cucumbers, and Japanese maples. Consider the age of the plant as well, says Eric. He once sold insecticidal soap to a customer who used it on his seedlings and killed off every one. Make sure your plants are sufficiently mature before you spray them with soap or any other control.

Another reason to use soap sprays carefully is their effect on beneficial insects, says Virginia Hayes of California's Lotusland. As Dr. Silva explains, long-term, high-dose use can harm butterflies, and though it won't hurt ladybugs, it can destroy their larvae. Bob Stewart of Arrowhead Alpine Nurseries in Michigan has a very practical reason for avoiding soap sprays. "I've tried them dozens of times and they don't make a bit of difference," he says.

HOMEMADE VERSUS COMMERCIAL SPRAYS Many of the experts express reservations about homemade soap concoctions. Household detergents can contain perfumes and other additives that could be toxic to plants, says Dr. Sharon Douglas, a disease control specialist at Connecticut's Agricultural Experiment Station. And Eric Sideman of the Maine Organic Farmers and Gardeners Association warns that homemade mixtures may not be as effective as store-bought ones, since some fatty acids—the active ingredient in soap and soap sprays—work better than others. If saving money is a priority, he recommends whipping up your own batch and testing it first on a small part of the plant you're targeting. Here's a simple recipe from Dr. Silva: Add 1 teaspoon of dishwashing liquid to 2 cups of cold water and mix thoroughly.

When using soap sprays, start at the base of the plant and spray upward to reach the bugs that hide on the undersides of the leaves.

SOAP SUCCESS

If you don't use soap sprays properly, they won't work very well. Here are ways to make them more effective:

❧ When mixing your soap spray from a concentrate, use soft water, suggests David Ittel of Illinois's Alternative Garden Supply. It enhances the effectiveness of the fatty acids (the active ingredient).

❧ To be sure and hit the thousands of bugs on the undersides of leaves, use this technique from Dr. Bastiaan Drees, professor and extension entomologist at Texas A & M University: Use a pump sprayer that works like a fountain, casting its spray upward rather than sideways, and starting at the base, spray in a spiral all the way around the plant until you reach the top.

❧ Stake or cage sprawling plants such as tomatoes. You can't fully spray a plant that's lying on the ground, says Dr. Drees.

pest & disease control

ORGANIC CONTROLS

Many products derived from nature have potent pest- or disease-killing effects. Be careful, though: even though these products are organically acceptable, they are still potent. Read all labels and follow directions carefully. And use these controls only when you have to!

❨ Pyrethrum, made from the blossoms of the painted daisy, is toxic to most common vegetable pests.

❨ Neem oil, extracted from the neem seed, is used to control aphids, mealybugs, and scale, as well as powdery mildew, blackspot, and rust.

❨ Hot pepper wax repels aphids, whiteflies, and thrips.

❨ Garlic spray repels many insect pests.

These products are available in many forms at garden centers and through catalogs.

A Beneficial Bacterium

BT and its brethren • Timing its application • BT boosters • Caveats and cautions

Bacillus thuringiensis, or BT, is a bacterium that kills caterpillars and other insect pests but is not harmful to fish, birds, and mammals (including humans). It works extremely well and is the best-selling microbial insecticide in the world.

START WITH THE RIGHT SPECIES Because there are several strains of BT, you need to choose the right one for the pest you're targeting, says Dr. George Silva of the University of Michigan. The kurstaki variety of BT (also called BTK), for instance, controls tent caterpillars, gypsy moth caterpillars, cabbage loopers, tomato hornworms, and other leaf-eating caterpillars. The San Diego variety is effective on Colorado potato beetles, and BT Israelensis helps control mosquitoes and fungus gnats.

TIME IT RIGHT Timing can be crucial to achieving the best possible results with BT, says Dr. Silva. Bugs are much more vulnerable when they are in their larval stage. Knowing the life cycle of your pests can help you deal with them at the right time.

• Most beetles overwinter as larvae in the soil; they start feeding again in the spring and emerge as adults when plants begin to put out fruit. Asparagus beetles are a bit earlier, emerging in early spring when the first spears come out. If you're going after Colorado potato beetles, spray them when they're in their hatchling or larval stage, advises Gary Coull of Johnny's Selected Seeds, and only when the larvae are ¼ inch long or smaller.

• Cankerworm eggs hatch in spring. The larvae creep into the soil and stay there until early winter, when adults emerge. They are susceptible to BT only in their larval stage.

• Cabbage looper larvae emerge in May. They stay in that stage for only two to four weeks.

• Corn borer larvae are around for three to four weeks from late June to the middle of July.

• Gypsy moths can be treated with BTK in their caterpillar stage; spray at two- to three-week intervals. Caterpillars have a longer-than-usual cycle, lasting from mid-May to mid-July.

• Cutworm larvae should be treated from early May to early June.

• Cabbageworms lay eggs in early spring; they stay in their larval stage for two to three weeks.

• Spruce budworm, which attack several types of conifers, should be sprayed with BTK as soon as the larvae emerge in late summer.

BETTER BT To boost BT's effectiveness, Gary applies it with a sprayer, adding a bit of liquid seaweed and a drop of mild dish detergent. The seaweed helps the plant through the stress of being chewed on, and the soap helps the spray stay on the plants, he says. You can also add a feeding stimulant, which helps BT do its work faster, says Eric Vinje of Montana's Planet Natural. Available through catalogs and at some garden centers, feeding stimulants encourage insects to eat more heavily and thus consume more of the BT bacteria.

BT SAFETY BTK will kill any caterpillar, so it poses a serious threat to the beautiful and beneficial butterflies in your backyard. To lessen the threat, use BT only on plants affected by pests, advise Eric Vinje of Planet Natural and Eric Sideman of the Maine Organic Farmers and Gardeners Association. If you're going after cabbage loopers on your broccoli, just spray the broccoli, not the whole vegetable patch, says Eric Vinje. This is good advice for any control you use, says Virginia Hayes of California's Lotusland. "All of our controls are applied in the smallest possible area for the shortest possible period of time," she says.

BT can be dissolved in water and sprayed directly onto plants. Use as little possible, and direct the spray to the area where it's needed. Don't forget the undersides of the leaves.

pest & disease control

TAKING IN THE ILL

The first rule of smart shopping: Never buy an unhealthy plant. But what if you come across an extra-ordinary plant that you absolutely must have, even though it's not in the best of health? Here are some of the experts' suggestions:

❧ Determine whether or not the problem is systemic, affecting the whole plant, says Dr. Sharon Douglas. She might buy a plant with aphids or powdery mildew, but would think hard about more serious afflictions like root rot, crown rot, or borers.

❧ When you get your plant home, treat it imme-diately for whatever ails it and plant it in an isolated location, advises Byron Martin of Logee's Greenhouse in Connecticut. Watch it for two years before introducing it to the main garden, adds Peter Ruh of Ohio's Sunny-brook Farm. If problems haven't popped up again after two seasons, chances are they're under control.

❧ Don't propagate from diseased plants unless they're tested by a reputable lab.

Rough Going

Using diatomaceous earth • Diatomaceous downsides • The best use for DE

In use since the 1950s, diatomaceous earth (DE) is a fine powder made from diatoms—fossilized algae whose cell walls are made of silica (a glasslike mineral). You spread DE on the soil, and as pests crawl over the ground, the sharp particles of this powder scratch their skin or shells, wearing away the protective coatings on their bodies. Eventually the pests become dehydrated and die. For years, gardeners have used diatomaceous earth to control slugs and ants, but many have been dissatisfied. And there's a good reason for that, say the experts.

THE DRAWBACKS OF DE For one thing, diatomaceous earth could be deadly to beneficial insects as well as pests. That is, if it works. Many gardeners have discovered that DE doesn't seem to do a good job. If it gets wet, it becomes cakey and can become completely ineffective, says Eric Vinje of Montana's Planet Natural. So if you live in a rainy climate or you water your plants frequently, you're going to have to reapply it often. It also absorbs moisture from the ground, says Eric, and since slugs prefer moist conditions, they're not likely cross ground that's been treated with DE; unless DE is spread even over the whole garden, the pests will simply stay on the untreated spots.

pest & disease control

If slugs and snails are eating your plants, a bit of diatomaceous earth may deter them.

WHAT IS IT GOOD FOR? Like Kathy Hackim of Oregon's Natures Control, most experts use DE not against slugs but ants. If it's slugs you're after, DE is pretty much a waste of time, says Robyn Duback, whose Washington State nursery, Robyn's Nest Nursery, specializes in hostas, one of the favorite meals of slugs. For maximum effect against ants, apply DE on cracks in walkways where ants travel, not directly on anthills, advises Eric Vinje.

Oil Options

How horticultural oils work • Best uses • Vegetable varieties

Nontoxic to humans, pets, and wildlife, horticultural oils kill insect eggs and soft-bodied adults by smothering them. There are three types. Dormant oils are heavy-grade, viscous petroleum products that should only be used on dormant plants. The so-called superior oils, also made from petroleum, are less sticky and can be sprayed year-round. Even safer are the new vegetable-based oils.

BEST USES FOR HORTICULTURAL OILS Eric Vinje of Planet Natural finds oils most effective on insect eggs, but adds that they help control soft-bodied insects like aphids, mites, and scale. Eric Sideman of the Maine Organic Farmers and Gardeners Association highly recommends them for controlling mites on apple and other fruit trees. Though Virginia Hayes of California's Lotusland doesn't often use horticultural oils in her garden, she does use them in small doses for things that are out of control, especially sucking insects. Dormant oils can help keep scale and spider mites off roses, says Dr. Bastiaan Drees, professor and extension entomologist at Texas A & M University. He adds that superior oils work well against certain caterpillars, mealybugs, spider mites, whiteflies, and immature scale insects.

VEGETABLE OILS In the Seeds of Change gardens in Santa Fe, New Mexico, Howard Shapiro and his colleagues spray fruit trees with vegetable-based oils to control borers and moths. Because these oils come from cottonseed and other vegetable products, no chemical solvents are needed to extract them, which isn't the case with oils made from petroleum products. Vegetable oils are safe to use throughout the growing season, and they're less harmful to plants and beneficial insects.

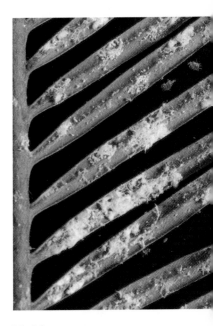

Mealybugs are easy to spot. They can be controlled with soap spray. You can also release lacewings in your garden to prey on mealybugs.

Cutworms attack young seedlings at the bases of their stems. Foil them by positioning seeds or transplants in paper cups or collars (above); the collar should extend a few inches above the soil. The plant will grow right through the collar (below right).

Set a Trap

The trap family and how they work • Realistic expectations • The right trap for you • Traps for monitors

Traps use a variety of tricks to capture troublesome pests. Some entice insects with color, shape, or scent. Baited traps give off the odor of a favorite food—the scent of potatoes seduces wireworms and beer brings on slugs. Pheremone traps attract pests with hormones that only the pests can detect. You can also capture pests by providing hiding places—a damp board will draw snails and slugs under its cover. Most traps have some means of restraining the invader, either with a sticky substance, by drowning them in liquid, or through some means of clever construction. But just how effective are traps in keeping pests out of the garden?

THE TROUBLE WITH TRAPS Ask an expert if traps succeed in attracting and restraining insects, and you're almost certain to get a yes. That doesn't mean, however, that they help cut down on insect populations.

Traps are very effective for the insects that get caught in them, says Dr. Bastiaan Drees, professor and extension entomologist at Texas A & M University. But unless they catch a lot of them, they won't make a difference. "We don't pretend that positioning a few traps around the garden is going to get rid of your pest problem," says Dr. Drees. Furthermore, traps often do a better job of attracting bugs than cutting down on their numbers. In small plots, pheromone traps do more damage than good, bringing insects into your yard from nearby meadows and woods or from your neighbors' gardens," says Eric Vinje of Montana's Planet Natural.

WHEN TRAPS WORK As with all means of pest control, the effectiveness of traps depends on your specific situation. Some traps work quite well at reducing pest populations. Pheromone traps (those that use hormones to attract insects) can be quite effective on large properties or in neighborhoods where everyone uses them. In southern California, where ips beetles have been wreaking havoc on native pine trees, traps baited with three separate pheromones have made a

To catch slugs and snails, set a shallow can into to earth, flush with the surface. Fill it with enough beer to drown the pests.

Sticky traps attract aphids, whiteflies, gypsy moths, beetles, and other pests. Buy commercial traps or make your own by coating a piece of cardboard with petroleum jelly. Simply hang the traps from tree branches or wrap them around the trunk. Dispose of them when they're coated with bugs.

PEST TRAPS

There's a certain satisfaction derived from trapping bugs that are determined to take more than their fair share of your crops. Here are a few traps the experts use.

❧ Kathy Hackim of Oregon's Nature's Control uses a portable vaccuum cleaner to reduce large whitefly populations. She shakes the plant until the whiteflies rise, then vaccuums the air. Never vaccuum the plant, she says; it will do more harm to the plant than the bugs ever did.

❧ You can lure large numbers of bugs with a single slice of melon or cucumber; it's easier than hand-picking. Just put a fresh-cut slice near your plants, then remove it, with all the bugs attached, about an hour later.

❧ Plant an inexpensive "trap crop" a few weeks before the main crop. For example, a small row of bush beans planted near your pole beans will keep bean beetles away from your longer-producing pole beans. Destroy the trap crop with the bugs still on it.

significant difference, says Virginia Hayes of California's Lotusland. If you have a large backyard and want to try pheromone traps, Eric Vinje suggests placing them in the center of your property. That way you'll be less likely to attract insects from nearby yards or from the wild. Traps that use color or edible bait as a lure are a wiser choice for small yards, Eric adds, since they're less likely to pull in pests from great distances. And they're also quite effective at controlling the specific pests they attract, according to Eric Sideman of the Maine Organic Farmers and Gardeners Association.

SNARING SLUGS AND SNAILS Of all the traps you can buy or make, slug and snail traps are among the simplest and the most effective. They're very good at reducing populations, says Dr. Drees, though they won't get rid of them entirely. For a few dollars, you can buy a beer-bait trap, or you can easily make your own. Take an empty tuna can, fill it with beer, and set it in the ground so that its rim is level with the soil surface. Slugs are suckers for the stuff. They'll dive right into it and drown. But Washington State hosta grower Robyn Duback of Robyn's Nest Nursery, Washington, a veteran of several slug wars, has a weapon that works even better. She sets an aluminum pie pan in the garden, fills it with beer, and lays a brick in the pan. Then she inverts another pie pan over the brick and places a second brick on top. Robyn invented this contraption after observing for several years that slugs prefer their beer straight up—if it's diluted, they tend to ignore it. The inverted pan prevents moisture from getting into the beer, and you catch more slugs and snails. Remember to check and empty traps daily until you've made a significant dent in the population.

ANOTHER TASK FOR TRAPS Like many garden experts, Eric Sideman and Eric Vinje find traps most useful in monitoring insect populations. If you're using a program of control aimed at a specific pest (or pests), traps will let you know whether your program is working. Eric Sideman uses pheromone traps to monitor corn earworms, white sticky traps for codling moths, and yellow traps for a whole slew of insects including thrips and cabbageworms. Here's his homemade trap for cabbage maggots: Just fill a yellow pan with soapy water. The color yellow attracts the maggots, and the soapy water keeps them from escaping.

Good Bugs

Do beneficial insects really work? • *Inviting them in* • *Keeping them happy*

Consider calling in the troops—troops of predatory and parasitic insects, that is—to help fight pests. Ladybugs will search out and eat aphids. Trichogramma wasps have a different tactic. They lay their eggs in a host's body, where the next generation lives part of its life cycle, much to the detriment of the host insect. There are several beneficial insects that may prove to be useful soldiers in your war against garden pests.

THE BEST BUGS Some beneficial insects do a better job than others. The experts offer their star picks:

• Eric Vinje of Montana's Planet Natural sells an array of beneficials through his Planet Natural catalog. He's especially enthusiastic about lacewings, which love to eat soft-bodied insects, and he likes minute pirate bugs, which feed on thrips, spider mites, scale insects, aphids, and leafhoppers. For mealybugs, he recommends *Cryptolaemus montrouzieri*, a beetle considerably smaller than its name but with a very big appetite.

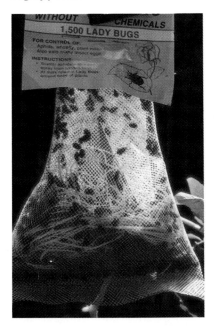

If your garden isn't full of ladybugs, you can buy them by the bagful.

LET 'EM LOOSE

Whats the best way to release beneficial insects into your garden? Should you let them all go at once? Or should you free a few at a time? And when's the best time to introduce them to your garden? Here are some tips from the experts:

☙ Beneficial insects are most effective when released at the first sign of pest problems, says Kathy Hackim of Nature's Control, a biological pest control company in Oregon.

☙ If you're sending trichogramma wasps after caterpillars, you need to get the wasps (shipped as eggs) into the garden during the caterpillars adult stage (moth) and then periodically thereafter, according to Eric Vinje of Montana's Planet Natural.

☙ To fight aphids with lacewings, you may need to make two releases. Though lacewings can consume 60 aphids an hour, aphids reproduce equally fast.

☙ For best results with encarsia wasps, stagger their release over a four-week period, says Eric.

SMART RELEASING

When ordering beneficials, ask about any special considerations that might be necessary for their release. According to Kathy Hackim, the best time to release most beneficial insects is in the evening or early morning. At that time, temperatures are usually cooler and the bugs are much less active. They will have time to settle into their new home before they get the urge to fly away.

• David Ittel of Illinois's Alternative Garden Supply praises predator mites for their effective control of plant-feeding mites, and says whitefly parasites (tiny wasps that lay their eggs in immature whiteflies) work well.

• John Jeavons, author of *How to Grow More Vegetables*, recommends trichogramma wasps, which lay their eggs in moth and butterfly larvae; tachnid flies, which help control caterpillars, Japanese beetles, earwigs, gypsy moths, brown tail moths, tomato worms, and grasshoppers; and syrphid flies, which attack aphids and help pollinate crops.

Other beneficials to consider are true bugs (for control of thrips, mites, aphids, and whitefly pupae), encarsia wasps (for whiteflies), and beneficial nematodes. Nematodes aren't actually insects—they're tiny, hollow worms. Some nematodes are harmful and can damage plant roots, but the beneficial ones will attack black vine weevils, fungus gnats, grubs, and wood borers.

OVERRATED GOOD BUGS Two of the best-known beneficial predators, ladybugs and praying mantids, get lukewarm reviews from the experts. Praying mantids eat everything, good and bad, and they're preyed on heavily by birds, says Eric Vinje. John Jeavons suggests using them only in infestation emergencies. Ladybugs, unlike mantids, aren't likely to attack the beneficial insects in your garden, but you can't count on them to stay for very long. For this reason, Eric Sideman of the Maine Organic Farmers and Gardeners Association recommends them mainly for greenhouse situations.

BUY THEM OR LURE THEM If you've decided to give beneficials a try, the next step is getting them into your garden. For specific pest problems that need immediate attention, the fastest means is to buy the beneficials you need. Biological control companies sell a wide variety of beneficial insects, mostly by mail (see "Sources" on page 362). While most companies don't guarantee success in your garden, they should promise that your predators will be in good shape when they arrive at your doorstep. Before you order, make sure that you can get a refund or credit if things go wrong en route.

If you're not in a hurry and are looking for a long-term solution to pest problems, bring beneficial insects to your garden by creating

Bright colors, like the gold petals of these rudbeckias, attract beneficial insects to your garden.

conditions they like. Howard Shapiro and his colleagues at Seeds of Change in Santa Fe have planted specific sections of their fields with plants that will attract beneficials. They've had the best success with sorghum, corn, sunflowers, and other members of the composite family (which includes daisies, asters, coneflowers, and black-eyed Susans). "We've found that insects like a big, yellow platform—it looks safe to land on," he says. To attract the greatest variety of insects, Howard suggests planting flowers that grow to a wide variety of heights. Some insects like to stay close to the ground, others like to be higher up, he explains. Virginia Hayes of California's Lotusland not only provides refuge for predator insects, she harvests them with a special tiny vacuum, available through specialty horticulture supply outlets and then releases them where they're needed most. Don't try this with a regular vacuum; it will quickly kill all the bugs. But you can snip off a leaf with a good population of good bugs and transfer it to another part of the garden, says Kathy Hackim of Nature's Control in Oregon.

Of course, if your garden draws beneficial insects, it's also attracting less desirable ones, but according to John Jeavons author of *How to Grow*

For many years, experienced gardeners have sworn that marigolds repel certain pests. Scientific evidence has proven them to be right in some circumstances.

More Vegetables, this isn't the problem it seems. If you want to keep beneficial insects in your garden, they need food, and, of course, they feed on exactly those insects that you don't want in your garden. No pests, no beneficials. However, if you have both, you'll have a balance, John notes, so the beneficials will prevent the pests from becoming a problem.

KEEPING THE TROOPS HAPPY Once you've released beneficial insects into your backyard, you'll want them to stay as long as possible. The best way to do this is to create a bug-friendly environment by planting nectar-producing plants. In addition, biological control companies are beginning to offer lures that not only attract predatory insects to your garden but also help keep them there. Eric Vinje says that ladybug lures do a good job of encouraging ladybugs to stick around (though they don't work as well at attracting them from the wild).

Plants That Partner in Pest Control

The great debate on companions • Marigolds—the nematodes nemesis
• Other plants that repel pests • Attracting beneficials

You may have noticed this in your own backyard. Certain plants seem to benefit each other when they're grown together. Though science is skeptical about whether or not companion planting works, many gardeners swear by it. Plants do give off aromas in order to attract certain insects, and the roots of many plants secrete substances that seem to repel or even kill pests, but whether these lead to genuine pest control continues to be debated.

EXPERT OPINIONS Not all of the experts endorse companion planting. Dr. Bastiaan Drees, professor and extension entomologist with Texas A & M University, cites studies done in California that showed companion plantings could have an effect on pests, but that in order to reduce the number of pests significantly, so many companion plants had to be grown that yield from the garden dropped. In an ornamental garden, of course, this wouldn't be a problem, and it wouldn't make much of a difference in a vegetable garden where high yield isn't important. Certain plant combinations may be more effective than

Sage reduces cabbage moth and carrot fly populations; it also attracts beneficial insects to the garden.

others. John Jeavons, author of *How to Grow More Vegetables*, encourages home gardeners to experiment with companion plantings.

THE MAGIC OF MARIGOLDS The best-known of the pest-repellent plants is the marigold. For years, gardeners have sworn that it controls nematodes—tiny worms that feed on roots and leaves—but until recently, the evidence had always been anecdotal. A study conducted in the Netherlands, however, suggests that marigolds do help deter nematodes, at least to a degree. Dutch horticulturists planted more than 800 varieties and found that at least one, the French marigold (*Tagetes patula*), first attracted nematodes and then killed them with ozone gases exuded from the roots. The marigolds were most effective, however, when grown as a cover crop (see "Going for Cover" on page 283) for two successive seasons—more time than some gardeners would be willing to give. And according to Dr. Paul Steiner, professor and extension fruit pathologist at the Univeristy of Maryland, marigolds act on some nematodes, but not all of them. They're effective on those nematodes that harm margiolds, but not necessarily on the ones that are interested in the bean plant next door.

BENEFICIALS' FEASTS

If you want beneficial bugs to stay in your garden, make sure they can find the foods they like. Some of their favorite categories:

❧ Aromatic plants such as sage, thyme, rosemary, and basil; these attract the beneficials with scent.

❧ Members of the Asteraceae (composite) family—including daisies, asters, feverfew, marigolds, and sunflowers—have bright yellow centers that attract beneficials.

❧ Parsley, dill, carrots, and other members of the Apiaceae family are food for ladybugs and lacewings.

Plants are the main sustenance of sucking beneficials like ladybugs and lacewings, but many other useful insects eat only other bugs. Keeping a balance of good and pesty insects in your garden will allow one population to control the other. Getting rid of every bug in your garden—an impossible task to begin with—would also mean destroying the beneficial insects that naturally control pest populations.

GOOD COMPANIONS

Want to give companion planting a try in your backyard? Here are some recommendations from John Jeavons, author of How to Grow More Vegetables:

✤ For blackflies: stinging nettle.

✤ For cabbageworms: butterflysage, rosemary, hyssop, thyme, mint, wormwood, and southernwood.

✤ For moths: sage, santolina, lavender, mint, and a variety of herbs.

✤ For plant lice: castor bean, sassafras, and pennyroyal.

✤ For potato bugs: flax and eggplant.

✤ For squash bugs: nasturtium.

✤ For weevils: garlic.

Howard Shapiro from Seeds of Change in Santa Fe believes in the power of marigolds. "We've sold nematode marigolds to people who grow Easter lilies, and they've worked very well," he says. If you want to give marigolds a shot, Howard recommends *Tagetes minuta*. Traditionally used to control nematodes in vegetable gardens in Mexico, especially as a companion to radishes, carrots, and broccoli, *T. minuta* bears clusters of tiny yellow flowers.

PLANTS THAT REPEL INSECTS Though we don't have scientific proof, certain plants do seem to deter pests, says John Jeavons. It may be a while before scientists find a way to prove these relationships, but that doesn't mean that they don't exist. Nasturtiums and garlic appear to repel aphids. White geraniums and datura keep Japanese beetles away. Eggplant and green beans may control Colorado potato beetles, and radishes seem to ward off the striped cucumber beetle. To reduce the number of nematodes around his fruit trees, Paul Steiner plants Kentucky 31 tall fescue. Fescue contains an endophyte fungus that won't harm the trees but wreaks havoc on nematodes. To kill nematodes before planting, Paul recommends sowing rapeseed, which produces a cyanidelike compound deadly to the tiny worms. Sow the rapeseed in the fall and let it grow over winter; then turn it under in spring. For best results, Paul recommends planting a second crop two weeks later.

PLANTS THAT BRING IN GOOD BUGS You can use companion planting to attract beneficial insects to your garden. Try growing flowers from the Asteraceae or composite family, suggests John Jeavons. Asteraceae is one of the largest flowering-plant families and includes daisies, sunflowers, asters, and pot marigolds (calendulas). Composite flowers are excellent attractants for predatory insects because their large supplies of pollen serve as a food source, says John. And you don't need rows and rows of them. Two to four plants per 100 square feet will probably suffice, says John. (For more on composites and their effect on pests, see "Good Bugs" on page 309.)

In addition to sunflowers and their kin, Virginia Hayes of California's Lotusland recommends any plant thats highly attractive to butterflies (including butterfly bush, butterfly weed, and milkweed). The nectar that entices butterflies is likely to attract a wide variety of other insects, as well.

Four-Legged Pests

Deterring deer • Ridding your yard of rabbits, mice, and voles
• Banishing birds

They may be cute, but our winged and four-legged friends can become
our enemies when they feast on the flowers and vegetables in our
backyards. And as we continue to develop and encroach on once-wild
areas, animals are sure to become an increasing problem in the garden.

DEER If you live anywhere near a wooded area, you've probably had
to contend with these graceful, intelligent, and voracious creatures.
The only way to keep them out of your garden completely is to fence
them out, but if you only see them occasionally, you can try some less
drastic measures. Deer tend to be deterred by the scent of humans or
dogs, or by anything that gives off an unpleasant odor.

Jack Crittenden of Missouri's Stark Brothers Nurseries recommends
placing bars of soap, mothballs, or a sock filled with hair in your
garden. But you must rotate these items on a regular basis, says Jack, or
the deer will get used to and ignore them. Peter Borchard of

If you're serious about
keeping deer out of your
beds, fencing is the only
solution. Deer can jump an
8-foot fence, so build your
fence high or enclose your
fencing with a "roof."

pest & disease control

pest & disease control

DEER DETERRENTS

As deer populations expand, experts work harder to develop products and procedures to get rid of them. Some of these—such Deer-Off™, Not Tonight, Deer™— have rotten eggs and hot peppers as their main ingredients. Other products, such as Hinder, use ammonium soap, whose odor deer hate.

You can create your own deer deterrents from the same ingredients. Experiment with different combinations of soap, egg, and hot pepper mixed in a water solution and spread them around the garden. Note which combinations work best with the deer in your area and adjust your recipe. Avoid coconut-based soap—deer seem to like it.

Another way to deter deer is to place plants they dislike among those that they do. Plants that are rarely browsed by deer include yarrow, lantana, lavender, mints, foxglove, ferns, barberry, boxwood, oleander, mountain laurel, spruce, pine, and rosemary, and the old standby, daffodils.

Companion Plants, who deals with a large and hungry deer population in his Ohio backyard, places wolf fur around the perimeter of his propery. (He gets the fur from a neighbor whose dog is part wolf.) You can also try dog fur. Even if it doesn't keep the deer from chomping at your azaleas, it will enrich the soil as it decomposes.

If you can't deter them through their sense of smell, try their sense of hearing. Donald Ledden of New Jersey's Ledden Brothers Seed Company keeps deer at bay with a portable radio, protected from the weather and tuned to a talk station. Or try singeing their taste buds by spritzing plants with hot pepper spray, available at garden centers and through mail-order catalogs. However, as Peter Ruh of Ohio's Sunnybrook Farm warns, "If you handle a plant that's been sprayed with hot pepper and then put your hand near your eye, you'll never want to use hot pepper again."

FENCE THEM OUT You can try it all, but with deer it comes down to fencing, says Richard Pillar, whose Wild Earth Native Plant Nursery in central New Jersey has seen its share of hungry deer. His own fence is 6 feet high, and deer rarely jump it, though they did once, in a severe drought, he says. The larger and hungrier the deer population, the higher your fence will need to be, says Richard. If you don't like the look of an 8-foot fence, try Peter Ruh's secret deer deterrent. He covers the area around his garden with a double layer of flattened cardboard boxes, first cutting any weeds or brush down to the ground. Then he lays long, thin poles (about 8 feet long and 3 inches in diameter) on top of the cardboard and stretches chicken wire over the poles. "It's the most effective way I know of keeping deer out of the garden," he says, though it's not appropriate for an ornamental garden.

RABBITS, MICE, AND VOLES They're small, furry, and cute, and they can wreak havoc in your garden. Mice and rabbits can girdle and kill a tree, says Jack Crittenden of Missouri's Start Brothers Nurseries. To stop them, he uses tree guards: 18-inch lengths of chicken wire for rabbits and a finer wire for mice. Richard Pillar traps rabbits and takes them away from his home (you can buy or rent traps that don't hurt the animal and are easy to use). But keep in mind that rabbits are quick studies. Unless you catch them the first time they see the trap, you won't be successful, warns Jack.

Richard Pillar, who once controlled the vole population in his nursery with poison, stopped the practice as soon as he discovered that it was killing beneficial snakes as well. "So now we just feed a few wild cats, and that's helped the vole problem," he says.

BIRDS If you grow berries or fruit trees, you know what a menace birds can be. In a small garden, commercial netting keeps birds out of your berries, says Douglas Clark of Washington State's Modern Agri-Products, but he admits that it can be time-consuming to use on large areas. And he warns that netting can entrap ground snakes, which play a critical part in the ecosystem in certain areas. Another option, Douglas says, is Birdscare flash tape—a silver and red metalized mylar ribbon—that apparently looks like flames to many birds. It's especially effective with flocking birds such as starlings, crows, woodpeckers, and geese.

Don't banish your pets from the garden! Your cat or dog's scent will scare off mice, voles, and rabbits. But make sure that the plants in your garden are not harmful to your pets before you turn pets loose.

pest & disease control

Discolored spots on foliage are a sign of disease. Act quickly to diagnose the problem and, if it is one that can spread to other plants, remove it from your garden.

DESTROYING DISEASE

Visible bugs are not the only culprits when it comes to causing problems in your garden. Viruses and bacteria attack plants the same way they attack humans, causing symptoms of distress and sometimes even killing their hosts. Keeping your garden free of soil- and plant-borne disease is as important as keeping deer or beetles from chewing up your vegetables.

Directions for Diagnoses

The importance of being early • Bacteria, fungi, viruses, and nematodes • Picking up clues • Reading symptoms

Not every dead plant in your garden is diseased; drying up and dying off is part of the normal cycle of nature. There are, however, ways to distinguish between the inevitable and the avoidable.

MONITOR REGULARLY Make monitoring a regularly scheduled part of your gardening activities. Look under leaves, up and down stems, and at the base of the plant. "Take notes," says Debby Kavakos of Stoneledge Farm in New York. "If something is growing rapidly and suddenly stops, I look at it more closely. If foliage starts to look a little off-color, I make a note to check it carefully the following week."

KNOW WHAT YOU'RE LOOKING FOR Most garden diseases are caused by pathogens, tiny organisms that infect the plant and can spread from one plant to another. These pathogens are divided into four groups: fungi (which cause powdery mildew, damping off, blackspot, and early and late blight); bacteria (which cause fireblight, crown gall, and bacterial wilt), viruses (which cause rose mosaic and other leaf discolorations), and nematodes (some of which are beneficial).

Symptoms to look for when inspecting your plants include:
• Dark or sooty patches on foliage, caused by blackspot.
• White, discolored areas on foliage, caused by powdery mildew.
• Sudden wilting and withering, often caused by botrytis or early or late blight.
• Leaf discolorations, which can be caused by any of several plant pathogens.

• Mushy, oozing cankers on branches. Pay careful attention to these; some cankers can kill a tree.

• Discolorations on leaves, especially if they are raised or curled; these can be caused by rusts or viral diseases or by lack of water.

• Spongy or soft roots, which are symptoms of fungal diseases.

Prevention is the Best Medicine

Keeping things clean • Keeping pathogens out of your garden

Once a pathogen has entered your garden, it's difficult to eradicate it. It's much easier to keep it out in the first place.

SANITATION IS SMART Weedy, debris-filled gardens are havens for all sorts of pathogens. Pathogens, particularly fungi, breed in areas with poor air circulation. Anything you can do to keep air flowing between your plants will help avoid plant disease. Proper pruning, weeding, and spacing not only help your plants grow better, they also keep diseases from attacking. Garden debris belongs in the compost pile, not wherever it happens to fall.

KEEP IT DRY, BUT NOT TOO DRY Moist, waterlogged plants are prone to a slew of diseases. Try to water at a time when the moisture on the leaves will evaporate quickly. Jeff Edwards of Home Harvest Garden Supply in Virginia recommends a drip irrigation system that gets water into the soil rather than on the foliage and bark. This is ideal. On the other hand, plants that are stressed by lack of water are also vulnerable to both insect and disease infestation.

WATCH WHAT YOU BRING IN Plant pathogens live in plants. If your garden is healthy now and you want to keep it that way, inspect every plant that you bring into your garden. Look under the leaves, check the roots for mushiness, and make sure the foliage is vigorous and clean.

ACT QUICKLY If you do find a problem, take care of it immediately, before it can spread. Prune out all infected areas of the plant and take them far away to be burned or buried. Don't put them in your compost pile unless it is very hot—over 160°F. And if the plant still seems sick after a few weeks, get rid of it. It's not worth risking the rest of the garden.

ORGANIC DISEASE CONTROL

If you catch a disease in its early stages, the following products can prevent it from spreading. Many of these are toxic; read label directions carefully. Early detection and treatment is critical.

❧ Copper is effective against early and late blights on tomatoes and potatoes, and against many other diseases. It is, however, toxic and should be used with great care.

❧ Sulfur can be used to reduce the effects of blackspot, applescab, and powdery mildew.

❧ Bordeaux mix, discovered by French grape growers in the nineteenth century, is a mixture of lime and copper sulfate that protects food plants from fungi.

❧ A mixture of horticultural oil and baking soda can control blackspot and powdery mildew on roses.

pest & disease control

Espaliering works very well for fruit trees because it ensures good air circulation. Starting when the tree is young, select the strongest branches and tie them to the support. Prune off all other branches.

SPECIAL-CASE CONTROL

The easiest solution to pests and diseases is to grow plants that are resistant to them. But sometimes you simply have to have a plant, despite all the difficulties of growing it. If you've ever grown fruit trees or roses, you know the problems they present, but you also know the rewards. What could be more satisfying than picking a ripe peach off your own tree or gathering a lavish, fragrant bouquet of roses from your backyard? It was once thought that you couldn't grow good-looking roses or bountiful fruit trees without dousing them with chemical insecticides and fungicides, but no more. There are a few organic secrets that can keep your special plants looking special.

Fruit and Nut Trees

Choosing resistant varieties • *Good garden maintenance*
• *Keeping your backyard clean* • *Organic pest controls*

Fruit and nut trees produce fragrant blossoms in spring, a bountiful harvest in summer and early autumn, sculptural beauty in winter—and more pest and disease problems than almost anything else you could grow in your backyard. But don't despair. Whether you have a small orchard or a single fruit or nut tree, the experts' no-spray secrets can help boost the health of your trees and the heft of your harvest.

SELECT RESISTANT VARIETIES If you're planting fruit trees for the first time or adding new ones to an established orchard, choose your trees for their ability to resist pests and diseases. Variety selection is your number-one angle for pest-free anything, says Dr. Bastiaan Drees, professor and extension entomologist at Texas A & M University. (See "Super Fruits" on page 320 for a selection of resistant fruit-tree varieties.)

IMPROVE YOUR SOIL As John Jeavons, author of *How to Grow More Vegetables* puts it, "The soil needs your energy, rather than the insect." This truth applies throughout the garden, but even more so to fruit and nut trees. A tree grown in a healthy soil with good tilth and availability of organic matter will be more resistant to insects and diseases, says Gerry Donaldson of Michigans Hilltop Nurseries.

PRUNE REGULARLY In addition to increasing fruit production, regular pruning can help decrease infestation and infection. Be especially rigorous in pruning out all weak, dead, and dying limbs and branches, which can harbor high populations of scale insects and fungal and bacterial pathogens, says Dr. Paul Steiner, professor and extension fruit pathologist at the Univeristy of Maryland. If you're growing peaches or nectarines, Dr. Steiner advises cutting out any weak or thin interior shoots immediately after harvest. They usually die in early winter and serve as points of invasion for *Cytospora* canker fungus, he says. When you prune, make cuts that will help keep the canopy open, advises Missouri fruit-tree grower Jack Crittenden. This allows air to circulate and the sun to penetrate the canopy, which reduces the moisture that fungal diseases need in order to breed.

Apple trees at the Rudolf Steiner Fellowship Foundation orchards are pruned to allow maximum air circulation between the branches.

SUPER FRUITS

If you're looking for fruit trees that are highly resistant to pests and diseases, Dr. Paul Steiner, extension fruit pathologist at the University of Maryland, recommends the following apple and pear varieties. This list is by no means comprehensive.

Reputable growers should be able to answer any questions about the pest and disease resistance of their trees. If your're planting peaches or nectarines, try to find varieties that are resistant to bacterial spot disease.

Apples resistant to fire blight: 'Golden Delicious'; 'Red Delicious'; 'Stayman'; 'Winesap'.

Pears resistant to fire blight: 'Honeysweet'; 'Magness (immune)'; 'Maxine'; 'Moonglow'; 'Seckel'.

Apples resistant to apple scab: 'Freedom'; 'Jonafree'; 'Liberty'; 'Prima'; 'Priscilla'; 'Redfree'; 'Sir Prize'.

FERTILIZE CAREFULLY According to Gerry Donaldson of Michigan's Hilltop Nurseries, excessive fertilization can lead to too-rapid growth, which in turn makes a tree more susceptible to pests and diseases. Be especially wary of high-nitrogen fertilizers (including manure), says Paul Steiner. High nitrogen levels in the soil encourage high populations of aphids and psylla insects, and they can can lead to severe limb damage if fire blight develops, he says. Sucking and chewing insects damage a plant's cell structure, which allows fire blight and other disease an easy way in.

WEED REGULARLY Weeds not only compete for water and nutrients, they also harbor vast populations of insects. In winter, they provide the perfect nesting site for mice that feed on bark and roots, says Dr. Paul Steiner. If nematodes are a problem in your orchard, Dr. Steiner recommends planting Kentucky 31 tall fescue under your trees. It carries an endophyte fungus that seems to suppress nematodes, he says. (See page 327 for other nematode controls.)

KEEP IT CLEAN Keeping a clean garden helps prevent pest and disease problems from developing in general, but it's even more important if you're growing fruit or nut trees. After harvest, remove all fallen leaves, says Dr. Paul Steiner. They harbor the overwintering stages of several insect pests, he says, as well as the spores that initiate apple and pear scab in the spring. In addition, Paul recommends collecting and destroying any fruits that fall from the tree too early, since premature fruit-drop is often caused by pests or fungal diseases that linger in the rotting fruit. For the same reason, don't allow any unharvested fruit to remain on the tree.

Roses

Resistant varieties • Getting rid of aphids • Baking soda for diseases • Keep your rose bed tidy

Until recently, growing roses meant spraying them with chemical pesticides to control scale, aphids, chafers, Japanese beetles, and midges, and with chemical fungicides to control blackspot, powdery mildew, rust, and leaf spot. One popular gardening book, first published in the 1960s, recommended 19 separate chemicals for

Roses are less disease-prone if they are carefully pruned to promote good air circulation.

maintaining optimum rose health. But there are safe and effective organic ways of growing healthy, fragrant, beautiful roses.

PLANT RESISTANT ROSES The best way to cut down on pest and disease problems in your rose garden is to plant disease- and pest-resistant cultivars, says Louise Clements, proprietor of Oregon's Heirloom Old Garden Roses. And as gardeners clamor for resistant varieties, more and more growers are breeding them. Louise loves 'Babylove', a highly resistant rose with small yellow blooms.

pest & disease control

FRUITFUL CONTROLS

Even in the most carefully tended orchard or backyard, pests and diseases can crop up. To deal with them effectively, make sure your control targets the specific insect or disease you're fighting. Some suggestions:

❧ Eric Sideman of Maine Organic Farmers and Gardener's Assocation uses apple maggot traps to catch the adult stage of apple maggot.

❧ To kill apple maggot pupae in the ground, Eric Vinje of Montana's Planet Natural recommends beneficial nematodes. Spread them by hand over the soil and then water them in.

❧ Around fruit trees, Eric Sideman likes to use yellow sticky traps, which attract and ensnare a wide variety of insects.

❧ Predatory insects can be helpful in the orchard, says Hunter Carleton of Washington's Bear Creek Nursery.

❧ Gerry Donaldson of Michigan's Hilltop Nurseries recommends dormant oils for fruit-tree pest problems. The safest are the new vegetable-based oils.

Keeping your rosebushes well-pruned and deadheaded will not only result in less disease—it will also increase blossoming.

ATTACKING APHIDS No matter what variety of roses you grow, resistant or not, they're probably going to get aphids. These little suckers are especially prevalent in spring, as they favor the tender new growth at the tips of branches. You can successfully remove them with insecticidal soaps (see "Wash Pests Away" on page 300) or with the help of beneficial insects, especially ladybugs (see "Good Bugs" on page 309), but Louise Clements and many of the other experts prefer to simply handpick them. "I just crush them with my fingers," says Louise. You can also knock them off with a strong burst of water from the hose.

For diseases, apply baking soda. In addition to relieving your upset stomach and rendering your fridge odor-free, baking soda helps combat two of the most common rose diseases: powdery mildew and blackspot. For mildew, which shows up as a fine white powder on leaf surfaces, a sprayed-on solution of baking soda, water, and horticultural oil can work magic, says Judy Megan of Connecticut's historic Glebe House. Her secret formula combines a gallon of water, 2 1/2 table-spoons of horticultural oil, and a tablespoon of baking soda. Dr. Sharon Douglas, a disease control specialist with Connecticut's Agricultural Experiment Station, recommends applying oil at the first sign of symptoms. But before you spray, pick off all infected leaves, place them in a plastic bag, and dispose of them. To keep mildew from returning the following season, Richard Boonstra of Bluestone Perennials in Ohio suggests jotting down the date of its first appearance and then spraying just before that date next year.

Baking soda may also help prevent or reduce blackspot, says Louise Clements. This disease produces small dark spots on leaves closest to the ground, which eventually yellow and drop off. Don't wait for the blackspot to appear before spraying. As soon as your bushes have fully leafed out, start spraying your rosebushes with baking soda as described above; this will prevent the disease from infecting your roses in the first place. Once a week should be sufficient, unless you get heavy rains.

BE PRUDENT ABOUT PRUNING Good air circulation is the best disease prevention, says Louise Clements. Fungi need moisture to grow, and freely moving air prevents moisture from lingering. Don't crowd your roses, and prune them regularly to keep them open.

SEARCH FOR AND DESTROY DEBRIS As with fruit trees, you can prevent the spread of disease by keeping your rose beds clean. In the fall, after dormancy, rake up all debris, even reaching into the bush and pulling out any leaves that are stuck on the canes, says Louise Clements. The spores of blackspot and powery mildew overwinter on leaf debris, and will be ready to pop up and infect your roses come spring. Unless you know your compost pile is hot enough to kill off these spores and any other diseases that might be lurking on the leaves, bag them tightly in plastic and dispose of them.

Some roses are naturally less prone to disease than others. 'Tausenschoen', a vigorous rambler, is resistant to powdery mildew and blackspot.

THE EXPERTS' TOP GUNS

Every pest and disease control has both advantages and disadvantages. How do the experts control pests or diseases in their own gardens? Here are some methods they find useful.

THE CONTROL	THE PROBLEMS IT CONTROLS	HOW THE CONTROL WORKS	COMMENTS FROM THE EXPERTS
Trichoderma	Root diseases, such as root rot and club root	Trichoderma is a fungus sold under the name Root Shield. It enters the roots of plants and blocks the entrance of destructive fungi. See "Sources" on page 362.	Trichoderma is recommended by Dr. Sharon Douglas, plant disease specialist with Agricultural Experiment Station, Connecticut.
Garlic	Whiteflies, mites, leafrollers, and aphids on both edible and ornamental plants	The odor deters pests from attacking plants.	Recommended by Gary Coull, Johnny's Selected Seeds. Several products are available at garden centers or through catalogs. Or, make your own: Soak 3 ounces of garlic in mineral oil for 24 hours, then strain, add 1 pint of water, and a tablespoon of liquid soap. Spray on affected plants.
Hot pepper wax	Mites, aphids, whiteflies, leaf hoppers, codling moths, and other insects	Capsaicin, the substance that makes hot peppers hot, repels insects.	Recommended by Gary Coull, Johnny's Selected Seeds. Several products are available at garden centers or through catalogs. Or, grind up the seeds of very hot peppers; sprinkle the dust on plants or mix with soap and water. Wear gloves!
Bantam chickens	Slugs	Chickens eat slugs, and eight to ten chickens on two acres will reduce slug population significantly.	Robyn Duback of Washington's Robyn's Nest Nursery says: "They're my number-one control."

THE CONTROL	THE PROBLEMS IT CONTROLS	HOW THE CONTROL WORKS	COMMENTS FROM THE EXPERTS
Birds	All pests	Many birds are insectivores. Spread bird feeders throughout your garden to attract them, or grow plants that birds like.	Louise Clements of Heirloom Old Garden Roses in Oregon and Howard Shapiro of Seeds of Change in Santa Fe both find that pest problems are reduced when bird populations increase.
Aerating sandals; shoe attachments with steel spikes, usually advertised for aerating lawns.	Grubs	Researchers at Colorado State University strapped on the sandals and walked over test lawns three to five times. They found that the sandals killed more than half the grubs present in the plots, which makes them better than many chemical insecticides marketed for grub control.	Recommended by Eric Vinje of Planet Natural in Montana.
Milk	Root maggots on cabbage and broccoli	After transplanting your cabbage and broccoli seedlings, give them a good watering, then pour a cup of milk around the stem. The sticky casein in the milk seals the soil, creating a barrier that eggs can't penetrate.	It's safe and reduces mortality by 95 percent, says Byron Martin of Logee's Greenhouses in Connecticut.
Floating row covers	Most flying insects and animal pests on vegetable plants	Place row covers over plants right after transplanting. Anchor well into soil to create a physical barrier between pests and plants. Remove for pollination when crop flowers.	Debby Kavakos of Stoneledge Farm in New York finds that row covers are an effective control.

7
PROPAGATION
TIPS & TRICKS

*"Propagating plants is the most fun you can have
with your clothes on."*
DALE HENDRICKS, NORTH CREEK PERENNIALS

Whether you start your plants from seed, order them by mail from a catalog, or pick them up as starts from the local garden center, sooner or later you're going to think about propagating your own. Propagation is the most inexpensive way to get your garden growing, and it's enormously satisfying. Imagine having two or three (or more) of your favorite rosebush (or your neighbor's, if she's willing). Consider the joy (and the economy) of a forsythia hedge propagated from a single shrub. And what could be nicer than growing annuals from seed you've harvested from your own plants?

In this chapter, the experts will show you just how easy propagation can be and describe their own yard-tested methods for turning a single plant into a landscape. You'll discover everything you need to know about taking stem, root, and leaf cuttings, division (dividing a single plant into several smaller plants), layering (placing a section of the plant's stem underground and allowing it to root), and seed collection. You'll learn the secrets of when to propagate, and how to dry and store seeds. In addition, the experts suggest their favorite easy-to-propagate plants.

HERE'S WHAT YOU'LL FIND IN CHAPTER 7

TRUE COLORS?

Not all plants produce seeds that are true to their type—that is, the new plants may not be identical either in form or color to the parent, points out Peter Borchard of Ohio's Companion Plants. The reason? Usually, it's because of cross-pollination with another plant in the same family. 'Opal' basil planted near green sweet basil, for example, will produce widely varying offspring—some purple, some green, some mottled purple and green—says Peter. If you have a gambler's sensibility, you don't need to worry about cross-pollination. But if it's important to you to get a specific plant from the seed you sow, make sure your plants are isolated from similar plants in the same family.

SEED SAVING

Your own backyard is a bountiful source of free seeds. Saving seeds allows you to preserve those you like best, without relying on seed companies that frequently sell only those seeds that do well in all parts of the country. Many people like to save seeds that have been handed down from generation to generation; for more about heirloom seeds, see "How about Heirlooms?" on page 96.

Seeds to Save

Good reasons for saving seeds • Which seeds are best

You can save seeds from just about any plant in your backyard, but some will be a little trickier to work with than others. Consider beginning with some of the simpler vegetable, herb, and flower seeds recommended by the experts.

THE EXPERTS' FAVORITES With experience, you'll learn which plants you can rely on for good seeds and which ones produce not-so-usable seeds. For beginners, some of the easiest seeds to collect and propagate are cleome, coriander, cosmos, dill, mallow, marigold, morning glory, nasturtium, petunia, string bean, and sunflower. The experts share some of their other favorite picks:

• If you want to grow vegetables, Garry Coull of Johnny's Selected Seeds recommends beans, peas, and tomatoes.

• Sarah Gallant of Maine's Pinetree Garden Seeds saves radish, squash, and cucumber seeds.

• Jim Becker of Oregon's Goodwin Creek Gardens harvests seed from a variety of annual and perennial herbs, including amaranth, basil, chives, lavender, lovage, parsley, and thyme.

• Among flowering plants, Dale Hendricks of Pennsylvania's North Creek Perennials likes to save the seeds of blue-star (*Amsonia tabernaemontana*), foam flower (*Tiarella cordifolia*), fringed bleeding heart (*Dicentra eximia*), and wild indigo (*Baptisia tinctoria*).

• Noah Schwartz of Matterhorn Nursery in Spring Valley, New York, finds that tiny seeds, like those of begonias, lettuces, and carrots, are the hardest to save.

• Craig Dremann of the Redwood City Seed Company in California saves seeds of any vegetable that's particularly tasty.

Gathering and Storing Seed

Collecting seeds from your garden • Cleaning and drying seeds
• Storing seeds • Treating tomato seeds

From the tiny, hairlike seeds of marigold to the substantial pods of nasturtium, seeds come in an extraordinary variety of forms and dimensions. Nevertheless, the same principles of collecting, preparing, and storing apply to nearly every seed—with a few notable exceptions.

COLLECTING SEEDS For Tessa Gowans of Washington's Abundant Life Seed Foundation, seed-saving is, as she puts it, "a mission." She and her colleagues wait until seeds are totally mature and dry on the plant, and then they collect them. "Seed maturation generally takes a month after the flowers fade," says Peter Borchard of Ohio's Companion Plants.

Another way to tell if seeds are mature is to shake them. "When seeds are ready, they're loose. If you have trouble dislodging them, you're too early," says Neil Diboll of Wisconsin's Prairie Nursery. Some seedpods, including those of impatiens and cleome, will actually explode when touched if they're ripe.

You won't have trouble finding and saving seeds of sunflowers (below left) and cosmos (above).

Seeds can drop and scatter in the wind in a few seconds. Rather than take the chance of losing the seeds, wrap the seedpod in closely woven gauze; when the pod pops, the seeds will be saved.

Linda Gay of the Mercer Arboretum in Texas recommends checking seeds regularly to see how they're maturing. If you're afraid of having them pop before you can get to them, she advises tying the seedpod in a piece of pantyhose or cheesecloth. "When the seed falls, it will drop into the cloth," she says.

SEED PREPARATION After you collect your seeds, clean off any pulp by hand, and then put them on a napkin in a tray for drying, advises Linda Gay. Dale Hendricks of Pennsylvania's North Creek Perennials dries his seeds on newspapers set well out of the sun. Jim Becker of Oregon's Goodwin Creek Gardens slips his into paper bags. When they've lost all residual moisture, he rubs them by hand, sieves them, and blows away the husks.

STORING SEEDS After cleaning and drying, Tessa Gowans stores her seeds in airtight containers in a cool, dark place. Dale Hendricks recommends Tupperware or similar plastic containers. After making sure the container is completely dry, he puts the seeds inside and places the container in the refrigerator. You can also use zipper-lock bags, as Jim Becker does or, like Linda Gay, store your seeds in individually labeled envelopes. Don't put them in the freezer, warns Linda—freezing can damage the fragile seed embryo. And keep seeds out of the crisper drawer, where moisture can settle and encourage the growth of mold.

Seeds will keep well in foil packets, stored in plastic containers in the refrigerator. Don't forget to label the packages.

STARTING SEEDS INDOORS

Nature has a neat trick for successful germination: She simply produces so many seeds that at least a few are sure to sprout. If you're starting seeds indoors, however, you'll need some more practical secrets to ensure their germination. Fortunately, the experts have many: the best containers and growing media, efficient lighting, plus tips on watering and fertilizing.

Cleanliness Is Next to Godliness

Sterilizing pots and tools • Cooking your soil

If you've ever nursed a seedling only to watch it wither and die, you can probably blame it on damping-off. Though it sounds like a problem of overwatering, this number-one killer of seedlings is actually a fungal disease. Fungi and other disease-causing organisms can also ruin your cuttings if they happen to get inside the stem at the point of the cut. The way to prevent these problems is to use sanitary propagation techniques.

STERILIZING TOOLS, POTS, AND OTHER MATERIALS Like many of the experts, Dale Hendricks of Pennsylvania's North Creek Perennials recommends working with sterile tools when propagating. To keep them germ-free, he dips the tools in rubbing alcohol or diluted bleach. For truly fuss-free sterilization, Jeff Epping of the Olbrich Botanical Gardens in Wisconsin simply sprays his tools with Lysol and then rinses them with plain water. New pots or planting packs probably don't need sterilizing, but if you're reusing containers, clean them with a 50 percent solution of bleach in plain water.

PLANTING MEDIA To protect your seeds and seedlings from damping-off, you'll need a sterile planting medium that's free of fungi, bacteria, and other disease-producing organisms. Nurseries often sterilize their soil with fancy equipment like autoclaves, but since you probably don't have one of those at home, do as Dale Hendricks does and pop your seed-starting medium in a hot oven. Place the seed-starting medium in a pan and "cook" it for 30 minutes at 180°F. Though some

Keep a small container of 50% bleach, 50% water near your propagation supplies. A quick dip may save your future plants.

A clean spot where air can circulate is ideal for growing seedlings. Many professional growers place their flats on wire grids. Dirt and debris fall through the cracks and air flows freely from the bottom.

gardeners sterilize their soil in the microwave, most experts advise against it. It's messy, it smells bad, and there's no solid research that shows it works. "The only thing you should ever microwave is a cup of coffee," says Sarah Gallant of Maine's Pinetree Garden Seeds.

Sterilizing is the oven is not fun, either, and leaves a lingering odor. The easiest way to make sure your growing medium is sterile is to buy a sterile soilless mix from a nursery or garden center, says Kate Burroughs of California's Harmony Farm Supply.

Finding the Right Flat

Flats • Individual containers

Garden centers and catalogs offer a variety of seed-starting containers, from individual peat pots to fiberboard trays for multiple seedlings, and each has its advantages. To find what works best for you, try a few of the experts' favorites. Or follow seed purveyor John Schneeberger's lead and make your own seed starting containers.

FLATS AND TRAYS Flats are shallow boxes, sometimes divided into individual sections known as cells, that are used to start multiple seedlings. Often set into trays (which can be filled with water to keep roots evenly moist), flats are available in a variety of materials. Here are several options that the experts like:

• Alice Krinsky, trial garden manager at Shepherd's Garden Seeds, suggests Kord fiber flats, which are small (6 × 10 inches) and lightweight, making them easy to use. If you don't let them get too wet, you can reuse them for several years.

• If you're concerned about harming your seedlings during transplanting, consider plug flats, a favorite of both Bill McDorman of Idaho's High Altitude Gardens and Pennsylvania horticulturist Dr. Michael Orzolek. The flats' cells are shaped like inverted pyramids, which encourages plants to form neat, root-filled soil plugs. "They make nice, tight little bundles that transplant very well," says Dr. Orzolek.

• Pressed-fiber pots are widely available, and they're useful for their ability to hold moisture, but John Schneeberger of Montana's Garden City Seeds warns that they make an excellent breeding ground for bacteria, which can compete with plants for nutrients.

Plug flats produce neat little bundles, shaped like inverted pyramids, that are ready to take off as soon as they hit the ground. Each flat holds two hundred or more seedlings.

Styrofoam flats can be floated over a bed of water. The styrofoam is water-permeable, allowing water to be delivered to the bottom of the seedlings.

• Davy Dabney of Kentucky's Dabney Herbs recommends floating flats—styrofoam flats that sit on top of a "bed" of water. The water slowly rises into the bottom of the soil, keeping it evenly moist. These flats are particularly useful if you're not able to water your seedlings on a regular basis.

• If the flimsiness of plastic and pressed fiber puts you off, Bill Bruneau of California's Bountiful Gardens recommends cedar flats. "They're hard to find," he says, "but they're excellent for starting seeds, and they last."

INDIVIDUAL CONTAINERS While Bill McDorman prefers to go directly from plug flats to the garden, planting his seedlings out after only two or three weeks indoors, many gardeners choose the intermediate step of transplanting into larger containers. If you decide to go this route, you'll need to transplant seedlings from flats into small individual pots. Or do as herbalist Bertha Reppert of Pennsylvania's Rosemary House does, and start your seeds in pots. Her germinating secret is to fill the bottom half of a 4-inch pot with styrofoam peanuts, then top it with 2 inches of potting soil and a final layer of perlite. To keep the soil from leaking out, place a "net" of nylon pantyhose between the styrofoam and the drainage hole. After sowing, cover the pot with a clear plastic bag; remove it as soon as the seeds sprout.

Aileen Lubin, director of Maine's Merryspring Park, recommends peat pots—containers made from biodegradable peat—for "do not disturb" species, including peas and beans, that don't take well to transplanting. But watch out! Peat pots can dry out quickly, warns Jeff Edwards of Home Harvest Garden Supply in Virginia. In fact, any pot that's 4 inches in diameter or larger will need more frequent watering, says Jeff. For ease of germination, he likes Jiffy 7s—disks of peat moss surrounded by netting—that serve as both pot and planting medium in one.

If you're planting rare or hard-to-sprout seeds, try Bertha Reppert's secret for foolproof germination: Fill petri dishes (available at large drugstores or through medical supply catalogs; see "Sources" on page 362) tightly with perlite, water the perlite well, and then sponge off excess moisture. After dropping in your seeds, cover the dishes securely. Remove and transplant the seedlings as soon as they sprout.

propagation tips & tricks

HOMEMADE CONTAINERS

Gardeners have been making their own containers for centuries, and many of them work as well as the commercial varieties. Take a cue from John Schneeberger and try paper or Styrofoam cups or milk containers cut in half. You can also use a shoebox lined with aluminum foil (which does a neat job of catching and reflecting light and heat). Or, for a minor investment, you can get yourself a potmaker (available from Johnny's Selected Seeds and other catalogs), which allows you to transform old newspapers into compact little seedling pots. As with all homemade containers, make sure you create a hole for drainage.

You'll find a wide selection of containers for seed starting at garden supply centers. Some of them accommodate small seedlings, others large. You can also make your own containers from shoeboxes, egg cartons, or newspaper.

THE TIME OF YOUR LIGHT

Does it make a difference at what time of day you provide light for your seedlings? None at all, says Jeff Edwards of Home Harvest Garden Supply in Virginia. "If it's better for you to provide light during the nighttime hours—because you like to keep the house cool during the day, for example—your plants won't mind at all," Jeff says. What is important, Jeff points out, is that it be consecutive hours, not a few hours here and there. And not only the light periods need to be consecutive; plants that need darkness need it in uninterrupted periods as well.

Shedding Light on Your Seeds

Outdoor light • Types of artificial light • Seeds that germinate in the dark

Many seeds—including fennel, nasturtium, and sweet pea—prefer to sprout in the dark. Others—such as columbine, impatiens, and peppers—do best under light. However, all seedlings, once sprouted, need light to grow and thrive. If you're unsure about how to provide the right lighting, the experts can shine some light on the matter.

WHEN THE SUN'S ENOUGH Although some seeds will sprout with nothing more complicated than the light through a sunny window, most do better with a little help. If you don't want to bother with artificial lighting, you can do as Kate Burroughs of California's Harmony Farm Supply and Mary Harrison of Mary's Plant Farm do: Start your seeds in an outdoor greenhouse or coldframe (see "Hardening-Off Seedlings" on page 113). Both coldframes and greenhouses provide a warm place for your seeds to sprout while exposing them to lots of outdoor light.

MAKING MORE LIGHT Even though Aileen Lubin, director of Maine's Merryspring Gardens, starts her seeds in the greenhouse, she prefers to use artificial light for her seedlings. "I can control it better, and I get stockier seedlings," she explains. "My lighting setup isn't fancy—just gray metal utility shelves and shop lights hung from chains to make the height adjustable." Minnesota nurserywoman Ainee Busse of Busse Gardens germinates her seeds under shop lights set 8 to 10 inches above the flats. After the seeds sprout, she hardens the seedlings off under natural light.

For homeowners, it's most economical to use fluorescent bulbs for seed-starting. Jeff Edwards of Home Harvest of Virginia recommends bulbs at least 4 feet long. "Anything less isn't very efficient because you lose about 4 to 6 inches of usable light on each side," he says. Jeff's secret is to group two to four bulbs and set them 2 to 4 inches above the plants. "But make sure you raise the lights as the plants grow," he says. He advises keeping the lights on for 14- to 18-hour stretches daily. "Light is cumulative. If you shut it off in the middle, you haven't given the plant what it needs," he says.

DARK SECRETS What if some of your seeds need light to germinate while others sprout best in darkness? Don't worry, you don't have to invest in two setups. "You can accommodate any seeds that need darkness to germinate by placing a humidity dome over them and covering the dome with newspaper," says Sarah Gallant of Maine's Pinetree Garden Seeds. Mary Harrison of Mary's Plant Farm germinates a variety of seeds side by side, covering those that need darkness with a sheet of black plastic. See "Special Treatment" on page 109 for a list of light requirements of vegetable plants.

Warm Surroundings

The importance of soil temperature • *Warming the soil from beneath*

"Every seed has its own set of requirements," says Sarah Gallant. Just as some prefer to sprout in darkness and others in light, certain seeds like cool soil while others need warmth. (Check seed packets for specific heat and light requirements.) To thrive, they need to have these requirements met.

ROOM TEMPERATURE VERSUS SOIL TEMPERATURE According to Ray Pevitt of Astoria-Pacific, Inc., in Oregon, "Soil temperature is much more important than room temperature, and the source of heat should be on the bottom." Don Ledden of New Jersey's Ledden Brothers

DIFFERENT LIGHTS

According to Lydia Anderson of Worm's Way, a garden supply company in Indianapolis, seeds germinate best under blue-white light. Lydia and her colleagues use a metal halide system. When seedlings have sprouted, she switches to a sodium system—a full-spectrum light source. "To take plants through the rest of their life, they need full-spectrum light, which promotes fruiting and flowering," explains Lydia.

propagation tips & tricks

Heating mats provide all-important bottom heat evenly and safely.

SPECIAL HANDLING

Most of the seeds you find in commercial packets need little special care before planting. But some benefit from—or require—soaking, stratifying, or scarifying.

❧ Soaking seeds overnight (but never for more than 24 hours, warns Sarah Gallant of Pinetree Garden Seeds) in a glass of tepid water usually helps speed germination.

❧ The seeds of certain plants, including lupine and honey locust, need scarification—breaking of the seed coat—before sowing. Gallant recommends using a file or small knife to do the job; cut away from the embryonic end of the seed.

❧ Unless you're planting lots of fall-bearing fruit trees from seed, you probably won't need to do much stratification, a process that involves subjecting the seeds to a period of cold dormancy. Ken Asmus and his colleagues at Missouri's Oikos Tree Crops stratify most of their seeds by placing them in lightly damp peat moss and storing them for three to four months in a refrigerator set to 37°F.

makes sure his soil is a constant 75°F—the ideal temperature for germinating, he says.

FROM THE BOTTOM UP You can create bottom heat by placing your flats or containers on an inverted pan set on top of a radiator, but that's a bit risky; radiators don't deliver constant, even heat, which is what seeds need. Lydia Anderson of Worm's Way, a garden supply company in Indianapolis, prefers to use electric heating mats—thin plastic films with embedded wires that plug into a socket. Heating mats raise the soil temperature by about 15 degrees. "They make a real difference in germination time," Lydia says. Maine seed-seller Sarah Gallant uses heat cables—waterproof electric cables that snake underneath flats. If your seeds need cool soil, the best way to get it is with a room air-conditioner.

It's Not Just the Heat, It's the Humidity

Domes • Tents • Other solutions

Most experts find that a humid environment boosts seed germination, and it's essential for rooting cuttings. You can create humidity by misting your plants regularly, but the experts offer some easier methods.

DOMES Available at garden centers and by mail order, humidity domes work like miniature greenhouses, recycling moisture back into the soil and boosting humidity in the air around your seeds. Many of the experts use them, including New Jersey nurseryman Don Ledden. To encourage transpiration, which is the process by which plants give off water, you'll need to vent the domes occasionally by lifting the lid, says Lydia Anderson.

TENTS Plastic tents work the same way domes do. Bob Stewart of Arrowhead Alpines in Michigan rigs up a simple tent by draping clear plastic over bent wire hangers. Dennis Neimeyer of North Carolina's We-Du Nursery uses tents over his rooted cuttings, but covers them with translucent cloth or paper to provide the necessary shade. As with domes, you'll need to create venting. One or two small slits in the plastic will do, says Peter Linsner of Illinois's Morton Arboretum.

A SIMPLE SOLUTION The easiest way to increase humidity around seeds and seedlings is Peter Linsner's preferred method: He fills his flat to one inch below the top with germination mix, waters it thoroughly, then sows seed on top of the mix (this only works with fine seed). After that, he simply covers the top of the flat with ordinary plastic wrap. "If it doesn't cling, I use a rubber band to hold it in place," he says. He makes one or two small slits in the plastic, places the flat under artificial light or in a north-facing window, and as soon as the seeds germinate, he removes the plastic wrap. "The advantage of this

Plastic domes like this one keep the air around germinating seedlings moist. Be sure to lift the dome daily to vent.

Special nozzles, available at garden centers and through catalogs, spray a fine stream of water that increases humidity in the air.

system is that you don't have to mist the flats constantly," he says. Sarah Gallant of Maine's Pinetree Garden Seeds says you can also use pieces of clear painter's drop cloth instead of plastic wrap. One note of warning: Keep plastic-covered seeds out of direct sunlight, or they might get cooked.

Best Soil for Seeds and Cuttings

Best commercial growing media • Homemade mixes • The downsides of peat
After years of seed-starting and rooting, the experts have arrived at a number of first-rate soil or soilless mixes, some of them homemade, some storebought.

COMMERCIAL MIXES Easy, efficient, and inexpensive, commercial mixes are the top choice of many of the experts. Most actually contain no soil and virtually all are sterile, which means you won't have to worry about losing your seedlings to disease. Many of the most popular mixes contain synthetic fertilizers and chemicals; look for soil mixes that are labelled "organic."

Lydia Anderson of Worm's Way, a garden supply company in Indianapolis, sells several soilless mixes made from a variety of ingredients including coconut fibers and worm castings. If you're looking for a super-sterile mix, she recommends rockwool, a spun fiber made from volcanic material. "You have to be careful not to overwater it, however, because it absorbs a lot of water," she warns.

HOMEMADE MIXES If you'd like to try making your own growing medium, here are some of the experts' secret formulas:

• Linda Gay of the Mercer Arboretum in Texas starts with a commercial mix and adds perlite to increase porosity. "The most important factors in ensuring seedling survival are drainage and porosity," she says.

• Peter Linsner, a propagator with Illinois's Morton Arboretum, has found a 50-50 mix of screened peat moss and medium-grade vermiculite to be highly effective for a wide variety of annuals, perennials, and woody seedlings. For rooted cuttings, he uses 30 to 40 percent screened peat moss combined with 60 to 70 percent coarse perlite. "It's a sterile, well-aerated mix that promotes rooting and helps prevent stem rot," he says.

• Aileen Lubin, director of Maine's Merryspring Park, likes a 50-50 mix of sand and peat moss for cuttings.

• Dexter Merritt of Vermont's Green Mountain Transplants swears by his own mix, which consists of equal parts of peat moss, perlite, vermiculite, and finely ground bark.

• Noah Schwartz, propagation specialist at Matterhorn Nursery in New York, uses a standard potting mix for seedlings, but adds about 25 percent vermiculite to improve drainage. He prefers vermiculite to perlite, which he finds difficult to work with and too large and porous.

PEAT MOSS? PERHAPS NOT While peat moss has its good qualities, not all the experts are enthusiastic about it. According to Craig Dremann of the Redwood City Seed Company in California, peat promotes the growth of algae. And Penn State horticulturist Dr. Michael Orzolek

propagation tips & tricks

SEED-STARTING MIXES

If you want the strongest, healthiest seedlings, the experts advise using a soilless mix. Widely available under a variety of brand names, these mixes are porous, fine-textured, moisture-retentive, and above all, sterile. To sterilize a mix, manufacturers expose it to intense heat, a process that kills off any existing microorganisms. Unsterilized soil can be a breeding ground for molds and bacteria. If you make your own mix, sterilize it before use.

Because they're easy, efficient, and inexpensive, most experts prefer to buy prepared organic mixes rather than work up their own. Many mixes contain fertilizer, which means you won't have to fertilize until the transplants are about 6 weeks old. "Contrary to popular belief," says Craig Dremann of California's Redwood City Seed Company, "soil mixes aren't all alike; a superior mix will give you superior plants. Try a variety of mixes until you find one that works well for you."

When mixing a seed-starting medium, add ingredients that will improve drainage, such as (clockwise, from top center) sand, vermiculite, rocks, and perlite. Most standard potting mixes (far left) already include some of these ingredients.

believes that it can make mixes overly acidic. In addition, peat moss is an endangered natural resource.

For an alternative, Tim Sharp of Oklahoma's EZ Soil recommends coir pith bricks, which expand to 12 times their size when you add water. "Coir is a short fiber that provides good aeration, it's easier to transport than peat, and it doesn't use up a nonrenewable resource," says Tim.

Water Ways

How and when • Frequency

Naturally, seedlings need water to grow, but because they're susceptible to fungal diseases like damping-off, you'll need to exercise some caution when watering.

HOW TO WATER Watering seedlings from the bottom can help keep fungal problems at bay. Set your pots or flats in containers of water, and moisture will slowly seep into the soil. Bottom watering probably isn't necessary if you use a sterile mix, says Kate Burroughs of Harmony Farm Supply, who uses a watering wand on her seedlings.

WHEN TO WATER According to Dale Hendricks of Pennsylvania's North Creek Perennials, the best time to water is in the morning, especially if it's sunny. To avoid damping-off, don't let water sit on leaves overnight.

HOW OFTEN It's a good idea to get your plants on a watering schedule, advises Kate Burroughs, who waters twice a day during hot spells. But even with a schedule, check soil conditions regularly, unless you're germinating in a climate-controlled environment. "Seedlings need more water when it's hot, dry, and sunny," says Kate. Growers Mary Harrison and Ainie Busse both suggest watering only when the surface of the soil feels dry to the touch. They add that to keep your seedlings from drying out, you'll have to check them frequently.

A layer of sphagnum moss can help keep your potting mix evenly moist.

Food for Naught?

Whether or not to fertilize • Best fertilizers

In their eagerness to get seedlings off to a good start, many gardeners try to boost and hasten growth with fertilizer, but this can be disastrous. Before you tear open your bag of fertilizer, read what the experts have to say.

TO FERTILIZE OR NOT? "Seeds don't need fertilizer; they're a food storage system in themselves," says Lydia Andersonof Worm's Way, a garden supply company in Indianapolis. Seeds can't take up fertilizer and can be burned by it. The time to add nutrients is after the seeds have sprouted. Sarah Gallant of Maine's Pinetree Garden Seeds fertilizes her seedlings after they get their second set of true leaves. (The first set of leaves, called cotyledons, are produced essentially to feed the plant and usually don't resemble the mature foliage.)

FERTILIZING SEEDLINGS You wouldn't feed chili and onions to a newborn, so why would you offer your seedlings fertilizer meant for mature plants? In other words, don't use a fertilizer high in nitrogen, which can overstimulate seedlings and produce weak, leggy growth,

STARTING TREES FROM SEED

Guy Sternberg of Starhill Forest Arboretum in Illinois starts trees from seed because he enjoys the pleasure of watching his plants develop. Many trees can be grown from seed with only a little more effort than annuals; the main ingredient that must be added is patience.

When propagating oaks and other tap-rooted nut trees from seed, stratify the seed until germination begins and then pinch off the tip of the young root. It will branch at the broken end, making a seedling with many roots and that will make it easier to transplant the next year.

says Dennis Neimeyer of North Carolina's We-Du Nursery. Instead, Dennis recommends a balanced fertilizer in liquid form (so you can easily control the amount you offer), and he says to apply it at half the indicated rate.

Jeff Edwards of Home Harvest Garden Supply in Virginia recommends the following three organic fertilizers in particular: Seastart, Superthrive, and Startup, all of which contain B vitamins. B vitamins relieve stress and reduce transplant shock in seedlings and new transplants.

Dennis Neimeyer likes well-diluted compost tea, which you can make by scooping a spadeful of compost into a burlap sack, tying the sack securely, and then letting it steep in a bucket of water for two or three days. For seedlings, the tea should be very light brown in color; if necessary, add clear water until you get the desired shade.

Ainee Busse of Busse Gardens in Minnesota has her own secret for healthy seedlings: Start them on a 10 percent solution of water-soluble fertilizer with a nitrogen-phosphorus-potassium ratio of either 2-1-2 or 1-0-1. When seedlings are five to six weeks old, she switches to a 1-1-1 or 1-2-1 fertilizer, which she offers weekly until the plants are established in the garden.

This large greenhouse at Matterhorn Nursery in New York includes mirrors to increase light and fans to circulate air, and it is domed to keep things humid. You can do the same on a smaller scale at home by using small fans, mirror tiles, and humidity domes.

STARTING FROM STEMS

Another popular way to propagate plants is to take stem cuttings. One of the advantages over seed propagation is that, with a cutting, you know you'll get an exact replica of the parent plant. It's also a handy way to get woody plants from the gardens of friends and neighbors.

The Right Cut

Types of cuttings • When to take cuttings • How to cut • Removing leaves

There are three basic types of stem cuttings: hardwood, taken from fully mature wood; semihardwood, taken from a stem that's just started to harden off; and softwood; taken from wood that's still green and supple. Different plants grow best from different cuttings. For example, dogwood, euonymus, forsythia, grape, hydrangea, privet, and willow will root fairly easily from hardwood cuttings, while broadleaved evergreens like rhododendron and holly root best from semihardwood cuttings. And a large number of popular shrubs— including azalea, magnolia, privet, rose, and spirea—root most successfully when cuttings are taken from soft, young wood. See "Propagation: An Overview" on page 356 for more information on the best type of cutting for different kinds of plants.

CUT ACCORDING TO THE SEASON Once you've determined the best kind of cutting to take from the plant you're propagating, you'll be able to figure out when to make your cuttings. You should take softwood cuttings early in the season, when new growth is still soft, says Doris Taylor of the Morton Arboretum in Illinois. "They shouldn't be so soft that they flop over," warns Brian Thomas, propagator for Connecticut's Sunny Border Nursery, who advises that you look for stems that have some snap to them when bent. Doris recommends that you take semihardwood cuttings toward the end of the summer and hardwood cuttings in autumn or early winter.

WATCH THE WEATHER If at all possible, take your cuttings on a day when the weather is relatively mild. "Don't take cuttings when it's 95°F out; do it when it's 80°F or below," says Maryland horticulturist Harry Swartz. And because cuttings—especially those taken from

Begonias root easily from leaf cuttings. Just cut a leaf in half and press it into soil. It will soon form new roots.

soft-wood—are useless if they dry out, try to take them on a day that's slightly overcast, preferably in the morning.

WHERE AND HOW TO CUT Cut the stem at its base, where it joins either the trunk of the shrub or another, larger stem. For hardwood cuttings, make the cut at an angle, advises Harry Swartz. "Hardwood doesn't root easily because of the woody tissue," he says. When you take an angled cut, however, you're exposing more of the soft tissue in the center of the branch.

THE LENGTH OF THE CUTTING How much you cut depends in part on the kind of cutting you're taking. For softwood cuttings, Doris Taylor of the Morton Arboretum in Illinois removes a 2- to 3-inch section of stem. For semihardwood cuttings, she takes a slightly larger piece—about 3 or 4 inches. And for hardwood cuttings, she goes longer still—about 8 or 9 inches.

Even more important than the cutting's length is its number of nodes (the slightly raised sections of the stem from which the leaves grow). "It's important to get at least one node. Take a multiple-node cutting when you can," says Maryland horticulturist Harry Swartz. (Or, in the words of propagator Brian Thomas, "if you get the node, you've got it made.") A cutting without any nodes won't root.

Cuttings can be taken from just about any plant; this Persian shieldleaf needs a trim, anyway.

Use a sterilized, sharp clipper to make an angled cut. Make sure you get at least one node.

Strip off some of the lower leaves, then cut the leaves that are left. The cutting needs some leaves so that it can transpire, but not many because it has no root system to support them.

LEAVING THE LEAVES After you've taken your cutting, strip off some, but not all, of the leaves. "Keeping too many leaves drains the plant. However, the new plant needs at least a few leaves to transpire (release waste-water into the air)," explains Dennis Niemeyer of North Carolina's We-Du Nurseries. Doris Taylor suggests keeping one or two of the lower leaves and stripping the rest.

Finding Their Roots

How to root the cuttings • The best medium for rooting • Watering and retaining humidity • The importance of warmth

Like seedlings, cuttings need a good medium to grow in and a high-humidity environment.

GROWING MEDIA Unlike the mature plants you've taken them from, cuttings don't need a rich soil—in fact, say the experts, they don't need soil at all. While some gardeners root their cuttings in straight perlite, Brian Thomas, propagator for Connecticut's Sunny Border Nursery, cautions against it. "You need something to coarsen up the perlite and keep it from retaining too much moisture," he says. He recommends a 50/50 mix of peat and perlite or sand and perlite.

Use a stick or pencil to make a hole and gently press the cutting into a prepared, moistened soil mix.

OTHER WAYS TO PROPAGATE

Leaf cuttings A few plants, including African violet, begonia, gloxinia, and stonecrop, will root from a leaf. While some plants can root from the leaf alone, it's best to take both a leaf and at least 1/2 inch of the petiole (leaf stalk). Insert the petiole into the planting medium and root as you would a stem cutting.

Root cuttings You can propagate plants with fleshy root systems by cutting off 2- to 4-inch root sections and placing them, narrow side down, in potting soil or a peat and soil mix. After an initial watering to thoroughly wet the soil, keep the soil damp but not overly wet, to discourage fungal infection. Most root cuttings will do fine on any bright windowsill.

Baldassare Mineo recommends the "little covered wagon" method: Make a hoop with wire, place it over the cuttings, and anchor it in the soil. Then slip the cuttings into a plastic bag—instant miniature greenhouse.

You can use almost any kind of container—a plastic pot is good. If you're reusing a container, you should sterilize it (see "Cleanliness Is Next to Godliness" on page 333). After filling the pot with growing medium, water it thoroughly and wait until all the excess water has drained out. Then insert the cutting at least an inch down into the medium. For the greatest chance of rooting success, Brian recommends burying a node.

CREATING ATMOSPHERE You'll need to provide a comfortable environment for your cuttings—one that's humid but not wet, and warm but not torrid. Baldassare Mineo of Oregon's Siskiyou Rare Plant Nursery recommends heating pads or cables to provide bottom heat (see "Warm Surroundings" on page 339) for hardwood cuttings.

Humidity is even more important than warmth. You don't want to drench the medium, which can lead to rot, but you do want to keep it moist. And the air around the cutting should be consistently humid. Professional growers create a humid environment with high-humidity chambers that can cost hundreds, even thousands, of dollars. But Maryland horticulturist Harry Swartz has a low-cost alternative that's as good as the real thing. All you'll need are two sections of plastic sheeting—one clear and one white (to reduce the brightness of the light); some chicken wire; and a fan or hair dryer. Make a U-shaped tent with the chicken wire, then tuck the plastic around the wire, making a tight seal but leaving a small area open for the fan or hair dryer. With the fan or hair dryer, inflate the space between the pieces of plastic, then complete the seal.

DIVIDING PERENNIALS

The easiest way to increase your store of perennial plants is to divide them. In fact, many perennials need to be divided periodically to keep them healthy and free-flowering. Dividing is just what it sounds like: taking a whole plant and separating it into several smaller plants. If you've held off on dividing because you're afraid to hurt your plants, hesitate no longer. The experts have the secrets to make division fast, fun, and foolproof.

When to Divide

Determining when a plant needs division • What time of year is best?

Ask three gardeners how often to divide a particular plant—say, daylilies—and you're likely to get as many different answers, even among the experts. For example, Peter and Jean Ruh of Ohio's Sunnybrook Farm's Homestead Division divide their daylilies every four years, while Gail Korn of Nebraska's Garden Perennials allows a little more latitude, dividing every three to five years. And Mary Harrison of Mary's Plant Farm in Ohio has left some of her daylilies undisturbed for as long as fifteen years. So how do you know when to divide? And what's the best time of year to make your divisions?

LISTEN TO YOUR PLANTS The secret to successful division is to watch your plants. A healthy plant that's growing vigorously and blooming freely probably doesn't require division—unless it's too large for its allotted space. "Generally, a plant will tell you by its looks when it needs to be divided," says Kim Hawks of North Carolina's Niche Gardens. Brian Thomas, propagator for Connecticut's Sunny Border Nursery, recommends dividing when the plant declines in volume; healthy plants are supposed to increase in size each year. Of course, even if your plant is bigger, it may not necessarily be better. Doug De Luca of Mississippi's De Luca Nursery recommends dividing plants "if they're congested with greenery but not willing to bloom." After a number of years' growth, daylilies and other plants may not have enough root surface to pick up the nutrients they need to produce flowers. Doug also looks at the center of the plant: If it's weak, faded, or dying out—as is often the case with overgrown ornamental grasses—it's time to divide.

PLANTS TO DIVIDE

Most perennials benefit from division, and some require it. Lobelias, for instance, will die if they're not divided. New York State grower Phyllis Farkas divides hers every other year. According to Doug De Luca of Mississippi's De Luca Nursery, sago palm offsets (baby plants that grow off the main root) will actually drill through the mother plant and kill it if they're not removed. Instead of asking which plants to divide, it makes more sense to ask which you shouldn't divide. Don't divide plants that have single tap roots, says Ohio grower Mary Harrison. And don't try splitting plants with single stems like Artemisia 'Powis Castle', warns Brian Thomas, propagator for Connecticut's Sunny Border Nursery. Among the many dividable plants are daylily, iris, peony, chrysanthemum, aster, veronica, coral bells, bleeding heart, spiderwort, phlox, peony, hosta, canna, calla lily, ginger, and amaryllis.

propagation tips & tricks

DIVIDING SEASONS There are plenty of rules about when to divide specific plants; the only problem is that they often contradict one another. Though some plants seem to prefer being moved and divided at specific times of the year—peonies in mid-fall, for example—you can divide most perennials anytime throughout the growing season.

Brian Thomas of Connecticut's Sunny Border Nursery divides most of his plants in spring. "That way, you give them a season to reestablish themselves," he says. Doug De Luca, on the other hand, prefers fall. "You don't have the heat stress then, and the plants don't need to put out new growth—they can concentrate their energy on growing new roots," he says.

Dr. Patricia Holloway, a horticulturist at the Georgeson Botanical Garden in Alaska, frequently fields questions about when to divide. "We have a really short growing season, so I suggest to people that they divide either really early, when the plant starts showing the first signs of growth, or late, but not so late that the new plants can't put out roots," she says. If you're planning to collect seeds, she advises waiting until the plant has set seed before making your divisions. Otherwise, her general rule for all gardeners couldn't be more straightforward: "The only time you don't want to divide during the growing season is when the plant is in bloom."

To divide a clump of primroses, simply dig them up and pull them apart, making sure to keep a few viable roots in each division.

Replant each division carefully, allowing room for it to grow. Watch the new plants carefully for a few weeks, supplying water, nutrients, and shade until they are established.

How to Divide

Making divisions • The best tools for dividing • How many roots to leave in each division • Preplanting care for newly divided plants

Though they may look delicate, perennials are hardy plants. They can withstand the kind of abuse that would wither an annual or destroy a shrub—including being dug up with a sharp spade and pried apart with eager fingers. That's why they take so well to division—and why division is so easy to learn.

TOOLING UP You don't need complicated tools to divide your perennials. Phyllis Farkas of Wildginger Woodlands in New York State uses a spade for big plants (like Joe-Pye weed) and for plants with large root systems (like irises). Otherwise, she just uses a trowel. "I go through a couple of trowels a season," she says. Doug De Luca of Mississippi's De Luca Nursery cuts into his plants with a sharp machete, dividing them while they're still in the ground and pulling up the divisions by hand. If the plant is in loose, loamy soil, he dispenses with the machete and uses his hands to make the divisions, working his fingers through the soil and into the roots. Alaska horticulturist Dr. Patricia Holloway prefers to lift her perennials with a large fork before dividing them. "I like the control it gives me—I can see what I'm getting in each division," she says.

LAYERING

The stems of some plants, including rhododendron and forsythia, will root when still attached to the mother plant—a process known as layering. There are several ways to layer, but simple layering is the most popular. When plants begin to grow in spring, bend a low, pliable branch so that the top 6 to 8 inches are standing straight up. Cut a small notch into the bent portion of the branch, then insert the bottom 3 or 4 inches into the soil. Use a piece of strong wire to keep it in place. By next spring, you'll be able to separate the layered branch from the main plant and replant it in the garden.

TAKING ROOTS The number of leaves you take in each division is less important than the amount of roots you retain. "Some plants, such as garden phlox and poppies, will even grow from pieces of root left in the soil," says Ainee Busse of Minnesota's Busse Gardens. She tries to keep a hand's length of roots on each division. But don't panic if all of your divisions don't have a thick, full network of roots. "You don't need a whole lot of roots—2 to 3 inches of good fiber is generally enough," says Connecticut propagator Brian Thomas. When dividing tuberous plants like irises and daylilies, Mississippi's Doug De Luca isn't overly concerned with the roots but takes great care to keep the eye—the budlike swelling on the tuber—intact. For peonies, Patricia Holloway makes sure that each division contains at least three eyes.

CARE BEFORE REPLANTING Most newly divided perennials can be replanted without much additional fuss. But it's always a good idea to get rid of any dead or decaying matter, advises Brian Thomas. And if the soil you're replanting in is particularly poor, Patricia Holloway recommends amending it with organic matter—but only if you're dividing in spring. For a natural rooting boost, Phyllis Farkas soaks several willow branches overnight in a bucket of water, then dips the roots of her divisions in the water before planting. "Willows contain a natural rooting hormone," she explains. After planting your divisions, keep them watered well, as you would any newly planted perennial.

Dividing Bulbs

Division time • Bulb division techniques
• Cautionary tips • Replanting

Like perennials, bulbous plants like daffodils and lilies can get overgrown. When your bulbs stop flowering or lose vigor, it's time to divide them.

WHEN TO DIVIDE According to Maryland bulb grower Kitty Washburne, the best time to divide bulbs is after the leaves have turned brown and the plants have been adequately "fed" through a season of photosynthesis. If you divide bulbs soon after they've flowered, they will not be able to take in enough nutrients to last through the winter and flower strongly the next season.

HOW TO DIVIDE Dig out the bulbs, taking care that you don't slice through them. "Some can be quite deep, so inch your way downward," warns Kitty. When you can see the full clump, lift it and gently separate each bulb. Then store the bulbs in a mesh bag in an area where they'll receive adequate air circulation. Replant in the fall. Because summer-flowering bulbs like lilies need moisture during storage, Kitty recommends replanting them as promptly as possible. If they can overwinter in the ground, divide them after flowering and replant them immediately.

CORMS AND TUBERS Some popular bulbous plants, such as crocuses and gladioli, actually grow from corms rather than bulbs. These corms form smaller structures around their bases that can be easily lifted off and divided. When the plant has finished blooming, lift it from the ground and pull the small corms (called cormels) from the base of the withered large corm. If the plant is hardy in your area (check its Hardiness Zone), you can replant the cormels immediately. If not, store as described in "Weathering Winter" on page 186. Tubers on plants such as dahlias and tuberous begonias can be separated by pulling them apart. If they are matted or difficult to separate, they can be cut with a knife. Be sure to leave at least one eye on each new division. Plant the new divisions immediately if they are hardy, or store indoors over winter if they are tender in your region.

Tubers (far left) and corms (near left) are easy to divide. Simply pull apart the separate structures and replant each one. If they are matted and difficult to separate, use a knife.

PROPAGATION: AN OVERVIEW

There are many ways to propagate plants; some are better than others for specific plants. This chart lists the most common propagation methods and the plants that are best propagated with each method.

METHOD	HOW IT'S DONE	PLANTS IT WORKS FOR
Planting from seeds	Collect, save, or purchase seeds. Sow them indoors in seed-starting mix, or outdoors directly in the garden. For more information, see "Seed Saving" on page 330 and "Starting Seeds Indoors" on page 333.	Most plants, even trees, can be started from seeds, but some do not germinate easily or they take a very long time to mature from seeds. Also, plants started from seed may be different from the parent plant. Almost all annuals and vegetables can be started from seed; potatoes and sweet potatoes are the exceptions. Perennials that are easily started from seed include columbine, *dianthus* spp., gaillardia, lady's-mantle, and purple coneflower .
Taking cuttings	For more information, see "The Right Cut" on page 347	
Hardwood cuttings	Cut an 8- to 9-inch section from where it is attached to the branch; the cut should be angled. Include at least one node (the raised area where leaves are attached). Cutting should be made from mature, hardwood. Take cuttings in autumn just after leaves have fallen or in late winter before bud break.	Boxwood, butterfly bush, dogwood, euonymus, forsythia, grape, privet, Russian olive, and willow.
Semi-hardwood cuttings	Cut a 4- to 6-inch section from where it is attached to the branch; the cut should be angled. Include at least one node. Take cuttings in late summer, when stem is woody but still pliable.	Broadleaved evergreens like rhododendron and holly; daphne, magnolia, and viburnum.
Softwood cuttings	Cut a 2- to 3-inch section of a sideshoot from new, soft growth.	Arborvitae, azalea, beautyberry, camellia, clematis, cotoneaster, crab-apple, juniper, magnolia, privet, rose, snowbell, spiraea, viburnum, and yew.

METHOD	HOW IT'S DONE	PLANTS IT WORKS FOR
Stem cuttings	Cut a 6- to 8-inch long section of stem. Include several nodes.	Most annuals and perennials, including shrubby plants like lavender and candytuft.
Root cuttings	Cut a section of roots at least 1/4 inch in diameter and 1 1/2 to 2 1/2 inches for perennials, 4 to 6 inches for trees and shrubs. Plant the pieces vertically or horizontally.	Blackberries, raspberries, bottlebrush buckeye, flowering quince, lilac, trumpet creeper, and summer phlox.
Dividing Perennial division	Dig up the entire plant while it is dormant. Divide clumps of roots by pulling them apart. Large tangled clumps may need to be divided with shovels or garden forks. Replant each division.	Artemisia, aster, astilbe, beebalm, blanketflower, chrysanthemum, columbine, coreopsis, daylily, delphinium, spiderwort, summer phlox, violets, and yarrow.
Shrub division	Some shrubs form roots like perennials and can be divided. Dig up the entire plant in early summer and divide as for perennials; it is best done in spring. Plants that produce suckers can be divided by removing rooted suckers from parent plant and planting in moist soil.	Barberry, blueberry, deutzia, lilac, mock orange, and sweet pepperbush. clethra, lilac, and kerria can be propagated from suckers.
Bulb division	Most bulbs can easily be divided into sections by detaching offsets, each of which can be replanted.	Daffodils, dahlias, lilies, and tulips. Peonies can and should be divided, but do so infrequently; they do not appreciate being disturbed.
Layering Simple layering	Bend a low branch and insert the bottom 3 or 4 inches into the soil; keep it in place with wire. The next spring, separate the layered branch, which will have formed its own roots, from the main plant. Replant it in the garden. (For more information, see "Layering" on page 354.)	Boston ivy, camellia, cotoneaster, crabapple, forsythia, grape, holly, lilac, magnolia, maple, rosemary, smokebush, and wisteria.

THE EXPERTS' GARDEN CALENDAR

It's impossible to predict exactly when gardening tasks will need to be done. But after years of experience, the experts have a pretty good handle on what will need to be done when.

MONTH	NORTHEAST	MIDDLE ATLANTIC	SOUTHEAST	SOUTH CENTRAL
January	Make plans, order seeds, repair tools.	Make plans, order seeds, repair tools. Sow slow-growers indoors.	Make plans, order seeds, repair tools. Plant bare-root roses. Sow seeds indoors.	Make plans, order seeds, repair tools. Plant bare-root roses.
February	Prepare to start seeds. At the end of the month, sow seeds indoors for cool-season vegetables and slow-growing annuals.	Plant some hardy annuals outdoors if you don't mind risk. Start seeds for all annuals.	Prepare all beds, amending soil with compost and mulching. Plant cool-season root crops and sow hardy seeds outdoors.	Start cool-season crops under lights indoors. Plant peas if you can protect them. Prune grape vines.
March	Harden-off vegetable and annual transplants. Plant evergreens; make sure to keep them well watered. Prune fruit trees. Cut back perennials if you didn't do it in fall.	Begin to plant cool-season crop transplants outdoors. Prune fruit trees. Prepare perennial beds.	Plant all cool-season transplants. Move perennial seedlings to larger pots. Cut back and prune perennials and hardy herbs. Divide perennials. Prune trees and shrubs.	Plant out cool-season crops, but be prepared to protect them. Sow warm-season seeds indoors. Prune flowering shrubs.
April	Plant potatoes and all cool-season crops. Prune flowering shrubs. Divide perennials. Prepare garden beds by amending soil and mulching.	Frost-free date in much of this region is the middle to the end of the month; don't plant tender annuals and vegetables until it is safe. Watch new seedlings; protect if necessary.	Frost-free date has passed; plant out tender annuals. Watch for sudden frost. Water new transplants until they are established.	You can't assume that there will not be another frost. Don't plant out tender vegetables and annuals until the end of the month.
May	By the end of the month, soil will be warm enough to plant warm-season vegetables and annuals. Don't cut back spring bulb foliage until it turns brown.	Continue watching new transplants; water as necessary until they are established. Continue monitoring for pests.	If you haven't begun a sanitation and monitoring program, do so now. Continue planting summer crops for continuous harvests.	Plant out all warm-season crops. Weed as necessary to keep air circulating in humid weather.

NOTE: These times and tasks are meant to serve as a rough guide for each region. There are serveral different climates within each region—there are even microclimates within each backyard—that will determine how your garden grows. Watch your garden for more exact clues.

MIDWEST	NORTH CENTRAL	SOUTHWEST	NORTHWEST
Make plans, order seeds, repair tools.	Make plans, order seeds, repair tools.	Active growing season; water in times of drought.	Make plans, order seeds, repair tools. Plant bare-root roses.
At the end of the month, start slow-growing seeds indoors.	Prepare coldframes and other season-extending equipment.	Continue watering and caring for crops; be prepared to protect them in case of sudden frost.	Start seeds for all annuals and perennials. It's still too wet to work much outdoors, except for pruning.
Start seeds for all crops at the end of the month. Remove mulch from fall-planted bulbs. Prune fruit trees.	Start seeds for cool-season crops indoors at the beginning of the month. Prune fruit trees and vines.	Plant and harvest last warm-season vegetables. Amend beds with organic matter to help them retain water in warmer months.	Plant out perennials and all vegetables. Divide perennials as necessary. Prune fruit trees and flowering shrubs.
Start warm-season vegetables. Prune flowering shrubs and trees at the end of the month. Prepare perennial beds.	Plant out cool-season crops. Prune flowering shrubs and trees at the end of the month.	Harvest last of warm-season crops. Cut back perennials. Pay attention to new plants that are not yet established and water if there is a drought. Divide perennials.	Prepare new beds and plant new perennials and shrubs.
Divide perennials. Plant new perennials and hardy annuals. By the end of the month, soil should be warm enough for tender annuals and warm-season crops.	By the end of the month, plant out warm-season crops with protection. Divide and plant new perennials.	As the hottest time of the year approaches, cut back shrubs and perennials to allow air circulation and prevent disease. Water new perennials in dry spells.	Continue planting for continuous harvests. Monitor for pests and diseases. Water as necessary. *(Continued on page 360)*

The Experts' Garden Schedule *(continued)*

MONTH	NORTHEAST	MIDDLE ATLANTIC	SOUTHEAST	SOUTH CENTRAL
June	Start seeds for fall crops. Monitor for pests and other problems. Weed the garden and keep it clean. Irrigate in dry spells.	Start seeds for fall crops. Keep the garden weed-free and water during dry spells. By the end of the month, plant fall crops.	Plant out fall crops; keep them well watered so they will tolerate heat. Keep the garden well-weeded and free of debris.	Plant out fall crops. Thin foliage to keep air circulating. Monitor for pests and diseases.
July	Pick beans so they will continue producing. Continue to monitor, weed, and water. Mulch to conserve water.	Pick beans so they will continue producing. Continue to monitor, weed, mulch, and water.	Plant succession crops. Continue to monitor, weed, and water.	Plant succession crops. Continue to monitor, weed, and water.
August	There's less work, but don't forget to maintain the garden. Keep it weeded, watered, and mulched. Plant out fall crops.	Keep maintaining the garden. Keep it weeded, watered, and mulched. Plant out fall crops.	Keep the garden weeded, watered, and mulched. Take cuttings of tender plants.	Keep the garden weeded, watered, and mulched. Take cuttings of tender plants.
September	Finish harvesting summer vegetables. Cut back summer perennials. Start preparing new beds for next spring.	Finish harvesting summer vegetables. Cut back summer perennials. Start preparing new beds for next spring.	Plant perennials for next year; they will have time to establish before winter.	Plant perennials for next year; they will have time to establish before winter.
October	Harvest fall crops. Plant garlic. Take cuttings of tender plants. Put in cover crops as necessary. Cut back perennials and clean the garden for winter.	Harvest fall crops. Plant garlic and fall bulbs. Take cuttings of tender plants. Put in cover crops as needed. Cut back perennials. Clean the garden for winter.	Harvest fall crops. Put in cover crops and prepare beds for spring. Lift tender bulbs and take cuttings of tender annuals.	Harvest fall crops. Plant garlic and fall bulbs. Take cuttings of tender plants. Put in cover crops as needed. Cut back perennials. Clean the garden for winter.
November–December	Plant spring bulbs by mid-November. Start a compost pile with fall leaves. Mulch tender plants.	Plant spring bulbs by mid-November. Start a compost pile with fall leaves. Mulch tender plants.	Plant spring bulbs by late November. Start a compost pile with fall leaves. Mulch tender plants.	Plant spring bulbs by late November. Start a compost pile with fall leaves. Mulch tender plants.

MIDWEST	NORTH CENTRAL	SOUTHWEST	NORTHWEST
Plant out warm-season crops at the beginning of the month. Remove row covers as soon as plants blossom. Prune flowering trees that blossom on old wood.	Plant out warm-season crops at the beginning of the month. Remove row covers as soon as plants blossom. Prune flowering trees that blossom on old wood.	Plant some heat-tolerant annuals. Dead-head flowers so they will rebloom during the summer. Keep the garden free of weeds. Water in dry spells.	Plant out fall crops; keep them well watered so they will tolerate heat. Keep the garden well-weeded and free of debris.
Monitor for bugs and other problems. Start seeds for fall-season crops.	Monitor for bugs and other problems. Start seeds for fall-season crops.	Watch for heat-related problems. Water and prune as necessary.	Plant out succession crops. Continue to monitor, weed, mulch, and water.
Plant out succession crops. Monitor for pests; keep the garden weeded, watered, and mulched.	Plant out succession crops. Monitor for pests; keep the garden weeded, watered, and mulched.	Mulch heavily to conserve water. Start seedlings for fall plantings.	Keep the garden weeded, watered, and mulched. Take cuttings of tender plants.
Plant perennials before September 15. Direct-seed pansies and other annuals. Dig up tender bulbs. Prune shrubs.	Plant perennials before September 15. Direct-seed pansies and other annuals. Dig up tender bulbs. Prune shrubs.	Plant out fall vege-tables. When it cools down, begin planting annuals and perennials for fall and winter. Prune flowering shrubs.	Plant perennials for next year; they will have time to establish before winter.
Prepare beds for spring. Put in cover crops. Plant fall beds. Close down the garden for winter, mulching plants that have not yet become established.	Prepare beds for spring. Put in cover crops. Plant fall beds. Close down the garden for winter, mulching plants that have not yet become established.	Harvest fall vegetables and replant for a winter crop. Plant new annuals and perennials; mulch and water as they begin to grow.	Harvest fall crops. Plant garlic and fall bulbs. Take cuttings of tender plants. Put in cover crops as needed. Cut back perennials and clean the garden for winter.
Mulch tender plants. Wrap or protect trees as necessary. Start a compost pile with fall leaves.	Mulch tender plants. Wrap or protect trees as necessary. Start a compost pile with fall leaves.	Harvest and replant vegetables. Keep flowerbeds mulched and weeded.	Plant spring bulbs by late November. Start a compost pile with fall leaves. Mulch tender plants.

SOURCES

The ever-growing gardening industry consists of thousands of sources. Inclusion on this list does not constitute a recommendation, and there are many fine sources that have not been included on this list.

COMPUTER GARDENING

For those who enjoy using them, computers have become a major source of gardening information. Many valuable internet sites are available, among them:

Garden Web, which lists dozens of other gardening-related sites as well as hosting forums and chat rooms for amateur and professional gardeners: http://www.gardenweb.com/

Garden Gate, which includes links to other webs as well as articles and forums: http://garden-gate.prairienet.org/

Web garden, which is geared to Midwest gardening: http://www.hcs.ohio-state.edu/webgarden.html

Virtual garden, which includes a huge encyclopedia of plants: http://www.vg.com/

Garden.com, which includes catalogs of many major gardening retailers: http://www.garden.com/

Also available are software products that contain amazing amounts of gardening information. Listed here are some of the best ones.

Burpee 3D Garden Designer allows you to type in your zip code and find a list of plants suitable for your area and to design and see 3D views of your garden in all seasons. Available from W. Atlee Burpee & Co., Warminster, PA, 18974, (800)888-1447

Complete LandDesigner includes a 4,000-plant database and allows you to design and "walk around in" your future garden in 3D. Also includes a deck designer and a personal garden planner. From Sierra Home Products, available in software stores.

Desert Landscaping: Plants for a Water-Scarce Environment covers 600 low-water-use plants and how to care for them. Available through Native Seeds/SEARCH, 2509 Campbell Avenue, Tucson, AZ 85719.

Microsoft Gardening includes a plant encyclopedia and

listmaker, a problem solver, and interactive animations of techniques. Available in software stores.

Plantmaster, designed for landscape design professionals, is an electronic horticultural journal and plant portfolio builder. Available from Acacia Software, 2899 Agoura Rd. Suite 652, Westlake Village, CA 91361 (805) 499-9689.

Sprout! was developed specifically for designing vegetable gardens; it allows you to calculate amount of seed needed, spacing, and yield and includes cultural information for dozens of vegetables. Available through Territorial Seed Company, PO Box 157, Cottage Grove, OR 97424; (541) 942 9547

PLANT AND SEED SOURCES

Abundant Life Seed Foundation
P.O. Box 772
930 Lawrence Street
Port Townsend, WA 98368

Adventures in Herbs
P.O. Box 23240
Mint Hill, NC 28227

Allandale Farm
259 Allandale Road
Chestnut Hill, MA 02467

Allen Plant Company
P.O. Box 310
Fruitland, MD 21826

Anderson Nursery & Garden Centre
9666 Tecumseh Road
E. Windsor, ON Canada

Andre Viette Farm & Nursery
P.O. Box 1109
Fishersville, VA 22939

Antique Rose Emporium
Rte 5, Box 143
Brenham, TX 77833

Antonelli Brothers, Inc.
2545 Capitola Road
Santa Cruz, CA 95062

Arborvillage Farm Nursery
P.O. Box 227
Holt, MO 64048

Arrowhead Alpines
P.O. Box 857
Fowlerville, MI 48836

B & D Lilies
330 P Street Port
Townsend, WA 98368

Bear Creek Nursery
P.O. Box 411
Northport, WA 99157

Beaver Creek Nursery
7526 Pelleaux Road
Knoxville, TN 37938

Bluestone Perennials
7211 Middle Ridge Road
Madison, OH 44057

Bountiful Gardens
18001 Shafer Ranch
   Road
Willits, CA 95490

W. Atlee Burpee
   Company
300 Park Avenue
Warminster, PA 18991

Bundles of Bulbs
112 Green Springs
   Valley Road
Owings Mills, MD
   21117

Busse Gardens
5873 Oliver Avenue SW
Cokato, MN 55321

Butterbrook Farms
78 Barry Road
Oxford, CT 06478

Carroll Gardens
P.O. Box 310
444 E. Main St.
Westminster, MD
   21158

Catnip Acres Herb
   Farm
67 Christian Street,
Oxford, CT 06478

Coastal Gardens &
Nursery
4611 Highway 707
Myrtle Beach, SC
   29575

Companion Plants
7247 N. Coolville
   Ridge Road
Athens, OH 45701

Country Carriage
Nursery & Seed
Company
P.O. Box 536
Hartford, MI 49057

Crocker Nurseries
1132 Route 137
Brewster, MA 02631

Crosman Seed
   Company
P.O. Box 110 or
407 W. Commercial
   Street
East Rochester, NY
   14445

Dabney's Herbs
P.O. Box 22061
Louisville, KY 40252

Early's Farm & Garden
   Centre
2615 Lorne Avenue
South Saskatoon, SK,
   Canada

Edgewood Farm &
   Nursery
1186 Middle River
   Road
Stanardsville, VA 22973

Fieldstone Gardens
620 Quaker Lane
Vassalboro, ME 04989

French's Bulb Importer
P.O. Box 565
State Rt. 100N
Pittsfield, VT 05762

Garden Perennials
Route 1
Wayne, NE 68787

Garden City Seeds
778 Hwy 93N
Hamilton, MT 59840

Good Hollow
   Greenhouse
50 State Rock Mill Rd
Taft, TN 38488

Goodwin Creek
   Gardens
P.O. Box 83
Williams, OR 97544

Green Mountain
Transplants
RR 1,
East Montpelier, VT
   05651

Greenlady Gardens
1415 Eucalyptus Drive
San Francisco, CA 94132

Greer Gardens
1280 Goodpasture
   Island Road
Eugene, OR 97401

Harris Seeds
60 Saginaw Drive
Rochester, NY 14623

Hartmann's Herb Farm
1026 Dana Road
Barre, MA 01005

Heather Acres
P.O. Box 850
1199 Monte-Elma Road
Elma, WA 98541

Heirloom Old
   Garden Roses
24062 NE Riverside
   Drive
St. Paul, OR 97137

High Altitude
   Gardens
P.O. Box 1048
308 S. River
Hailey, ID 83333

Homestead Division
   of Sunnybrook Farms
9448 Mayfield Road
Chesterfield, OH
   44026

Horticultural
   Goddess, Inc.
36 Sound Avenue
Riverhead, NY 11901

Jackson & Perkins
P.O. Box 1028
Medford, OR 97501

Johnny's Selected
   Seeds
Foss Hill Road
Albion, ME 04910

Joyce's Garden
64640 Old Bend
   Redmond Highway
Bend, OR 97701

Lamtree Farm
Route 1, Box 162
Warrensville, NC
   28693

Las Pilitas Nursery
Las Pilitas Rd.
Santa Margarita, CA
   93453

Le Jardin du Gourmet
P.O. Box 75
St. Johnsbury Center,
   VT 05863

Logee's Greenhouse
141 North Street
Danielson, CT 06239

Mary's Plant Farm
Lanes Mill Road
Hamilton, OH 45013

Matterhorn Nursery
227 Summit Park Road
Spring Valley, NY 10977

McClure &
   Zimmerman
P.O. Box 368
108 W. Winnebago
   Street
Friesland, WI

Mellinger Farms
2310 W. South
   Range Road
North Lima, OH 44452

Mesa Gardens
P.O. Box 72
Belen, NM 87002

Mileager's Gardens
4838 Douglas Avenue
Racine, WI 53402

Musser Forests
P.O. Box 340, 119
North
Indiana, PA 15701

Nature's Garden
40611 Highway 226
Scio, OR 97374

New England Seed Co.
3580 Main Street, #10
Hartford, CT 06120

Niche Gardens
1111 Dawson Road
Chapel Hill, NC 27516

Nichols Garden
Nursery
1190 N. Pacific
Highway
Albany, OR 97321

North Creek
Perennials
R.R. #2, Box 33
Landenberg, PA 19350

Oikos Tree Crops
P.O. Box 19425
Kalamazoo, MI 49019

Old House Gardens
536 Third Street
Ann Arbor, MI 48103

Oral Ledden & Sons
Centre & Atlantic Avenue
P.O. Box 7
Sewell, NJ 08080

Owen Farms
Route 3, Box 158-A
2951 Curve-
Nankipoo Road
Ripley, TN 38063

Pawnee Greenhouse
and Nursery
1901 Big Horn Avenue
Cody, WY 82414

Perennial Pleasures
Brickhouse Road, East
Hardwick, VT 05836

Pinetree Garden Seeds
Box 300
New Gloucester, ME
04260

Plants of the Southwest
Route 6, Box 11A
Santa Fe, NM 87501

Powell's Gardens
9468 U.S. Highway 70
E. Princeton, NC 27569

Prairie Nursery
P.O. Box 306
Westfield, WI 53964

Prentiss Court Ground
Covers
P.O. Box 8662
Greenville, SC 29604

Redwood City Seed
Company
P.O. Box 361
Redwood City, CA
94064

Richter's Herbs
357 Highway 47
Goodwood, ON,
Canada LOC 1AO

Robyn's Nest Nursery
7802 N.E. 63rd Street
Vancouver, WA 98662

Sandy Mush Herb Farm
316 Surrett Cove Road
Leicester, NC 28748

Seeds of Change
P.O. Box 15700
Santa Fe, NM 87506

Shepards' Garden Seeds
30 Irene Street
Torrington, CT 06790

Sleepy Hollow Herb
Farm
568 Jack Black Road
Lancaster, KY 40444

Southern Perennials
and Herbs
98 Bridges Road
Tylertown, MS 39667

St. Lawrence Nurseries
325 State Hwy 345
Potsdam, NY 13676

Stark Brothers Nurseries
P.O. Box 10
Louisiana, MO 63353

Stoecklin's Nursery
135 Critchlow Road
Renfrew, PA 16053

Sunshine Farm &
Gardens
Route 5 GB
Renick, WV 24966

Taylor Ridge Farm
P.O. Box 222
Saluda, NC 28773

Territorial Seed
Company
P.O. Box 157
Cottage Grove, OR
97424

The Bulb Crate
2560 Deerfield Road
Riverwoods, IL 60015

The Herb Farm
R. R. 4
Norton, NB, Canada,
E0G 2N0

The Rosemary House
120 South Market Street
Mechanicsburg, PA
17055

The Gourmet Gardener
8650 College
Blvd.
Overland Park, KS
66210

The Thyme Herb Seed
Company
20546 Alsea Highway
Alsea, OR 97324

Tripple Brook Farm
37 Middle Road
Southampton, MA 01073

Twombley Nursery
163 Barn Hill Road
Monroe, CT 06468

Van Engelen, Inc.
313 Maple Street
Litchfield, CT 06759

We-Du Nursery
Route 5, Box 724
Marion, NC 28752

Well-Sweep Herb Farm
205 Mt. Bethel Road
Port Murray, NJ 07865

Weston Nurseries
East Main Street, Rt. 135
Hopkinton, MA 01748

White Flower Farm
P.O. Box 50
Litchfield, CT 06759

Whitman Farms
3995 Gibson Road NW
Salem, OR 97304

Wild Earth Native
Plant Nursery
49 Mead Avenue
Freehold, NJ 07728

Wildginger Woodlands
P.O. Box 1091
Webster, NY 14580

Wilson Farms
10 Pleasant Street
Lexington, MA 02073

Woodlanders, Inc.
1128 Colleton Avenue
Aiken, SC 29801

Wrenwood of Berkeley
Springs
Route 4, Box 8055
Berkeley Springs, WV
25411

Yucca Do Nursery
P.O. Box 655
Waller, TX 77484

GARDENS TO VISIT

Ash Lawn-Highland
James Monroe Parkway
Charlottesville, VA
22902

Berkshire Botanical Garden
Rt. 102 & 183
Stockbridge, MA 01262

Botanica Gardens
701 North Amidon Street
Wichita, KS 67203

Brookgreen Gardens
1931 Brookgreen
Gardens Drive
Murrells Inlet, SC 29576

Callaway Gardens
US Highway 27
P.O. Box 2000
Pine Mountain, GA
31822

Chadwick Arboretum
Ohio State University
2001 Fyffe Courte
Columbus, OH 43210

Cheyenne Botanic Garden
710 South Lions Park
Drive
Cheyenne, WY 82001

Chicago Botanic Garden
1000 Lake Cook Road
Glencoe, IL 60022

Clemson Botanic Garden
Clemson University
Agricultural Station
Clemson, SC 29631

Denver Botanic Garden
909 York Street
Denver, CO 80206

Des Moines Botanical Center
909 East River Drive
Des Moines, IA 50316

Desert Botanical Garden
1201 North Galvin
Parkway
Phoenix, AZ 85008

Fairchild Tropical Garden
10901 Old Cutler Road
Miami, FL 33156

Foellinger-Freimann Botanical Conservatory
1100 S. Calhoun Street
Fort Wayne, IN 46802

Ganna Walska Lotusland
695 Ashley Road
Santa Barbara, CA
93108

Glebe House Museum
Hollow Road
Woodbury, CT 06798

Highstead Arboretum
127 Lonetown Road
Redding, CT 06875

John Bartram Garden
54th Street & Lindbergh
Boulevard
Philadelphia, PA 19143

Longwood Gardens
US Highway 1
Kennett Square, PA
19348

Maymount Foundation
1700 Hampton Street
Richmond, VA 23220

Mercer Arboretum & Botanic Gardens
22306 Aldine-Westfield
Road
Humble, TX 77338

Merryscape Gardens
7 Highland Avenue
Camden, ME 04843

Minnesota Landscape Arboretum
3675 Arboretum Drive
Chanhassen, MN 55317

Missouri Botanic Garden
4344 Shaw Boulevard
St. Louis, MO 63166

Morris Arboretum
9414 Meadowbrook
Avenue
Philadelphia, PA 19118

Morton Arboretum
4100 Route 53
Lisle, IL 69532

Mount Cuba Center
P.O. Box 3570
Greenville, DE 19807

New York Botanical Garden
200th Street & Southern
Boulevard
Bronx, NY 10458

Olbrich Botanical Gardens
3330 Atwood Avenue
Madison, WI 53704

Old Westbury Gardens
71 Old Westbury Road
Old Westbury, NY 11568

Powell Garden
1609 NW US Hwy 50
Kingsville, MO 64061

Queens Botanical Garden
4350 Main Street
Flushing, NY 11355

University of California, Santa Cruz, Farm and Garden
Santa Cruz, CA 95064

Wave Hill
675 W. 249th Street
Bronx, New York 10471

Washington Park Botanic Garden
Springfield Park
District
P.O. Box 5052
Springfield, IL 62705

SUPPLIES AND SPECIALTY PRODUCTS

Astoria-Pacific, Inc.
14600 SE 82nd Drive
Clackamas, OR 97015
Propagation supplies

Cook's Consulting
RD2, Box 13
Lowville, NY 13367
Soil testing service

Design 5
Cliff Rock Road
Marblehead, MA
Lighting design

EZ Soil Co.
Route 3, Box 176
Idabel, OK 74745
Soil amendments

Gardener's Supply Company
128 Intervale Road
Burlington, VT 05401
Supplies for organic gardens

Gardens Alive!
5100 Schenley Place
Lawrenceberg, IN
47025
Organic fertilizers, soil conditioners, and pest controls

Guano Company International
3562 E. 80th Street
Cleveland, OH 44105
Organic fertilizer

Harmony Farm Supply & Nursery
3244 Gravenstein Hwy
North
Sebastapol, CA 95472
Tools, soil conditioners, and fertilizers

Hobbs & Hopkins
1712 SE Ankeny
Portland, OR 97214
Alternative lawn seeds and supplies

Home Harvest Garden
  Supply, Inc.
13426 Occoquan Road
Woodbridge, VA 22191
Supplies for organic gardens

Miller Horticultural
  Consultants
113 W. Argonne Drive
St. Louis, MO 63122
Beneficial insects

Nature's Control
P.O. Box 35
400 Morton Way
Medford, OR 97501
Beneficial insects

Nitron Industries, Inc.
P.O. Box 1447 4605
Johnson Road
Fayetteville, AR 72702
*Soil conditioners, fertilizers,
and composting supplies*

Ohio Earth Food
5488 Swamp Street NE
Hartville, OH 44632
*Soil conditioners and amend-
ments, pest control, and soil
testing*

Planet Natural
1612 Gold Avenue
Bozeman, MT 59715
*Natural soil conditioners
and amendments, pest control*

Reotemp Instruments
  Corporation
11568 Sorrento Valley
  Road
San Diego, CA 92121
Compost thermometers

Ringer Corporation
1279 Trapp Road
Eagan, MN 55121
*Organic soil amendments
and pest control*

Symo-Life
Quarry Road
Gap, PA 17527
Organic soil amendments

Topiaries Unlimited
RD 2, Box 40C
Pownal, VT 05261
Topiary supplies

Woods End
  Agricultural Institute
Old Rome Road
P.O. Box 297
Mt. Vernon, ME 04352
*Cover crops, soil testing,
compost testing*

Worm's Way of Indiana
7850 N St.Rd.
Bloomington, IN 47404
Organic gardening supplies

LANDSCAPE DESIGNERS

A Garden for All
  Seasons
Angela Fabbri
478 La Grande Avenue
San Francisco, CA 94110

Bobbie's Green Thumb
Bobbie Schwartz
18405 Van Aken
  Boulevard
Cleveland, OH 44122

Boggs, Rick
4301 Woodlawn Drive
Raleigh, NC 27604

Buchholz Landscaping
John Buchholz
3020 Bridgeway #136
Sausalito, CA 94965

Caughlan & Son
  Landscapes
Robert Caughlan
914 Fleetwood Drive
San Mateo, CA 94402

Charles N. Sandifer &
  Associates
2886 Cela Road
Memphis, TN 38128

Design Concepts
Rob Layton
211 N. Public Road
Lafayette, CO 80026

Energyscapes, Inc.
Douglas Owens-Pike
3849 Pillsbury Avenue
Minneapolis, MN
  55409

Harvard and Associates
Deborah and Peter
  Harvard
4250 Fremont Avenue N
Seattle, WA 98103

Harvey, Kyrnan
  Horticulture
360 E. Shore Road
Great Neck, NY 11023

Hresko Associates, Inc.
Philip Hresko
110 Broad Street
Boston, MA 02110

Kirch, Jeffrey
2734 W. 44th Street
Indianapolis, IN 46208

Landscapes by Atlantic
  Nurseries
Gisela Schaeffer
694 Deer Park Avenue
Dix Hills, NY 11746

Living Landscapes
Loretta Spilker
12063 Laurel Oak Drive
Indianapolis, IN 46236

MDG, Inc.
Sara Edi Livingston
820 Santa Fe Drive
Denver, CO 80204

Marta Fry Landscape
  Architects
165 10th Street
San Francisco, CA
  94103

McGuire, Diane Kostial
85 E. India Row
Boston, MA 02110

Moss, Sue
2205 E. Newton
Seattle, WA 98112

Preview Residential
  Landscape
Alan Burke
1911 9th Avenue W
Seattle, WA 98119

Rice, Cynthia
2900 Glen Burnie Drive
Raleigh, NC 27603

Sculptured Landscapes
Suzanne Biaggi
1090 Eucalyptus
  Avenue
Petaluma, CA 94952

Secret Garden
Kathryn Mathewson
64 S Park St
San Francisco, CA
  94107

Shen & Associates
Janet Shen
104 S. Michigan
  Avenue
Chicago, IL 60603

Sorensen, Leigh
7 Ward Avenue
Rumson, NJ 07760

Sunlight Gardens, Inc.
Andrea Sessions
174 Golden Lane
Andersonville, TN
  37705

The Landscape Group,
  Ltd.
6856 Eastern Avenue
  NW
Washington, DC 20012

Thuesen, Carl
1925 Grand Avenue
Billings, MT 59102

Victoria Gardens
Tory Galloway
2506 N. 39th Street
Seattle, WA 98103

RECOMMENDED READING

BOOKS

The American Garden Guides. Pantheon/Knopf, New York: 1994-1997.

Ball, Jeff, and Liz Ball. *Rodale's Landscape Problem Solver.* Emmaus, PA: Rodale Press, 1989

Bartholemew, Mel. *Square Foot Gardening.* Emmaus, PA: Rodale Press, 1981

Bradley, Fern Marshall, and Barbara W. Ellis. *All-New Encyclopedia of Organic Gardening.* Emmaus, PA: Rodale Press, 1992

Brickell, Christopher, Elvin McDonald, and Trevor Cole, eds. *The American Horticultural Society Encyclopedia of Gardening.* NY: DK Publishing, 1993.

Bubel, Nancy. *The New Seed Starter's Handbook.* Emmaus, PA: Rodale Press, 1988.

Campbell, Stu. *Let It Rot: The Gardener's Guide to Composting.* Pownal, VT: Storey Communications, 1998

Clausen, Ruth Rogers, and Nicolas H. Ekstrom. *Perennials for American Gardners.* New York: Random House, 1989.

Coleman, Eliot. *Four-Season Harvest: How to Harvest Fresh Organic Vegetables from Your Home Garden All Year Long.* VT: Chelsea Green, 1992.

Damrosch, Barbara. *The Garden Primer.* New York, Workman Publishing, 1988.

DiSabato-Aust, Tracey. *The Well-Tended Perennial Garden.* Portland, OR: Timber Press, 1998.,

Dirr, Michael. *Dirr's Hardy Trees and Shrubs.* Portland, OR: Timber Press, 1997.

Ellis, Barbara W. and Fern Marshall Bradley. *The Organic Gardener's Handbook of Natural Insect and Disease Control.* Emmaus, PA: Rodale Press, 1992.

Ellis, Barbara W., ed. *Rodale's Illustrated Encyclopedia of Gardening and Landscaping Techniques.* Emmaus, PA: Rodale Press, 1990.

Garden Way Publishing, editors. *The Big Book of Gardening Skills.* Pownal, VT: Storey Communications, 1993.

Gilkeson, Linda, et al. *Rodale's Pest and Disease Problem Solver.* Emmaus, PA: Rodale Press, 1996.

Halpin, Anne. *Horticulture Gardener's Desk Reference.* New York: Macmillan, 1996.

Hill, Lewis. *Secrets of Plant Propagation.* Pownal, VT: Storey Communications, 1985.

Hynes, Erin. *Rodale's Successful Organic Gardening: Controlling Weeds.* Emmaus, PA: Rodale Press, 1995.

Jeavons, John. *How to Grow More Vegetables Than You Ever Thought Possible on Less Land Than You Can Imagine, 5th edition.* Berkeley, CA: Ten Speed Press, 1995.

Martin, Deborah L., ed. *1,001 Ingenious Gardening Ideas.* Emmaus, PA: Rodale Press, 1999.

Phillips, Ellen, and C. Colston Burrell. *Rodale's Illustrated Encyclopedia of Perennials.* Emmaus, PA: Rodale Press, 1993.

Riotte, Louise. *Carrots Love Tomatoes, 2nd edition.* Pownal, VT: Storey Communications, 1998.

Sunset Books and Magazine Staff. *Western Garden Book, 6th edition.* Menlo Park, CA: Sunset Publishing Corp., 1995

MAGAZINES

Common Sense Pest Control Quarterly, Bio-Integral Resource Center (BIRC), P.O. Box 7414, Berkeley, CA 94707.

Fine Gardening, The Taunton Press, Inc., Newtown, CT 06470.

Horticulture, Horticulture, Inc., 98 N. Washington Street, Boston, MA 02114.

HortIdeas, 250 Black Lick Road, Gravel Switch, KY 40328.

National Gardening, National Gardening Association, 180 Flynn Avenue, Burlington, VT 05401.

Organic Gardening, Rodale Press, Inc., 33 E. Minor Street, Emmaus, PA 18098.

ABOUT OUR CONSULTANTS

We thank, once again, the garden experts who so generously provided information for this book.

Regional editors

David Bar-Zvi
Horticulturist, Fairchild
  Tropical Garden
Miami, FL

Galen Gates
Manager of Horticulture
  Collections, Chicago
  Botanic Garden
Glencoe, IL

Kim Hawks
Owner, Niche Gardens
Chapel Hill, NC

Sean Hogan
Horticulturist and garden
  designer
Portland, OR

June Hutson
Horticulturist,
  Missouri Botanical
  Garden
St. Louis, MO

Mary Irish
Director of Education,
  Desert Botanical Garden
Phoenix, AZ

Susan Nolde
Horticulturist
Gaithersburg, MD

Michael Ruggiero
Senior Horticulturist,
  The New York Botanical
  Garden
Bronx, NY

Nelson Sterner
Director of Horticulture,
  Old Westbury Gardens
Old Westbury, NY

Consultants

Claire Ackroyd
Horticulturist and former
  nursery owner
Orono, ME

Richard Allen
Owner, Allen Plant
  Company
Fruitland, MD

Pam Allenstein
Horticulturist, John
  Bartram Garden
Philadelphia, PA

Lydia Anderson
Manager, Worm's Way
Bloomington, IN

Robert Anderson
Owner, Anderson
  Nursery & Garden
  Centre
Windsor, ON, Canada

Skip Antonelli
Owner, Antonelli
  Brothers, Inc.
Santa Cruz, CA

James Arnold
Horticulturist, Clemson
  Botanic Garden,
  Clemson University
  Agricultural Experiment
  Station
Clemson, SC

Ken Asmus
Owner, Oikos Tree
  Crops
Kalamazoo, MI

Kris Bachtell
Horticulturist, The
  Morton Arboretum
Lisle, IL

Gene Banks
Owner, Catnip Acres
  Herb Farm
Oxford, CT

Jim Becker
Owner, Goodwin Creek
  Gardens
Williams, OR

Joyce Belyea
Owner, The Herb Farm
Norton, NB, Canada

Inez Berg
Director, Washington
  Park Botanic Garden
Springfield, IL

Suzanne Biaggi
Landscape architect,
  Sculptured Landscapes
Petaluma, CA

Joe Bloski
Owner, Early's Farm &
  Garden Center
Saskatoon, SK, Canada

Rick Boggs
Landscape architect
Raleigh, NC

Richard Boonstra
Retired president,
  Bluestone Perennials
Madison, OH

Peter Borchard
Owner, Companion
  Plants
Athens, OH

Steven Brack
Owner, Mesa Gardens
Belen, NM

Alan Branhagen
Director, Powell
  Garden
Kingsville, MO

Stephen Breyer
Owner, Tripple Brook
  Farm
Southampton, MA

William F. Brinton
Researcher, Woods End
  Research Laboratory
Woods Hole, MA

Tom Brooks
Owner, Wilson Farms
Lexington, MA

Bill Bruneau
Owner, Bountiful
  Gardens
Willits, CA

John Buchholz
Landscape Architect,
  Buchholz Landscaping
Sausalito, CA

Donald Buma
Former director, Botanica
  Gardens
Wichita, KS
Current director,
  Norfolk Botanical
  Gardens
Norfolk, VA

Stanley Buol
Professor of Plant
  Sciences, The
  University of North
  Carolina
Chapel Hill, NC

Alan Burke
Landscape architect,
  Preview Landscape
  Architecture
Seattle, WA

Kate Burroughs
Owner, Harmony Farm
  Supply
Graton, CA

Ainie Busse
Owner, Busse Gardens
Cokato, MN

Tom Butterworth
Owner, Butterbrook
  Farms
Oxford, CT

Michael Cady
Horticulturist, Jackson &
  Perkins
Medford, OR

Hunter Carleton
Owner, Bear Creek
  Nursery
Northport, WA

Robert Caughlan
Landscape architect,
  Caughlan & Son
  Landscapes
San Mateo, CA

Louise Clements
Owner, Heirloom Old
 Garden Roses
St. Paul, OR

Peg Cook
Owner, Cook's
 Consulting
Lowville, NY

Leslie Cooperband
Professor of horticulture,
 University of
 Wisconsin
Madison, WI

Gerry Coull
Horticulturist, Johnny's
 Selected Seeds
Albion, ME

Jack Crittenden
Owner, Stark Brothers
 Nurseries
Louisiana, MO

Vicki Crocker
Owner, Crocker Nursery
Brewster, Cape Cod, MA

Davy Dabney
Owner, Dabney's Herbs
Louisville, KY

Doug De Luca
Owner, De Luca Nursery
Natchez, MS

Neil Diboll
Owner, Prairie Nursery
Westfield, WI

Gene Dickson
Owner, Prentiss Court
 Ground Covers
Greenville, SC

Gerry Donaldson
Owner, Hilltop
 Nurseries
Hartford, MI

Dr. Sharon Douglas
Extension agent,
 Agricultural Experiment
 Station
New Haven, CT

Bastiaan M. Drees
Professor, Texas A & M
 University
College Station, TX

Craig Dremann
Owner, Redwood City
 Seed Company
Redwood City, CA

Robyn Duback
Owner, Robyn's Nest
Vancouver, WA 98662

Jeff Edwards
Owner, Harvest Home
 Garden Supply, Inc.
Woodbridge, VA

Tom Eickenberg
Horticulturist, Johnny's
 Selected Seeds
Albion, ME

Jeff Epping
Director, Olbrich
 Botanical Gardens
Madison, WI

Angela Fabbri
Landscape designer,
 A Garden for All
 Seasons
San Francisco, CA

John Fairey
Owner, Yucca Do
 Nursery
Waller, TX

Phyllis Farkas
Owner, Wildginger
 Woodlands
Brewster, NY

Zach Finger
Director, Nitron
 Industries, Inc.
Fayetteville, AR

Chuck Flynn
Manager, Musser Forests
Indiana, PA

Andy Force
Horticulturist,
 Foellinger-Freimann
 Botanical Conservatory
Fort Wayne, IN

Virginia Frazier
Owner, Adventures in
 Herbs
Mint Hill, NC

Howard French
Owner, French's Bulb
 Importer
Pittsfield, VT

Marta Fry
Landscape architect, Marta
 Fry Landscape Architects
San Francisco, CA

Sarah Gallant
Horticulturist,
 Pinetree Garden Seeds
New Gloucester, ME

Tory Galloway
Landscape designer,
 Victoria Gardens
Seattle, WA

Stephen Garrison
Extension agent,
 Rutgers Cooperative
 Extension
New Brunswick, NJ

Linda Gay
Horticulturist, Mercer
 Arboretum & Botanic
 Gardens
Humble, TX

Diana Gibson
Owner, B & D Lilies
Port Townsend, WA

Barry Glick
Owner, Sunshine
 Farm & Gardens
Renick, WV

Lisa Glick
Director, Life Lab Science
 Program, University of CA
Santa Cruz, CA

Nancy Goldstein
Owner, Nancy Goldstein
 Design
Marblehead, MA

Tessa Gowans
Director, Abundant Life
 Seed Foundation
Port Townsend, WA

David Graper
Extension agent, University
 of South Dakota
Brookings, SD

Harold Greer
Owner, Greer Gardens
Eugene, OR

Amy Greving
Extension agent,
 University of Nebraska
Lincoln, NE

Flora Hackimer
Owner, Wrenwood of
 Berkeley Springs
Berkeley Springs, WV

Rolfe Hagen
Owner, Thyme Garden
 Seeds
Alsea, OR

Gail Haggard
Owner, Plants of the
 Southwest
Santa Fe, NM

Kathy Hakim
Director, Nature's Control
Medford, OR

William Hall
Owner, Country
 Carriage Nursery &
 Seed Company
Hartford, MI

Barbara Harris
Owner, Southern
 Perennials and Herbs
Tylertown, MS

Mary Harrison
Owner, Mary's Plant
 Farm
Hamilton, OH

Lynn Hartmann
Owner, Hartmann's
 Herb Farm
Barre, MA

Deborah and Peter
 Harvard
Landscape designers
Seattle, WA

Kyrnan Harvey
Landscape designer,
 Kyrnan Harvey
 Horticulture
Great Neck, NY

Virginia Hayes
Horticulturist, Ganna
 Walska Lotusland
Santa Barbara, CA

Frederick Held
Owner, Nature's Garden
Scio, OR

Joyce Held
Owner, Topiaries
 Unlimited
Pownal, VT

Philip Helmke
Professor, University of
 Wisconsin
Madison, WI

Dale Hendricks
Owner, North Creek
 Perennials
Landenburg, PA

Ursula Herz
Owner, Coastal
 Gardens & Nursery
Myrtle Beach, SC

Bobbie Holder
Owner, Pawnee
 Greenhouse and
 Nursery
Cody, WY

Christina Hopkins
Owner, Hobbs &
 Hopkins
Portland, OR

Matt Horn
Owner, Matterhorn
 Nursery
Spring Valley, NY

Alice Hosford
Owner, The Bulb Crate
Riverwoods, IL

Philip Hresko
Landscape architect
Boston, MA

Mike Hughs
Owner, Reotemp Corp.
San Diego, CA

Dorthe Hviid
Horticulturist, Berkshire
 Botanical Garden
Stockbridge, MA

Louise Hyde
Owner, Well-Sweep
 Herb Farm
Port Murray, NJ

David Ittel
Manager, Alternative
 Garden Supply, Inc.
Streamwood, IL

Don L. Jacobs
Owner, Eco-Gardens
Decatur, GA

Fairman and Kate Jayne
Owners, Sandy Mush
 Herb Farm
Leicester, NC

John Jeavons
Director, Ecology Action
Willits, CA

Kim Johnson
Horticulturist, Old
 Westbury Gardens
Old Westbury, NY

Steve D. Jones
Owner, Fieldstone
 Gardens
Vassalboro, ME

Rachel Kane
Owner, Perennial
 Pleasures Nursery
East Hardwick, VT

Sharon Kaszan
Manager of trial
 gardens, W. Atlee
 Burpee & Company
Warminster, PA

Debby Kavakos
Farmer, Stoneledge
 Farm
South Cairo, NY

Jerry Kay
Manager, Let's Get
 Growing website
San Diego, CA

Dana Keiser
Owner, Stony Hill Farm
Binghamton, NY

Niles Kinerk
Owner, Gardens Alive!
Lawrenceberg, IN

Jeffrey Kirch
Landscape designer
Indianapolis, IN

Patty Kleinberg
Associate Director, Queens
 Botanical Garden
Flushing, NY

Alice Knight
Former owner, Heather
 Acres
Elma, WA

Gail Korn
Owner, Garden Perennials
Wayne, NE

Alice Krinsky
Director, trial gardens,
 Shepards' Garden Seeds
Torrington, CT

Scott Kunst
Owner, Old House
 Gardens
Ann Arbor, MI

Rob Layton
Landscape designer
 Design Concepts
Lafayette, CO

Don Ledden
Owner, Oral Ledden &
 Sons
Sewell, NJ

John Lee
Owner, Allandale Farm
Brookline, MA

Rosie B. Lerner
Extension agent, Purdue
 University
Lafayette, Indiana

Rick Lewandowski
Horticulturist, Morris
 Arboretum
Philadelphia, PA

Dr. Richard Lighty
Director, Mount Cuba
 Center
Greenville, DE

Peter Linsner
Horticulturist, Morton
 Arboretum
Lisle, IL

Sara Edy Livingston
Landscape designer, MDG
Denver, CO

Ted Lockwood
Director, Highstead
 Arboretum
Redding, CT

Aileen Lubin
Director, Merry Gardens
Camden, ME

Justine Mapstone
Owner, Crosman Seed
 Company
East Rochester, NY

Julie Marks
Owner, Sleepy Hollow
 Herb Farm
Lancaster, KY

Byron Martin
Manager, Logee's
 Greenhouse
Danielson, CT

Kathryn Mathewson
Landscape designer,
 Secret Garden
San Francisco, CA

Robert McCartney
Owner, Woodlanders, Inc.
Aiken, SC

Bill McDorman
Owner, High Altitude
 Gardens
Hailey, ID

Rose Marie McGee
Owner, Nichols Garden
 Nursery
Albany, OR

Patrick McGinity
Manager, Ringer
 Corporation
Bloomington, MN

Dennis McGlynn
Manager, New England
 Seed Company
New Haven, CT

Diane Kostial McGuire
Landscape architect
Boston, MA

Bill McKentley
Owner, St. Lawrence
 Nurseries
Potsdam, NY

Judy Megan
Horticulturist, Glebe
 House
Woodbury, CT

Dexter Merritt
Owner, Green
 Mountain Transplants
East Montpelier, VT

Wayne Mezitt
Owner, Weston Nurseries
Hopkinton, MA

Kevin Mileager
Owner, Mileager's
Gardens
Racine, WI

Ken Miller
Landscape designer,
 Miller Horticultural
 Consultants
St. Louis, MO

Richard Miller
Owner, American
 Arborist Supplies
West Chester, PA

Lee Morrison
Owner, Lamtree Farm
Warrensville, NC

Sue Moss
Landscape designer
Seattle, WA

Bobby Mottern
Horticulturist,
 Brookgreen Gardens
Murrells Inlet, SC

Dennis Neimeyer
Owner, We-Du Nursery
Marion, NC

Diane Nolang
Professor, University of
 Illinois
Urbana, IL

Dr. Robert Nuss
Professor, Pennsylvania
 State University
University Park, PA

Janet Oberleisen
Professor, Ohio State
 University
Columbus, OH

Jan Ohms
Owner, Van Engelen, Inc.
Litchfield, CT

Joseph Oppt
Director of horticulture,
 Des Moines Botanical
 Center
Des Moines, IA

Dr. Michael Orzolek
Professor, Pennsylvania
 State University
University Park, PA

Edric Owen
Owner, Owen Farms
Ripley, TN

Douglas Owens-Pike
Owner, Energyscape, Inc.
Minneapolis, MN

Rick Pearson
Horticulturist, Chadwick
 Arboretum, Ohio State
 University
Columbus, OH

Frank Peterson
Owner, Good Hollow
 Greenhouse & Herbarium
Taft, TN

Ray Pevitt
Director, Astoria-Pacific,
Clackamas, OR

Richard Pillar
Owner, Wild Earth
 Native Plant Nursery
Freehold, NJ

Loleta Powell
Owner, Powell's Gardens
Princeton, NC

Larry Pozarelli
Owner, Guano
 Company International
Cleveland, OH

Floyd Ranck
Manager, Symo-Life
Gap, PA

Lanny Rawdon
Owner, Arborvillage
 Farm Nursery
Holt, MO

Rebecca Reardon
Manager, Saltwater
 Farms
Barre, ME

Cindy Reed
President, Great Plains
 Native Plant Society
Hot Springs, SD

Bertha Reppert
Owner, The Rosemary
 House
Mechanicsburg, PA

Cynthia Rice
Landscape architect
Raleigh, NC

Conrad Richter
Owner, Richter's Herbs
Goodwood, ON,
 Canada

Larry Ringer
Director, Ohio Earth Food
Hartville, OH

Nancy Rose
Horticulturist,
 Minnesota Landscape
 Arboretum, University
 of Minnesota
Chanhassen, MN

Peter and Jean Ruh
Owners, Homestead
 Division of Sunnybrook
 Farms
Chesterfield, OH

Charles Sandifer
Landscape Architect
 Charles N. Sandifer &
 Associates
Memphis, TN

Gisela Schaeffer
Landscapes by Atlantic
 Nurseries
Dix Hills, NY

Coreen Schilling
Owner, Joyce's Garden
Bend, OR

John Schneeberger
Owner, Garden City
 Seeds
Victor, MT

Bobbie Schwartz
Owner, Bobbie's Green
 Thumb
Cleveland, OH

Noah Schwartz
Propagation expert,
 Matterhorn Nursery
Spring Valley, NY

Norman Schwartz
Owner, Edgewood Farm
 and Nursery
Stanardsville, VA

Andrea Sessions
Garden designer,
 Sunlight Gardens
Andersonville, TN

Howard Shapiro
Director, Seeds of
 Change
Santa Fe, NM

Tim Sharp
Manager, EZ Soil Co.
Idabel, OK

Janet Shen
Landscape architect,
 Shen & Associates
Chicago, IL 60603

Mike Shoup
Owner, Antique Rose
 Emporium
Brenham, TX

Eric Sideman
Director, Maine Organic
 Farmers and Gardeners
 Association
Augusta, ME

George Silva
Professor, University of
 Michigan
Ann Arbor, MI

Peggy Singleman
Horticulturist,
 Maymount Foundation
Richmond, VA

Shannon Singletary
Manager, The Gourmet
  Gardener
Leawood, KS

Anthony Skittone
Owner, Greenlady
  Gardens
San Francisco, CA

Shane Smith
Director, Cheyenne
  Botanic Garden
Cheyenne, WY

Leigh Sorensen,
Landscape designer
Rumson, NJ

Loretta Spilker
Landscape designer,
  Living Landscapes
Indianapolis, IN

Lois Stack
Professor, University of
  Maine
Orono, ME

Mike Stansberry
Owner, Beaver Creek
  Nursery
Knoxville, TN

Paul Steiner
Professor, University of
  Maryland
Baltimore, MD

Philip Steiner
Owner, Mellinger Farm
  & Garden Supply
North Lima, OH

Guy Sternberg
Director, Starhill Forest
  Arboretum
Petersburg, IL

Bob Stewart
Owner, Arrowhead
  Alpines
Fowlerville, MI

Marc Stoecklin
Owner, Stoecklin's
  Nursery
Renfrew, PA

Allan Summers
Owner, Carroll Gardens
Westminster, MD

Harry Swartz
Professor, University of
  Maryland
Baltimore, MD

Ellen Talmage
Owner, Horticultural
  Goddess, Inc.
Riverhead, NY

Doris Taylor
Director of Education,
  Morton Arboretum
Lisle, IL 69532

Gunnar Taylor
Owner, Taylor Ridge
  Farm
Saluda, NC

Paul Taylor
Owner, Le Jardin du
  Gourmet
St. Johnsbury Center, VT

Brian Thomas
Director, Sunny Border
  Nursery
Kensington, CT

Carl Thuesen
Landscape Architect
Billings, MT

Joseph Tomocik
Chief Aquarian, Denver
  Botanic Garden
Denver, CO

Ken Twombley
Owner, Twombley
  Nursery
New London, CT

Ward Upham
Extension Agent, Kansas
  State University
Manhattan, KS

Peter van der Linden
Horticulturist, Morris
  Arboretum
Lisle, IL

Suzanne van Schroeder
Horticulturist, Winter
  Greenhouse
Madison, WI

Andre Viette
Owner, Andre Viette
  Farm & Nursery
Fishersville, VA

Eric Vinje
Owner, Planet Natural
Bozeman, MT

Kitty Washburne
Owner, Bundles of Bulbs
Owings Mills, MD

Ray Weil
Professor, University of
  Maryland
Baltimore , MD

Janet Whippo
Horticulturist, New York
  Botanical Garden
Bronx, NY

Lucille Whitman
Owner, Whitman Farms
Salem, OR

Mark Willis
Horticulturist, Harris
  Seeds
Rochester, NY

Celeste Wilson
Owner, Las Pilitas
  Nursery
Santa Margarita

Cathy Wilson
Landscape Designer,
  The Landscape Group
Washington, D.C.

Steve Witcher
Extension agent,
  Washington State
  University
Western Washington
Cooperative Extension
Tacoma, WA

James Wooten
Director of Horticulture,
  Ash Lawn-Highland
Chalottesville, VA

PHOTO CREDITS

All photographs
© Albert Squillace
except the following:

© Ian Adams: pages 17,
50 (top), 61, 92 (center),
151 (top), 158, 167, 168
(bottom), 172, 201, 212,
269, 275, 317.

© James Cuidon: page 71.

© Galen Gates: pages 35
(left), 89 (top), 90
(bottom), 142, 180 (left),
181, 230, 235 (right),
237, 239, 257, 273.

© John Glover: pages
27, 77 (bottom), 83, 88
(bottom), 106, 113, 151
(bottom), 153, 175, 177
(bottom), 189, 190, 191
(bottom), 199, 224, 225,
229 (top), 321, 352, 353.

© John Nemerovski:
page 13.

© Maggie Oster: pages
86, 101, 193.

© Jerry Pavia: pages 68,
227, 311.

© Diane Pratt: pages 55,
64, 66, 67 (bottom), 69,
155, 218, 315.

© Lori Stein: pages 78
(bottom), 79, 144.

© Chani Yammer: pages
177 (top), 138 (right),
164.

INDEX

Page references in *italic* indicate illustrations. **Boldface** references indicate photographs.

USDA Plant Hardiness Zone Map

This map was revised in 1990 to reflect the original USDA map, done in 1965. It is now recognized as the best indicator of minimum temperatures available. Look at the map to find your area, then match its pattern to the key above. When you've found your pattern, the key will tell you what hardiness zone you live in. Remember that the map is a general guide; your particular conditions may vary.

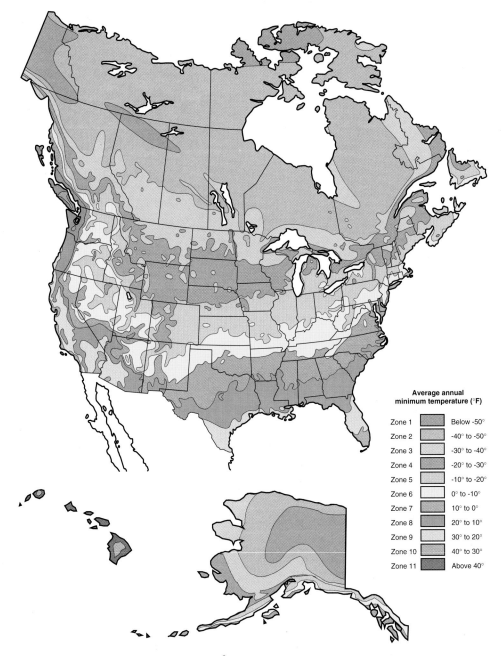

Average annual minimum temperature (°F)

Zone 1	Below -50°
Zone 2	-40° to -50°
Zone 3	-30° to -40°
Zone 4	-20° to -30°
Zone 5	-10° to -20°
Zone 6	0° to -10°
Zone 7	10° to 0°
Zone 8	20° to 10°
Zone 9	30° to 20°
Zone 10	40° to 30°
Zone 11	Above 40°